D1299518

SOUTHERN

CONGREGATIONAL

CHURCHES

Richard H. Taylor

Benton Harbor, Michigan

1994

SOUTHERN CONGREGATIONAL CHURCHES

A directory of Congregational and post merger churches in sixteen Southern states and the District of Columbia, with an overview of Congregational history in the area, including two groups of Independent Presbyterian Churches and information on the Congregational Methodist merger.

Benton Harbor, Michigan
      1994

Library of Congress Catalog Card No. 94-90333
ISBN: 0-9622486-2-2
Limited Edition

Copyright and Distribution Information:
Richard H. Taylor
1211 Seneca Rd.
Benton Harbor, MI, 49022

INTRODUCTION

When I was a boy I grew up at a Congregational Church in the northeast. I remember a conversation I had with the Pastor about a recent trip he took to the South. I asked about his visiting Congregational Churches. He chuckled and said, "there really aren't very many Congregational Churches in the South." Actually he was quite knowledgeable about the situation there, having served as the Pastor of former Christian Churches in North Carolina, and having visited such congregations as Circular Church in Charleston and Key West. But the impression stuck of Congregationalism being a non-entity in the South.

As a pastor myself, I have had lay people visit the South and make the same observation, only in a more inclusive way: "We couldn't find any Congregational Churches in the South at all."

It may seem strange to the reader then, to find an entire book listing thousands of Southern Congregational Churches. They really have existed. Some remain. Indeed Congregational penetration of the South has been very significant. When you put together the Puritan influences on the early South; the strength of the lowland South Carolina and Georgia churches, and their influence on both the American Revolution and the southern Presbyterian church; the significance of American Board Inidan missions; add the American Missionary Association College Churches and their involvement with much of America's emerging Black leadership; throw in a continued anti-Episcopal hemorrhaging from southern Methodism; and sprinkle in other miscellaneous churches and movements; you have a wide ranging and important part of southern life.

The difficulty is, of course, revealed by this very mix. There have, in fact, been several Congregationalisms in the South. One group would appear, have an impact, die or merge to another group, just when a new and very different Congregationalism was being born. Southern Congregationalism is a combination of many histories.

Therefore, unlike the other directories of Congregational Churches that I have published, this one needs more of a narrative history than the others. It also produces the longest bibliography.

Because of this multi-faceted reality, it has also been the most difficult directory to assemble. In other parts of the country Congregationalism, more or less, started and grew with one continuous history. Scholars can trace that development. Here we have many rises and falls. Even in the period from just before the Civil War to the present, when the national denomination monitored their related churches in the South, information is still hard to come by. In this period many of the state bodies were so weak that they could not publish their records, and these have apparently disappeared. This is further complicated by the fact that from 1885 through 1965 some of the state or similar bodies were racially segregated, thereby dividing a small group of churches into even smaller groupings where fellowship and record keeping were at a minimum.

Goals and Purposes of this study:

The purpose of this study is to compile a complete list of the churches of the Congregational Way in the South, from the time of the first separatist Puritan congregations down to the ecumenical mergers of the present century.

This continues the earlier work done by this author in my 1989 book The Churches of Christ of the Congregational Way in New England, and my 1992 book The Congregational Churches of the West.

Some of the lists of Congregational churches in this book are the first known attempts ever compiled for particular states. It is valuable to provide these lists now as the fellowship of Congregational Churches has been fractured by the debates over the issue of ecumenical merger.

It is my continued hope that the data I am putting together will help to provide the framework on which a careful long term study comparing church membership and population trends can be put together. It is also my desire to see this information used as a foundation for inventories of church records for genealogical and similar studies; local history studies of states, parts of states and counties and cities; ethnic histories as they relate to Anglo-Saxon Congregationalism; and studies in ecumenism as they relate to both federations and interdenominational local church unions on the one hand, as well as the Twentieth Century church unions of Congregationalism on the other. We would expect that these lists would be utilized to determine whether sociological studies of church history are drawn from truly representative samplings in regard to ethnic, geographic and social strata methods of study. By providing sources on bibliographic data we hope that we are helping future Congregational historians in the South, as well as Presbyterian and Methodist historians, and also provide a format for setting design parameters for a complete catalog of ministerial biography.

Focus and Definitions:

The focus of this study are the congregations part of the family and tradition of the Congregational Churches in the United States as derived from the original Pilgrim and Puritan congregations of New England or related thereto. This group begs an easy definition in the South before the Civil War, as we shall discuss. We have tried to include some information on all significant inter-relationships to the New England based family of churches and congregations in the South. During most of the period since the Civil War this group was clearly defined as a "denomination," having national publications and activities from the 1840's and 1850's, national Conventions in the 1850's and 1860's, and the National Council of Congregational Churches from 1871.

As indicated in the Cambridge Platform of 1648, which was the first major attempt of a group of congregations of this tradition in America to define their identity, the Congregational Churches are Christian congregations in the Reformed tradition. Indeed many of the early pre-Nineteenth century congregations were known by the name "Church of Christ."

A Congregational Church is Congregational in that it is part of the fellowship deriving from the Pilgrim congregations and is mutually recognized by the other congregations of that fellowship as such. This derived in the earliest forms through extending the mutual right hand of fellowship at services of covenanting for local churches. In later years churches organized by clearly denominational mission agencies were considered to be being organized as part of the fellowship. As local bodies of churches came into being, Associations and Conferences, it came to pass that all of the recognized churches were in fellowship with one of these bodies and membership in one such body constituted affiliation. The belief framework of the fellowship immediately following the Civil War can be seen in the introduction to the Constitution of the National Council of Congregational Churches formed in 1871.[1]

A congregation is not "Congregational" simply because it uses that name in its title. For example, a congregation of the Evangelical Congregational Church, a denomination headquartered in Pennsylvania and tracing its history to German pietistic Methodism, would not be included in this study. On the other hand a local church with a name such as Union or Community which never had the word "Congregational" in its title could still be a full member of the fellowship.

In the early part of the Nineteenth Century Unitarian churches also claimed the

INTRODUCTION

name Congregational. We have included references to Unitarian development in the South before 1850. Our definition of fellowship does become confusing, between Presbyterian and Congregational churches because of the Plan of Union which existed 1801 to 1852, and continued in some local congregations affiliated to the Presbyterian judicatories until 1870 or later, as well as because of interaction of these fellowships at earlier dates. We have tried to sort out these issues in the text which follows.

Where there has been a question as to whether to include a given congregation because of disagreements in sources, this author has uniformly included such congregations and then noted arguments about their inclusion in the appropriate text.

A Congregational Church is a Church in that it is a group of Christians who have consented together in covenant to submit themselves to worship and the ordinances of the Lord.[2]

In early New England most Congregational churches were formed in fellowship with ecclesiastical parishes or societies which were separate organizations that handled the secular affairs of the Church. These societies, under New England law, could be legally incorporated to hold property, and were composed originally of only male persons of the legal age. The officers of such societies were trustees. The Church, on the other hand, was made up of believers, accepted all sexes and people under age, and had Biblical officers: elders and deacons. Many writers confuse these two organizations and often describe the organization of a society as if it were a church. We have tried to avoid this error. Where we have discovered that some information refers to the parish or society we have tried to distinguish that data. It most modern situations the societies and churches have merged as one legal entity. This pattern did exist in the South, or in some variant form, but was declining in use by the time most of the congregations documented in this book were being formed.

The scope of territory covered in this book as the South includes three areas so designated by the United States Census: South Atlantic, East South Central, and West South Central. It includes sixteen states (Alabama, Arkansas, Delaware, Florida, Georgia, Kentucky, Louisiana, Maryland, Mississippi, North Carolina, Oklahoma, South Carolina, Tennessee, Texas, Virginia, West Virginia) and the District of Columbia. This definition includes the eleven states which were full parts of the Confederate States of America, as well as West Virginia (claimed by the Confederate state of Virginia), Kentucky (which had a rump Confederate government), and Oklahoma (whose territories related to the Confederacy). It also includes the slave areas of Delaware, Maryland, and the District of Columbia. It does **not** include Missouri, which was a slave state and also had a rump Confederate government, nor does it include Arizona and New Mexico, where territorial claims were made by the Confederacy. The decision not to include these two areas in this book is because: (1) they are not in the South as defined by the Census; (2) Congregational development in these areas primarily took place after the Civil War in conjunction with Plains state and western Congregational development, rather than with southern development.

Notes for the Introduction:
[1] - See Walker, Williston, <u>The Creeds and Platforms of Congregationalism</u>, (Pilgrim Press, Boston, 1960), pp.572-574.
[2] - <u>Cambridge Platform</u>, IV, see <u>*Ibid*</u>., pp.207-209.

PREFACE

The author is grateful for the help of a myriad of archives and libraries which made this work possible. In particular, my thanks goes to the Congregational Library, Boston, Massachusetts; the Archives of the United Church of Christ at Lancaster Theological Seminary, Lancaster, PA; the Presbyterian Historical Society, Philadelphia, Pennsylvania; the Library of the Andover Newton Theological School, Newton Centre, Massachusetts; the Library of the Chicago Theological Seminary, Chicago, Illinois; the Andover Harvard Library of the Harvard Divinity School, Cambridge, Massachusetts; and the Library of Marietta College, Marietta, Ohio.

My personal thanks is also expressed to several friends who have helped me along the way with inspiration, challenge, and comments essential to this work. My particular thanks goes to Lester E. Page Jr. for computer help and design. My thanks also goes to those who took time to read parts of this document and to make worthwhile comments including the Rev. Dr. Harold F. Worthley Jr., the Rev. Dr. T. Erskine Clarke, the Rev. Roger D. Knight, Mr. Albert H. Keller Jr., the Rev. Erston M. Butterfield, and the Rev. William T. Scott, Jr.. However, all errors in fact or understanding are purely my own.

On April 10, 1994 the Church of which I am currently the Pastor, the First Congregational United Church of Christ of Benton Harbor, Michigan, held a celebration of the Twenty-Fifth Anniversary of my ordination to the Christian ministry. Many gifts were received from Church members and from other friends and relatives around the country. These gifts have been used towards the publication of this book. My sincere thanks is given to all who have made this possible.

Naturally in a study of this magnitude some errors are bound to slip in. The author requests that any corrections be sent to him for use in future editions. Time will also cause some changes which you may wish to note in your copy.

The author intends to continue this study with similar publications covering other parts of the country and other branches of the United Church of Christ. Those desiring information, or having suggestions on that future work are also encouraged to write.

Richard H. Taylor
Benton Harbor, Michigan
September, 1994

WRITTEN FOR THE GREATER GLORY OF GOD

AND DEDICATED TO

MELINDA SUMMERBELL HUTTON

(1879-1957)

TABLE OF CONTENTS

TABLE OF CONTENTS

DEVELOPMENT OF THE SOUTHERN STATES

Generally initial Congregational penetration of an area depended upon its incorporation into the Anglo-Saxon dominated culture of the United States.

Therefore, an understanding of how this area developed presents a framework for the later development of Congregationalism.

The Southern part of the United States was an attractive area for many European powers throughout the Sixteenth Century.

French Huguenots made settlements at Charlesfort in South Carolina (1562) and Fort Caroline in Florida (1564) but were quickly turned out by Catholic Spain.

Spain made a permanent settlement at St.Augustine, Florida in 1565, and then marched westward through that territory, establishing Pensacola in 1696. Other settlements to the north at San Pedro (GA) and San Miquelde Gualdape (SC), and a Jesuit mission in Virginia were soon abandoned. To the west, Spain claimed Texas as early as 1513 and began to plant missions and forts in the area after 1583, but particularly after 1680.

At a late date, pushing down the Mississippi River from the north, France claimed the River valley. They established Fort Prudhomme, near Memphis, Tennessee in 1680, a settlement in east Texas in 1685, Fort Maurepas near Mobile, Alabama in 1699, and New Orleans, Louisiana 1717-1718.

England began settlement on the east coast, their first at Roanoke Island, North Carolina in 1585, but it was soon abandoned. However, the 1607 settlement at Jamestown, Virginia by the Virginia Company of London began the permanent settlement by English speaking peoples on the coast.

The Virginia Company's 1606 grant was revised in 1609 but revoked in 1624 when the colony was made a royal colony.

Bermuda settled from 1609 to 1612 was under the jurisdiction of Virginia to 1684, though supervised by its own company from 1615.

Virginia was divided into counties in 1634.

Puritans had intermingled with the early Virginia settlers. However, during the Puritan ascendancy in England (1649-1660) the Virginia government remained loyal to the Stuarts, although Parliament impacted local control of the Colony 1652-1660.

A grant to Ralph Hopton (Baron) was issued under Virginia in 1649 and fell to Fairfax in 1688, which gave titles in the north of the Colony a separate hold until abolished in 1785.

A grant in Virginia to Henry Bennet, Earl of Arlington and Lord Culpeper of 1673 was returned to the King in 1684.

The English crown made a grant of the Chesapeake Bay area to Lord Baltimore as Maryland in 1632, and it was settled in 1634. Counties began to be organized as early as 1637. It was made a royal colony in 1691, but returned to the proprietors in 1715.

Developing in a very different way was Delaware. Beginning in 1627-1628 Sweden began the settlement of New Sweden (organized in 1633) in Delaware and extending into Pennsylvania and New Jersey. In addition the Dutch New Netherlands Colony (begun 1614) set up a fort at the mouth of Delaware Bay. In 1655 the Dutch forced the Swedes to submit to their authority, absorbing their Colony. In 1664 the English conquered the Dutch territory making New Netherlands into New York. The Duke of York claimed the Dutch territories in Delaware "by conquest." A brief attempt by the Dutch to reclaim their lands (1673-1674) failed.

In 1682 the Duke leased Delaware to William Penn who attached it administratively to Pennsylvania (granted 1681). The crown took over Pennsylvania and Delaware in 1692, but restored them to the Penns in 1694. Delaware was set off as its own colony in 1701, still as a proprietary land. Delaware counties began to be set up in 1673.

Britain desired to press their settlements to the south, and granted a charter for Carolina to Robert Heath in 1629. However, in the crush of the English Civil War he did nothing. His charter was later revoked by Charles II for non-use. In 1663 a new charter was given for Carolina to Edward Hyde, Earl of Clarendon and seven others. It was enlarged in 1665. In 1670 the crown added the Bahama Islands (settled 1646) to the Carolina lands.

Meanwhile settlement began in the area. Virginia population overlapped into northeastern North Carolina between 1650 and 1653. A group of Puritans from New England, ship wreck victims, and refugees from Virginia were at Cape Fear possibly by c.1657. Settlement to the south at Charleston began between 1670 and 1680.

Carolina set up Palatinate counties in 1663. One of these passed to South Carolina at the split. The others began to be divided in 1670/1672 into sub units which became Counties, and the Palatinate Counties died out.

The wide distances in the Carolina Colony led to its division into two legislative areas, North Carolina and South Carolina in 1689. The provinces were divided in 1710 and separate governors were appointed in 1712.

In 1717-1718 the crown took the Bahamas off and made them a separate royal colony.

In 1719 a rebellion took place in South Carolina which led to the crown taking over that territory. The King made it a royal colony in 1721, and bought out the proprietors' charter in 1729. South Carolina had only one of the original Carolina Palatinate counties. Most early locations specify the Anglican parishes, which were set up in 1706.

North Carolina continued under the proprietors to 1729 when it became a royal colony. One of the proprietors, John Lord Carteret, heir to Sir George Carteret, refused to sell to the crown, and was finally given a separate title to a strip of land in 1744.

A charter was given by the crown to James Oglethorpe and others to Georgia in 1732 and it was settled in 1733. It was made a royal colony in 1752. Its southern boundary was pushed from the Altamaha River to the St.Mary's River in 1763. Initially Georgia was divided into Anglican parishes, but these yielded to counties in 1777.

Delaware, Maryland, Virginia, North Carolina, South Carolina, and Georgia all became part of the United States in 1776.

To the west the French territory in the Mississippi was lost by them to England in the French and Indian War in 1763. At the end of the War, all of Spanish Florida and French lands east of the Mississippi, came under English control. French territory west of the Mississippi and a few villages on the east bank of the lower part of the River came under Spanish control at the same time.

By the treaty ending the American Revolution in 1783, Florida and the coastal areas of the Gulf of Mexico to the Mississippi River were returned to Spain.

The United States was given the territory east of the Mississippi, but with no outlet to the Gulf of Mexico.

The opening of lands west of the mountains to American ownership reactivated claims of the eastern States to the west based on old Colonial charters.

Some settlements had already been made in the west, and settlers tried to set up independent governments. Vandalia was centered in West Virginia and started 1769. Transylvania was centered in Kentucky and began 1775. Neither of these were recognized. A group in Tennessee put themselves under the authority of North Carolina as the Washington District in 1776.

The Federal government encouraged the eastern states to give up their claims to land in the west. Virginia gave up its lands in Pennsylvania and northwest of the Ohio in 1781 (accepted 1784), but held on to Kentucky. New York gave up a claim to certain Indian lands throughout the south in 1782. South Carolina had a technical claim to western lands which, when laid out, was found not to really exist. However, this claim was given up in 1787.

North Carolina hesitated about its western lands. It gave them up in 1784, and then re-claimed them later in that year. This reversal led to the organization of the independent "state" of Franklin in east Tennessee in 1784. Unrecognized, it gave up in 1789. Finally in 1790 North Carolina gave up its control of Tennessee.

Georgia's land claim was set out in 1788, but was not ratified until 1802, when it was clear Georgia would retain its claim to the northwest corner of that State.

The Spanish-American border in Alabama and Mississippi was in dispute until 1795, when America was given land which brought it still closer to the Gulf.

In 1789 the Territory South of the Ohio River was set off, and organized in 1790. It included Tennessee and also claimed lands in Mississippi and Alabama also claimed by Georgia. When Tennessee was made its own territory in 1794, this Territory ceased to exist, although it continued a theoretical existence until 1802.

Virginia finally gave up Kentucky in 1792 and it immediately became a State. It already had counties dating back to 1776, established by Virginia. Kentucky's boundary was incorrectly drawn in 1780, giving a long strip of its land to Tennessee, and that was confirmed in 1820.

Tennessee Territory was begun in 1794 and became a State in 1796. It had counties organized by North Carolina from 1777.

The new Federal Constitution called for a Federal capital district. The District of Columbia was taken from Virginia and Maryland in 1790 and created in 1791. Its lands taken from Virginia were returned to that State in 1846.

In 1798 Mississippi Territory was organized in the lands secured in the 1795 boundary settlement with Spain. By 1804 it was enlarged to take in the land from its original area north to Tennessee.

In 1800 Spain ceded to France the "Louisiana" territory from the Mississippi River west to Texas. France in turn sold the area to the United States in 1803. The boundary between it and the Spanish territory to the west was clarified by a treaty in 1819. It included all of later Arkansas, Louisiana west of the River, plus the area east of the River below Lake Ponchartrain, and Oklahoma except for its panhandle. In 1804 the Louisiana sections of the territory were organized as the Territory of Orleans. The areas north were designated at the District of Louisiana in the same year, and made a Territory in 1805.

With Spanish Florida now cut off from Spanish Texas, Americans began to move into the Spanish Peninsula. The rest of modern Louisiana east of the Mississippi was taken from Spain in 1810, and added to the Territory of Orleans. The Territory was then organized as the State of Louisiana in 1812, the western boundary being then clarified. It had French-Spanish "Parishes" which dates from 1763 and were reorganized under the American government in 1805.

Also in 1812 the old District Territory of Louisiana became Missouri Territory.

In 1812 and 1813 respectively the "heels" of Mississippi and Alabama, which had been taken from Spain in 1810 (and claimed from 1803), were added to the Mississippi Territory.

In 1817 the Mississippi Territory was divided and the western portion became the State of Mississippi that year. It had counties dating from 1799 organized by the Territory.

The eastern portion of Mississippi Territory was reorganized as Alabama Territory in 1817. It became the State of Alabama in 1819, having its earliest county dating back to 1800 when organized by the old Territory.

In 1819 the remainder of Spanish Florida was ceded to the United States, and it was taken possession of in 1821. It was organized as a Territory in 1822, although its first county dates from 1821. It became a State in 1845.

Also in 1819 Arkansas Territory was set off from Missouri. It included that part of Oklahoma to its due west, while Oklahoma's northern strip, due west from modern Missouri, remained in the Missouri Territory. Arkansas' oldest county was functioning from an old French Parish by 1810, and was restructured 1813. Arkansas became a State in 1836, when its land in Oklahoma to the west was cut off as unorganized territory.

Missouri became a State in 1821, which cut off its territories to the west, making the northern strip of Oklahoma also unorganized.

The Spanish territory on the west coast of the Gulf became part of Mexico (which had begun to rebel in 1810) when it became independent in 1821. American settlement began to penetrate the area in 1821. In 1826 the Americans failed in a try to establish an independent republic called Fredonia. In 1836 Texas was declared independent and it won its independence in a War with Mexico. It claimed to include the Oklahoma panhandle, as well as lands to the north and west. Texas was received as a State in 1845. In 1850 (paid for 1853) it sold lands beyond its current boundaries to the Federal government, including the Oklahoma panhandle, which became unorganized territory.

Texas' first counties date from the 1835-1837 period.

With the absorption of Texas in 1845, the United States had control of all of the territory in this study.

After the election of Abraham Lincoln in 1860, withdrawal of several southern states began. South Carolina withdrew in 1860. It was followed in 1861 by Mississippi, Florida, Alabama, Georgia, Louisiana, Texas, Virginia, Arkansas, North Carolina, and Tennessee. The Confederate States of America was organized the same year. In Kentucky the regular government stayed with the Union, but a rump pro-Confederate government was organized in 1862 and recognized by the Confederacy. (The same happened in 1861 in Missouri, a Plains state.)

Both the Federal and Confederate governments claimed the Indian lands in the unorganized territory of later Oklahoma. Most of the Indian tribes supported the Confederacy, but a large minority clung to the Union.

In the entire area only Delaware, Maryland, and the District of Columbia were not claimed by the Confederacy.

In Virginia there was much opposition to secession. An 1861 Convention led to the organization of Kanawha, a pro-Union government in much of the State. This government was recognized by Lincoln as the Virginia government in exile. In 1863 this government gave most of its counties permission to leave Virginia, and that area was organized as West Virginia and admitted as a State that year. That State was enlarged by the addition of Berkeley and Jefferson Counties in 1866. A small pro-Union Virginia government continued in that part of the State in the suburbs of Washington, DC.

As the Civil War moved along, first the rump Confederate governments and then several of the State governments collapsed.

In 1864 Lincoln recognized new pro-Union governments in Arkansas, Louisiana, and Tennessee. After Lincoln's death and the end of the War, President Johnson recognized new governments in the other seven States. Congress, however, did not recognize these new bodies. It agreed to re-admit Tennessee in 1866, but held back on the rest.

Louisiana, Arkansas, Florida, Alabama, South Carolina, and North Carolina were re-admitted in 1868. Virginia, Mississippi, Texas, and Georgia were re-admitted in 1870 (although Georgia's votes had been accepted in the 1868 election.)

The final steps in the organization of the south revolved around what was to become Oklahoma. As early as 1820, when most of this area was part of Arkansas Territory, Indian tribes began to be assigned lands in this area. An act of 1830 made the area an intended home for American Indians. Almost all of Oklahoma was originally set aside for the five so called "civilized nations:" the Cherokee, Creek, Choctaw, Chickasaw, and Seminole. After the Civil War they were stripped of some of their land. Additional reservations were set up. The five main tribes were confined to the south and the east (except the Cherokees had an unattached "Strip" in the northwest, but not including the panhandle.) The panhandle always remained unassigned to a tribe. Some lands in the center of the modern State were never assigned to a tribe after the reorganization of tribal lands following the Civil War.

Although the area was commonly called "Indian Territory" there never was any such governmental organization. Therefore the land often appeared on maps merely as "Unorganized Territory," or as "Indian Land." Each of the five main tribes, however, maintained there own ongoing government. After the organization of the Kansas Territory in 1854 this land became at least visually a single piece.

Beginning in 1889 the government began to open large sections of the area to non-Indian settlement. The panhandle, and a miscellaneous collection of lands running from the Kansas border through the center of the present State to the southwest were assigned to the newly open areas. It was made the Territory of Oklahoma in 1890, with counties beginning that year. The Cherokee "Strip" along the Kansas border, which was separate from the tribe's main holdings, was taken from them and attached to Oklahoma in 1893. The original Oklahoma lands included the area of several Indian reservations which were made jurisdictions under the new Oklahoma government until opened for non-Indian settlement.

Greer County, in the southwest corner of present Oklahoma below the north fork of the Red River had long been claimed by Texas. It was organized as a Texas County and acted as part of their government. It was assigned to Oklahoma by the 1889 plan, but did not come under Oklahoma control until an 1896 court case.

Only the lands of the five main tribes and a small Indian enclave in the northeast corner of the present state remained outside the new territory.

The remaining five tribes and the small group in the northeast petitioned to be admitted as a State of Sequoyah but were denied the opportunity.

Finally in 1907 the Indian lands were added to Oklahoma which was made a State that year.

COUNTIES AND EXTINCT COUNTIES

ALABAMA - Georgia attempted to organize a Houston County here in 1784 which did not survive. The oldest surviving County was begun in 1800 as part of Mississippi Territory. All Counties organized before 1817 were part of Mississippi. The Mississippi County of Wayne included land here before 1817. Baine County (1866-1867) was abolished, but was reorganized as Etowah in 1868. Jones County (old) (1867-1867) was abolished but was reorganized as Sanford in 1868. The following Counties changed their names: Baker became Chilton; Benton became Calhoun; Cahawba became Bibb; Cotaco became Morgan; Hancock became Winston; Sanford became Lamar; Covington became Jones (new) and later Covington again.

ARKANSAS - Arkansas' Counties derive from Districts of the 1805 Louisiana Territory which became the Missouri Territory in 1812. New Madrid District begun 1804, became a County in 1812, and btwn.1815 & 1819 was restricted to present day Missouri. Arkansas District descended from a French District of Louisiana set up by 1763, and was re-organized as a County in 1813. Miller County (original) was organized in 1820, but served only a part of Texas after 1828, and was abolished c.1838. Dorsey County became Cleveland; Clayton became Clay; Sarber became Logan; and Searcy (old) became Marion. Lovely County (1827-1828) is extinct. Washita is an alternative spelling for Ouachita.

DELAWARE - Delaware has counties dating from 1673. St. Jones County became Kent; and Deale became Sussex.

DISTRICT OF COLUMBIA - The District was divided into two counties in 1801. However, Alexandria County was returned to Virginia in 1846. The one remaining County (Washington) was thereafter absorbed into the District/City government.

FLORIDA - The first County was created in 1821. These Counties have changed their names: Hernando became Benton and again became Hernando; Mosquito became Orange; New River became Bradford; and Saint Lucie (original) became Brevard.

GEORGIA - Georgia's Counties began to be set up in 1777, growing from earlier Anglican Parishes. Campbell and Milton Counties were attached to Fulton County in 1932. Cass County became Bartow; Kinchafoonee became Webster; and Randolph became Jasper. Walton County (original) (1803-1812) was found to be entirely in North Carolina and was abolished.

KENTUCKY - All counties organized before 1792 were part of Virginia. A Virginia County named Kentucky (org.1776) was divided in 1780. Josh Bell County became Bell County.

LOUISIANA - The present Louisiana Parishes date from a county/parish reorganization of 1805. These were based on earlier French Parishes begun by 1763. Some of these, such as Illinois (1763) and Arkansas (1805) are now outside the limits of the present state. Others such as Cabanoose and Venauela were extinct by 1805. Some French Parish names such as St.Francis, St.Gabriel, St.Louis, and others were dropped in 1805. Others, such as Ascension, Assumption, St.Bernard, St.Charles, St.James, St.John the Baptist, St.Landry, and St.Martin were revived as basic units in 1807. Acadia (original; Ascension and St.James Parishes), Attakapas (St.Martin Parish), German Coast (St.Charles, and St.John the Baptist Parishes), and Opelousas (St.Landry Parish) were temporary names for county/parishes from 1805 to 1807. The 1805 Parishes of Iberville, Lafourche, Natchitoches, Orleans, and Point Coupee were direct reorganizations of French Parishes. The 1805 Parish of Rapides, and the 1807 Parishes of Avoyelles, and Baton Rogue also claim to have derived from French Parishes. Baton Rogue Parish became West Baton Rogue. LaFourche Interior is the same as LaFourche, and New Orleans is the same as Orleans. Carroll (org.1832) was divided into East Carroll and West Carroll in 1877. Feliciana (org.1812) was divided into East Feliciana and West Feliciana in 1824. Washita is an alternative spelling for Ouachita. Louisiana has kept the designation "Parish" rather than "County" for its divisions.

MARYLAND - Counties began here as early as 1637. Providence County became Anne Arundel. Old Worcester County, begun 1658 disappeared in the 1690's. Baltimore City is an independent city cut off from the County of the same name in 1851.

MISSISSIPPI - Georgia set up a Bourbon County here in land claimed by Spain in 1785. It came to an end in 1788. The first surviving Counties were organized within the Territory as early as 1799. The Counties of Baldwin and Washington (original), assigned to Alabama in 1817, included land in current Mississippi before the division. Pickering County became Jefferson, Sumner County became Webster, and Colfax became Clay.

NORTH CAROLINA - Initially the Carolina Province was divided into three Palatinate Counties (Albemarle 1663/1664;Clarendon 1664;Craven (old) 1664). The population of Clarendon abandoned the area in 1667, and the County died. Craven eventually became South Carolina. Albemarle was divided into precincts in 1670/1672 many of which eventually became Counties on their own. Bath County was set up 1696 but related to the Albermarle General Assembly. It was discontinued in 1705 when it was divided into precincts. At the division of the colony all precincts were part of the Albemarle General Assembly. In 1739 all the precincts became Counties, and Albemarle became extinct. We have not bothered to show every change in name from precinct to county. Several other early Counties became extinct: Bute (1764-1779); Dobbs (1758-1791); Fayette (1784-1784); Tryon (1768-1779). The Georgia County of Walton served on land here 1803-1812. When Tennessee was cut off (1790), its Washington County was laid out in such a way as to claim land in present North Carolina for a few years. Glasgow County became Greene, Archdale became Craven (new), Pamptecough became Beaufort, and Wickham became Hyde. Authorization to set up Hooper County (1851) and Lillington County (1859) was never approved.

OKLAHOMA - The Arkansas Counties of Lawrence, Pulaski, Clark, and Miller (original) claimed to serve land here before 1828. Greer County was laid out by Texas in 1860 and organized in 1886 on land currently in Oklahoma. It functioned as a part of Texas, but was claimed by Oklahoma from 1889. It was awarded to Oklahoma in an 1896 court case. Other modern Oklahoma Counties began in 1890. Day County (1890-1907) is extinct.

SOUTH CAROLINA - When South Carolina's legislature was separated from North Carolina in 1689 it took over Craven Palatinate County. The colony serviced local areas through the Anglican Parishes set up in 1706, and a few isolated Districts such as Craven (1683-1769) and Granville (1700-1769). The colony was divided into defined Districts in 1769, and from there South Carolina begins a peculiar and unique County organizational history. In 1785 the Districts were subdivided into smaller units called Counties. We refer to these as Sub Counties to avoid confusion with the later Counties. We call Districts with Sub Counties General Districts during the period when they were divided. Eventually most of these smaller Counties became Districts on their own without subdivisions. A few of the general Districts also became Districts on their own without any subdivisions. The following General Divisions are extinct: Camden (1769-1799), Ninety-Six (1769-1799), Cheraws (1769-1799), Pinckney (1791-1799). Most sub counties were created in 1785. Those not made into Districts were abolished in 1799, as follows: Bartholomew, Berkeley, Charleston (also the name of a General District), Claremont, Clarendon, Granville, Hilton, Kingston, Lewisburg, Liberty, Lincoln, Marion (not the same as the later District), Orange, Shrewsbury, Washington, Winton, and Winyaw. Salem existed 1791-1799. Some sources also indicate that there was a sub county named Dorchester. Many of these were never really organized, and steps to abolish them began earlier. Lexington and Williamsburg sub counties were also abolished in 1799, but reorganized as Districts in 1804. Georgetown, Marion, and Orangeburg Districts through 1800, and Sumter through 1810 were treated as General Districts by the Census. Kingston, Lewisburg, Lexington, Liberty, Orange, Williamsburg and Winyaw were treated as sub counties by the Census through 1800, as were Claremont, Clarendon, and Salem in 1800 and 1810. Waccamaw is the name of a Census area in 1800 not organized by the State. Pendleton sub county (1789) became a District in 1799/1800 and extinct in 1826. Spartan is an alternative name for Spartanburg. All Districts were renamed Counties in 1868. We have not shown these 1868 name changes, they can be assumed.

TENNESSEE - All Counties organized before 1790 were part of North Carolina. Washington District of 1776 became a County in 1777. Christiana County became Loudon. Tennessee County (1788-1796) and James County (1871-1919/1920) are extinct. The following Kentucky Counties claimed to serve in Tennessee for some period before the boundary was secured in 1820: Lincoln, Christian, Logan, Warren, Barren, Cumberland, Caldwell, Wayne, Pulaski, Knox. The 1791 Census also included population for an area south of the French Broad River not in any county.

TEXAS - The earliest Counties developed from Mexican municipios in 1836/1837. The Louisiana County of Natchitoches claimed to serve land in modern Texas to 1812, as did the Arkansas Counties of Hempstead (to 1827), Lafayette (to 1836), and Miller (original,to c.1838). Cass County became Davis, and then again became Cass. Buchanan County became Stephens, Navasota became Brazos, Somerville became Somervell, Harrisburg became Harris, Wegefarth became Donley, and Willacy (original) became Kenedy. Buchel (1887-1897), Dawson (original) (1858-1866), Encinal (1856-1899), and Foley Counties (1887-1897) are extinct as are Bexar and Young Districts, both created by 1870 and abolished 1876.

VIRGINIA - Virginia Counties began in 1634. The early Counties of Accawmack (or Accomac) became Northampton, and Warrosqueyoacke became Isle of Wight. Illinois County (org.1778) which served land given up in 1784, is extinct. Yohogania County (org.1776) was mostly on land given to Pennsylvania in 1784 and was discontinued in 1785. Norfolk County (old) of 1636 was divided 1637. Lower Norfolk (1637-1691) was replaced by Norfolk (new). Rappahannock (1656-1692) is extinct. Alexandria County, received from the District of Columbia in 1846, became Arlington County. Charles River County became York, Upper Norfolk became Nansemond and Dunmore became Shenandoah. The following present West Virginia Counties served land currently in Virginia after 1789 and prior to 1863: Pendleton, Monroe, and possibly Mercer. Three of the State's early Counties included the word "City" in their title: Charles City County, Elizabeth City County, and James City County. In addition to these Virginia has set up a system where "independent cities" are separated from Counties. In 1990 there were 95 Counties and 41 independent cities. The Census has not always clearly distinguished between cities in counties and independent cities. Only four cities appear separately in some Censuses before 1890, although fifteen had been formed by then. Because of these confusions and the rapid growth in the number of independent cities after 1892, most religious studies have continued Virginia information on the basis of the old county boundaries with the independent cities taken from them added to the county data. A few independent cities have expanded through time to include land in counties in addition to those they were originally taken from, but we have continued to place them with the original counties. Five Counties have been completely replaced by their independent cities and are now extinct, but we unite the information under the old County name. These are: Elizabeth City County (1634-1952) absorbed by Hampton City; Nansemond County (1637-1972) replaced by Suffolk City; Norfolk County (1693-1963) replaced by Chesapeake, Norfolk, and Portsmouth Cities; Princess Anne County (1691-1963) consolidated with Virginia Beach City; and Warwick County (1634-1952) replaced by Warwick City, later absorbed by Newport News City. The following independent cities are extinct: Manchester, Nansemond, South Norfolk, and Warwick.

WEST VIRGINIA - All Counties begun before 1863, and in the eastern panhandle before 1866, were part of Virginia. In addition these Virginia Counties at some time served land currently in West Virginia after 1789 and prior to 1863: Russell, Wythe, Montgomery, Botetourt, Augusta, Tazewell, Bath, and Giles.

MINOR CIVIL DIVISIONS

As was done in our New England volume, it has been our desire to indicate church location by minor civil division in each County, where such information is available.

DEVELOPMENT OF THE SOUTHERN STATES

In the South, the United States Census continues to break down Counties by state determined minor civil divisions in the seven States of Arkansas, Louisiana, Maryland, Mississippi, North Carolina, Virginia, and West Virginia. In Mississippi these divisions are unusually shaped gerrymandered Districts which begin in center cities and fan out to edges of the county. These are of such unusual shape as to be of little use, and, therefore, have not been used by us. However, in the remaining six States, we have tried to indicate present minor civil division where possible. These are Townships in Arkansas and North Carolina, Wards in Louisiana, and Districts in Maryland, Virginia, and West Virginia. Former divisions have not been explored unless they appear as a former location of the Church. (The Work Projects Administration studies have often included Township information in some Tennessee counties for Church entries. We have included that information which they offer. We have also included a few former Oklahoma Townships where that information is reflected in church names.)

An asterisk next to a minor civil division name (District, Ward, Township, etc.) indicates the church was never known by that name. An asterisk next to a community name in the index indicates that this is a minor civil division shown in the text but which was never used as the name of a Church location. (An asterisk may appear next to the name for a minor civil division for one church at its entry, but not in the index, because it was used for another church's location. An index asterisk indicates that all church entries with that name use an asterisk.)

Where a minor civil division is known only by a number or by a name and a number, the number identification is shown only at the church entry and is never used in the index.

A HISTORY OF SOUTHERN CONGREGATIONALISM

PURITANISM

When English settlement began in Virginia in 1607 no separate group called "Congregationalists" existed. Instead a large faction within the Church of England was calling for reforms, and were known collectively as Puritans. This group had no clear agreement on the polity of the Church. Many supported some type of modified Presbyterian polity which had been developing among Reformed and Calvinist Churches on the continent. Others were willing to maintain a modified episcopacy within the Church of England if reforms were made. Still others favored a system with more local autonomy. Indeed there had been Brownist separate churches in England as far back as the 1580's. Other independent congregations, usually underground, came and went in England. Congregations in exile, particularly in Holland, experimented with various forms of organization.

The great ferment created by Puritanism in England extended into the new American colonies. A well known Anglican Puritan, Alexander Whitaker became the first pastor of the Henrico Parish (Richmond) in 1611. There were other Puritan pastors in established Parishes in Virginia as well.

Tradition holds that an independent Puritan congregation existed in Warwisqueake Parish by 1621. It is claimed that the noted Separatist Henry Jacob, founder of an independent church in London in 1616, served this congregation before his death. Others dispute whether he came to America.

With the arrival of the Pilgrims at Plymouth in 1620, and the Puritans at Salem in 1629, a large number of specifically Puritan congregations came to life in America. The New England churches claimed to be a reformed Church of England, and hoped to model a reformed church for the English homeland.

Early Puritan development in America rose and fell in response to the events in England. By 1641 the English Civil War had begun between the Puritan Parliament and King Charles I. At the Westminster Assembly (1641-1652) a Presbyterian position was taken in Church polity. A clearly Congregational position was put forward by a minority at the Assembly. These two positions helped to define the episcopal Puritan faction as well.

In New England the Cambridge Synod (1646-1648) supported the faith stance of the Westminster Assembly, but offered a staunch defense of the Congregational view of church polity.

As Puritanism broke into visible denominational groups in England, the same forces were at work in Virginia. In 1641 a petition was sent to New England by a group of Virginia residents. They contended that there were sufficient people of Puritan sentiment to organize three congregations in the colony, and they requested that New England pastors be sent to them. New England leaders responded, and three Pastors were sent to Virginia in 1642 (Thomas James, John Knowles, and William Thomson (or Tompson)).

However, the Virginia government supported the King. An Anglican tax supported establishment had existed in Virginia since 1619. Now it was tested, and the idea of independent non-conforming congregations met with fast and swift opposition. Two of the three pastors were expelled in six months. Thomson continued, but remained as the named Pastor of his Church in Braintree (Quincy), Massachusetts, and, after 1644 also helped a Puritan congregation starting up in Maryland.

An independent Puritan Church had emerged in Nansemond County, VA by 1641. It was led, first by Thomson, and then by two Anglican clergy from nearby Parishes who left the established church to become Independents: Thomas Harrison of Elizabeth River Parish in Norfolk County in 1644, and Thomas Bennett of West Parish in Nansemond County in 1648. The Virginia government took a more and more belligerent attitude to these outbreaks as the war in England increased in ferocity. Thomson spent little time in Virginia after 1644. Both Bennett and Harrison were banished in 1648. So was most of the independent congregation, the majority of which fled to Providence, Maryland in 1649, where they amalgamated with the earlier group led by Thomson. Tradition holds that a small portion of the Nansemond Church continued underground to 1660, when the return of the Stuart monarchy in England, caused them to flee. This situation made Congregationalism an anathema in Virginia (or Virginia an anathema to Congregationalists), and the family of churches avoided the Virginia/West Virginia area before the Civil War, and for the most part from then until the 1931 merger.

Maryland had begun as a colony under a Roman Catholic proprietor. There is some indication that the independents fleeing there contemplated beginning an independent colony of their own. There is no doubt that in the first decade or so they had a very strong presence in Maryland and dominated the government 1654 to 1657. A satellite settlement to Providence was begun on the Patuxent River in 1650. There was also a mixed English and Scottish Puritan settlement in Charles County by 1659, and also some occasional Puritan preaching elsewhere in the colony. These latter movements have left little trace. After the return of the Stuarts to power in England, the Patuxent River property was taken over by the Anglican Church, but the congregation continued and developed into the Upper Marlborough Presbyterian Church. The main Providence settlement later moved to Annapolis. It came under both Quaker and Anglican influences and was absorbed by the Protestant establishment.

Delaware, originally Swedish, then Dutch, then under the control of the Quaker proprietors of Pennsylvania developed differently from the rest of the South. An old Swedish Lutheran Church at New Castle (New Amstel) had been organized in 1642. It became a mixed Protestant church including Dutch Reformed, as the latter's government took control of the colony (1655). After England took over the colony (1664), English settlers began to move into the community. By about 1698 this congregation had re-organized as an English speaking Calvinist Church, including Scottish settlers and New Englanders.

By 1700 only the Upper Marlborough, MD, and New Castle, DE churches existed in the southern states north of Virginia with any Puritan elements. However, a Scottish and Scotch-Irish Presbyterian Calvinistic settlement had begun on the Delmarva peninsula in the 1670's. Two Irish ministers had come to serve them, William Traill (c.1682-1688) and Francis Makemie (from 1683). Makemie itinerated in several colonies and began a correspondence with Puritan leader Increase Mather in 1684. We shall continue this upper South development below.

THE LOW COUNTRY CHURCHES BEGIN

Possibly as early as 1657, but clearly in the early 1660's a Puritan settlement emerged near Cape Fear, NC. The settlement may have included refugees from the underground church in Nansemond, VA. Also involved were some escapees from a ship wreck, and a few settlers directly from Barbados and New England. With a new charter given to Carolina in 1663, the possibility of a Puritan colony to the South of Virginia appealed to many. When it became clear that the new colony's city would be Charleston, the Puritans removed there. Perhaps in 1680 or 1681 an independent Puritan congregation began in Charleston. This was the second church of any denomination in what would become South Carolina (proceeded only by the first Anglican church in the city). Initially this congregation "on Meeting Street" became a meeting place for all types of non-conformist Protestants in addition to the Cape Fear group, including Huguenot refugees from France, as well as Puritans from England and New England. Eventually they were joined by Scotch-Irish and Scottish settlers, and German and Swiss Reformed people.

The opening of South Carolina became attractive to many New Englanders. In 1695 a portion of the Dorchester, MA Church met in Charleston, MA to organize a new church, which then settled Dorchester, SC in 1696. Another Puritan Church emerged at Wappetaw between 1695 and 1699. By 1703 Puritan preaching had begun at South Edisto River. These were strong, well supported and large settlements.

By 1686 or 1687 the Huguenots in Charleston were sufficient in number to organize their own church. By 1700 four other Huguenot Churches had started in the colony (Goose Creek; Orange Quarter; Santee-Jamestown; St.John's Par.:Berkeley).

It was clear that a large non-Conformist population was streaming into South Carolina.

THE RISE OF THE ANGLICAN ESTABLISHMENT

We have already pointed out how Virginia banished Puritan development.

Pressures from the late Stuart kings in England had increased against Puritan New England between 1679 and the Glorious Revolution in 1688. This was when South Carolina development was still rather feeble. It was thought that the new House of Orange would be more receptive to Reformed and Calvinist ideas. However, that did not prove to be the case. Steps were taken to confirm crown control over Massachusetts and the Plymouth colony. The new Massachusetts and New Hampshire governments forbade the meeting of Puritan Synods, thereby shutting off the cooperative power of the churches.

In 1701 the Society for the Propagation of the Gospel was chartered in England. It became clear very quickly that the purpose of the S.P.G. was to bring all American dissenters into conformity with the Anglican church. Funding was put into sending high church clergy to the colonies to press for Anglican congregations and Anglican establishment.

Governmental power also pushed the establishment of tax supported Anglican parishes. An act dating from 1694 in New York, began to be fiercely enforced after 1704 in parts of that colony, requiring tax supported Anglican churches. Existing Congregational or Puritan Churches in Queens and Westchester Counties were suppressed or destroyed.

A similar Anglican establishment was adopted for Maryland in 1692.

An Anglican establishment began to appear in Charleston in 1698, and was extended across the colony by two strong acts in 1704. Shortly thereafter the rural Huguenot churches submitted to Anglican control.

Anglican establishment was also imposed on North Carolina in 1715.

Georgia, the last English colony to be organized on the coast began in 1732/1733. Between 1743 and 1755 it became attractive to non-Conformist settlers of various nationalities, as South Carolina had two generations earlier. However, again the crown stepped in, and an Anglican establishment was imposed on Georgia in 1758.

Therefore, except for Delaware, the entire English South had become officially Anglican.

These establishments allowed non-conformist congregations the freedom to worship. However, taxes supported the Anglican churches. Also most non-conformist churches were prohibited from receiving charters and clear title to their property. In many places non-conformist church members were prohibited from voting, and other forms of persecution were entered into from time to time.

The strongest protests to Anglican power came from the Low Country non-conformist churches. However, their valor did not overcome their isolation. In each case, following Anglican establishment, most English Congregational or Puritan settlement ended. The Churches had to survive on their own.

EFFECTS OF THE ESTABLISHMENT ON NON-CONFORMING CHURCHES ELSEWHERE

In England the restoration of the Stuarts in 1660, and the expulsion of non-conforming clergy from the Church of England in 1662 had seriously changed the Puritan movement. Many had conformed to the Anglican establishment. Those Presbyterians and Independents who refused to conform were drawn more and more to each other in a united dissent. After the Glorious Revolution they were able to come together and in London many clergy adopted a united "Heads of Agreement," in 1691, bringing most dissenting Reformed churches into a loose cooperation. Puritan congregations in America, at this point mostly English in background, cooperated with the unity forces there. English Presbyterians coming to America joined Congregational congregations and fellowships. Scotland developed differently. The Presbyterian Church was established there by law in 1690.

THE NON-CONFORMISTS ORGANIZE TO DEFEND THEIR FREEDOMS

Beginning in the 1690's the Mathers and other New England leaders began to encourage all Reformed peoples in the colonies to unite to defend their rights from the imposition of Anglicanism. Massachusetts proposals in 1705 to better organize the Churches in that colony were opposed by the government. Connecticut, however, was able to call a Synod at Saybrook in 1708 and form a strong inter-church organization.

Steps were taken by Baptists to organize, their first Association dating from 1707.

The Mathers' influence also led in 1706 to the organization of a Presbytery in Philadelphia with Makemie as the leader. Trinterud contends that three of the seven founding members of the Presbytery were from New England. It was a loosely organized body, without a clear creed or the need of churches to submit to its power. Both the New Castle and Upper Marlborough churches became parts of this new Presbytery, which was really a mix of Congregationalists and Presbyterians. The unionist tendencies of such documents as the "Heads of Agreement" were supported in the new body.

A group of Welsh Independents (Congregationalists) settled at Pencader in Delaware in 1710, and affiliated with the Presbytery in 1713 or 1714.

However, the low country churches in South Carolina were far from Philadelphia , and did not affiliate with the Presbytery. But the same forces were at work there. A Presbytery of Charlestown (sometimes called South Carolina, which is the designation we use in the tables for easy identification) was organized sometime about 1722(60,61;1723(71);by 1733(58)). It was also a loosely organized body and included pastors of both English Puritan and Scottish Presbyterian congregations.

DEVELOPMENT OF THE LOW COUNTRY CHURCHES

As we have seen above, by 1703 four strong Puritan congregations (Charleston, Dorchester, Edisto, Wappetaw) had emerged, as well as the Huguenot Church in Charleston. These resisted the encroachment of the establishment.

These were soon joined by other Reformed populations entering the growing colony. Just as Makemie served some of the first Scottish and Scotch-Irish settlers on the Delmarva peninsula, some Scottish elements began to penetrate South Carolina. An unsuccessful Scottish colony existed at Stuart's Town on Port Royal Island (Beaufort County) from 1683 to 1686. After their demise their membership scattered. Their Pastor preached occasionally at the Independent Church in Charleston. In 1700 Archibald Stobo, an Edinburgh graduate from Scotland became Pastor in Charleston. Over the next decade he brought New England, English, Scottish, and Scotch-Irish settlers together in forming other churches nearby Charleston, and strengthening some of the existing churches. His position was basically unionist and he called his congregations "British Presbyterian."

Another element entering the area was a German and German/Swiss Reformed populace. Their earliest settlements date from 1732. While their first few congregations buckled under to the Episcopal establishment, congregations from 1737 on, often aided by the other independent Calvinist congregations, also began to stand outside the Anglican establishment.

The Low Country churches, while representing a real ethnic mix, were able to be recognized as a common group because of their opposition to the Anglican establishment, their common Reformed and Calvinist heritage, and because of commonalities shared in the development of a new low country culture. The low country areas (basically Beaufort, Berkeley, Charleston, Colleton, Dorchester, Hampton, and Jasper Counties in SC, later joined by Bryan, Chatham, and Liberty Counties in Georgia) developed a social system independent of the rest of the south. While the area's wealth was highly dependent upon the ports of Charleston and Savannah, it was also developed by the growth of the rice and indigo harvests in the swampy, almost tropical lands nearby. The plantation economy of the area was so specialized (not like the cotton or tobacco areas of much of the rest of the South), that it became very much its own independent producer of valuable goods.

Around the early churches there developed a group of sister churches with Reformed ideas. These churches were of mixed backgrounds. By 1710 congregations had started at Wilton, James Island, and Johns Island. By 1745 there were additional churches at Cainhoy, Pon Pon, Stoney Creek, and Beaufort, and a Scottish Presbyterian Church was formed in Charleston from a group coming out of the Independent Church. When Georgia became open for settlement, some similar churches began there between 1743 and 1755 at Vernonburg (White Bluff), Midway, and Savannah. A later church began at Saltcatcher, SC in 1766. Another Huguenot congregation began up the Savannah River at New Bordeaux in 1764.

These congregations were all more or less autonomous. They had New England, English Puritan, Welsh, Scottish, Scotch-Irish, Huguenot, Dutch, German, and Swiss members, in differing proportions. With the exception of the two specifically Huguenot congregations, this group of churches were English speaking. Every one of these churches went through long periods when they were not under any judicatory.

It was this group of churches that the Presbytery of Charlestown tried to pull together.

(We have not included in our study the Scottish Presbyterian Church in Darien, McIntosh Co., GA, begun 1736, which died 1823. It probably had no Presbytery affiliation until 1809. Nor have we included the Presbyterian Church in Altamaha, Tattnall Co., GA, begun about 1761, and dying sometime after the Revolution. It was for a while supplied from Midway, and apparently never belonged to a Presbytery.)

CONTROVERSIES IN THE REFORMED CALVINIST CHURCHES

However, the pre-Revolutionary eighteenth century English speaking Puritan world was wracked by two controversies which diverted attempts towards unity.

The first was known as the "subscription controversy." After 1690 candidates for ordination in Scotland were required to subscribe to the doctrines of the Westminster Confession. (Literally sign ("subscribe") the Confession vowing complete unqualified acceptance.) About 1717 in Scotland there were even forces that wanted to force candidates to subscribe to particular interpretations of the Confession. Moves were afoot in northern Ireland from 1697 to follow Scotland's lead in subscription. In both places subscription was the will of the majority.

In England, however, the unionist ministerial groups had less of a doctrinaire stance. In 1719 when suspicions arose about some Unitarian views being expressed, the London ministers decided to address the issue. A paper was put forward requiring specific adherence to the Trinity. One faction, including most English Independents, adhered to the statement. This group became known as the "subscriptionists." Another faction, including most English "Presbyterians" opposed adherence. The latter group argued that if the Bible was a sufficient rule for faith and practice, and people accepted the Bible, why was some particular theological interpretation required? This group became known as the "non-subscribers." The debate was so divisive that the London clergy on either side stopped meeting with each other. A minority of Independents began to meet with the non-subscribers, while a minority of the "Presbyterians" began to meet with the subscribers. This returned to the English dissenter community two distinct groups, but now with a mixed polity on either side of a theological issue. It also placed the English "Presbyterians" almost to a person in a group far distant from the Presbyterian majorities in Scotland and Ireland.

In actual effect subscription never became as strong an issue in England as it did elsewhere. Since most of the subscriptionists in England were Independents, there was no Synod to enforce subscription over time. While the Independents were perhaps more evangelical than the non-subscribers, they were able to encourage evangelicalism on a one by one basis, looking for individual faith and commitment in ordination councils. Local churches could do the same in their autonomous individual church covenants.

But in America subscription became an important issue.

In New England, where there were no Synods after Saybrook, there were few forums in which to press subscription. Evangelicals worked on a personal basis as they met in ecclesiastical councils to consider ministerial candidates.

But the Synod of Philadelphia (which was a 1717 expansion of the 1706 Presbytery) was, as we have seen, a mixture of New England and Scottish forces. It had expanded into the northern New Jersey and New York area, adding many formerly English Puritan congregations, particularly after 1707 when the Anglican Governor of New York had arrested Makemie and another Presbytery member for preaching without a license.

But far more significant growth was taking place in the Delmarva peninsula and in Pennsylvania from the arrival of the Scotch Irish. After the English Parliament had taken actions in 1699 which destroyed the woolen industry in Ireland, and acts of 1704 were passed to try to force Presbyterians in Ireland to submit to the Anglican church, a large wave of immigration began to come to America. Delaware, New Jersey, and Pennsylvania, which had no religious establishment were particularly popular.

However the differences between subscriptionist Scottish Presbyterianism on the one hand, and the autonomous traditions of the New Englanders soon strained the Synod. Attempts were begun in 1719 to move the Synod towards a more European structure by adopting some type of a creedal statement and increasing the power of the Synod. A compromise was reached in 1722. Then in 1729 the Westminster Confession was adopted by the Synod, but with allowances by which any candidate could indicate any "scruples" that they might have against specifics in the Confession, and still be considered orthodox and ordained. This act also admitted that some sections of the Confession were non-essential, and only "recommended" Westminster for use by other bodies in the Church. However, in 1736, when a Scotch Irish group had clear control of a majority of the Synod, this was modified. All references to scruples and non-essentials were removed. Subscription had become the rule.

The end result of this was obvious. By 1741 one Presbytery had withdrawn, and by 1745 they were joined by most of the New Englanders in a new Synod of New York (commonly called the "New Side" or the "New Lights.")

Aiding in this cause was the second great theological debate of the period, revivalism and the Great Awakening. The pro-revival, pro-Awakening group had coalesced with the non-subscriptionists. Because the Awakening issues have been explored in such great detail by other authors, we shall not run through them here again. It does need to be said that in New England, however, where local autonomy allowed for more diversity, there were both pro and anti revival factions.

A HISTORY OF SOUTHERN CONGREGATIONALISM

SOUTHERN NON-CONFORMITY DURING THE PERIOD OF CONTROVERSY

What happened to the Synod of Philadelphia also happened to the Presbytery of Charlestown. In the late 1720's Hugh Fisher, Pastor of Dorchester sought a subscription rule in the Presbytery. He was opposed by Josiah Smith of Cainhoy (later at Charleston) and Nathan Bassett, the Charleston Pastor. The Presbytery agreed to subscription, and Bassett and Smith withdrew. This was probably also an incentive for the organization of the First Presbyterian Church ("Old Scots") in Charleston in 1731.

These actions removed the most important church from the deliberations of the Presbytery. After the subscription controversy Charleston, Wappetaw, and Cainhoy broke from the Presbytery. Dorchester followed after Smith ended his term as Pastor (1734). The Georgia churches, when formed, also remained outside the Presbytery. Edisto, James Island, the Scots Church in Charleston, and Wilton were the mainstays of the Presbytery. Except for about a decade and a half Johns Island also was loyal to the Presbytery. The Presbytery also added some churches of Scotch Irish derivation in South Carolina beyond the low country area. During this period the Presbytery churches, actually culturally mixed but subscribing, came more and more to be called Presbyterian, while those outside the Presbytery became the nucleus of southern Congregationalism.

Both of the Low Country groups made overtures towards the new German and Swiss population. The Presbytery of Charlestown licensed or ordained John Ulrich Giessendanner the younger for service in the German Church in Orangeburg in 1738. In 1778 we find the Frederickan German Church at Cattle Creek treated as if under the care of the Presbytery.

But the independent churches also had a strong voice in the German community. John Joachim Zubly, a native of Switzerland came to America in 1744, and became the first Pastor of the Vernonburg (White Bluff) Church in GA. Originally a German congregation, that Church later became Congregational and Presbyterian. He also organized a German Church at Frederica, GA, and served one at Amelia, SC. However his talents soon attracted the Independent churches. He became Pastor at Wappetaw, and probably at Cainhoy. He often lectured in the Charleston Church. He then returned to GA where he became the first Pastor of the Independent Church in Savannah (1760-1781), probably also supplying White Bluff.

Savannah became another Church of great importance. Modern writers have tried to connect it directly to the Church of Scotland. The Westminster Confession and the doctrines of the Church of Scotland are mentioned early in its records. However, it first incorporated only as the Independent Church, the word Presbyterian only being added to its name at a later date. After the long service of a German Reformed Pastor that it called from a Congregational Church in SC, it later turned to other Low Country independents or New Englanders for its Pastors. When a Church in Presbytery was organized in Savannah (1827), it took the telling name "First Presbyterian Church of Savannah," implying the lack of Presbyterianism in the Independent Church. Even Thompson (Vol.I,p.401) admits that this Church had a Congregational background.

Meanwhile another movement was taking place which would have a profound effect on southern Congregationalism. As we have seen the Synod of Philadelphia had divided and a New Side Synod of New York had been created. This latter group was strongly influenced by New England forces, and was generally tolerant and non-subscribing in its sentiment. It was also fiercely revivalistic and mission oriented. After 1732 a large Scotch Irish immigration began in the Shenandoah Valley and related sections of Virginia. Despite the proximity of the Scotch Irish Synod of Philadelphia and their churches, they did not respond to the new settlements. Instead the Synod of New York began a vigorous mission work in Virginia. While the population there was

Scotch Irish, many of the clergy had New England connections, and were partial to the sentiments of that area. It is in Virginia Presbyterianism that some of the most vigorous movements would arise for American independence, and in opposition to the Anglican establishment.

As Scotch Irish population pressed south from Virginia, the New Side Synod followed. Hanover Presbytery, organized in 1755 supplied churches in both Carolinas. Orange Presbytery begun in 1770 began more vigorous church work into South Carolina. There was a South Carolina Presbytery in the Synod by 1784. This southern penetration was now bringing the Synod into contact with the low country Presbytery of South Carolina and the independent Low Country Churches.

UNITING TO OPPOSE THE MONARCHY

During all this time the Anglican establishment persisted in the South, and, as we have seen, even extending and growing into Georgia in 1758.

As the colonies gained economic independence from the crown, a desire followed for political independence. This was strongly supported by the various Reformed Churches who coined the motto "A Church Without a Bishop; A Country Without A King."

Steps were taken to unite the Churches as strong resilient bodies. In 1758 the two branches of the main Presbyterian Church reunited as the Synod of Philadelphia and New York. In this body the missional effectiveness of the New Side, and the influence of their new college at Princeton combined to give toleration a momentary period of ascendancy.

From 1766 to 1775 the Presbyterian Synod and Congregational bodies in New England held joint conventions, mainly to work against the Anglican establishment.

These types of moves also strengthened the Presbytery of Charlestown.

The Pon Pon Church, which had been connected directly to the Church of Scotland, made its way into the Presbytery, as did the newer churches at Stoney Creek, Beaufort, and Saltcatcher. During this period the Pastor at Wappetaw also reentered the Presbytery. As the spirit of unity prevailed, the Presbytery even began to explore membership in the Presbyterian Synod in 1770, but nothing came of it.

During the Revolutionary War the Presbytery was unable to meet. By the end of the War it had ceased to exist. But a new day was beginning for the Churches.

INDEPENDENCE AND ITS EFFECTS

After the Revolution there was no attraction to the Anglican establishment and its Tory sympathies. Steps were quickly taken to abolish it.

The most famous ordinance in this regard was Virginia's act of religious freedom (1785). All Virginia establishment laws were repealed by 1802. North Carolina took steps to end its establishment in 1775, and later removed requirements that state officers had to be Protestant. Maryland granted religious freedom to Christians in 1776, and to Jews in 1826. South Carolina adopted a general establishment of Protestantism in 1778, but moved in 1790 to no establishment. Georgia established freedom of conscience in 1777, and had repealed all aspects of the establishment by 1789.

Another factor brought about by the Revolution was that now non-conformist churches could get charters and have clear titles to their property. This freedom led many of the German Churches both Lutheran and Reformed to go their own way, separate from the help they had had from the English churches. In 1780 the Anglicans took over the Huguenot Church at New Bordeaux, but part of the membership affiliated with a local Presbyterian Church and later reorganized as a French Presbyterian Church.

In South Carolina a new Charleston Presbytery was organized in 1790. This body was clearly influenced by Scottish and subscription standards. However, by this time independence and autonomy had caught on in the Low Country, and there was strong opposition to the new Presbytery. Edisto fired their Pastor after he joined the group. Stoney Creek Church formally protested their Pastor's membership. Pastors at Dorchester, Pon Pon, and Wilton apparently also belonged without the approval of their congregations. Old Scots Church in Charleston was the most committed to the new group. James Island was served by it for three years, then went elsewhere for leadership. Johns Island was in, left, then later returned. Beaufort belonged until 1800, Saltcatcher until 1811. The Huguenot Church in Charleston was briefly served by a member of this Presbytery 1816-1818. It also included some churches in the state outside the Low Country area. However, it never gained a strong foothold. It engaged in conversations to join a local Synod of the Presbyterian General Assembly in 1800 and 1804, but it was denied in 1805. Again it voted to join the General Assembly in 1811, but was never received. It finally died in 1819 or later.

The obstinacy of the new Presbytery left the territory open for the expansion of the idea of independency on one hand, or the extension of the Presbyterian General Assembly into the area. The General Assembly was a 1789 reorganization of the old Synod of Philadelphia and New York.

After the War, the independent churches in Georgia took Pastors who affiliated with the New York Presbytery of the General Assembly. It was the Presbytery most influenced by New England, and the churches remained virtually autonomous with their Pastors' Presbyteries so far away.

The unity which had helped to create the Revolution by bringing Reformed Churches together began to dissipate after the War. Not only had the ethnic churches moved away, but also Jacob Green led a schism in New Jersey and New York towards the organization of "Associated Presbyteries." These bodies reasserted some of the key New England ideas of autonomy, and non-subscription, mingled with a pro-revival and social action stance. Largely New England settled parts of New York, and some similar parts of New Jersey left the Presbyterian Church. However, many of the oldest and most cosmopolitan churches remained keeping some Congregational viewpoints alive in the main Presbyterian fellowship.

UP THE SAVANNAH RIVER

Initially South Carolina and Georgia Presbyterianism was heavily influenced by the independent and autonomous spirit fostered in the Low Country. Some churches, such as Camden in Kershaw County, and Beersheba in York County had Congregational Pastors. Others, such as Waccamaw in Horry County, Rocky Springs in Laurens County, Waxhaw in Lancaster County, and the St.Andrew's Church in Charleston (1814-c.1823) spent much of their history independent of Presbyteries.

The Bullock family, once connected to Charleston's Independent Church helped organize the Bullock's Creek Church in northern South Carolina. When it was chartered in 1784, it took the name "Presbyterian or Congregational Church of Bullock's Creek."

These influences were most clear up the Savannah River valley. A Church in Brier Creek, GA had been the first in that colony to affiliate with the Presbyterian Synod (by 1766). But when it was chartered in 1790 it chose the name Independent Congregational Church of Waynesboro. In 1810 it absorbed another Presbyterian Church by merger.

In 1819 two Presbyterian churches across the River in SC reorganized as Congregational (Rock/Rocky Creek, and Old Cambridge). By the next year another Congregational Church existed in nearby Beech Island, SC.

Another independent church began to meet in St. Marys, GA by 1808.

On the other hand the General Assembly was also trying to extend its hegemony in the deep South. Its South Carolina Presbytery divided in 1800. The Hopewell Presbytery (organized 1796) served Georgia. South Carolina work was extended in the new Harmony Presbytery (organized 1809) which also included the old Presbyterian Church at Darien, GA, and the Augusta, GA Church (1804). Eventually Pastors from Independent Churches in the Low Country joined Harmony Presbytery. The pastors of the Georgia coastal churches became part of the Georgia Presbytery (begun 1820), while Waynesboro's Pastor is found in the Hopewell Presbytery after 1821. These churches, though, remained independent, and were usually not even listed in the Presbytery minutes.

In Low Country South Carolina a few Pastors connected themselves with Presbyteries in the General Assembly before 1822: Dorchester (1794-c.1800), Wappetaw (c.1818-1820), James Island (1796-1801,1816-1822); Johns Island (1792-1798,c.1820-1822); Saltcatcher (1811-c.1816) and Old Scots in Charleston (1819 (possibly 1810)-1822).

THE CHARACTER AND POLITY OF THE LOW COUNTRY CHURCHES

By this point the reader may be amazed as to why I have given such a relatively expansive treatment to a group of churches which appear to be so few in number. Indeed, the number of Low Country churches, even including those in Appendix VII., was always less than two dozen.

But their strength and power can not be underestimated.

First it needs to be said that the country churches were plantation churches. At the center of each parish was a large meeting house used by everyone in the winter. However, in the long hot summers when mosquitoes and disease ravaged the swampy land, the wealthy property owners moved to summer villages in more friendly locations. There small meeting houses or house churches served parts of the congregations. Many of these "branch" churches were much larger than full congregations of other denominations at the time. One congregation and their out-stations could cover huge sections of land. To indicate this we have included all branches of the plantation churches with letter entries under the main church at its entry point. The parishes were so large that many of the branches are in other counties. When that is the case we still list them under their main church, but you can use the index to find where the entries should be. Later, when the plantation economy fell apart most of the branch churches became independent congregations on their own. The branch organization pattern was so successful that it was copied by the city churches as well.

Their highly educated ministry took key leadership roles in the community. They also inspired ministry as the professional choice of many young parishioners. Perhaps hundreds of pastors, mostly Presbyterians, came from the low country churches.

Also, we can not say enough about how these congregations influenced the development of South Carolina and Georgia. Many of the key leaders of these colonies and states for generations were members of these churches. After the Revolution, when many Episcopalians were labeled as Tories, the leadership posts in the communities fell to members of the Low Country churches. A whole host of important figures in these states and in the nation, came from or were descendants of members of these congregations. For example, of the four individuals elected to the Continental Congress from Georgia, three came from the Midway or Savannah congregations, two of whom (Lyman Hall, and J.J. Zubly) had been ordained as ministers! The Midway Church claims four of the early Governors of Georgia.

Any student of American history must admit that there was something of a spirit of autonomy and independence that was in stronger in South Carolina, and particularly the Charleston area, than in other parts of the South.

Were these Churches Congregational? To me it is clear that the central core of churches were indeed Congregational. Some say no because of the multiplicity of names.

Indeed in 1775 the Independent Church in Charleston voted:
"This Church has never adopted any distinguishing Name, Platform, or Constitution in a formal manner, nor declared of what denomination of Dissenters it is; but suffered itself to be called either Presbyterian, Congregational, or Independent, sometimes by one of these names, sometimes by two of them, and other times by all three." (Edwards, p.32)

While this may seem like a disclaimer, we need to clarify what those words meant at that time. Independent was the name used by Congregationalists in England and Wales. It was the preferred name there since it meant "independent" of the establishment of the Church of England. The churches in New England that called themselves "Congregational" were established and tax supported. Therefore this church was independent in the sense that it was outside a tax supported establishment, but Congregational in that it was autonomous. It was Presbyterian in that it highly regarded the authority of its teaching elders (pastors). In this latter regard it was on the same ground as most of the churches in Connecticut at that time, and many others in New England, that called themselves Presbyterian in the same sense. Those churches, though, also did not recognize the power of judicatories, and are considered Congregational today, and historically. Such is the case here.

C.K.Shipton said:
"The seventeenth century ministers here [in the colonies] would have said that they were ordained in the presbyterian manner over churches of the congregational polity. They usually called themselves Independents or Congregationalists, but would have laid claim to being Presbyterians... In the southern and middle colonies the Dissenters usually took the name Presbyterian because of the large proportion of Scotch among them. They differed in no way from the New England churches until they were swamped by the Scotch." (quoted in Edwards, pp.32-33.)

In 1789 several churches joined with the Independent Church in organizing the "Society for the Relief of Elderly and Disabled Ministers and the Widows and Orphans of the Clergy of the Independent or Congregational Church in the State of South Carolina." It was chartered by the state, and initially included delegates and received contributions from many churches.

Finally in 1801 a Congregational Association of South Carolina was organized. This was the only such group in the South before the Civil War. It ordained Pastors for two of the Georgia churches (Waynesboro and White Bluff), and ten or eleven South Carolina churches also had pastoral connections to this body. The Independent Church in Charleston (now beginning to be known as Circular Church) always served as the anchor. During the life of the Association several other churches (notably Wappetaw, Edistoe, and the Huguenot Church in Charleston) remained independent.

The heart of the Association was made up of clearly Congregational Churches.

THE RACE QUESTION

But there is another reason why most Congregational historians have written off this group of churches.

Up to this point we have failed to mention one more ethnic group present in these churches, indeed the largest ethnic group. For most of their history many of these churches had far more Black members than European. Indeed some had many times the number of Black members that they had of European members. But the Black members were second class members. Most were slaves. The Europeans ran the churches.

21

A HISTORY OF SOUTHERN CONGREGATIONALISM

The great wealth of these congregations was built on slave labor. It could be argued that the rice and indigo economy was even more labor intensive than the cotton and tobacco crops in the rest of the South. The Plantation churches were exactly that: Plantations. When the European owners departed to their ocean front summer homes, the African Americans stayed in the heat of the swamps, surrounded by mosquitoes and disease.

It is true that these churches considered themselves the moderate and caring wing of southern society in regard to the race issue. In many cases they broke southern law and educated their slaves. They hired seminary trained pastors to preach to and care for them. The owners considered themselves "enlightened."

But slavery is still slavery. Pastors of these churches attended Harvard or Yale and traveled back and forth to New England pulpits with no one questioning the morality of slavery. It is probably this blot on the Congregational denomination, which later heralded itself as the great champion of justice, that caused historians to bury this history under a basket. Modern Congregationalists would rather not have the light shone on this part of their history. But there it is.

We shall return to the Low Country churches after we have explored some other Congregational influences in the expanding South.

OTHER EARLY SOUTHERN CONGREGATIONALISM

At the end of the French and Indian War, England gained control of much formerly French territory reaching the Mississippi River. Soon two Congregational pastors made their way to the Natchez (MS) area, and a Congregational Church began there in 1773, the first Protestant Church in the old Southwest. The Church, however, did not last out the Revolutionary War.

After America took over Louisiana, some Congregationalists made their way to New Orleans, where a Church was begun on a New England model in 1818.

For the most part, though settlement from New England or of English and Welsh Puritans was slow in the South. The New England element was never very strong. The reasons for this were somewhat geographic. Most population movement inland from the coast tended to be due west. When one realizes that New England is east of New York (and not north of it), one realizes that New Englanders had a lot farther to go before they reached the center of the continent. When Yankee settlement was filling in central and western New York, southern coastal settlers were more than half the way to the Mississippi River.

The few Congregationalists that did arrive continued, for the most part, the cooperation with the Presbyterians already begun. Two factors undergirded and strengthened this process: The Plan of Union and united Missionary Societies.

CONGREGATIONAL AND PRESBYTERIAN COOPERATION

In 1801 the Presbyterian General Assembly and the General Association of Connecticut entered into a Plan of Union to work in a united way on the opening western frontier. This was later approved by the other New England state Congregational bodies. It provided that Congregational and Presbyterian churches would not be organized in the same frontier territory. Instead people would cooperate to form mixed churches which could mingle elements of both polities as well as people. In addition Presbyterian churches could call Congregational pastors and Congregational churches could call Presbyterian pastors. The process of appeal in difficult questions would be according to the denominational traditions of the Pastor. It needs to be pointed out that in 1801 much of the Presbyterian General Assembly leadership had New England connections or ancestry. It was a move by the cooperative end of the Presbyterian Church.

A HISTORY OF SOUTHERN CONGREGATIONALISM

This was further extended by the Accommodation Plan adopted by the Presbyterian Synod of Albany (NY) in 1807/1808. Under this plan the Synod admitted an entire Congregational Association, composed entirely of Congregational churches into membership in the Synod. These churches were allowed to maintain their own local forms of organization. Many did not even have ruling elders, but merely sent delegates to Presbytery or Synod. This open plan made the Presbyterian church very cooperative. Therefore an era of good feeling set in. With the exception of a few bodies in New York state clinging to the New England boundary, one by one every Congregational body in the wider country either disbanded or merged with its local Presbyterian body. The Congregational denomination ceased to exist. But at the same time the Presbyterian Church became a cooperative body tolerating many local forms, covenants, and ideas.

These actions which effected church forms were enforced by issues of pastoral supply.

As early as 1774 the General Association of Connecticut began to send missionaries to the frontier. Later Missionary Associations were set up to continue this work. Those who were expecting to settle in the west were generally advised that Congregational institutions and styles could not be perpetuated on the frontier, therefore they were encouraged to unite with Presbyterians where they settled and join Presbyteries. Later, after Congregationalism did gain a foothold in the west, Congregational historians tried to prove how ridiculous this argument was. However, these arguments have failed to understand the timing of these recommendations. Up to 1834 in Massachusetts (and a few years earlier in Connecticut, New Hampshire, and Maine) Congregational churches were established churches supported by taxation. Meetinghouses were owned by the towns. Pastors' salaries were paid by taxes. Churches not worrying about such financial obligations could use charity to expand on the mission field. So, while strong missionary aid was provided, the west could not be expected to be like New England. Obviously tax support could not come to be the case in the new west. Established Congregationalism could not expand.

Two types of Missionary Societies were created. One type, which served "foreign" missions, including Indian tribes in America will be explored below. The other type of Society focused on sending missionaries to the new frontiers or strengthening existing churches. The earliest of these included regional groups such as the Society in Morris County for the Promotion of Learning and Religion (1787, in NJ, founded by the Morris County Presbytery, a Congregational body), the Berkshire and Columbia Missionary Society (1797;on the NY/MA border), and state groups like the Missionary Society of Connecticut (1798, controlled by the General Association), and the Massachusetts Missionary Society (1799). The Presbyterian General Assembly, and some of its judicatories, like the Connecticut Congregationalists, had also appointed missionaries to the new territories. They created a Standing Committee on Missions in 1802, which became the Board of Missions of the General Assembly in 1816. However, the individual societies prospered much more quickly than that of the General Assembly, and people seeking pastors were more inclined to write to a society that could send help, than one that couldn't.

Several smaller Societies in New York united in 1822 as the United Domestic Missionary Society (UDMS). Then, in 1826, the American Home Missionary Society was organized (AHMS). The AHMS absorbed the UDMS and some other groups. Before 1833 its major support came from "Presbyterians" primarily in New York State. However, this constituency was primarily mixed churches in Presbytery under the Plan of Union or Congregational or formerly Congregational Churches in Presbytery under the accommodation plan. The southern and Scotch Irish elements in the Presbyterian Church had little involvement. Between 1828 and 1832 each of the New England state societies became auxiliaries of the AHMS. They soon became the primary contributors.

Under the new auxiliary arrangement the state societies continued and were autonomous, and were responsible for missionary activity within their state. But, income above and beyond that was sent to the AHMS for work in states that were not self supporting. (There was also more minor support from Dutch Reformed Churches and the Associate Reformed Presbyterian Church.)

One can not read the history of the Presbyterian Church in almost any part of the country that began to develop between the Revolutionary and Civil Wars and not encounter New England missionaries arriving and founding churches. This was even true in the South. Indeed, perhaps a majority of early Presbyteries had churches that could trace New Englanders in the earliest congregations. In the earliest days you find references to the New England missionary societies, such as Connecticut. Later you find references to the AHMS.

However, as we said above, at least in the South, the missionaries encountered few other New England settlers. We are forced to conclude that many churches they organized probably had mixed forms of polity with some Congregational influences, just as we have seen how Congregationalism in the South Carolina low country influenced Presbyterianism in other parts of that state. However, Presbyterian historians have rather uniformly covered up any such instances in the South. A few have been discovered almost by pure chance. We therefore must report that there were probably some other churches with Congregational forms in southern Presbyteries that are not reported in this book.

Parker (1988), for example, shows how the New England theology of Hopkinsinianism was widespread among Presbyterians in east Tennessee. He documents the importance of New England born and/or trained Pastors in the area. He indicates that the area had a strong anti-slavery streak, and a pro-Union majority during the Civil War. We also know that Presbyteries in the area admitted Indian congregations which had local Congregational forms into membership. We can not conclude that New Englanders in the area made the area anti-slavery and pro-Union. It may have been that the anti-slavery and pro-Union sentiments in the area made it attractive to New Englanders. Nonetheless, there was a clear Congregational presence in southern Presbyterianism that is hard to codify or count.

UNITARIANISM

One aspect of New England that most Congregationalists would probably have wished never reached the South was Unitarianism. Beginning particularly about 1805 or 1806 Unitarian thought, which denied the Trinity, began to split New England congregations. The movement peaked in 1825 with the organization of the American Unitarian Association. Some other local schisms continued until nearly 1850, so we have viewed the period through that year as the period of the Unitarian departure from Congregationalism.

The South became part of the battleground. When William Ellery Channing of Boston's Federal Street Church gave an ordination sermon in 1819 in Baltimore for Jared Sparks, on the title "Unitarian Christianity," it became the platform of the new movement.

Southern Unitarian Churches often called themselves Congregational, and to this day it is common in some parts of the South to equate Congregationalism with Unitarianism.

The movement did impact the southern churches. The Independent Church in Charleston was divided, and an old branch broke off and became a Unitarian congregation. The First Church in New Orleans, which had already adopted Presbyterian forms and joined Presbytery, had a hard time displacing a Pastor with Unitarian ideas. It also divided with both the continuing Presbyterian and Unitarian factions seeking their historic origins in the older church.

A HISTORY OF SOUTHERN CONGREGATIONALISM

Other Unitarian churches began before the Civil War in several southern cities, and those started by 1850 are documented in Appendix I.

THE INDEPENDENT PRESBYTERIAN CHURCH

Another unusual Congregational influence on southern Presbyterianism began at the Bullock Creek Church in northern South Carolina. As we have indicated earlier, that congregation had been influenced by the Low Country churches and was chartered as a "Presbyterian or Congregational" Church.

The Rev. William C. Davis, a Pastor in the Bullock Creek area, near the SC/NC border, from 1789, was deposed from the Presbyterian ministry in 1810. Two congregations then served by Davis were divided, and three new congregations were begun sympathetic to his views. These five formed the General Convention of the Independent Presbyterian Church in 1813.

The new group was theologically loyal to Davis, whose views are hard to characterize. However, all authorities agree that its polity was clearly Congregational. Its Constitution provided that each "congregation...(is) sovereign and independent." The General Convention functioned in a way similar to a Congregational Association. The group also expressed some anti-slavery thought.

In addition to the two founding states, the group spread into Tennessee, and later Mississippi and Alabama.

In 1836, after the deaths of most of the early leaders, a plan was suggested to revise the organization of the group. Adopted in 1838 the plan brought the group more in line with the thought of Old School Presbyterian Churches in the area. Culturally peace also began to be made with the slave system.

The Feemster family, relatives of Davis, had taken the lead in organizing the Mississippi and Alabama churches. There, in 1842, they took a strong anti-slavery stand. Between then and 1844 the western churches broke away from the main body. These churches were forced into exile during the Civil War. After the War the Pastor returned and two of the three western Churches evolved into predominantly Black Congregational Churches.

Meanwhile the remaining General Convention Churches tried to unite with the Old School Presbyterians in 1857. The latter group rejected the merger, but a move to unite with the Presbyterian Church in the Confederate States (later the Presbyterian Church in the United States) was approved in 1863.

Even in that group the Congregational order still persisted. Individual congregational votes were needed to approve the merger. Initially three of the then thirteen churches opposed the union, but one of these agreed to go along with the majority. Eventually the other two followed as well.

We have included all these churches in Appendix VIII. Those that reorganized as Congregational after the Civil War, are also shown again in the main lists.

(The history of this group is drawn from two different historical trails, drawn together here for the first time. The most extensive material is found in Parker (69, 1972). He had access to the diary of one of the later leaders of the group as well as the minutes of the Conventions of 1836, 1844, 1855, 1856, 1858, and 1860. Russell Hall's cards (75) are based on Parker's work. The other trail begins with a paper written by Samuel Calvin Feemster about 1875 (67). It explains the feelings of the western anti-slavery group and is found at the Presbyterian Historical Society in Philadelphia. That document refers to many enclosures not there. Punchard's (16) treatment seems to be based on Feemster's work, as it touches many of the same themes. Punchard, however, also adds some specific church information that the Feemster document alludes to, but which is not found in Philadelphia. Copies of the General Convention minutes of 1833 and 1834 (68) are also found in Philadelphia.)

CHARLESTON UNION PRESBYTERY

The Plan of Union reached the only Congregational Association in the South in 1822. In that year the Association merged with the Harmony Presbytery (org.1809) which was part of the General Assembly. A provision of the merger was that a new Presbytery be set off for the Low Country area, and that came to pass with the setting up of Charleston Union Presbytery (CUP) in 1823, "Union" as a Plan of Union Presbytery. However, unlike union Presbyteries in the north where Congregational churches were listed as full members, the CUP in a southern environment had trouble deciding how to deal with its many types of congregations. In its 1826 report to the General Assembly (for c.1825) it listed ten churches as if all were full members. But the next year it listed only four member churches and the other six were designated "under pastoral care of ministers of Presbytery,... but have not put themselves under care of the Presbytery." It became a very unique body. (When names of studied churches were shown with the pastor's name in this Presbytery, we have shown the churches as listed here, even if it was not a full member of this Presbytery. We have followed this policy with studied Georgia churches as well.)

In 1823 a young Andover Seminary graduate came from New England to begin services in Saint Augustine, FL, where the first Presbyterian or Congregational Church in that state was organized the next year by the CUP.

The Georgia Presbytery set up in 1820/1821 also took on elements of a union Presbytery. Pastors from Midway, and sometimes White Bluff, Waynesboro, and the Independent Church of Savannah were found to be members of this Presbytery.

THE PRESBYTERIAN DIVISION

The era of good feeling did not last long. As the Presbyterian Church continued to grow in areas primarily populated by descendants of Scottish and Scotch Irish settlers, the center of gravity began to shift in the Church. The desire for strict subscription to the Westminster standards rose again. This was at a time when other "liberal" theologies, such as those of Samuel Hopkins, and Nathaniel Taylor began to spread in churches with New England contacts. Also Princeton Seminary came clearly under the control of the conservatives in the Presbyterian Church. Strict Presbyterian constructionists charged that the existence of local churches without sessions and ruling elders in Presbytery (mixed or accommodation plan churches) was in violation of the General Assembly Constitution.

The anti-slavery movement was also spreading in the north and causing greater divisional controversy. The Congregationally dominated states of Massachusetts, New Hampshire, and Connecticut had joined Pennsylvania in being the first to outlaw slavery after the Revolution. Massachusetts Pastor Manasseh Cutler had also been instrumental in writing the Northwest Ordinance of 1787 which outlawed slavery in five Great Lakes States. This heritage began to make New Englanders unwelcome in southern pastorates, and southern pastorates unattractive to New Englanders.

Issues of the Missionary Societies also grew. In 1828 the Presbyterian General Assembly had strengthened their Board of Missions for ministry in the west. Since it was operating in the same territory as the AHMS, in 1830 a move was made to merge the work. This effort, retried the next year, failed. Now there was a way to start new Presbyterian churches unsoiled by Congregational influences.

All of these factors reached a head in 1837 when the conservative majority at the Presbyterian General Assembly voted to throw out of the church four entire synods (three in New York and one in Ohio), which were the most contaminated by mixed and accommodation plan churches. Other Presbyteries and Synods were also warned and censured. After an attempt to reseat the four Synods failed, they and their allies organized a new Presbyterian General Assembly in 1838. The new Assembly became popularly known as the New School.

The older Assembly came to be known as the Old School. It ended its cooperation in the Plan of Union. It insisted on local Presbyterian forms in all congregations. It withdrew support from the inter-denominational missionary societies. It set up its own Board of Foreign Missions.

The New School continued with the Plan of Union, and the support of the cooperative societies. It, of course, included just about all of the accommodation plan and mixed congregations. But we do find even the Old School Charleston and Georgia Presbyteries listing churches or pastors who were serving churches with Congregational forms. These few technical violations of Old School Presbyterian law were done to probably convince the churches to become Old School. There were probably other churches that were tolerated as well.

But the New School was not entirely New England in orientation. An argument was put forward that since Presbyterian government was based on a series of judicatory courts, where charges and appeals could be levied, to excise four synods without a trial or hearing was a violation of Presbyterian law. Therefore a large group of strict Presbyterians calling themselves "Constitutional Presbyterians" affiliated with the New School. This group was further strengthened by an insistence on the part of many Old School bodies to require Presbyterial votes to approve the excising of the Synods. This became a type of subscription to the acts of the Old School majority. Many felt that they could have reservations or mis-givings about those actions, but still want to stay in a unified Presbyterian Church. However, this insistence and requirement drove some committed Presbyterians into the New School.

On the other side many Congregational churches in Presbytery began to fear that, if the General Assembly could by fiat throw people out of the Church, and the New School still had the same Constitution that allowed that in the Old School, then there was no future for them in the Presbyterian Church at all. Therefore large numbers of accommodation plan and mixed churches began to leave New School Presbyteries. The Waynesboro, GA church, for example, withdrew from Presbytery in 1840. In parts of the country where there were more Congregational Churches, Congregational Associations and Conferences were established and Congregationalism again became a national church group.

Because of the way that population was distributed, and considering that Congregational rising opposition to slavery was part of the problem to conservative southern Presbyterian churches, the South was strongly Old School. A minority of New School Presbyteries did exist in the South. Parker (1988) has pointed out that these Presbyteries were primarily in areas strongly influenced by New England thought.

The presence of some southerners in the New School, however, thwarted that organization and made it afraid to take strong stands on slavery or to be carried away with its unity with the Congregationalists. Unable, therefore, to find a clear identity, the New School faced a constant drain of churches and an inability to grow.

Other Presbyterians ended up outside of both General Assemblies. Chief among these were the Charleston Union Presbytery and a short lived independent Presbytery in GA, Etowah (1839 to btwn.1842 & 1844). The CUP divided in 1839, with the Old School withdrawing and taking the name Charleston Presbytery. The Old School claimed they were the majority, because most of the clergy in the continuing CUP were serving churches which were "not Presbyterian Churches at all." (Smyth) Therefore, the Plan of Union and the era of good feeling had apparently not even happened. The CUP tried to find for themselves a middle position. They said that when the Old School faction had tried to get the old CUP to consent to the actions in excising the four synods, that they opposed it. Such a consent was not needed and was not an issue of faith. They said that the Old School had left, claimed the Presbytery seats at Synod and been accepted by the Old School majority in the Synod. They stated that they wished to stay in the Synod and General Assembly even though they disapproved the excising action. (Report and Resolutions... 1845) The CUP also objected to an anti-Hopkinsinian stand taken by the Synod of South Carolina. They called it "a new test of orthodoxy." (71, Vol.I)

The CUP documents present an intellectual quandary. On the one hand you can see the shadow of slavery in their actions. They wanted to maintain a southern unity, and felt the possibility of national division on the horizon. (Afterall, they were centered in Charleston,SC.) Eventually their paper advocated an independent southern church. (71, Vol.I) But they also had the problem of their churches with Congregational forms. How did they expect to continue to serve them in a General Assembly that insisted on Presbyterian forms? The plea for toleration of a minority on the excising issue had about it the plea for a general toleration.

In Appendix VII. we have listed Presbyterian churches in the CUP during its independent phase: 1839-1852. Also included in that list are a few independent churches usually associated with the CUP, and notes on later Black congregations organized from these churches.

Controversy continued. Despite the presence of New School churches in the South, the AHMS was unable to serve them. Fewer northerners, either Congregationalists or New School Presbyterians were willing to go South. The AHMS had a vocal minority which agitated against support to churches including slave owners. During the 1840's the number of AHMS missionaries in slave states declined to only a handful.

Radicals also drew away some of the AHMS support. In 1846 several small groups joined together to form the American Missionary Association (AMA) committed to work against slavery and not to support or aid churches that had admitted to membership any slave holders.

In 1852 a national Convention of Congregationalists was held in Albany, NY. It revoked the Plan of Union, and encouraged a denominational Congregationalism. Congregationalism, however, still remained the primary supporter of the AHMS and the ABCFM. Several mixed and accommodation plan churches still continued to be members of New School Presbyteries, so the Plan of Union continued with them.

In 1847 the New School General Assembly set up its own Committee on Home Missions. It began to compete for support with the AHMS, and New School support for the AHMS declined. In 1853 the Southern Aid Society was created, a new missionary society aimed at supporting New School Presbyterian and Congregational Churches in the South. It was a move to continue independent societies, but indicated the failure of the older societies in the South. In 1857 the AHMS cut off all support to churches which included slave holders in their membership. In that same year most of the New School Presbyteries in the South left that church and organized the United Synod of the South, a New School southern church.

RADICAL CONGREGATIONALISM

After the reappearance of Congregationalism beyond the New England/New York areas, it made a few attempts to spread into the South before the Civil War. A church was begun in Newark, DE in 1836 and lived about seven years before being absorbed by a New School church. A short lived church also existed around this time in Wheeling, WV (then VA). Two attempts were made to organize a Congregational Church in Washington, DC in the 1850's.

The most significant work of this type was the ministry of John G. Fee. Ordained in the 1840's by the New School Synod of Kentucky, Fee seceded in opposition to slavery. He organized a handful of Kentucky churches on abolitionist grounds, and founded Berea College in Berea, KY in 1855 as an integrated school. Fee considered himself a non-denominational Christian, but received support from the AMA, and after the War most of his still surviving churches were treated for a period as

Congregational churches.

THE COLLAPSE OF LOW COUNTRY CONGREGATIONALISM

With the continued growth of anti-slavery sentiment in the Congregational Churches, the slave holding churches in the South found themselves more and more isolated. In 1852 the Charleston Union Presbytery gave up its separate existence and joined the Old School Presbytery of Charleston. In their minutes of 1853 the Presbytery reported:

"Within a comparatively small compass are not less than eight Congregational and Independent Presbyterian churches identified in interest with us; which must be supplied with pastors from us; and which, though making the Presbyterian church in some measure the channel through which their charities are disbursed, have never formally committed themselves with us in Ecclesiastical bonds."

They then went on to invite the eight to join them. This minute indicates that three of the congregations are "influential, wealthy, and large" churches in the City of Charleston. The James Island Church responded by joining the Presbytery later that year. In 1854 the invitations were repeated and the First Presbyterian Church of Charleston, the Presbyterian churches on Edisto Island, Circular Church in Charleston, and Wappetaw, Dorchester, and Stony Creek, were asked to join. If we assume that there were two churches on Edisto Island, then the seven listed here, plus James Island would equal the eight churches counted in 1853. However, since we know of no other churches on Edisto at this time, and since the 1853 vote referred to three congregations in the City of Charleston, we assume that the Huguenot Church of Charleston is actually the eighth church referred to. The Beaufort and Cainhoy churches were long dead. The Walterboro Church had become Old School around the time of the 1838 division, and the Wilton Church had followed in 1850.

In Georgia the Waynesboro church joined an Old School Presbytery in 1853. Midway was also being served by a member of an Old School Presbytery, but remained independent, as did the White Bluff and Savannah Independent Churches.

The 1789 Society for the Relief of Elderly and Disabled Ministers and the Widows and Orphans of the Clergy of the Independent or Congregational Church in the State of South Carolina had originally served several churches. However, during the era of good feeling, other churches dropped out of support and the organization became dominated by the Circular Church of Charleston. The Society loaned money to the Circular Church for its extensive building plans. In 1834 the Society's By Laws were amended to direct its support to that one congregation. In 1854 members at Wappetaw began a court case saying that amendment was improper and that the funds should be made available to clergy from a wider area. In 1854 the Stony Creek Church also petitioned for a similar claim. They were not willing to wait, however, and in 1855 Stony Creek was reorganized as a Presbyterian Church. Finally in 1859 the court ruled that the money was meant for the Congregational denomination in South Carolina, but it was essential that Congregationalism be re-established in the state, and that attempts be made to reorganize a Congregational Association.

The Society began to respond. In 1859 it made a loan to the Wappetaw church to prevent the selling of their Mount Pleasant branch building to the Presbytery for its organization as a Presbyterian Church.

In 1860 the Society's By Laws were revised and sent for approval to the Congregational Churches in the state, which were named as Circular Church in Charleston, Wappetaw, and Dorchester.

Circular Church was listed in the 1860 Congregational Quarterly as a Congregational Church in that state.

But then came the Civil War. The Low Country was a chief target of Sherman's March to the Sea. Circular Church also burned in 1861. The eradication of the slave economy destroyed the plantation churches. Heavily dependent on slave labor, their economies could not survive. The Midway, Dorchester, and Wappetaw churches all died as a result of the War. The Whites settled in the old summer branch churches, which were now reorganized as Presbyterian. The Blacks seceded and organized their own congregations. (We have listed the first Black churches drawn off of the old plantation congregations, following the branch lists with letter designations under the parent churches. We have also listed as notes two Black Presbyterian Churches in Charleston drawn from several city congregations.) Edisto Island reorganized as a fully Presbyterian Church in 1870. The First Presbyterian and the Huguenot Churches in Charleston, the Independent Church in Savannah, and White Bluff continued as independent churches served by members of southern Presbyteries. Only Circular Church continued as a Congregational remnant of the once mighty Low Country dynasty, and it emerged from the War meeting in a Sunday School building behind the burned out ruin of a Church.

PRESBYTERIAN REORGANIZATION

After the outbreak of the Civil War the Old School Presbyterians also split North and South. The Presbyterian Church in the Confederate States of America began in 1861. In 1864, the United Synod of the South, the southern New School body, united with the Old School body. After the Civil War it became known as the Presbyterian Church in the United States.

In the North the remaining Old School and New School General Assemblies reunited in 1869/1870. The new united church insisted upon local Presbyterian forms in all churches. The remaining mixed and accommodation plan churches either left at this time, in another secessionist wave to Congregationalism, or, accustomed to Presbyterian connections, conformed themselves to Presbyterian usage. Presbyterian and Congregational cooperation was over.

From 1869 to 1881 or 1882 a few pastors in the Charleston area, led by the Pastor at Old Scots Church tried to recreate the Charleston Union Presbytery. However no churches ever affiliated with it, and it did not long survive.

With the exception of one congregation in Charleston and Fee's work in Kentucky, all the Congregational efforts in the South were now living in Presbyterian institutions.

INDIAN MISSIONS

Similar to domestic missions, Indian missions also arose as a combined effort of Presbyterian and Congregational bodies.

Initial interest in organizing for Indian missions surfaced in New England but was thwarted before the Revolution by opposition from the crown. A 1762 Society had royal interference to their charter.

After the Revolution that changed. Among early independent societies aimed primarily at Indian work were the Society for Propagating the Gospel among Indians and others in North America (MA,1787), the New York Missionary Society (1796), the Northern Missionary Society (NY,1797), and the Western (Foreign) Missionary Society (NJ,1800). These were mostly supported by Congregational, and later by Plan of Union and accommodation plan churches. Many of the independent Societies, with the approval of the Presbyterian General Assembly, combined their work as the United Foreign Missionary Society (UFMS) in 1817.

But the chief player on the Indian Mission scene was to be the American Board of Commissioners for Foreign Missions (ABCFM) founded in 1810. It began first with an inspiration to start mission work outside of the United States. It was originally planned to be a body under the control of the Congregational ministerial bodies in

Massachusetts and Connecticut. However, Presbyterians asked if they could participate in the new endeavor, so by 1812, the Board was chartered as a free standing self perpetuating Board serving several denominations. Again the strongest mission support came from New England. The UFMS was troubled by debt in 1826 when its operations were taken over by the ABCFM. It became quickly the center of all Indian work for both Presbyterians and Congregationalists.

The first Presbyterian or Congregational Indian mission work in the south was begun in southwestern Mississippi serving the Chickasaw tribe in 1799. The work was conducted by a New Englander under a commission from the New York Missionary Society. The effort was abandoned in 1807, but the white membership of the mixed congregation became a continuing Presbyterian Church. Some consider this mission to be the parent of the later Choctaw missions in the state.

In 1803/1804 the Presbyterian General Assembly planned and opened a mission to the Cherokee tribe in Tennessee. It was supported by the Western Missionary Society of New Jersey, and New England sources, basically Congregationalists. It was discontinued in 1810.

In 1817 the ABCFM picked up the interest in Cherokee missions, beginning at Brainerd in Tennessee. The eastern Cherokee mission spread into Alabama and Georgia. The mission included eleven sites and nine churches were organized. Seven of these belonged to Presbytery, two did not. We know that the church at the main station at Brainerd had specifically Congregational forms, even while in Presbytery. It is probably the case that many, if not all of the others did as well. The mission continued until 1839.

In 1818 the ABCFM began a mission to the Choctaws in Mississippi, eventually extending to fourteen sites. Only five churches were organized, four becoming part of Presbytery, the only one not in Presbytery having died before there was a Presbytery operating in the area. It is likely that this mission had more of a Presbyterian flavor than the Cherokee mission. This mission persisted until 1833.

The New England influence on the Indian missions is obvious in all the ABCFM work. Mission stations had names like Brainerd, Dwight, Eliot, Mayhew, Lenox, Stockbridge, names that touched on New England Indian history. However, it is clear that the Cherokee mission always seemed the closest to the New England heritage, while the Choctaw was predominantly Presbyterian.

In 1821 the Presbyterian Synod of South Carolina and Georgia began a mission among the Chickasaw in Mississippi, spreading into Alabama and Tennessee at five sites. In 1827 they transferred this work to the ABCFM. Only two churches were organized. Neither church was in Presbytery, but they were isolated in an area before Presbytery came to be. The work was abandoned in 1835, but the White members of one of the previously mixed churches continued as a Presbyterian Church.

Initially the Cherokee mission was quite successful, and the Choctaw also, but to a lesser extent. However, the pressure for white settlement into Indian territory increased. Great acts of injustice were forced onto the southern tribes. The government took action to force the tribes into the Indian Territory (now Oklahoma). The Choctaw and the Chickasaw left first. However Cherokee resistance was strong and was aided by the missionaries. The government of Georgia invaded the mission and arrested the missionaries. Appeals were made, with some ABCFM support, all the way to the Supreme Court where the decision was in favor of the tribe. However, President Andrew Jackson refused to heed the Court, and forced the Cherokees to leave. The great "trail of tears," where the Cherokees made their way to Oklahoma in terrible conditions is one of the great tragic injustices of American history. The missionaries went with the Cherokees, and probably gained the increasing ire of White southerners.

Actually a western Cherokee mission had been begun by the ABCFM in Arkansas in 1820. In 1829 it was removed into modern Oklahoma. There were two sites in Arkansas, one with a church, and seven in Oklahoma, six with churches. None of these churches ever belonged to Presbytery, and they probably all had Congregational forms. We know that in the 1840's the missionaries were connected in a Congregationally defined Indian Mission Association, but little information is available about it.

But there was a problem. Years of living in a southern culture had acquainted the "five civilized tribes" (Cherokee, Creek, Chickasaw, Choctaw, Seminole) that dominated the Indian Territory, with southern culture. Powerful members of each of the tribes owned slaves. There was increasing pressure from the North to separate from the work of supporting churches with slave owners. Finally in 1860 the ABCFM decided to transfer the Cherokee work to the Old School Foreign Mission Board. However, the missionaries protested and became independent of all Boards. This work floundered during the Civil War. In 1870 one of the main churches was taken up as a mission of the newly reunited northern Presbyterian Church. They eventually revived two of the other stations.

The western Choctaw mission in modern Oklahoma was begun by the ABCFM in 1832. It became the largest mission, with twenty-five sites and eighteen churches founded before the Civil War. (One brief Choctaw mission was on Chickasaw land.) Fifteen of the churches were in Old School Presbyteries, and two of those that weren't were among the earliest and shortest lived. Quite early most of these churches joined the Arkansas Presbytery, and in 1840 they became part of a new Indian Presbytery. In 1845/1846 the Old School began some Choctaw mission work of their own, outside the ABCFM. In 1859 the ABCFM transferred all of their work to the Old School Board. In 1861 it all came under the sway of the new southern Presbyterian Church. The main part of the Choctaw work continued under that sponsorship.

In 1872/1873 the ABCFM tried to again have a Choctaw mission. They began to aide one of the older sites, a site begun before the War, probably by the Old School, and two new sites. This was, however, very isolated, and in 1876 the work was again turned over to the southern Board. The northern Presbyterian Church took over a few of the Choctaw sites beginning in 1886.

The ABCFM sponsored one Creek mission in Oklahoma 1829 to 1837. The Church was never in Presbytery, but was quite early for that. The work was abandoned.

The ABCFM sponsored one mission to a group of Chickasaws living on Choctaw land in Oklahoma beginning about 1841. The Church joined Presbytery, and in 1853 the work was transferred to the Old School Board.

The Old School Presbyterians also began their own Creek mission in 1841/1842 and a Seminole mission in 1848, both in Oklahoma. These became part of a Creek Presbytery organized in 1849. This work was to be transferred to the southern Presbyterian Church, but was discontinued during the Civil War.

The UFMS had begun missions to the Osage and Neosho tribes in Oklahoma in 1819/1820. Faced with financial difficulties, the work was transferred to the ABCFM in 1826. The one church was not in Presbytery, but was probably too early for that. The work was abandoned in 1837.

Because it is not always easy to tell which ABCFM missions had Congregational forms, and which had Presbyterian forms, all of these missions are listed together in Appendix V. We have not listed those missions specifically under the Old School Presbyterians without ABCFM connections.

NEW OCCASIONS TEACH NEW DUTIES

While the ABCFM Indian work drew to a close, and low country Congregationalism was collapsing, the Civil War brought two new Congregational incursions into the South.

Two new efforts appeared. The first, and most vigorous of these was the work of the American Missionary Association.

A HISTORY OF SOUTHERN CONGREGATIONALISM

Before the War the AMA had been a competitor of both the AHMS and the ABCFM on anti-slavery grounds. With slavery fading away, the purpose of the AMA may have been in doubt. But its Board had a clearer vision than waiting on a new future. Chaplains and missionaries followed the Union armies into the South. The AMA set as its task the education and evangelization of the former slaves. This was to be done in a cooperative and integrated way.

Already in 1864 the AMA supported the return of John Fee to Berea, and the refounding of his anti-slavery and integrated College and churches. In the same year a mission effort was begun at Hampton, VA which led to the establishment of Hampton Institute.

A National Congregational Council was held in Boston in 1865. One of the major results of that Council was a decision to raise a large amount of money to provide schools in the South for the freed slaves. The AMA became the agent for this historic work, and over five hundred schools were set up in the next few years. While the AMA also accepted donations from other denominations, it was primarily a Congregational endeavor.

Many of the smaller grammar schools could be started by one person. But the higher level Academies and Colleges demanded the importation of large groups of teachers into the communities. Immediately new racially-mixed Congregational churches arose adjacent to these schools. The teachers could not join nor support racially segregated churches that had supported slavery only a few years earlier. But neither were they happy in the new fast spreading Black denominations which did not have educated ministries. The new churches were racially accepting but stressed education.

In addition to Fee's work in Kentucky, the AMA also took up contact with the Feemster family's reorganization of two formerly Independent Presbyterian Churches in Mississippi, along Congregational lines, and primarily serving Blacks.

Fee's integrated work was also extended into east Tennessee where work was begun among the mountain people. East Tennessee had been pro-Union during the War. Also its Presbyterian Churches, as we have indicated, had been strongly influenced by Congregationalism before the War. Most of these new churches were predominantly White, but were emotionally connected to Berea and AMA sentiments.

Another important growth center for the new Black churches was in the South Carolina and Georgia Low Country. Blacks had been the majority of the members in most of the Low Country Churches before the War, but had no control over the congregations. After the War they seceded and organized their own churches. Because the Low Country churches had allowed education for their slaves, these congregations emerged at a strong educational level, often capable of self support. The majority of the new Low Country Black churches became Presbyterian. Some were started with help from northern Presbyterian missionaries. Others joined the southern Presbyterian church, and by 1872, two thirds of the predominantly Black congregations in that church were in the Low Country. These churches, however, transferred to the northern church in 1878, making the combined northern Presbyterian presence there one of its largest minority centers down to the 1983 merger. However, strong Congregational churches were also organized. The 1867 Plymouth Church in Charleston was a direct secession of Black members from Circular Church. Other strong Black Congregational Churches were born with large memberships in Savannah and Midway.

Another important area for the founding of the earliest Black churches was in the old Roman Catholic area of southern Louisiana. This area had been won by Union forces early in the War. New Black Congregational churches were a way for the population to relate to what seemed like "Americanized" institutions. One of the new Congregational Churches in Louisiana chose as its name "Equal Rights Congregational Church." But most of these Churches revealed their Catholic heritage with names more from that tradition, such as "Saint Mary's."

In 1867 an attempt was made to absorb by merger a group of churches that had recently been formed in southeast Tennessee and northwest Georgia. This went so far as to have the churches listed in the Quarterly. However, the plan fell through. We have listed these churches separately in Appendix VI..

The most important predominantly Black schools to come out of AMA work were Howard University in Washington, DC; Hampton Institute, VA; Atlanta University, GA; Fisk University, Nashville, TN; LeMoyne College, Memphis, TN (later LeMoyne-Owen); Talladega College, AL; Tougaloo College, MS; Straight University, New Orleans, LA (later Dillard); Tillotson College, Austin, TX (later Huston-Tillotson). In each of these communities churches also arose.

A word needs to be said about the geography of this mission activity. Congregationalism emerged from the War not only as a denomination almost entirely northern, but also in the northern parts of those states that bordered the South. In states like Pennsylvania, Ohio, and Illinois, most of the Congregational strength was in the northern part of the states. On the other hand, most slaves were in the deep South and not in the border states. Therefore, this new Black southern Congregationalism developed without any geographic overlap with the existing churches.

The other new entry of Congregationalism into the South, was northern whites moving South for a variety of reasons. Some of these were governmental freedmen agents. Others were business people quick to make a fortune in rebuilding the South. Others were veterans of the Union Army and others attracted by the southern climate. Collectively they have become known as "carpet baggers." The 1863/1864 Church in Memphis now known as First Congregational was formerly called the "Church of the Strangers." It received some support from the AHMS, as did short lived congregations in New Orleans and Chattanooga.

Welsh miners began to move into the South, and Welsh Congregational churches appeared in Maryland, Virginia, and Tennessee.

Congregationalists near the northern states formed a few churches which joined with northern Congregational church bodies. These included Baltimore, MD (1865); Huntington, WV (1872), and Newport, KY (1869). An inter-racial, but predominantly White First Congregational Church was organized in Washington, DC in 1865.

In 1869 twenty seven churches sent delegates to a meeting in Chattanooga, TN to plan a southern strategy for the AMA. Those attending included two White churches supported by the AHMS. The meeting endorsed the need for new churches, and "a church beside the school" policy was articulated for growth and expansion. It was also decided to organize three Conferences of Churches to be centered in the New Orleans, LA, Nashville, TN, and Atlanta, GA areas.

SOUTHERN CONGREGATIONALISM STARTS TO ORGANIZE

After the Civil War there was a move throughout Congregationalism for stronger organization. National Councils were held in 1865, and 1870, the latter calling for an ongoing national body. The National Council of Congregational Churches was created in 1871.

Similarly, trying to be a national denomination, Congregationalism set its sights on a growth in the South.

Churches along the border with the North became part of groups there. Maryland churches originally were part of Welsh groups in Pennsylvania, but became part of the New Jersey body when it was organized. That body also included churches in the District of Columbia, Virginia, eastern West Virginia, and later Delaware. Churches along the Ohio River in West Virginia and Kentucky became part of the Ohio organization. The Missouri group began to serve north Arkansas in 1881. These inter-church bodies were integrated and remained so.

(In the Bibliography section of this book we list each of the state level Congregational inter-church bodies which served in the South. Years are given and the changes in names of the various groups are noted. Look there for fuller data.)

A Southwestern Conference (later Louisiana) was organized in the New Orleans area in 1869. A Central South Conference (later Tennessee) centered at Nashville began in 1871. Plans for a Southeastern group around Atlanta in 1874, fell through, but a Georgia Conference was functioning by 1878. Other groups followed in Alabama (south of the Tennessee River) in 1876, North Carolina in 1879, Mississippi in 1883, and Florida in 1883/1884.

Except for Louisiana, the original southern bodies west of the Mississippi River were regional and very weak. A Texas body, centered in the southern part of that state began 1871 but was inactive from c.1884 to 1894. A Red River Association serving along the Indian Territory/Texas border began by 1880, but was replaced by the North Texas Association in 1882. Some churches in northern Arkansas formed an Association in 1887.

All these bodies were meant to be inclusive. The TN group was the most mixed, while the LA group included at least one White Church. The Red River group was centered in the AHMS mission to the Indians (see below), but expanded to include White and BLack congregations in Texas. The Arkansas group was predominantly White, and the Florida group included all predominantly White churches. On the other hand, the GA, AL, MS, and NC groups included only predominantly Black churches.

A State Association of Christian Churches and Ministers of Kentucky was listed as Congregational by 1870, and was centered around Fee's Churches and Berea. In 1879 its Secretary reported to the denomination that it was not a Congregational body, and in 1880 it was dropped. A few years later Berea College also withdrew from AMA support, Fee feeling that the AMA had become too denominational in its interests. However, most of the Churches in the Christian Association eventually made their way back into the Congregational family, Kentucky churches initially connecting to Tennessee. Fee's main church in Berea was later listed by the American Christian Convention (with whom the Congregationalists merged in 1931), and later became a Community church.

By 1872 the AHMS work in the South had been transferred to the AMA. The AMA was also instrumental in beginning the first church in Florida, a White congregation in 1875/1876. In 1876 a meeting of AMA missionaries in Atlanta vowed to be more aggressive in church starts, not only in schools. They felt the "large Negro denominations" were doing little to elevate what they called a "low moral level." They wanted to see "pure churches."

The period after the Civil War was a time of great tumult for the mission agencies. The ABCFM was giving up much of its Indian work to Presbyterian Boards. By about 1875 the AMA had become the mission arm for the South and the AHMS for the North. But soon tensions and turf battles would begin.

A NEW INDIAN MISSION

In 1876 the AHMS decided to undertake mission work in the Indian Territory. In that year a congregation was begun in the Choctaw Nation. In 1879 a congregation was begun in the Cherokee Nation. This ministry extended to include ten congregations and one mission in the Choctaw Nation, and five churches in the Cherokee Nation. Some of the Cherokee Churches became part of the Missouri Congregational body.

This was probably not exclusively Indian work. The Choctaw Nation churches were closely aligned with White and Black churches on the other side of the Red River, and were probably of mixed membership themselves during some of this period.

This work was not very successful. The Choctaw work faltered, but a few congregations lasted perhaps until 1902. The Cherokee work was transferred from the AHMS to the AMA in 1884, when the AHMS gave up its experiment in Indian work. The main Cherokee Church soon became predominantly English. The Church lasted until 1947.

We show the above churches with the Indian ethnic code (In) although many were probably mixed.

Only two other attempts were made to minister to southern Indians.

From 1895 to 1905 the AMA sponsored a work among the Cheyenne and Arapahoe people near Darlington, OK. A Church was begun, but the property was sold to the Baptists.

A congregation probably serving the Coushatta tribe joined a Louisiana body in 1901. It was always small and isolated from the rest of the denomination's Indian work. The Church has probably been inactive in recent years.

All these churches are shown on the main lists.

ATLANTA AND THE MISSION BOARDS

In 1882 a new White congregation was begun in Atlanta (then Piedmont Cong., now Central). It applied to and was granted support from the AHMS. The President of Atlanta University and others protested this Board support for a division of Congregational work in the City. The AMA also joined the complaint and charged that operations by two Boards in the South would create a segregated Congregationalism. They said that racial harmony had characterized and made Congregationalism distinct in the South up to this point.

The supporters of the AHMS said that many Whites in the South, and some from the North as well, could not risk the social ostracism that would result from membership in the existing churches, but desired a "progressive theology," and Congregational polity. (One can see here, perhaps, an early case of what was to become a great debate in Congregationalism. The Piedmont church was theologically liberal, but socially conservative. The AMA churches were theologically conservative but socially liberal. If Congregationalism began to characterize itself as liberal, in what way was it liberal?)

This racially based debate fired up the national church. Entire issues of missionary magazines were devoted to the question as to whether two Boards could function side by side serving racially different churches, and not cause a division in the churches?

In December 1883 a meeting was held in Springfield, MA to try to iron out the difficulties between the two Boards. The AHMS agreed to only aid churches that were willing to receive Negro members. But it was also agreed that both Boards could start churches, but "not in area of others without mutual conference and agreement."

The meeting failed to iron out all the difficulties, so another was held in June, 1884 in Boston. It tried to transfer some works from one Board to another to make work more consistent. However, a move to transfer the care of Atlanta's Piedmont Church from the AHMS to the AMA was only agreed to "if the Church will consent." The Church, of course, did not consent.

The results of the 1883 meeting would be quoted again and again. Officially the denomination would only support churches willing to integrate racially. However, the rhetoric and the actuality often were at odds. One change can be seen in the way integration was described by the White Churches. Eventually one finds references that they were willing to receive "qualified" Negroes. That is about the same language used to allow for Black voting in the South before the Civil Rights movement. "Qualified" usually meant no one qualified.

What we have here is a classic case of the debate of social stance versus church growth. The arguments were carried on by, and to sustain the reputation of the large bureaucratic boards. Of course, in these days, there were two boards, one to take each side. One wonders what that means for the church in a day when their are large "united" boards which make church policy decisions? As we shall see the position of church growth over social stance was the position that won out. However, as we shall also see, not a lot of real church growth resulted from this decision. The denomination had compromised its identity, and stood with little clarity to offer the South.

The AHMS began to be more active in the South. After 1883 the new Jacksonville pastor, Sullivan F. Gale was named as the southern agent of the AHMS. He helped organize the new Florida state body, and began a vigorous Church extension in that state.

In 1885 the White Churches in the Atlanta area created a new inter-church body, outside the state body, known as the Atlanta Congregational Union. It was never seated by the National Council, but the 1887 Yearbook does acknowledge its existence. The prediction of the AMA that support from two Boards would lead to a segregated Congregationalism was on its way to being fulfilled. But what began as a dispute in Atlanta, fueled by the interests of the two Societies, soon spread like wild fire over most of the South.

THE CONGREGATIONAL METHODIST CHURCH

Eager to extend White Congregationalism in the South, Sullivan Gale came into contact with a denomination known as the Congregational Methodist Church. Gale promoted a merger with that group. Modern Congregational historians have merely noted the encounter with the Congregational Methodists as one of the first steps in the ecumenical growth of the denomination. It is heralded as a progressive step in Christian understanding and unity.

However, those types of remarks really cover up the role of this event in introducing segregation and racial division into organized Congregationalism.

The Congregational Methodist Church was organized in 1852 by a group of local preachers who left the Methodist Episcopal Church South. A debate had been brewing in that Church for two years over the role of "local ministers." The itinerant method of the Church had created two classes of clergy: itinerants (or circuit riders) and local preachers. The local preachers were subject to the circuit riders. For example, local preachers could hold and organize revivals, but they had to wait for the arrival of a circuit rider before the new converts could be received as members of the churches. The wide territory of the circuit riders also meant that many churches had preaching only on weekdays. They could have Sabbath services if more local preachers were given permission to lead churches. They gave five reasons for organizing the new body: (1) they favored Sabbath preaching; (2) they were opposed to all government in the church being in the "same hands;" (3) they believed lay people have a role in the government of the Church; (4) they opposed the division of the clergy into circuit and local classifications; (5) they believed the Methodist Episcopal Church South would not change on these issues. For further explanation of these issues see McDaniel (37).

However, there are a few other aspects of what were some of the roots of the controversy not directly addressed by McDaniel. First is the anti-missionary movement. McDaniel describes the early Methodist Church as a "missionary" and migratory emphasis with "but few regular churches." That situation, he argues, favored strong circuit rider leadership. But he also argues that the missionary period is over. Intertwined with desire for local control, was opposition to large assessments to support the establishment episcopacy. The rise of the Congregational Methodists was closely aligned with the anti-mission movement in much of rural America. While the new Church did not specifically denounce mission boards, its thinking was influenced by that train of thought. Secondly, we are, at this stage, just at the beginning of the period when the Methodist churches were founding colleges and seeking better education and salaries for their elders (circuit riders). Intrinsic to the Congregational Methodist argument was a view of the clergy closer to the farmer/pastor of the Baptist and restorationist traditions. There was resistance here to the high paid educated clergy coming into vogue.

The new body was also very Methodist in its original polity. It was organized by a group of clergy, before any congregations existed. As part of the organization the group adopted a Book of Discipline and instituted a system of references and appeals. Power to ordain and license clergy was held by the District Conferences.

From its origins in west central Georgia the group spread into Alabama in its first year. Churches were added in Mississippi in 1853, Florida in 1872, and Missouri in 1874. By 1890 other churches had been added in Arkansas, Illinois, Louisiana, North Carolina, Tennessee, and Texas. Colored Congregational Methodist Churches also existed in Alabama and Texas by 1890.

Interestingly, you will find little on the Congregational Methodist schism in regular Methodist historical sources. McDaniel (37) suggests (p.28) that the Methodist Episcopal church had a policy to say nothing about the movement. He suggests that there was a gag rule in place. This was very effective, because even in modern histories of the Methodist Churches in states effected, one can find hardly a word about the movement.

THE CONGREGATIONAL METHODIST MERGER

In October, 1887 a convention was held at Central Church in Atlanta (formerly Piedmont, then Church of the Redeemer) to pursue a merger of the Atlanta Congregational Union, the Congregational Methodist State Conference of Georgia, and the Free Methodist Protestant State Conference. The latter body was organized in 1881 as a schism from the Methodist Protestant Church. The Congregational Methodist body claimed to continue the original District Conference begun in 1852. It included a few churches in Alabama. Four Churches in the Union were represented, six in the Free Methodist Protestant group, and thirty-six from the Congregational Methodists. They planned to organize a United Congregational Conference of Georgia, and it came into being in 1888. Many Congregational Methodist Churches were not represented. Even though the Congregational Methodists had a General Conference to serve the entire country, this "merger" was arranged not by either national group, but only by certain congregations in this limited area. A group of Congregational Methodist Churches continued as the State Conference and never acknowledged the "merger."

All of this was done without consultation with the older Georgia Association. It had been formed, as had similar bodies in most smaller states by a convention of the churches of the state. In 1889 it voted to either (1) admit all the churches of the United Conference into its membership, or (2) dissolve itself, if it could be assured that its churches would be welcome in the United Conference, or (3) dissolve itself, and sit down with the United Conference to organize a new state body. The United Conference refused these overtures and instead went to the 1889 National Council and asked to be seated as a state body from Georgia.

Then a war of words began. The AHMS and their agents contended that the Congregational Methodists were true Congregationalists, lovers of Pilgrim ideals, and a natural group to merge with. It is interesting to see a Missionary Society here supporting a group born partly because of the anti-mission movement!

There were also technical questions raised. It was contended that the existing Georgia Association was not a state body because it was not big enough to be one! It was also contended that it was normal Congregational practice to have overlapping bodies serving the same territory. This was true regarding German, Welsh, and American Indian inter-church bodies, but by this date these language groups were sub groups of common state bodies with English bodies. There had also been a theological dispute in New York City which led to two competing bodies in that area from 1889 to 1896. Unwilling to lose some large New York congregations, the National Council seated delegates from both groups until the division was healed. That sad and unique case was also used as justification for setting up segregated bodies in the South. It was also argued that the idea that there should be only one inter-church body functioning in an area was an introduction of Presbyterianism into the Church. True Congregational freedom would allow for segregation. Of course, if the 1883 meeting between the Boards was really true, then neither group favored segregation and the need for two bodies was very obscure. The 1889 National Council welcomed the Congregational Methodist merger, but seated the delegates of the United Conference only as "honorary delegates." The Association was still the recognized body from Georgia.

But while the majority of the delegates to the National Council recoiled at the idea of accepting segregation, Sullivan Gale continued to press for more absorption of White churches into the denomination. The United Conference expanded in Georgia by adding new District Conferences during the 1890's. In Alabama it was reported that "Superintendent Gale went through the state reorganizing the Congregational Methodist Conferences as Congregational." (Clark)

A United Congregational Conference of South Alabama was organized in 1890, and a United Congregational Conference of North Alabama in 1891. These were also White bodies, and were organized without contact with the older Alabama Association. These White bodies were consolidated as the General Congregational Convention of Alabama in 1892. Some Alabama Congregational Methodists stayed out of these bodies. In that year this group also showed up at the National Council and requested to be seated. In that year the National Council seated delegates from the local White bodies that were part of the General Convention, and the Black Association delegates. However, the delegates from the General Convention itself were not seated, since, as a state body, they did not include the Association.

Other Congregational Methodist groups continued to become Congregational. In 1893 the Florida Western District Congregational Methodist Conference (west of the Apalachicola River) divided into three sub groups which joined the Florida Congregational body. In the same year the Taylor Conference of Congregational Methodists (in Baker and Columbia Counties,FL, and Charlton Co.,GA) reorganized as the St. Mary's River Conference in the FL state Congregational body.

The Golden Valley Conference in North Carolina became Congregational in 1890, and the Piedmont Conference in that state followed in 1892. These merged in 1897, then the new body died in 1900, but a few White churches continued outside the General Association.

A White West Central Association appeared in Louisiana 1889 to 1895, then these churches went into the older Association.

The Florida churches were part of an all White state body. It was in Alabama and Georgia that the segregation battle was fought.

The issue then became confused with another issue. In New England most state bodies had been made up of delegates from regional groups. In the rest of the country Congregational state bodies had direct representation from churches. As transportation services improved, and there was a desire to make denominational structure similar from state to state, the five larger New England state bodies moved to the direct church representation system between 1892 and 1895. The National Council recommended this as a uniform structure for the Church.

However, Gale had suggested that the new White bodies in Alabama and Georgia follow the old Massachusetts pattern of representation from district bodies. This made some sense among the old Congregational Methodist churches which were, on average, so poor and so small, that they could not afford to attend state wide meetings. But they came into the fellowship just as this type of structure was being abandoned and this issue added to the controversy of their acceptance. Alabama Whites still opposed direct representation in 1899, and only gave way in 1908.

Pressure was being put on the Alabama and Georgia churches to come to a solution. In 1890 the Georgia Association (Black) agreed to become a separate sub group within the new General Congregational Convention of Georgia, organized that year. While they could maintain their own fellowship, they were, at the state level, swamped out by the White majority.

In Alabama, however, the Black Churches made a valiant effort to be treated with respect. In 1891 they invited all the new White churches that had appeared in the Yearbook to their meeting. None came. In 1892 they proposed a joint meeting of all White and Black churches. It failed. In 1894 a new plan of union was proposed whereby the Black churches would be part of the local District Associations. The Black congregations opposed this plan by a vote of 3 yes, 12 no, 3 not voting. (Alabama Churches...) Then the Black Association proposed either all White Churches joining the Association or both the White and Black bodies disbanding and having all churches join a new body. This was rejected by the White Churches. In 1895 the Association had no delegates at the National Council, and the General Convention delegates were seated "pending further action." In 1898 and 1901 the National Council refused to seat either delegation and urged them to unite with representation from the churches. E.C.Silsby contended that the White churches had to be recognized as capable of forming their own state organization, since some of their churches dated back before 1876, when the Black Association was formed! Of course, at that time they were Congregational Methodist and Gale had not reorganized them as Congregational. The injustice occurred when those reorganizations took place with no regard to the existing Congregational churches and bodies in Alabama.

Meanwhile in Georgia the plan for the Black Association to be part of the state United Conference was not working out well.

SEGREGATION TRIUMPHS

In 1903 the long dispute gave way. The White churches in Georgia left the General Convention, leaving that an all Black body. The Whites reorganized as the United Congregational Conference of Georgia, which merged to the Florida state body in 1905 to become the General Congregational Association of Florida and the Southeast. These new arrangements, as well as Alabama segregation, were accepted by the 1904 National Council. Segregation had won the day.

It is true that in all this time the AHMS supported White bodies claimed that they only aided churches willing to accept Black members. But when the Georgia Whites set up a paper in 1894 they said it would illustrate "Congregationalism from a Southern standpoint." They went on, "[we] will oppose and expose all efforts looking to the amalgamation of the races in the line of church life and work, as well as that of social equality."(Wright) In 1908, when a book promoting Anglo Saxon Congregationalism in the South was published (20), it includes a long section on "the race question" which regards Blacks as inferiors and confines them to agricultural and industrial work. Race was clearly the issue.

Once Georgia/Florida and Alabama segregation was recognized, it spread across the rest of the South. A new state body was created in Kentucky in 1898 (after an abortive attempt in 1896). It was White, while the Black churches continued to be related to Tennessee. A White body was created in North Carolina in 1910, and another in South Carolina in 1917. These two merged in 1918. A White body was created in Louisiana in 1914. Tennessee was finally segregated in 1915.

Arkansas' Association had died in 1894. During its life, Black churches had been affiliated with Tennessee. White churches were transferred to Missouri, and some were later related to Oklahoma.

Texas' bodies had been split geographically. The North Texas group was integrated, while the Southwestern group was entirely Black. After 1904 the Southwestern group died. Sometime between 1900 and 1917 a new Black Conference was created in Texas, and the former North Texas body evolved into an all White state body.

DISAFFECTION IN THE DEEP SOUTH

While segregation triumphed, the condition of having anti-mission churches with uneducated clergy eventually caught up to the denomination.

The peninsula churches in Florida were mostly formed by re-settled New Englanders. Their connection with the former Congregational Methodist churches in the northern part of the state and Georgia became strained. In 1918 the Georgia and Florida bodies divided. The St. Mary's River Conference in Florida (formerly Congregational Methodist) had died in 1914. In 1919 all the churches in West Florida (also from Congregational Methodist sources) were transferred to the Alabama body.

Meanwhile in Alabama some type of division took place. The actual facts seem to have been covered up. By 1922 the Alabama minutes report that their own minutes for 1918, 1920, and 1921 are missing. By 1922 all the District Associations in Alabama had been reorganized, and it was clear that some of the earlier groups had not cooperated with the merger.

Many sources have alluded to churches of Congregational Methodist background leaving the Congregational fold and returning to the parent body. Much of that must have happened at this time.

In 1927 E.W.Butler gave a fascinating address to the White Churches in Alabama. Suddenly he had discovered that the Congregational Methodists were really unlike the Congregationalists. He discovered the anti-mission origins of the group and their slogan "we are taxed without representation." He notes that from 1850 to 1890 they had no zeal for missions or Sunday Schools or theological schools. He notes that by 1927 all their churches are rural or dying, and that none of them are in cities. He suggests that the merger was really engineered by Gale. He then gives some startling statistics on the White Churches in Alabama in 1927: one half had no Sunday School; 80% have church worship services only once a month!; 90% collect no offering; most ministers are not trained, only four having some training. It is no wonder that the merger did not work!

THE LATER CONGREGATIONAL METHODIST CHURCH

Many Congregational Methodist Churches never went along with the Congregational merger. These included all the Colored Churches, and all the White Churches in Arkansas, Mississippi, Tennessee, and Texas, and large minorities in Alabama and Georgia. (It is not clear if some Congregational growth in southern Illinois in the late nineteenth century came from the Congregational Methodist churches, or was an unrelated effort.) The group later spread into Indiana. It is not clear how many churches once part of the Congregationalists made their way back to the parent group. The Congregational Methodist Church made plans to incorporate in 1937/1938. This led to a division in 1941, with two groups claiming to continue the original body. They also suffered two other schisms which have since died out. The Reformed New Congregational Methodist Church began in 1916 in Indiana and Illinois. The Cumberland Methodist Church began in Tennessee in 1950. Another group, the New Congregational Methodist Church was begun in 1881 by a direct schism from the Methodist Episcopal Church South. However, several of this group's local churches eventually affiliated with the main Congregational Methodist body. The New

41

Congregational Methodist group, as well as both parts of the 1941 schism continue to this day.

OKLAHOMA

As we have seen, the original missions in the Indian Territory developed as a continuation of the work further East with the southern tribes.

However, when the central part of what would be Oklahoma was opened for non-Indian settlement, the denomination made a different approach. In 1889 Congregationalism was well established in the Plains states, but weak in Texas and Arkansas. Congregationalists joined with others in the great land rushes into the new territory. The approach was driven from the Plains settlements to the north and was conceived of as an extension of that work. Large numbers of Congregational churches were organized both in the original open area in central Oklahoma and in the Cherokee strip, which was opened in 1893. However, the majority of settlers in the new territory did not come from the prosperous Plains, but from the poor, rural South. Except in a few counties the Congregational churches did not grow. There are few places in the country where a more extensive mission enterprise led to such few surviving churches.

In the areas along the Red River and in the continuing Indian Territory to the east, few churches were organized. Beginning in 1901, about a dozen White churches were begun in the Indian Territory before it was united with Oklahoma in 1907.

Black congregations were also begun. Following the southern style a segregated Black sub-group was organized about 1910 as part of the state general body.

WHITE CHURCH DEVELOPMENT

After the triumph of segregation, the AHMS (which became the Congregational Home Missionary Society) put much effort into the White churches in the South.

Colleges were begun: Rollins College, Winter Park, FL (1885); Kingfisher College, Kingfisher, OK (1894); Piedmont College, Demorest, GA (1897). An Atlanta Theological Seminary was begun in 1901, but it became only a Foundation during the Depression, and was later amalgamated to the Methodist Seminary at Vanderbilt in Nashville.

Following the northern pattern, attempts were made to organize Home Missionary Societies in southern states. At least three were begun: Florida Home Missionary Society (1885), Georgia Home Missionary Society (1888), Oklahoma Home Missionary Society (plan 1898, organized 1899). None of these were ever able to become self supporting, so none ever became full auxiliaries of the national Society.

Isolated from the rest of Texas, the western county of El Paso had its churches transferred to a New Mexico affiliation between 1913 and 1915, and have remained so.

In Florida, and in isolated locations elsewhere new churches were formed by New England settlers moving South. Also a few groups influenced by new liberal theological ideas broke away from established churches and became Congregational. Most of these were in urban settings.

BLACK CHURCH DEVELOPMENT

After the White merger with the Congregational Methodists and Free Methodist Protestants, Black leaders pursued the same goal. Between 1893 and 1895 a large number of formerly Methodist Black congregations in east central Georgia and central North Carolina became part of the Congregational fellowship. This doubled the number of churches in the latter state, and increased the number almost as much in Georgia. This also put these two states in the place of being the most important Black Congregational states. The original strength in Louisiana and Tennessee was now eclipsed.

Unfortunately historians have not given us a clear picture of this group of churches. We don't even know from which Methodist group they came. Except for a church in Charlotte, NC these were mostly small and rural churches. Although not noticed by most historians, these churches changed some of the nature of the southern Black churches. These were really not "churches by the schools," but rural churches, with a tradition of home grown leadership, and a Wesleyan theological slant.

The two mergers (White and Black) both began to give southern Congregationalism a more Wesleyan than Calvinist position.

To some degree ignoring these Wesleyan and rural connections, the AMA set as its goal to "lay claim on the Black elite." (33,p.74) This work was aimed at the urban churches and the churches connected to the schools. Knighton Stanley (33) goes on to suggest that the AMA "never maintained that it was against a system of class," "nor would it...clearly recognize that it was more disposed to the social elite." (p.76)

Yet even with that goal, large amounts of money did not continue to flow South. No account was made for economic burdens peculiar to Black life in the South. Instead the denomination began to abandon the higher percentage of support that had been needed to get Black churches going (as compared to White churches in the West). Black membership in the South went into decline. (See 33,pp.89-90). The needs of the higher level schools being great, monies were concentrated there, and many churches withered.

The Black inter-church groups also declined. In 1925 the Black churches in Oklahoma were detached from its Association and joined to those in Texas. In 1929 the Mississippi Association was merged to that in Alabama.

OTHER ETHNIC CHURCHES

In many ways the South had the most mixed ethnic complexion of Congregationalism in any part of the country, but in other respects it was the least ethnically mixed.

Black churches were more numerous, and a higher percentage of the churches in the South than in any other part of the country. Also the Indian work here was more extensive than in any other area, except the Plains states.

But the South had the fewest number of other ethnic groups. We have already mentioned interconnections with Huguenot and German and Swiss settlers in the low country. We have also discussed an early Welsh settlement in Delaware, and other Welsh mining congregations formed after the Civil War.

Hispanic work began among Mexicans in Texas in 1892. Cuban work began in Florida in 1897, and soon included work on the island of Cuba as well.

German Churches, particularly among Germans from Russia, became one of the largest ethnic ministries in national Congregationalism. A national General Conference was begun for these churches in 1883. It included local Associations which were also part of their respective state bodies. A shaky start was made for these churches in Oklahoma in 1903. In 1915 this work was strengthened under the Colorado German group. This work spread to Texas in 1924/1925. In 1926 a Southern German Congregational Conference was organized serving these two southern states as well as Kansas. Unlike the other local German bodies, this never became part of any state body. It continued to be related to the denomination until 1964.

In 1924/1925 the Evangelical Protestant Church of North America united with the Congregational Churches. This was a unitive German group with liberal theology. It brought into the fellowship three congregations in Kentucky, the oldest dating back to 1847. These were part of a separate Evangelical Protestant Conference until 1947 when they became affiliated with Ohio. All German churches in Kentucky were affiliated with this group.

Beyond this, there was one Slovak church in Virginia, and one Creole church in Louisiana. No other ethnic groups were represented in the South.

THE CONGREGATIONAL CHRISTIAN MERGER

In 1931 the National Council of Congregational Churches united with the General Convention of the Christian Church to form the General Council of Congregational (and) Christian Churches.

These two groups began to publish their statistics together in 1929. However, churches were distinguished between Christian and Congregational backgrounds through 1933. Beginning in 1934 all new churches were Congregational Christian. Churches founded through 1933 as Congregational appear in the main lists. Churches listed as Congregational Christian are shown in Appendix II. (We have not listed Christian churches listed up to 1933 in this study.) Two new joint mission starts begun in 1932 in the South are also included in Appendix II. Two Christian churches in the South joined Congregational bodies by 1929, they are shown in brackets in the main list. Two Congregational churches in the South also joined Christian groups in 1930 and 1931, and these dual alignments are mentioned in their entries. There were two mergers of Congregational and Christian local congregations in Georgia in 1931.

The southern branch of the Christian connection had begun as the Republican Methodists, a schism from the Methodist Episcopal Church opposing the powers of the bishops. It continued with a Wesleyan theology. This reinforced the Wesleyan tendencies already present in southern Congregationalism in the new fellowship.

Much of the Christian strength was in the South, but it was also segregated. We therefore, will continue the history in segregated sections.

WHITE CONGREGATIONAL CHRISTIAN CHURCHES

At the time of the merger some White Christian churches in border states were part of regional Conventions centered in the North. The Metropolitan Christian Convention included some churches in Delaware which were transferred to the Middle Atlantic (formerly New Jersey Congregational) body. However, their churches in western Maryland opposed the merger and withdrew. They also had two local Conferences in West Virginia, both of which also opposed the merger.

The Central Christian Conference included a West Virginia presence connected to an Ohio group. This church continued, affiliated to Ohio. In Kentucky there were two entire Conferences. One of these opposed the merger and withdrew. The other initially opposed the merger in 1934, but reaffiliated with the merged group as the Kentucky North Conference in 1938. However, it was not active in the denomination, and was finally dropped in 1948.

The major group, though, was the large Southern Christian Convention. The Christian connection had split between North and South in 1854, and the Southern Convention had acted like its own denomination for many years. In 1890 it again began an affiliation with the northern churches, though complete merger did not take place until 1922. This group was very strong in North Carolina and Virginia. It had a few congregations in eastern West Virginia, and another center in west central Georgia and eastern Alabama. It had one church in eastern Maryland which was transferred to the Middle Atlantic Conference.

The Southern Convention was so large and powerful that a plan was put into place to unite to it all the White Congregational Christian Churches, not only in Virginia and North Carolina, but also in Georgia, Alabama, and Tennessee. The Congregational Churches in Tennessee never sent any delegates to the Conventions exploring this possibility. Georgia and Alabama, however, spent about three years exploring the plan. However, what finally emerged was a Southern Congregational Christian

Convention centered in North Carolina and Virginia. White Congregational Churches were joined to the enlarged Christian group.

Christian Churches in Alabama and Georgia were added to the Congregational bodies in those states, but were the dominant group in some areas.

In Florida, particularly after the Second World War, the churches began to grow, enjoying the large influx of retiring and vacationing northerners.

Most of the other new churches in the South during the Congregational Christian period were in the formerly predominantly Christian areas.

Where there were large numbers of Christian congregations, new churches were also begun in this period. However, in the rest of the South the Churches languished. As a result inter-church bodies also became too weak to continue. The Tennessee and Kentucky groups were united in 1941. In 1947 the Louisiana, Oklahoma, and Texas churches were united in a Central South Conference. In 1949 the Kentucky/Tennessee, Georgia (including South Carolina), and Alabama (including west Florida) groups united as a Southeast Convention of Congregational Christian Churches.

In Louisiana in the 1940's several White congregations began to become distraught with the national Church fellowship's liberalism. Some churches began to withdraw. A group eventually known as Bible Conferences and Missions benefited most from this schism.

BLACK CONGREGATIONAL CHRISTIAN CHURCHES

The Black part of the Christian Church was also quite large in the South in 1931. The Afro-Christian Convention had begun in 1892. Although the Black churches had grown out of secessions from the White churches, they gained their chief financial support from the northern branch of the Church. They had absorbed a group of Black Methodist Protestants early in the Twentieth Century.

It brought to the merger a large group of congregations in North Carolina and Virginia, a Conference in Maryland, and some congregations in New York and New Jersey. The Maryland group opposed the merger and withdrew.

In 1932 the Black Congregational and Christian Churches in North Carolina were united in one body. However, the Congregational Churches were still kept in their own local sub-group distinct from the Christian churches. This internal separation later proved a problem.

The Virginia, New York, and New Jersey congregations stayed together with the Afro-Christian name until 1939 when Virginia became its own group.

The lack of support of southern Black churches continued during the Congregational Christian period. There were further declines in the churches. Of twenty four new Black congregations in the South from 1934 to 1960, twenty were in the heartland of the old Christian Churches in North Carolina and Virginia. Of the four begun in other parts of the South, three were begun between 1957 and 1960, after the start of the Civil Rights movement and the earliest steps towards the United Church of Christ. Support for urban churches, or children congregations of the "churches by the schools," had come to an end.

In 1948 the Louisiana and Texas/Oklahoma groups were united as a Plymouth Conference.

Finally in 1950 a Convention of the South was set up to unite all of the Black work in the South. It included the Afro-Christian group in New York and New Jersey, as well as the Black bodies in Virginia, North Carolina, Georgia (including South Carolina), Tennessee (including north Alabama, Kentucky, and Arkansas), Alabama/Mississippi, and Plymouth (LA,OK,TX). Interestingly, Black congregations of Congregational background in Delaware and the District of Columbia continued to be related to the Middle Atlantic Conference.

THE UNITED CHURCH OF CHRIST

In 1957 the General Council of Congregational Christian Churches united with the Evangelical and Reformed Church to form the United Church of Christ.

Congregational Christian Churches had to vote on whether or not to be part of the new Church, and most did that through voting in 1960 and 1961 on the Constitution of the United Church. A list of approving churches was released in the summer of 1961. The statistical reports for 1961 are the first to distinguish clearly between Congregational Christian Churches that became United Church of Christ, and those that did not. Therefore, we have shown any churches listed through 1960 as Congregational Christian. Churches listed 1961 and on are shown as United Church of Christ, and are shown in Appendix III. An exception to that includes seven new church starts in 1958, 1959, and 1960 jointly begun by both parts of the newly merged Church. These are shown in Appendix III., and marked "early start." In addition, there was one merger in the South of a Congregational and an Evangelical and Reformed Church before 1961.

The United Church Constitution allowed Congregational Christian Churches not part of the United Church of Christ to continue as members of Associations and Conferences. These have been reported in two groups: Schedule I Churches (shown as Schedule II in the 1962 Yearbook) includes churches which have not voted on whether to join the United Church, or which have voted to abstain from making a decision; Schedule II Churches (shown as Schedule III in the 1962 Yearbook) are churches which have voted not to be a part of the United Church of Christ.

Opposition led to the formation of two "continuing" denominations which are active in the South.

The Congregational Christian Churches, National Association, was formed in 1955, and began to act as a denomination in 1961 by declaring itself the successor to the General Council. At that date it had already entered two southern states.

The Conservative Congregational Christian Conference was formed in 1948 and entered the South between 1951 and 1955.

New congregations, first shown with either of these groups, or as Schedule I or Schedule II churches are shown in Appendix IV.

Two formerly Evangelical and Reformed congregations in the South became part of continuing Congregational Christian groups and are shown in Appendix IV. in brackets. One United Church of Christ congregation in Appendix III. became part of the National Association.

In 1960 the Evangelical and Reformed Church had congregations in all states and districts covered in this study except Delaware, Georgia, and South Carolina. Their strength was concentrated in Maryland, North Carolina, Texas, Virginia, and Kentucky. (We have not included in this study Evangelical and Reformed congregations listed by 1960.) These churches included three Synods concentrated in the South: Potomac, Southern, and Texas. Six predominantly northern Synods included congregations in nearby southern areas. There was also a non-geographic Magyar Synod which served Hungarian churches in most of the country, including the South. (For detailed information on the service of these Synods, see the annotated bibliography.)

Almost all of the Evangelical and Reformed Churches were German in background, the main exception being the congregations in the Magyar Synod. They were, therefore, all White. They had no Black congregations in the South.

THE SEGREGATION ISSUE

The United Church of Christ was formed just a few years after the Brown versus Board of Education decision. The idea of "separate but equal" was under attack. Much of the new United Church of Christ became intertwined with the Civil Rights movement. The new Constitution therefore provided that, after the initial reorganization of Associations and Conferences, that they would be composed "without regard to race, language, or culture, of congregations or local churches in a geographical area..." The new Church set itself to end segregation in the South. The results should not be surprising.

BLACK RESPONSE TO THE MERGER

As we have already indicated, the North Carolina Black congregations had remained separated along Congregational and Christian lines. Stanley (34) explains some of the animosities between the two groups. As a result, a little more than a quarter of the North Carolina State Conference (the Congregational body) seceded in 1960 and declared itself the continuing body. A few years later it became one of only two regional groups to gain "Affiliate" status with the National Association. It also later attracted two formerly Christian Churches, and two Congregational Christian Churches formerly in predominantly Christian local bodies into membership. A total of fifteen congregations have been involved in this group at some time, and they are the only organized continuing Black Congregational Christian inter church body in the nation outside the United Church of Christ. Their churches are rural, and many trace back to the regions received from the Methodist merger in the late 1890's.

Enthusiasm from the rest of the Black community, was nonetheless slow in coming for the United Church. The problems cited by Stanley (34) still left a suspicion towards the denomination. When voting was tallied in July, 1961, less than half of the remaining Convention of the South churches had joined the United Church, the third lowest support rate among Congregational Christian Conferences. However, as the United Church commitment to Civil Rights increased, the Commission on Racial Justice was formed, and it set up a regional office in North Carolina and Virginia, the vast majority of Black congregations did move into the United Church. Only a few remain in the Schedule I or II categories. A few also became independent, but not enough to monitor any trend.

Following the United Church merger Black church expansion began to be more adapted to the realities or urban life, and covered a wider geographic area than had existed for sometime.

WHITE RESPONSE TO THE MERGER

Initially most White bodies gained majorities (if just barely) in favor of the new United Church. The strongest support was in peninsular Florida, where the majority of churches had northern origins, and many had begun only recently; in Texas, where the few White congregations were very urban; in the border areas where churches belonged to northern inter church bodies; and in Tennessee and Kentucky, where a more liberal tradition had existed for sometime.

Non-German White churches in Oklahoma were a mixed bag, with notable opposition coming from Oklahoma City and a few rural churches, but the majority of the other rural churches, dating back to the Plains state immigrants, entering the United Church.

Elsewhere race became the issue. When the reality of reorganizing Associations and Conferences along non-racial lines finally became the agenda, churches that had joined changed their minds.

Every Oklahoma and Texas Church in the Southern German Conference stayed out of the United Church. It is likely that they have continued their group as an independent body.

In Louisiana only one White congregation favored the merger, all the rest withdrew.

In eastern Virginia there was initially strong United Church support. However, in 1969, when the Black and White bodies finally merged, a large minority of the White churches withdrew and formed their own group. They have since been joined by other withdrawals.

In North Carolina a majority of the White congregations initially entered the new Church. However, since then, particularly in the integrated Eastern North Carolina Association, almost all the White congregations withdrew. Now more than half of the formerly Christian White churches in North Carolina have left the United Church. Among formerly White Congregational Churches in this state, a majority was maintained for the United Church, although most of these are in retirement centers developed in this century by former northerners.

In both Virginia and North Carolina Congregational Christian Churches formed between the two mergers were far more positive in their support for the United Church, possibly because of their urban settings, or because of recent significant help from the denomination.

But it was in the Southeast that the segregation battle became the most obvious. Before the merger there were three Black Associations in the area (Georgia/South Carolina; Tennessee (including Kentucky, and northern Alabama) and Alabama/Mississippi.) There were six White bodies(Georgia/South Carolina; Tennessee/Kentucky; East Alabama; North Alabama; Central Alabama; South Alabama-West Florida.)

Beginning in 1953 a church in west central Georgia had transferred to the East Alabama group. From 1959 on there was an increasing move of White churches in that part of Georgia into that group. Also, by 1963 a South Georgia Association of Congregational Christian Churches had been reorganized outside the new United Church. Every single White Church in the southern part of that state joined the new group. It became the only other body to gain "Affiliate" status with the National Association. In 1969, after the large majority of White churches had left their fellowship, the few remaining churches in the White Georgia/South Carolina group merged with the Black group.

In Tennessee and Kentucky there was much more ease in integration, and the two groups united in 1965.

In 1969 the Black group in Alabama/Mississippi, three of the four Evangelical and Reformed Churches in the Southeast Conference, and a few individual White Congregational Christian churches in Alabama united with the Tennessee/Kentucky group as the Alabama/Tennessee Association. However, the other four regional bodies in Alabama merely refused to integrate. Most of these contained many, in some cases a majority of churches, in the Schedule I and II categories. Thus a gerrymandered Association pattern came into being in Alabama, and the true goal of the United Church Constitution has not been achieved to this day.

Nonetheless, this arrangement did not prove wholly satisfactory to the non-UCC congregations. In 1977 the majority of the Central Alabama group seceded and organized the Alabama Association of Congregational Christian Churches, all of whose congregations joined the National Association. The Central Alabama group continued with only two churches, until it was absorbed by the East Alabama group in 1990.

In 1989 all but one of the remaining churches in the North Alabama group seceded and that group collapsed. The schismatic churches organized an Alabama Conference of Independent Congregational Christian Churches.

Churches in the National Association also were able to organize an Association in Florida around 1977. The Conservative Conference gained a small body in North Carolina and Virginia in 1985.

Many of the leaving churches have become totally independent or went to other groups.

In Georgia, west Florida, Louisiana, and the German Churches of Texas and

Oklahoma the majority of living White Congregational Christian Churches are not in the United Church of Christ. This is the only part of the country where this is the case. Nearly half of the Alabama Churches, and a majority of the formerly Christian White churches in North Carolina, and a large minority in southern Virginia also fall into the same category. Then, we need to remember that many United Church congregations in Alabama, Georgia, and west Florida are in gerrymandered segregated Associations. Interestingly opposition is the strongest in areas where Congregational Methodist roots are the most obvious, and secondarily among formerly Christian Churches. The history of segregation can be clearly seen as the key issue. A one hundred year experiment has been found wanting.

After the merger the United Church of Christ has grown in the South, particularly in Florida, where more new churches have appeared than in any other state.

NEW ETHNIC GROUPS

The Evangelical and Reformed Church's Magyar Synod also refused to reorganize along non-ethnic lines. It has added new Magyar/Hungarian churches in the South since the merger.

After a hiatus of several decades the United Church began Hispanic work in Florida in 1978. Hispanic work in Texas has continued and expanded.

Filipino congregations were formed in 1978 in Florida and in 1985 in Texas.

Samoan congregations appeared in Texas in 1988.

On page 48, the second full paragraph from the top of the page should read:

In North Carolina a majority of White congregations initially entered the new Church. However, since then, particularly in the integrated Eastern North Carolina Association, many of the White congregations have withdrawn. Now more than half of the formerly Christian White churches in North Carolina either never joined, or have left the United Church. Among formerly White Congregational Churches in this state, a majority was maintained for the United Church, although many of these are in retirement centers developed in this century for former northerners.

THE CHURCH LISTS
COLUMNS A THROUGH E EXPLAINED

Each church is located at the city or town in which it worships or worshiped at the time it was part of the fellowship. Where cities or towns have changed their name, the present town name, if known, is used even if it was not the name during the life of the church. Open country churches are located at the name of the nearest town or city used by the congregation for identification.

Churches which have changed their location within a state are located at their last place of worship. Churches which have changed location over state lines are located twice, separately in each state. This, however, does not include mission churches covenanted in one place to be immediately removed to a new location. These are shown only in their new location.

Listings are by state and county. Each state listing begins with the state name followed by its U.S.Census two-digit computer number.

Under each state, counties known to have had Congregational churches are listed in alphabetical order. Each county is followed by the year in which it was locally organized (sometimes later than being set apart by the state.) It is then followed by a three-digit U.S.Census number. In cases where Virginia data has been joined together under an extinct county name, the first three digits are the traditional digits, the last three are those used in most modern sociological studies.

At the end of the regular state lists the names of counties with no known Congregational Churches are shown, including the counties' organization dates and computer numbers. Listing and not listing information in county identifications refer to appearances in the U.S.Census.

Within each county each town or city is listed in alphabetical order. Within each town or city, each church is listed in alphabetical order by name.

The church lists are shown in five columns labeled A to E.

The consecutive church numbers and town names for alphabetical listing are shown in column B.

However, it is **column D** which provides the research backbone on which the ribs of the churches are attached.

The primary sources for this study are the church lists published by the national church and the various state or state equivalent bodies.

Column D shows the years a church was listed. Years listed means the years in which a church was published in the church lists. Churches appeared in the listings which would follow their own state organization pattern (see the listing in the annotated bibliography). (If this is not the case an explanation would appear in column B).

Once a church has been initially listed, periods of not listing indicate that the specific church is not listed. When an entire Association or Conference is not reported, but the church appears on both sides of the missing report, the church is shown as continually listed.

Churches which were never listed in these listings are shown as not listed (nl.) in column D.

Incorrect double or triple listings are shown in the text (column B.) Long periods of not being listed may suggest a temporary withdrawal from the fellowship or being closed for a while, but shorter periods are generally listing errors.

If discrepancies appear between the state and national lists they are treated in one of these ways: problems for the entire state or state body, such as dates of reporting, are discussed in the bibliography; individual church problems are taken up in the text (column B).

In Kentucky listings, an asterisk (*) in column D is used to identify six congregations dropped in 1880 because their inter-church body decided it was not Congregational.

Column E indicates the current status of the church or its history after listing ended. United Church of Christ churches are shown as such. Congregations listed at any time as Schedule I, Schedule II, National Association or Conservative Conference are shown here as such with the years listed. Corrections regarding actual voting dates are shown here or in the text (column B).

Churches transferred to other denominations or withdrawn are indicated, except that since no clear data is available on churches returning to the Congregational Methodist Church, all such possible churches are shown as extinct.

Extinct congregations are identified. It may be assumed that a church became extinct in the year it was dropped from listings (last figure in column D) unless another date is given here. Dates specifically shown here are clear dates, while dates shown here in parentheses are indicated by some sources but not accepted by this author.

Information on dual alignments with other denominations is also included here, as are debates on subsequent life of the church. Where there is much information for this column, the statement "see text" indicates that further information from this column is printed in column B.

Column A indicates any special ethnic or language group with which the congregation was identified at some part of its history.

Ethnic churches are those where one ethnic group was a clear majority of the congregation's membership.

Language churches are those where the main worship service was held in some language other than English.

Some language churches eventually became English-speaking ethnic.

Ethnic/language abbreviations may be found in the abbreviations section of this book.

Column C shows the year in which the church was organized. Where it is known, this is the date of the covenanting of the local church, usually as recognized by council. If that did not happen, the closest parallel date is given.

This date is best found in the records of the local church. For this column we have been forced to use secondary sources. The first date given is the best possible date (indicated as directly from the church records, or the most widely used date in the most responsible sources.) The first date given is supported by all exhaustive resources unless otherwise reported. Other alternative dates follow. If a more detailed history indicates the origin of these dates, that designation is given. If the reason for a conflicting date is not given, we merely indicate its source.

When the date shown is for a specific reason (such as Society organized, preaching begun, etc.) a colon (:) before the source indicates that they say that this date is for the reason shown. When a semicolon (;) separates special information from a source, it indicates that while the date is for the reason shown, the source mentioned sees that date as the church organization date.

Reorganization dates are also shown in this column.

Merged churches are so noted. The date here is the date of the merger, although most of these churches prefer to use the age of their earlier part in describing their age.

When there is too much information for this column, "see text" indicates it is described in column B.

Column B is the main text for each church.

The first item given is the town or city name in which the church is located (or nearest if in the open country), either at present, at the time of the 1934 change in listings, or when the church was dropped. Location means primary place of worship.

This is followed by the current legal name of the church (except that since the listing of new Congregational churches ended in 1933, in some cases the name at that time is inserted to make sense of the order of the listings. This is noted if not otherwise obvious.) Churches which were never incorporated or for whom legal status is obscure are listed by their best known name. The word "church" or the listing of the town of its location are generally eliminated from the printed church name in the list unless needed to make sense.

Following in parentheses is this information:

Popular current or historic alternative names for the church are shown, including translations of ethnic names when known.

Former formal names of the church are also noted if substantially different than the present name. Minor rearrangements of words are not shown. The most recent name is given first, following in reverse chronological order until the most ancient name which is given last. We have uniformly not included changes from Congregational to Congregational Christian or United Church of Christ, or from Congregational Christian to United Church of Christ, which would be obvious where the latter name is used in a given historical setting. If the town name changed that is shown here.

Information on the origin of merged churches is given.

Information on Federations is given.

Post office addresses, and notes and corrections to the listing and post merger listings are noted here.

A few branches, not related to plantation churches are discussed here.

Information on confusing treatments in various references, exclusion in exhaustive references, and any confusing factor in the church's history are discussed here. Information from other columns too extensive to fit there, is often shifted to this column.

Affiliations of churches in Presbyteries are specified.

An underlined place or post office name indicates that the church at some point appeared in the listings alphabetically under that name.

Information on minor civil divisions, if different from the location shown, are provided in the states of Arkansas, Louisiana, Maryland, North Carolina, Virginia, and West Virginia. A few former divisions in Tennessee are also given. Quadrant locations in the District of Columbia are shown for most churches.

Churches within each county are numbered consecutively.

Notes are shown alphabetically between churches. These usually regard missions or claimed churches that can not be fully recognized as Congregational Churches.

For plantation churches, their various branches follow the main branch list and are labeled "B," "C," etc.. After the branches, Black congregations which broke off from these churches and did not become Congregational Churches with full standing are also listed using the next consecutive letters. These entries are made under the main plantation church, even if they are not in the same County.

Merged churches formed 1934 or later deriving from a congregation in the main lists are shown under their older partner (except where they maintain the location or sometimes name of the newer partner, then there) with the designation of "M.".

Any church may be identified by a ten-digit code as follows: Listing (one digit - zero or appendix numeral); State (two digits); County (three digits); and church (four digits - three for the consecutive number and one for a letter M.) Churches with two or more mergers under the number (shown as M1, M2 etc. in the text) can be identified as N,O, etc. here for complete coding.

In all columns, numbers shown with the symbol # refer to the one-, two-, or three-digit numbers of churches in the county being discussed (if not otherwise noted.) This symbol is also used for numbered minor civil divisions. All unexplained two-digit numbers are bibliographic references, as are the forms "01K," "01S," and "01N." (See annotated bibliography.)

THE CHURCHES

ALABAMA (01)

A	B	C	D	E
	AUTAUGA COUNTY (org.1818)	(001)		
	1. Golson, First Cong.(1.01N;1.01S:1890-1891)	1890	nl.	X af.1891
	2. Kingston, Mount Creek Cong.;(f.First Cong.;1.01S:1890-1891)	1889	1892-1916	X
	3. Prattville, Cong.(Pratt City)	1898 / 1895(08)	1898-1899	X (1898:08)
	BALDWIN COUNTY (org.1809)	(003)		
	1. Fairhope, Cong.	1902	1901-1907	X
	2. Gateswood, Cong.	1903	1903-1904	X
	BARBOUR COUNTY (org.1832)	(005)		
	1. Clio, Concord Cong.(1.01S:1889-1891)	by 1890	nl.	X af.1891
	2. Clio, New Hope CC	1891	1892-on	UCC
	BIBB COUNTY (org.1818,f.Cahawba Co.to 1820)	(007)		
B1	1. Blocton, Cong.(Blockton)	1889 / 1890(08)	1892-1900	X (1898:08)
	BLOUNT COUNTY (org.1818)	(009)		
	1. Bangor, Cong.(f.l.Nectar;merger of # 5 & # 6)	1903 M	1903-1908	X
	2. Chepultepec, Cong.	1895	1895-1899	X
	3. Cleveland, Tidwell Cong.(f.Concord Cong.of Tidwell;1.01S: 1890-1891)	1891	1892-1908	X
	4. Harkness, Sardis Cong.(1.01S 1890-1891)	by 1891	1892-1895	X
	5. Tidmore, High Rock Cong.(1.01S:1890-1891)	1890	1892-1903	Merged to # 6 to form # 1(q.v.)
	6. Tidmore, Nectar Cong.(1.01S:1890-1891)	1891	1892-1903	Merged to # 5 to form # 1 (q.v.)
	7. Tidwell, New Hope Cong.(1.by 01N)	1895	nl.	X prob.soon (1896)
	BULLOCK COUNTY (org.1866)	(011)		
	1. Omega, Morgan's Chap.Cong.(m.1890:01S)	1892(prob.r.)	1892-1893	Merged to # 2 to form # 3 (q.v.)
	2. Perote, Cong.	1891	1891-1893	Merged to # 1 to form # 3 (q.v.)
	3. Perote, Cong.(Josie,Pike Co.PO;merger of # 1 & # 2)	1893 M	1893-1911	X

ALABAMA - continued

BUTLER COUNTY (org.1819) (013)

A	B	C	D	E
1.	Georgiana, Union Cong.(f.l.Avant)	1882	1891-1923	X
2.	Leon(Crenshaw Co.PO), Liberty Cong.(1.01S:1889-1891)	1887(s.01) by 1890	nl.	X af.1891

CALHOUN COUNTY (org.1832,f.Benton Co.to 1858) (015)

A	B	C	D	E
B1				
1.	Anniston, First Cong.(Affl.TN 1874-1876)	1875	1874-1968	UCC; X
2.	Oxford, Smith's Chap.Cong.	1893	1893-1901	X
3.	Oxford, Union Grove Cong.	1890	1891-1909	X

CHAMBERS COUNTY (org.1832) (017)

A	B	C	D	E
1.	Dadeville(Tallapoosa Co.PO), Pleasant Hill Cong.(1.by 01S specifically here)1889-1891)	by 1890	nl.	X af.1891
2.	Five Points, State Line Cong.(f.Mount Pisgah Ch.of Standing Rock;f.l.Stroud;f.l.Fredonia;1.01S:1889-1891;incor.l. Tallapoosa Co.1890;j Cong.Meth.1852)	1852	1892-1925, 1933-on	Sch.I

CHEROKEE COUNTY (org.1836) (019)

A	B	C	D	E
B1				
1.	Tecumseh, Cong.	1884	1883-1886 or 1887	X (1888:08)

CHILTON COUNTY (org.1868,f.Baker Co.to 1874) (021)

A	B	C	D	E
1.	Clanton, Cong.(1.01S:1890-1891)	1890 1891(s.01)	1892-1901	X
2.	Clanton, East View Cong.(f.l.Coopers)	1919	1919-1958	X
3.	Clanton, Mountain Springs Cong.(f.l.Mountain Creek;1.01S: 1890-1891)	1891	1892-1909, 1910-1950	X
4.	Clanton, Union Point Cong.(1.01S:1890-1891)	1874	1892-1897	X
5.	Clanton, Well's Chap.Cong.(1.01S:1890-1891)	by 1891	nl.	X af.1891
6.	Lomax, Cong.	1884	1892-1895	X
7.	Lomax, Cong.	1899	1900-1907	X
8.	Marbury(Autauga Co.PO), Union Cong.(f.l.Mountain Creek;f.l. Lightwood,Elmore Co.)	1879 1891(s.01) 1881(s.04)	1892-1977	UCC 1961-1970; Sch.II 1970-1977; NA 1977-on
9.	Mountain Creek, Pleasant Hill Cong.(f.l.Marbury,Autauga Co.)	1903	1904-1911, 1912-1915	X
10.	Thorsby, United Prot.(in 1902 bldg.)	1905	1905-1962	Sch.I; X
11.	Verbena, Union Cong.(1.01S:1890-1891)	1892(s.01)	1891-1913	X

	A	B	C	D	E
		ALABAMA - continued			
		CLAY COUNTY (org.1866)	(027)		
	1.	Ashland, Bethel Cong.(f.l.Millerville)	1892 / r.1910	1892-1908, 1910-1985	Sch.II; X
	2.	Ashland, Cong.	1894	1894-1923	X
	3.	Ashland, Pleasant Hill Chr.Home Cong.	1907	1907-1919	X
	4.	Barfield, Cong.	1894(s.01)	1896-1903	X
	5.	Cragford, Mount Carmel Cong.(f.l.Bluff Springs;f.l.Ashland; f.l.Millerville;f.l.Goldville,Tallapoosa Co.)	1891 / 1892(s.01)	1892-1963	Sch.I; X
	6.	Delta, Wesley's Chap.Cong.(f.l.Christiana,Randolph Co.,& reported as in that Co.)	1894 / 1892(s.01) / 1896(s.01)	1894-1963	Sch.I; X
	7.	Enitachopeo, Cooley Cong.	1903	1903-1905	X
	8.	Mad Indian, Cong.	1894	1894-1895	X
	9.	Mellow Valley, Cong.	1898	1898-1903	X
		CLEBURNE COUNTY (org.1866)	(029)		
	1.	Edwardsville, Salem Cong.(f.l.Heflin)	1890	1890-1912	X
	2.	Fruithurst, Cong.	1899	1899-1904	X
	3.	Heflin, Chulafinnee Cong.(poss.Fairview Ch.)	1891	1893-1923	X
	4.	Heflin, Flowery Grove Cong.(f.l.Arbacooche)	1896	1896-1913	X
	5.	Hightower, Lofty Cong.	1896	1897-1909	X
	6.	Rosewood, Cong.	1894	1894-1897	X
		COFFEE COUNTY (org.1841)	(031)		
	1.	Elba, Curtis Cong.	1904	1904-1910	X
	2.	Elba, Pleasant Hill Cong.(f.l.Curtis;f.Cong.of Opp,Covington Co.;see Covington Co.# 12)	1901	1901-1913	X
	3.	Elba, Union Hill Cong.	1909	1909-1910	X
	4.	Elizabeth, Salem Cong.(1.01S:1889-1891)	by 1890	nl.	X af.1891
		COLBERT COUNTY (org.1867;X 1867;r.1869)	(033)		
B1	1.	Sheffield, First Cong.	1900 / 1901(08,s.01) / 1902(30)	1902-1929	X
		CONECUH COUNTY (org.1818)	(035)		
	1.	Castleberry, New Hope Cong.(f.l.Volina)	1894	1894-1925	X
	2.	Gravella, Cong.	1903	1903-1906	X

ALABAMA – continued

COOSA COUNTY (org.1832) (037)

A	B	C	D	E
1.	Equality, Hebron Cong.(1.01S:1889-1891)	by 1889	nl.	X af.1891
2.	Goodwater, Oak Hill Cong.(f.l.Millerville,Clay Co.;in 1891 bldg.)	1892	1892-1963	Sch.II; X
3.	Goodwater, Shady Grove Cong.(f.Holmes;f.Meadow;f.l.Mountain Meadow,Clay Co.;f.l.Hillabee,Clay Co.)	1880(s.01) 1870 1874(s.01) 1875(s.01) 1886(s.01)	1892-1930	X

COVINGTON COUNTY (org.1821,f.Covington to 1868,f.Jones(new) to 1868) (039)

A	B	C	D	E
1.	Andalusia, Antioch Cong.(f.l.Hilton;1.01S:1889-1891)	1890	1891-on	UCC
2.	Andalusia, Coldwater Cong.	1873(s.01) 1925	1925-1965	Sch.II;prob.withdrew
3.	Andalusia, New Home Cong.(f.l.River Falls)	1923(s.01) 1894	1895-1965	Sch.II;prob.withdrew
4.	Andalusia, Shady Grove Cong.	1907	1908-1910	X
5.	Brooks, Cong.	1901	1901-1907	X
6.	Florala, Cong.(lt.1907-1908)	1904	1904-1909	X
7.	Florala, Pearl Chap.Cong.(or Purl;f.l.Ponds;lt.1907-1908)	1905 1906(s.01) 1895(s.01) r.1918(01)	1905-1908, 1918-1923	X
8.	Florala, Pilgrim Rest Cong.	1906	1907-1908	X
9.	Hilton, Hickory Grove Cong.(1.01S:1889-1891)	1882	1892-1893	X
10.	Opp, Bethel Cong.(f.l.Laurel Hill,Okaloosa Co.,FL;f.l.Henley)	1898 r.1903(01)	(FL)1898-1903;(AL) 1903-1906, 1908-1911	X
11.	Opp, Bradley Chap.Cong.	1909	1909-1913	X
12.	Opp, Cong.(f.l.Hallton;see also Coffee Co.# 2)	1887	1891-1902	X
13.	Opp, Pleasant Grove Cong.	1890(s.01) 1915	1915-1928, 1931-1934	X
14.	River Falls, Mount Olive Cong.(1.Andalusia)	1916(s.01) 1903	1903-1912	X
15.	Rose Hill, New Hope Cong.(f.l.Dozier,Crenshaw Co.)	1890	1891-1923	X

CRENSHAW COUNTY (org.1866) (041)

A	B	C	D	E
1.	Brantley, Indian Creek Cong.	1919	1919-1953	Merged to # 8 to form M.(q.v.)
1M.	Brantley, Indian Creek CC(f.Com.;merger of # 1 & # 8)	1953 M	1953-on	sch.I 1961; UCC late 1961-on
2.	Brantley, Liberty Cong.(Theba;f.l.Leon)	1887	1893-on	UCC

A	B	C	D	E
	ALABAMA - CRENSHAW COUNTY - continued			
3.	Brantley, Live Oak Cong.	1932	1933-1948	X
4.	Brantley, Oak Grove Cong.(f.l.Bullock)	1874 1890(s.01) r.1911	1892-1908, 1909-1910, 1911-1919	X
5.	Dozier, Smith's Chap.Cong.(f.l.Searight)	1909	1909-1948	X
6.	Glenwood, Bethel Cong.(New Bethel)	1909	1909-1950	X
7.	Luverne, Union Grove Cong.	1921	1921-1928	X
8.	Rutledge, Com.(f.Little Creek;f.l.Luverne)	1913	1913-1953	Merged to # 1 (q.v.)
	CULLMAN COUNTY (org.1877) (043)			
1.	Garden City, Garden City CC	1918	1918-on	UCC
2.	Hanceville, Mount Grove CC (f.l.Steppville;l.01s:1890-1891)	1890 1891(s.01)	1892-on	UCC
	DALE COUNTY (org.1824) (045)			
1.	Echo, Friendship Cong.	1893	1893-1906	X
2.	Ewell, Florence Cong.	1904	1904-1905	X
3.	Midland City, First Cong.(f.Chr.Hill Cong.;f.l.Art;f.l.Echo)	1893	1893-1985	UCC; X
4.	Ozark, Cong.	1896	1896-1899	X
5.	Ozark, Union Hill Cong.(f.l.Asbury)	1894	1894-1915	X
6.	Ozark, Zada(h) City Cong.(f.l.Ewell;f.l.Art)	1895	1895-1906	X
	DALLAS COUNTY (org.1818) (047)			
B1 1.	Beloit, Union Cong.(f.Olivet Cong.;f.l.Selma;f.l.Riverside Pltn.)	1886 1889(s.08) r.c.1917(08)	1884-1943	X (incor.1893:AMA)
B1 2.	Selma, First Cong.(East(01N);affl.TN 1871-1876)	1872	1871-1975	UCC; X
B1 3.	Summerfield, Cong.	1886	1884-1897	X
	DE KALB COUNTY (org.1836) (049)			
B1 1.	Fort Payne, Emmanuel Cong.(m.1891:01S)	1890	1892-1903	X
2.	Fort Payne, First Cong.(f.Mission School Ch.)	1889	1891-1904	X (1905:08)
3.	Fort Payne, Pleasant Grove Cong.	1897	1899-1908	X
4.	Fyffe, Ten Broeck Cong.	1891	1891-1915	X
5.	Guest, Cong.	1896	1897-1899	X
6.	Henegar, Pilgrim Cong.(Henagar)	1905	1906-1923	X
7.	Lebanon, Cong.	1892	1892-1893	X
8.	Lebanon, Cong.	1896	1897-1899	X

ALABAMA - continued

ELMORE COUNTY (org.1866) (051)

A	B	C	D	E
	1. Central, Equality Cong.(f.l.Central Institute;1.1889-1891: 01S;in 1850(s.01) or 1859(s.01) bldg.)	1890	1891-1925	X
	2. Deatsville, Stony Point Cong.(f.Pine Grove)	1897 1896(s.01) 1894(s.01)	1897-1930	X
	3. Eclectic, Union Cong.(f.l.Kidd(now Santuck))	1896	1896-1951, 1952-1960	X
	4. Eclectic, Watson's Chap.Cong.(f.l.Cotton(or Cotton's Store); f.l.Tallassee)	1892 1850(s.01) 1897(s.01) 1898(s.01)	1898-on	sch.II 1961-1979; UCC 1979-on
	5. Seman, Com.Cong.(Eclectic PO)	1933 1939(s.04) 1969(s.04)	1933-1977	sch.II 1961-1977; NA 1977-1992;prob.X
	6. Seman, Cong.	1922	1922-1923	x
	7. Tallassee, First Cong.(1.1889-1890:01S)	1890	1891-1929	X
	8. Tallassee, Mount Olive Cong.(f.l.Burlington;f.l.Kent;1.1889-1891:01S)	1890 1886(s.04)	1891-1977	UCC 1961-1970; sch.II 1970-1977; NA 1977-on
	9. Tallassee, Texas Union Cong.	1894	1894-1901	X
	10. Wetumpka, Balm of Gilead Cong.(f.l.Seman;f.l.Central Institute;f.l.Dexter;1.1889-1891:01S)	1890 1873(s.04) 1868(s.04) 1860(s.04) 1896(s.01) 1900(s.01)	1891-1977	sch.I 1961-1977; NA 1977-1990; X

ESCAMBIA COUNTY (org.1868) (053)

A	B	C	D	E
B1	1. Alco, Cong.(now part of Brewton)	1889	1889-1897	X (1898:08)
	2. Bradley, Cong.(f.l.Union Plains,f.incor.l.Union Springs, Bullock Co.)	1892 1894(s.01) 1895(s.01)	1895-1900, 1902-1908	X
B1	3. Bradley, Stokes Cong.	1905	1905-1907	X
	4. Brewton, Burkett's Chap.Cong.	1932	1932-1935	X
	5. Brewton, First Cong.	1895	1895-1906	X (1909:08)
	6. Hammac, Pleasant Hill Cong.	1914	1914-1916	X
	7. Wallace, Ebenezer Cong.	1903	1903-1908	X
	8. Wallace, Providence Cong.(in 1879 bldg.)	1897 1901(s.01)	1898-1908, 1909-1911, 1912-1923	X

A	B	C	D	E
	ALABAMA - continued			
	ETOWAH COUNTY (org.1866,f.Baine to 1867,X,r.1868)			
B1	1. Aurora, Cong.	1893	1893-1895	X
	2. Gadsden, Cong.	1893	1893-1950	X
		1894(01N,08)		
		1886(s.01)		
		1873(s.01)		
	GENEVA COUNTY (org.1868)	(061)	(055)	
	1. Hartford, Wright's Chap.Cong.(f.l.Dundee)	1894	1896-1939	X
		1893(s.01)		
	2. Malvern, Pleasant Ridge Cong.(f.Verden;f.l.Light;f.l.Taylor, Houston Co.)	1897	1899-1911	X
	HENRY COUNTY (org.1819)	(067)		
	1. Headland, Blackwood CC (Sch.I incor.,prob.Sch.II)	1894	1894-1992	UCC 1961-1964; sch.I 1964-1992; withdrew
	HOUSTON COUNTY (org.1903)	(069)		
	1. Cottonwood, Mount Zion Cong.	1900	1900-1906	X
	2. Cottonwood, Oak Grove Cong.	1896	1896-1903	X
	3. Dothan, Cong.(Dothen)	1897	1898-1916	X
	4. Taylor, Watford Cong.(f.l.Wicksburg)	1893	1893-1923	X
		1897(s.01)		
	5. Wicksburg, Cong.	1896	1896-1902	X
	JACKSON COUNTY (org.1819)	(071)		
pB	1. Fabius, Chr.Home Cong.(in 1906 bldg.)	1908	1908-1923	X
	2. Fabius, Flat Rock Cong.	1908	1908-1915	X
	3. Long Island, Sand Mountain Cong.(f.l.Porter's Bluff;l.01s: 1874-1875;affl.TN 1874-1882,1883-1894,1895-1896 or 1897, affl.AL(B1)(dual)1878-1879,1887-1890;unassociated(natl.: 01)1892-1895;l.(natl.)with AL(white) 1901-1907,but no reports submitted during that period;we assume Black by earlier listing,& that late natl.l.incor.)	1875	1875-1883, 1886 or 1887-1908	X (1902:08)
	4. Nat, Cong.(Bending Oaks)	1899	1899-1915	X (1914:08)
	5. Section, New Hope Cong.(f.l.Tip;in 1879 bldg.)	1902	1902-1913	X
		1892(s.01)		
	6. Section, Plymouth Cong.	1904	1904-1923	X
	7. Section, Seab Cong.	1904	1904-1906	X

A	B	C	D	E
	ALABAMA - JACKSON COUNTY - continued			
8.	Tip, Talley Cong.(f.l.Section)	1900	1900-1906	X
	JEFFERSON COUNTY (org.1819) (073)			
Bl 1.	Belle Sumpter, Cong.	1892	1892-1900	X (1898:08)
2.	Birmingham, Central CC	1932	1932-1933	X
Bl 3.	Birmingham, First Cong.	1883	1882-on	UCC
4.	Birmingham, Pilrgim Cong.(f.United Com.;dual align to Chr. 1930)	1882(s.01) 1887(s.01N) 1903 r.1928 r.1931(01)	1903-1923, 1928-on	UCC (dual Cong.& Chr. 1930-1934)
Bl 5.	Ensley, Christ Cong.(f.First)	1916 c.1917(08) 1919(s.01)	1916-1943	X
6.	Gate City, Cong.	1890 1880(s.01)	1890-1911	X
	LAMAR COUNTY (org.1867,f.Jones(old) to 1867,X 1867,r.1868,f.Sanford Co.to 1877) (075)			
1.	Sulligent, New Prospect Cong.(Pine Spring(s)PO;in 1875 bldg.)	1891	1892-1913	X
2.	Sulligent, Union Ridge Cong.	1898	1898-1902	X
3.	Vernon, Cong.	1908	1909-1911	X
	LAUDERDALE COUNTY (org.1818) (077)			
Bl 1.	Florence, First Cong.(affl.TN,dual AL(Bl)1876-1877,1879-1882, 1886-1890,1898-1902)	1876 1874(s.01) 1872(s.01)	1875-1940	X
	LAWRENCE COUNTY (org.1818) (079)			
1.	Caddo, First Cong.(f.Friendship of Trinity,Morgan Co.)	1903 1902(s.01)	1903-1989	UCC 1961-1989; withdrew
2.	Hillsboro, Cong.	1892	1892-1894	X
3.	Moulton, Cong.	1892	1892-1899	X
4.	Moulton, Jones' Chap.Cong.(f.Mount Moriah Cong.;f.l.Hatton; f.l.Courtland)	1896	1897-1915, 1917-1989	Sch.I 1961-1989; withdrew
5.	Pool(e), Cong.	1902	1902-1907	X
6.	Town Creek, Old Liberty Grove Cong.;(f.Liberty Grove Cong.; f.l.Courtland)	1891	1892-1927, 1930-1989	Sch.I 1961-1989; withdrew

ALABAMA - continued

LEE COUNTY (org.1866) (081)

A	B	C	D	E
B1 1.	Lively, Brownville Cong.(l.as if in Russell Co.1889;affl.GA 1888-1889;at 1887 GA Conv.as Cong.Meth.)	1886	1888-1890	X
2.	Opelika, Mount Jefferson Cong.(affl.GA 1888-1889;lt.1889-1890;at 1887 GA Conv.as Cong.Meth.)	1855 1856(s.01) 1895(01N)	1888-1891, 1895-1910	X

LIMESTONE COUNTY (org.1818) (083)

A	B	C	D	E
B1 1.	Athens, Trinity Cong.(affl.TN,dual AL(Bl) 1876-1877,1879-1882,1886-1890;nl.01S 1894-1895;incor.l.with white(natl.) 1901-1902)	1871 1876(30,s.01)	1870-on	Sch.I 1961; UCC late 1961-on

MARION COUNTY (org.1818) (093)

A	B	C	D	E
B1 1.	Bexar, Friendship Union Cong.	1905	1906-1927	X
2.	Hackleburg, Fairview Cong.(in 1880 bldg.)	c.1912(08) 1891	1893-1989	Sch.I 1961; UCC late 1961-1989; withdrew
3.	Hackleburg, First Com.Cong.	1912 1913(s.01)	1913-1952	X
4.	Hackleburg, Prospect Cong.(1.01S:1890-1891)	by 1891	nl.	X af.1891
5.	Haleyville(Winston Co.PO), Union Grove Cong.	1891	1892-1989	Sch.I 1961-1989; withdrew
6.	Hamilton, Mount Carmel Cong.(f.l.Barnesville)	1899	1900-1954	X

MOBILE COUNTY (org.1812) (097)

A	B	C	D	E
B1 1.	Citronelle, Charity Cong.(also l.as prps.1884-1885)	1885	1885-1888	X
B1 2.	Mobile, First Cong.	1876	1875-1937	X

MONTGOMERY COUNTY (org.1816) (101)

A	B	C	D	E
B1 1.	Lapine, Cong.	1894	1895-1901	X
B1 2.	Montgomery, First Cong.(f.Plymouth;affl.TN 1870-1876)	1869 1872(s.01,18, 30,08) 1868(s.01)	1869-on	UCC

MORGAN COUNTY (org.1818,f.Cotaco Co.to 1821) (103)

A	B	C	D	E
B1 1.	Decatur, First New Plymouth Cong.(f.l.New Decatur;affl.AL 1887-1890,TN 1889-1894(lt.01S 1889-1890))	1887	1886 or 1887-1900	X (1901:08)

62

A	B	C	D	E
	ALABAMA - MORGAN COUNTY - continued			
B1	2. Decatur, Second Cong.(f.l.New Decatur;affl.AL)	1887	1886 or 1887-1890	X
	3. Trinity, Oak Grove Cong.	1916	1916-1949	X
	PERRY COUNTY (org.1820)	(105)		
B1	1. Marion, First Cong.(affl.TN 1870-1876)	1870	1869-on	UCC
	PIKE COUNTY (org.1821)	(109)		
	1. Goshen, Cong.	1907	1907-1919	X
	2. Goshen, Wesley Chap.Cong.(f.l.Troy;f.l.Henderson;1.01S:1889-1891)	1890	1892-1940	X
	3. Josie, Webster Cong.(1.01S:1889-1891)	by 1889	nl.	X af.1891
	4. Linwood, Carr's Chap.Cong.(f.l.Catalpa;1.01S:1889-1890)	1891(prob.r.)	1891-1909	X
	5. Tarentum, Cong.	1900	1900-1903	X
	RANDOLPH COUNTY (org.1832)	(111)		
	1. Lamar, Cong.	1893	1893-1901	X
	2. Newell, Milner Cong.	1892	1893-1923	X
	RUSSELL COUNTY (org.1832)	(113)		
	1. Phenix City, Bethany Cong.(Phoenix;l.as if in Lee Co.1890-1891)	1886	1889-1929, 1932-1950	X
	2. Phenix City, First Cong.	1905	1905-1906	X
	3. Phenix City, First CC (f.United)	1929 1920(s.01)	1929-1990	UCC 1961-1983; sch.II 1983-1990; withdrew
	SAINT CLAIR COUNTY (org.1818)	(115)		
	1. Riverside, Cong.	by 1892	1892-1893	X
	2. Steele, Mount Lebanon Cong.	1905	1905-1982	UCC 1961-1982; withdrew to a sect
	SHELBY COUNTY (org.1818)	(117)		
	1. Calera, Pilrgim Cong.	1906 1905(s.01)	1906-1923	X
	2. Calera, South Cong.(1.01S:1890-1891)	1890	1892-1913	X
	3. Shelby, Ch.of the Covenant,Cong.	1890 1891(s.01)	1890-1907, 1908-1915, 1930-1949	X

A	B	C	D	E
	ALABAMA - SHELBY COUNTY - continued			
B1 4.	Shelby, First Cong.(f.Iron Works;lt.08)	1878 / 1879(s.08) / 1872(s.08)	1877-1929	X (1893:s.08)
	TALLADEGA COUNTY (org.1832) (121)			
B1 1.	Alpine, King's Chap.Cong.(f.First;f.l.Kinston;f.l.Kymulga (Kymulee);affl.TN 1874-1876;j UCC late 1961,incor.l.Sch.I late 1961-1962,was UCC)	1873 / 1874(01N,s.01)	1873-on	Sch.I 1961-1962; UCC 1962-on
B1 2.	Childersburg, Coosa Cong.	1903	1903-1908	X (1910:08)
B1 3.	Childersburg, First Cong.(affl.TN 1874-1876)	1874 / 1875(s.01)	1874-1925	X
B1 4.	Ironton, Beard Chap.Cong.(Ironaton;f.First Cong.;l.01S:1885)	1885	1883-1925	X
B1 5.	Jenifer, King's Chap.Cong.(f.First;f.l.Alabama Furnace;affl. TN 1874-1876;lt.08)	1874 / 1871(s.08)	1873-1925	X (incor.s.1884:08)
B1 6.	Lawsonville, First Cong.(f.of Lawson; Talladega PO;nl.1883-1884:01S)	1877 / 1876(08) / 1879(s.01)	1877-1882, 1883-1896	Merged to # 11 to form # 12 (q.v.); (X 1899:08)
B1 7.	Sycamore, Hopewell Cong.	1904	1904-1923	X
B1 8.	Sylacauga, Cong.	1893	1893-1896	X (1898:08)
B1 9.	Sylacauga, Liberty Hill Cong.(in 1900 bldg.)	1905 / 1906(s.01)	1906-1913, 1922-1928	X
B1 10.	Sylacauga, Mignon Cong.	1925	1926-1928	X
B1 11.	Talladega, (The) Cove Cong.(affl.TN 1874-1876)	1874	1873-1896	Merged to # 6 to form # 12 (q.v.)
B1 12.	Talladega, Cove Cong.(merger of # 6 & # 11)	1896 M	1896-1924	X
B1 13.	Talladega, First Cong.(affl.TN 1870-1876)	1868	1867-on	UCC
	TALLAPOOSA COUNTY (org.1832) (123)			
B1 1.	Alexander City, Antioch Cong.(f.l.New Site;j Cong.Meth.1852)	1852 / 1853(s.01) / 1856(s.01)	1892-1928, 1935-1985	Sch.I; X
B1 2.	Dadeville, Cong.(prob.f.Oak Ridge Cong.l.01S 1889-1891)	1868	1892-1900	X
B1 3.	East Tallassee, CC (f.Liberty Cong.of Dadeville;f.l. Tallassee,Elmore Co.,PO;l.01S 1889-1891)	1890 / 1898(s.01)	1898-on	UCC
B1 4.	Jackson's Gap, Sturdevant Cong.	1858 / 1857(s.01)	1892-1908	X
B1 5.	New Site, Mount Vernon Cong.	1903	1903-1908	X
	WASHINGTON COUNTY (org.1800) (129)			
B1 1.	Fairford, St.Thomas Cong.	1892	1898-1919	X

64

ALABAMA – continued

WINSTON COUNTY (org.1850(f.Hancock Co.to 1858))   (133)

A	B	C	D	E
	WINSTON COUNTY (org.1850(f.Hancock Co.to 1858))		(133)	
1.	Addison, Bethel Cong.	1892 / r.1916	1892-1913, / 1916-1926	X
2.	Amos, Cong.	1899	1899-1902	X
3.	Arley, CC (f.Robertson's Chap.;f.Smith Chap.)	1900	1900-1989	Sch.I; withdrew
4.	Arley, Robinson's Chap.Cong.	1903	1903-1904	X
5.	Delmar, Cong.	1892	1892-1894	X
6.	Haleyville, Rock Springs Cong.	1930	1931-1955	X
7.	Houston, Liberty Hill Cong.	1892(01N,s.01) / 1879(s.01)	1892-1989	Sch.I; withdrew
8.	Melville, Cong.	1901	1901-1903	x
9.	Natural Bridge, Cong.(f.incor.l."Fla.")	1905	1905-1908	X
10.	Tavern, Cong.	1895	1899-1902	X
11.	Tavern, Mount Pisgah Cong.(Oakshade)	1905	1906-1910	X
12.	Upshaw, Hopewell Cong.	1892 / 1883(s.01)	1892-1905	X

UNLOCATED CHURCHES   (999)

A	B	C	D	E
B1 1.	Belle Ellen, Lopez Cong.(prob.Bibb or Tuscaloosa Co.)	1900	1900-1905	X
2.	Jacobs, Cong.(yoked Winston Co.# 1,12)	1899(01S)	1904-1907	X af.1891
3.	Mount Pisgah Cong.(Troy Dist.;1.01N;1.01S:1890-1891)	1903	nl.	X af.1891
4.	New Hope Cong.(1.01S:1890-1891;Rose Hill Dist.(But NOT Covington Co.# 15),poss.same as Conecuh Co.# 1)	1890 / by 1891	nl.	X af.1899
5.	Newton's Chap.Cong.(Echo Dist.;1.01S:1898-1899;poss.in FL)	by 1899	nl.	X
6.	Pleasant Ridge Cong.(1.01 & 08)	by 1893(01) / 1899(08)	1892-1893	X af.1899
7.	Saint John Cong.(Echo Dist.;1.01S:1898-1899;poss.in FL)	by 1899	nl.	X
8.	Spio, Cong.(Troy Dist.;yoked to Barbour Co.# 2,Bullock Co. #3,Dale Co.# 1,3,4,5) See Note below.	1891	1892-1902	X
9.	Tucker, Cong.(yoked DeKalb Co.# 4)	1892	1893-1897	X
10.	Woodbine, Cong.(yoked to Russell Co.# 1)	1905	1905-1908	X

17 of 67 Counties have no known Congregational Churches and are listed below.

Note: Since these pages were prepared for publication, it has been found that Spio was in Barbour County.

65

ARKANSAS (05)

ARKANSAS COUNTY (f.a French Par.r.:1813) (001)

A	B	C	D	E
?	1. Bayou Meto, Cong.(Bayou Meteo)	1869	1868-1870	X
	BENTON COUNTY (org.1836) (007)			
	1. Cherokee City, Cong.(affl.MO)	1882	1881-1886 or 1887	X
	2. Gentry, Cong.(affl.MO 1900-af.1917,OK by 1928-1939)	1900	1900-1939	X
	3. Rogers, Cong.(*Esculapia Twn.;affl.MO 1880-1887,1894-1911, AR 1887-1894)	1881	1880-1911	X
	4. Siloam Springs, Cong.(*Ball Twn.;affl.MO 1882-1887,1894-1902, 1882 AR 1887-1894)	1882	1881-1902	X
	BOONE COUNTY (org.1869) (009)			
	1. Batavia, Cong.(affl.MO)	1903	1904-1907	X
	CARROLL COUNTY (org.1833) (015)			
	1. Eureka Springs, Cong.(*Cedar Twn.;prob.affl.AR 1887-1891)	1885	1885-1891	X
	CLARK COUNTY (org.1818) (019)			
?	1. Curtis, Cong.(*Caddo Twn.;poss.affl.AR 1887-1888)	1881	1885-1888	X
	CRITTENDEN COUNTY (org.1825) (035)			
?	1. Grass Lake, Cong.(prob.Grassy Lake,prob.*Tyronza Twn.)	by 1868	1867-1868	X
	DESHA COUNTY (org.1838) (041)			
?	1. Davis Lake, Cong.	1867	1867-1868	X
	LONOKE COUNTY (org.1873) (085)			
?	1. Austin, Cong.(*Caroline Twn.)	1869	1868-1870	X
	MILLER COUNTY (org.1874/1875) (091)			
?	1. Texarkana, First Cong.(*Garland Twn.;affl.MO btwn.1918 & 1928-1956)	1908	1913-1956	moved to Texarkana, Bowie Co.,TX (q.v.)

ARKANSAS - continued
PULASKI COUNTY (org.1818) (119)

A	B	C	D	E
	1. Little Rock, Central Cong.(f.Peoples(01S):*Big Rock Twn.; affl.MO:1889-1890,1891-1893)	1891 (poss.earlier see text)	1891-1893	X
B1	2. Little Rock, First Cong.(*Big Rock Twn.;affl.TN 1881-1894, 1895-1955;MO 1955-on)	1881	1880-1898, 1901-on	UCC
	3. Little Rock, Pilgrim Cong.(f.Second;Mayflower in 01N;*Big Rock Twn.;affl.TN 1884-1885,MO 1892-1897,poss.AR 1887-1892)	1885(01) 1884(01N)	1884-1897	X
	4. Little Rock, Pulaski Heights Cong.(*Big Rock Twn.;01 says affl.MO,though nl.01S)	1911	1911-1915	X

SEBASTIAN COUNTY (org.1851) (131)

A	B	C	D	E
?	1. Fort Smith, Cong.(*Upper Twn.,or *Lon Norris Twn.)	1886	1885-1886 or 1887	X

WASHINGTON COUNTY (org.1828) (143)

A	B	C	D	E
B1	1. Fayetteville, First Cong.(*Prairie Twn.;affl.TN)	1883 1882(s.08)	1882-1894	X (1891:08)

UNLOCATED CHURCHES (999)

A	B	C	D	E
?	1. Exeter, Cong.(1.in 01N)	1883	nl.	X prob.soon (1884)
?	2. Fort Wayne Reservation, Cong.(1.in 01N)	1885	nl.	X prob.soon (1886)

63 of 75 Counties have no known Congregational Churches and are listed below.

DELAWARE (10)

KENT COUNTY (org. 1682,f.St.Jones[sic] to 1683) (001)

A	B	C	D	E
	1. Canterbury, First Cong.(also m.1863-1864;not affl.)	1864	1864-1866	X

NEW CASTLE COUNTY (org.1673) (003)

A	B	C	D	E
We	1. Glasgow, Pencader Pres.(f.Pencader Hundred,Welsh Tract;f.l. Newark;this Ch.with Welsh Cong.background quickly j Pres.; j Pres.1714 or 1715(Old Side 1745-1758);l.75:by 1773-on (NS))	1710 bf.1713(53)	nl.	Tr.to Pres.1714 or 1715
	2. New Castle, First Ch.(org.as Swedish Luth.,r.as New Amstel Dutch Ref.(1654 or 1657);then r.as a mixed Puritan Ref. English speaking ch.(1698 or 1700)with New England pastor (Trinterud),we show as Cong.;j Pres.1706(Old Side 1745-af. 1748; New Side by 1757-1758)(l.75:by 1773-on(OS)))	1642(Luth.) r.1657(65) 1654(24,99) 1685(64) r.1698(65) 1700(24)	nl.	Tr.to Pres. 1706
	3. Newark, Free Ch. (affl.NY)	c.1836	1836-1843	X 1845
	4. Wilmington, First Cong.(also m.1897-1898;affl.NJ)	1898 1897(s.01)	1898-1901	X

SUSSEX COUNTY (org.1682,f.Deale to 1683) (005)

A	B	C	D	E
Bl	1. Milton, First UCC	1926 1927(s.01) 1924(s.01)	1927-on	UCC

All 3 Counties are shown here.

DISTRICT OF COLUMBIA (11)

	B	C	D	E
	WASHINGTON (District org.1791,Washington Co.org.1801,became only part 1846)			(001)
1.	Washington, Central Cong. (m.16)	1869	nl.	Tr.to Pres.1869 (ab. by Assembly's Pres.)
2.	Washington, Cleveland Park UCC (NW;f.Cong.Com.)	1918	1918-1938, 1939-on	UCC
3.	Washington, Cong. (First Cong.or Cong.Soc.in 08;nl.08 1855-1858)	1852	1852-1855	X c.1858(1859:08)
4.	Washington, Cong.	1864	nl.	X 1864 (lived 3 mos.)
5.	Washington, First Cong.UCC (NW;affl.NJ 1869)	1865	1864-on	UCC
6.	Washington, Ingram Mem.Cong.(NE;f.Fifth Cong.,Ch.of the Pilgrims)	1886 r.1908	1888-1970	UCC 1961-1970; X
Bl 7.	Washington, Lincoln Mem.Cong.(NW;Little Temple;affl.NJ 1881)	1881 1869(s.01,18)	1880-1902	Merged to # 14 to form # 8 (q.v.)
Bl 8.	Washington, Lincoln Temple UCC (NW;f.Lincoln Mem.Cong.Temple; merger of # 7 & # 14)	1902 M 1901 M(08)	1902-on	UCC
Bl 9.	Washington, Mount Pleasant Cong. (NW;moved to Bethesda, Montgomery Co., MD, 1949 as Westmoreland Cong.(q.v.), incor.l.here 1949-1981)	1886 1888(s.01)	1886-1949	Moved (see text)
Bl 10.	Washington, People's Cong.(NW;People's First Cong.;r.of a Meth.Ch.)	1891	1891-on	UCC
Bl 11.	Washington, Plymouth Cong.(NE,f.NW;affl.NJ 1882)	1881 1882(s.01)	1880-on	UCC
12.	Washington, Tabernacle Cong.(not affl.)	1881	1880-1881	X
13.	Washington, Tabernacle Cong.(affl.NJ 1884)	1883 1885(s.01N)	1884-1894	X
Bl 14.	Washington, University Park Temple (NW;f.Temple Park)	1897	1897-1902	Merged to # 7 to form # 8 (q.v.)

The 1 county equivalent is shown here.

A	B	C	D	E
	FLORIDA (12)			
	ALACHUA COUNTY (org.1824) (001)			
1.	Melrose, Cong.	1886	1885-1889	X
2.	Tacoma, Cong.	1895	1895-1898	X
	BAKER COUNTY (org.1861) (003)			
1.	Glen Saint Mary, First Cong.	1907	1907-1912	X
2.	Macclenny, Cong.	1899	1899-1907	X
3.	Olustee, Cypress Grove Cong.(prob.divided from Cong.Meth. (1891)(49))	1893	1893-1898	X
4.	Sanderson, Oak Grove Cong.	1889	1892-1912	X
5.	Taylor, Pine Grove Cong.(prob.same as Cong.Meth.(1883)(49))	1884 1896(s.01)	1892-1912	X
	BAY COUNTY (org.1913) (005) [WEST]			
1.	Millville, Cong.(now part of Springfield)	1909	1910-1913	X
	BREVARD COUNTY (org.1844,f.Saint Lucie to 1855)		(009)	
1.	Malabar, Cong.(also l.as prps.1884-1885)	1885	1885-1891	X
2.	Melbourne, Cong.UCC (f.First)	1889 1887(s.01) 1890(49) 1899(s.01)	1888-on	UCC
	BROWARD COUNTY (org.1915) (011)			
1.	Hallandale, Cong.(in 1911 bldg.)	1913	1913-1921	X
	CALHOUN COUNTY (org.1838) (013) [WEST]			
1.	Blountsville, Chr.Home Ch.,Cong.(l.only in 49)	1900	nl.	X prob.soon (1901)
	CITRUS COUNTY (org.1887) (017)			
Nt	(41 cites a Cong.ch.here 1890 with no specific location and no further dates, not otherwise known)			
	CLAY COUNTY (org.1858) (019)			
1.	Orange Park, Cong.	1883	1882-1904	X (1906:08)

70

A	B	C	D	E
pB	Nt		nl.	X

FLORIDA - CLAY COUNTY - continued

			nl.	X
pB	Orange Park, Second Cong.(l.only by 08:1910-1914;prob.a mission)			

COLUMBIA COUNTY (org.1832) (023)

1.	Lake City, Olive Cong.of Sheardkin	1892	1892-1896	X

DADE COUNTY (org.1836) (025)

1.	Coral Gables, Cong.UCC (f.Com.)	1923(01) 1924(49)	1924-on	UCC
2.	Miami, Cong.(Union Ch.in 49)	1896	1897-1900	X (1898:49)
3.	Miami, First Cong.	1912	1912-1938	X
4.	Miami, Plymouth Cong.(Ch.in the Gardens;f.l.Coconut Grove; f.Union Cong.to 1916;lt.41)	1897 1879(s.01)	1897-on	UCC
5.	Miami Beach, Com.(lt.41)	1921	1921-on	UCC
6.	North Miami, First Ch.of North Miami,Cong.(f.Christ Union Cong.of Arch Creek,f.l.Miami Shores;lt.41)	1912 1902(s.01)	1911-on	UCC

DUVAL COUNTY (org.1822) (031)

1.	Jacksonville, Arlington Cong.(f.Union to 1956;49 says 1875 Cong.Ch.bec.Union 1876)	1875 1876(01N,s.01 16)	1875-on	UCC
2.	Jacksonville, King's Rd.Cong.	1908	1908-1911	X
3.	Jacksonville, Philips Cong.of South Jacksonville	1885 1886(01N)	1885-1934	X

ESCAMBIA COUNTY (org.1821) (033) [WEST]

1.	Cantonment, Sanford Cong.	1912	1912-1923	X
2.	Hurobo, Cong.(f.Forty Nine Pines;f.l.Pensacola PO)	1892 1891(s.01)	1892-1905	X

GLADES COUNTY (org.1921) (043)

1.	Lakeport, Cong.	1916	1916-1918	X
2.	Moore Haven, Cong.	1917	1917-1921	X
3.	Palmdale, Cong.	1915	1915-1921	X

HERNANDO COUNTY (org.1843,f.Hernando to 1844,f.Benton Co.to 1850) (053)

1.	Mannfield, Cong.	1886	1885-1900	X

FLORIDA - continued

HIGHLANDS COUNTY (org.1921) (055)

A	B	C	D	E
	1. Avon Park, Union Cong.(f.First;lt.41;pr.1890(18))	1893(49,01N) 1894(01) 1892(s.01)	1893-on	UCC
	2. Lakemont, Cong.Ch.Among the Lakes	1905	1905-1906	X

HILLSBOROUGH COUNTY (org.1834) (057)

A	B	C	D	E
	1. Tampa, First United (f.University Terrace Com.;also l.as prps.1884-1885)	1885	1885-1902, 1904-on	UCC
Nt	Tampa, Hope Cong.Mission (l.only by 41 as an undesignated ch.,prob.a mission;no dates)			X
	2. Tampa, Hyde Park Cong.	1915	1915-1918	X
	3. Tampa, Immanuel Cuban Cong.(f.l.Zebor City(poss.Ybor City))	1897 1890(s.01)	1897-1906	X
Sp	4. Tampa, Latin Cong.(f.Pilgrim Cuban of West Tampa;lt.41)	1911	1911-1945	X
Sp	5. West Tampa, Union Cong.(l.in Tampa by 49;l.01 as added again 1906,although already l.)	1903 1905(s.01) 1904(s.01) 1907(49)	1903-1923	X (1919:49)

HOLMES COUNTY (org.1848) (059) [WEST]

A	B	C	D	E
	1. Bonifay, First Cong.	1888 1889(s.01)	1888-1905	X
	2. Bonifay, New Effort Cong.(f.Long Pine Union;f.l.Careyville, Washington Co.)	1891 1888(s.01)	1891-on	UCC
	3. Bonifay, New Home Cong.	1904	1904-1923	x
	4. Bonifay, Tulip Cong.(f.Second)	1894	1894-1903	X
	5. Cerro Gordo, Cong.	1896	1896-1901	X
	6. Esto, Carmel Cong.of Potolo	1891(01N) 1892(01)	1891-1913	X
	7. Esto, Hutto Cong.(f.Pleasant Hill;f.l.Potolo;f.l.Coatesville)	1891(01N) 1892(01) r.1901	1891-1909	X
	8. Esto, Union Grove Cong.(f.l.Wrights)	1898	1898-1913	X
	9. Westville, Cong.	1895	1895-1911	X
	10. Westville, Open Pond Cong.	1909	1910-1913	X

INDIAN RIVER COUNTY (org.1925) (061)

A	B	C	D	E
	1. Sebastian, Cong.	1903	1902-1906	X

A	B	C	D	E
	FLORIDA - continued			
	JACKSON COUNTY (org.1822)	(063)		[WEST]
1.	Bascom, Cong.(1.AL:01s:1898-1899)	by 1899	nl.	X af.1899
2.	Cottondale, County Line Cong.	1896	1896-1913	X
3.	Graceville, Cong.	1898	1898-1906	X
4.	Inwood, Cong.	1908	1908-1913	X
5.	Malone, Cong.	1911	1913-1921	X
	LAKE COUNTY (org.1887)	(069)		
1.	Lane Park, Cong.	1885	1885-1889	X
2.	Mount Dora, Com.Cong.(lt.01N)	1883	1883-1977	Sch.I 1961-1977; NA 1965(j 1966)-on
3.	Tavares, Union Cong.(also 1.as prps.1884-1885)	1885(s.01) 1884(s.01) 1883(49) 1888(s.01) 1885	1885-on	UCC
	LEE COUNTY (org.1887)	(071)		
1.	Fort Myers, Thomas A.Edison Cong.(f.Edison Park Com.)	1925	1925-1978	Sch.I 1961-1978; NA 1979-on
	LEON COUNTY (org.1824)	(073)		
B1 1.	Tallahassee, The Pilgrim Cong.(affl.GA(B1))	1917 1918(08)	1921-1924	X
	MARION COUNTY (org.1844)	(083)		
1.	Belleview, Cong.	1888	1888-1900	X
2.	Lake Kerr, Cong.(f.1.Kerr City;incor.l.Lake Weir at drop)	1886	!886-1892	X
3.	Lake Weir, South Lake Weir Cong.(still m.1895:01S)	1886	1885-1893	X
4.	Moss Bluff, Cong.Com.(49 says Ch.X 1938,but SS alive 1942)	1894 1898(49)	1894-1944	X
	MARTIN COUNTY (org.1925)	(085)		
1.	Jensen, Cong.	1904	1904-1912	X
2.	Palm City, First Cong.(UCC)(f.Bible Union Cong.;incor.lt.41, once here & once in Palm Beach Co.)	1921	1921-on	UCC
3.	Stuart, Cong.	1914	1915-1920	X

73

A	B	C	D	E
	FLORIDA - continued			
	MONROE COUNTY (org.1823) (087)			
1.	Key West, First Cong.(First CC;j UCC 1962,incor.l.UCC late 1961-1962)	1892	1892-on	Sch.I 1961; UCC late 1961-on
	OKALOOSA COUNTY (org.1915) (091) [WEST]			
1.	Baker, Cong.	1911	1912-1913	X
2.	Baker, Cong.	1915	1915-1919	X
3.	Baker, Good Hope Cong.(f.l.Cottonville to 1931)	1922 1896(s.01)	1922-on	sch.II 1961-1962; UCC 1962-1971; sch.II 1971-on sch.II
4.	Baker, Pyron's Chap.Cong.	1897	1905-1906, 1912-on	
5.	Campton, Cong.(l.Crestview;Garden City PO)	1890(01N) 1891(01) 1892(s.01)	1890-1905, 1907-1908, 1913-1929	X
6.	Crestview, C of C (Christ's Ch.;lt.1907-1908;also l.as prps. 1890-1891)	1891 1890(s.01)	1891-1945	X
7.	Crestview, Silver Springs Cong.	1897	1897-1903	X
8.	Destin, Cong.(lt.1907-1908)	1900(01) 1896(49)	1900-1909, 1910-1923	X (1926:49)
9.	Dorcas, Cong.(l.Crestview;f.Shoal River)	1892 1893(s.01)	1892-1966	UCC; X
10.	Dorcas, Mount Olive Cong.(f.l.Deerland;nr.Crestview)	1895 1904(s.01)	1895-1923	X
11.	Galliver, Moore's Chap.Cong.	1914	1914-1916	X
12.	Laurel Hill, Central Cong.	1932(01) 1930(49)	1932-1948	X
13.	Laurel Hill, Children's Home Cong.	1920	1921-1925, 1926-1928, 1931-1943	X
14.	Laurel Hill, Cong.	1896 1899(s.01)	1898-1908	X
15.	Laurel Hill, Cong.	1920	1920-1923	X
16.	Laurel Hill, New Life Cong.	1906	1912-1917	X
17.	Laurel Hill, Pleasant Hill Cong.	1914	1914-1928	X
18.	Mary Esther, Cong.(lt.1907-1908)	1892 1891(s.01)	1892-1909, 1910-1921	X
19.	Milligan, Oak Grove Cong.(see Santa Rosa Co.# 6)	1897	1898-1904	X
20.	Milligan, Shady Grove Cong.(f.l.Cobb PO)	1900(s.01) 1900	1907-1908, 1911-1913	X
21.	Niceville, Cong.	r.1909(s.01) 1911	1912-1914	X

FLORIDA - OKALOOSA COUNTY - continued

A	B	C	D	E
22.	Svea, Cong.(lt.1907-1908)	1905 / 1902(s.01)	1905-1913	X

Nt (41 identifies a Union Cong.in this Co.,not otherwise specified.We suspect it is an lt.of one of the above.)

ORANGE COUNTY (org.1824,f.Mosquito Co.to 1845) (095)

A	B	C	D	E
1.	Apopka, First Cong.(m.1895:01S)	1885 / 1897(49)	1885-1893	X (1899:49;see text)
2.	Clarcona, Cong.	1886	1886-1893, 1895-1899	X
3.	Lakeville, Union Cong.(Clarcona PO)	1886	1885-1886	X (1920:49)
4.	Ocoee, Winter Garden Cong.	1891 / 1878(s.01)	1891-1906	X
5.	Orlando, First Cong.(also l.as prps.1884-1885)	1885	1885-1902	X
6.	Tangerine, First Cong.(Cong.C of C;Sch.II assigned in report, prob.did not vote)	1886 / 1885(49)	1886-1963	Sch.I 1961;Sch.II late 1961-1963; X
7.	Winter Park, First Cong.(f.Cong.Soc.to 1915;lt.41 as Hooker Mem.Cong.)	1884 / 1882(Soc.:49)	1883-on	UCC
8.	Winter Park, Knowles Mem.Chap.of Rollins College (l.by 49 & 41)	1931	nl.	X af.1942

PALM BEACH COUNTY (org.1909) (099)

A	B	C	D	E
1.	Jupiter, People's Ch.(People's Cong.)	1917 / 1918(49)	1918-1974	UCC 1961-1974; withdrew
2.	Lake Worth, First Cong.(f.Union Ch.to 1922:49)	1912 / r.1921 / 1917(s.01)	1921-on	UCC
3.	Lantana, Cong.	1896	1896-1899	X
4.	Palm Beach, Poinciana Cong.(f.l.Lake Worth;we assume this is the same as Royal Poinciana Chap.(41,49);also l.as prps. 1884-1885;during some of this time not fully org.:services in hotel for tourist season)	1885 / 1895(49)	1885-1904, 1907-1922, 1923-1937	X
5.	West Palm Beach, Union Cong.	1894 / 1895(s.01)	1894-on	UCC

PASCO COUNTY (org.1887) (101)

A	B	C	D	E
1.	Crystal Springs, Com.Cong.(f.Union)	1913(s.01) / 1912(s.01) / 1914(49)	1912-1942	X (1937:49)
2.	New Port Richey, Com.Cong.UCC	1921	1921-on	Sch.I 1961; Sch.II late 1961-1964; UCC 1964-on

A	B	C	D	E
	FLORIDA - continued			
	PINELLAS COUNTY (org.1911) (103)			
1.	Belleair, Cong.	1897	1897-1901	X
2.	Saint Petersburg, First Cong.(f.United Evan.;f.UCC)	1888 / 1889(s.01)	1888-on	UCC
	POLK COUNTY (org.1861) (105)			
1.	Fort Meade, Cong.	1885	1885-1889	X
2.	Haines City, Cong.	1890 / 1900(s.01)	1890-1904	X
	PUTNAM COUNTY (org.1849) (107)			
1.	Interlachen, First Cong.	1884 / 1988([sic]s.04)	1883-1989	UCC 1961-1989; NA 1987-on
2.	Norwalk, Cong.	1884	1883-1896	X
3.	Pomona Park, Pilgrim Cong.(f.Union of Pomona)	1882	1883-on	UCC
	SAINT LUCIE COUNTY (org.1905) (111)			
1.	Eden, Cong.(poss.lt.in Brevard Co.by 41;poss.continues 1890-1902 Union Ch.(49))	1894 / 1893(s.01) / 1902(49)	1894-1918	X (1907:49)
2.	Fort Pierce, Cong.	1902	1902-1906	X
Nt	Walton, Cong.(41, says Ch.here X by 1939, but gives no dates or other information.)			
3.	White City, Cong.	1894	1894-1898	X
	SANTA ROSA COUNTY (org.1842(in 1830 census)) (113)		[WEST]	
1.	Bagdad, Bethel Cong.	1891	1891-1894	X
2.	Bagdad, Zion Hill Cong.	1890(01N) / 1891(01)	1890-1904	X
3.	Holley, Antioch Cong.(f.East Bay;1.Milton;f.l.Pensacola, Escambia Co.PO;lt.1907-1908)	1892	1892-1943	X
4.	Milton, Cong.	1896	1896-1903	X
Nt	Milton, Cram Chap.Cong.(l.only by 41 with no dates, we assume this is a lt.of # 4)			
5.	Munson, Cong.	1914	1913-1914	X
6.	Oak Grove, Center Ridge Cong.(poss.a r.of Okaloosa Co.# 19)	1905	1907-1908	X
7.	Otahite, Cong.	1895	1897-1902	X
8.	Sullivan, Calvary Cong.	1897(s.01) / 1896	1907-1908	X

76

A	B	C	D	E
	FLORIDA - continued			
	SARASOTA COUNTY (org.1921) (115)			
1.	Laurel, Cong.	1907	1908-1912	X
	SEMINOLE COUNTY (org.1913) (117)			
1.	Alamonte, Palm Springs Cong.(also l.as prps.01S:1886-1887)	1887	1887-1901	X
2.	Cameron City, Cong.(in 1910 bldg.;Sanford PO)	1911	1910-1918	X (1917:49)
3.	Lake Brantley, Cong.(l.by 41 as Union Chap.in Orange Co.;49 & 18 suggest that the Alamonte Ch.(Appendix III.# 1) is actually this ch.;also l.as prps.01S:1886-1887)	1887	1887-1893	X
4.	Longwood, Cong.(also l.as prps.1884-1885)	1885	1885-1904	X (1906:49)
5.	Longwood, West Cong.(also l.as prps.1884-1885)	1885	1885-1900	X (1899:49)
6.	Sanford, First CC(f.People's,The Ch.of the People;lt.41;lt.NA 1968-1973(Full & Affl.))	1890 1889(49)	1890-1965	UCC 1961-1965; NA (Full)1966(j 1967)-on
7.	Sylvan Lake, Union Cong.	1887	1886-1898	X
	SUMTER COUNTY (org.1853) (119)			
1.	Panasoffkee, Cong.	1893	1893-1909	X
	SUWANNEE COUNTY (org.1858) (121)			
Nt	Petersburg, Cong.(This is m.by 41, but with no dates.Not otherwise known.)			
	UNION COUNTY (org.1921) (125)			
1.	Johnstown, Union Cong.	1917	1917-1929	X
Nt	Pearl Chap.Cong.Ch.(41 identifies as here with no exact location and no dates. Not otherwise known.)			
2.	Raiford, Elarbee Cong.	1902 r.1911	1902-1913	X
Nt	Sampson City(Bradford Co.PO), Long Bridge Ch.(Cong.)(l.by 41 (1939),with no dates,not otherwise known)			
	VOLUSIA COUNTY (org.1854) (127)			
1.	Daytona Beach, Seabreeze United (f.Tourist Ch.of Seabreeze; lt.41;f.First Cong.of Daytona Beach at Seabreeze to 1929; withdrew 1929 but still l.1929-1963;f.in Counc.Com.Chs. 1950-btwn.1961 & 1964;Sch.II assigned,ch.never voted;j UCC 1886(s.01,18) 1964)	1904 1905(s.01) r.1929	1904-1963, 1964-on	Sch.I 1961; Sch.II late 1961-1963; UCC 1964-on

A	B	C	D	E
bB	FLORIDA - VOLUSIA COUNTY - continued			
2.	Daytona Beach, Tubman-King Com.Ch.(f.First Cong.to r.;f.l. Daytona;lt.(separate natl.l.:01)1881-1882;01N implies 1880 was date ch.received;bec.predominantly Black c.1978)	1877 1878(s.01N, s.01) 1880(s.01N) 1884(s.01) r.1985	1879-on	UCC
3.	Hawk's Park, Cong.	1884	1884-1891	X
4.	Holly Hill, UCC (f.Union Cong.;lt.41)	1914	1928-on	UCC
5.	Lake Helen, First Cong.	1895(49) 1886(49,s.01) 1887(01N,18, s.01)	1885-on	UCC
6.	New Smyrna Beach, UCC(Cong.-Disc.)(f.Christ Fed.;f.Christ Cong.of New Smyrna;f.C of C;Fed.to First Chr.(Disc.)(1924) 1972-on;in Holmes Co.in 17)	1875(17,18) 1883(s.01) 1885(s.01)	1882-on	UCC
7.	Oak Hill, Cong.	1886 1887(01N) 1885(s.01)	1886-1918	X
8.	Orange City, First Cong.	1883 1885(s.01)	1882-on	UCC
9.	Ormond Beach, Ormond Beach Union Ch.,Cong.(f.l.Ormond;lt.41; s.in Counc.Com.Chs.)	1883 1888(49) 1887(s.01)	1890-on	UCC
10.	Port Orange, First Cong.	1880(01) 1881(s.01) 1885(49) 1886(01N)	1882-1903	X (1920:49)
	WALTON COUNTY (org.1824) (131) [WEST]			
1.	DeFuniak Springs, Cluster Springs Cong.(f.l.Ealum; f.l. Florala,Covington Co.,AL)	1911 r.1956	1911-1925, 1927-1943, 1957-1962	Sch.II 1961-1962; prob.withdrew
2.	Ealum, Cong.(or Ealurn)	1896	1897-1905	X
3.	Gordon, New Light Cong. (f.Wood)	1894	1894-1914	X
4.	Mossyhead, Stella Cong.	1903	1903-1925	X
5.	Oak Ridge, Bearhead Cong.(DeFuniak Springs,PO;l.as drop 1906 (01),but not done)	1905(s.01) 1892 1882(s.01) 1889(s.01)	1892-1908, 1912-1921	X
6.	Portland, Black Oak Cong.	1892 1894(s.01)	1892-1903	X
7.	Portland, Cong.	1890 1894(s.01)	1895-1903	X

A	B	C	D	E
	FLORIDA - WALTON COUNTY - continued			
8.	Portland, Rocky Bayou Cong.(Boggy)	1892(s.01) 1902(s.01)	1892-1903, 1907-1908	X
9.	Whitfield, Cong.(l.only by 01S,1894-1895)	by 1895	nl.	X prob.sonn (1896)
	WASHINGTON COUNTY (org.1825) (133) [WEST]			
1.	Caryville, Second Cong.(f.Union of Mayvieve)	1896	1901-1913, 1920-1923	X
2.	Chipley, Shiloh Cong.	1897	1896-1909	X
		1896(s.01)		
3.	Vernon, Cong.	1895(01N) 1897(01)	1895-1905	X
4.	Wausau, Harmony Cong.(f.l.Holmes Valley)	1891(01N) 1892(01)	1891-1905	X
	UNLOCATED CHURCHES (999)			
Nt	Fessenden, Cong.(l.only by 08 1917-af.1918,prob.a mission)		nl.	X
1.	Warnell, Cong.(in South FL Conf.,yoked to Sumter Co.# 1)	1892	1892-1899	X

pB 25 of 67 Counties have no known Congregational Churches and are listed below. Note also that Citrus and Suwannee Counties above have have no full churches.

79

GEORGIA (13)

APPLING COUNTY (org.1818) (001)

A	B	C	D	E
1.	Baxley, Crosby's Chap.Cong.	1904	1904-1907	X
2.	Baxley, Friendship CC	1892 1876(s.01,s.04) 1887(s.01)	1892-1985	Sch.II 1961-1985; NA(affl.)1966(j 1967)-1979,1991-on
3.	Baxley, Mount Olivet Cong.	1897	1897-1914	X
4.	Baxley, Pleasant Grove Cong.	1894	1894-1896	X
5.	Surrency, Cong.of Meridian(f.l.Mindian;lt.1902-1903)	1892	1892-1905	X
6.	Surrency, New Home Cong.of Meridian No.2	1905	1905-1922	X

ATKINSON COUNTY (org.1917/1919) (003)

A	B	C	D	E
1.	Pearson, Union Cong.(Union Hill;f.l.McDonald's Mills,(nr.Axson);f.l.Waycross,Ware Co.)	1892 1884(s.01) 1922(s.01)	1892-1985	UCC 1961-1970; Sch.II 1970-1985; NA(affl.)1966(j 1967)-on

BACON COUNTY (org.1914) (005)

A	B	C	D	E
1.	Medders, Williams Chap.Cong.	1904	1904-1907	X
2.	New Lacy, Cong.	1910	1910-1920	X
3.	Rockingham, Cong.(Leroy PO)	1913	1913-1920	X

BAKER COUNTY (org.1825) (007)

BARTOW COUNTY (org.1832,f.Cass Co.to 1861) (015)

A	B	C	D	E
B1 1.	Milford, St.Mark's Cong.	1886	1885-1892	X (1890:08)
B1 2.	Milford, Shiloh Cong.(f.St.Louis)	1886	1885-1888	X (1891:08)

BEN HILL COUNTY (org.1906) (017)

A	B	C	D	E
1.	Folsom, Cong.	1912	1912-1920	X

BIBB COUNTY (org.1822) (021)

A	B	C	D	E
1.	Fitzgerald, Plymouth Cong.	1905	1905-1906	X
1.	Lizella, Burgie's Chap.Cong.(or Burgey's Chap.;f.l.Burkett's Store;at 1887 Conv.as Cong.Meth.)	1886	1888-1894	X
B1 2.	Macon, First Cong.(affl.TN 1870-1877;incor.1.1990-1992)	1868 1898(s.08)	1867-1992	UCC (incor.X 1904:08);X 1990

GEORGIA - BIBB COUNTY - continued

A	B	C	D	E
3.	Macon, Hopewell Cong.(at 1887 Conv.as Cong.Meth.)	1875	1888-1894	X
4.	Macon, Second Cong.(f.Cong.Meth.;at 1887 Conv.as Cong.Meth.)	by 1887	1888-1890	X
B1 5.	Rutland, Cong.of <u>Walden</u> (First Cong.)	1885	1884-1927	X

BLECKLEY COUNTY (org.1912/1913) (023)

A	B	C	D	E
1.	Cochran, Pleasant Hill Cong.(Cohren;Cohran)	1897 1898(s.01)	1898-1947	X

BRANTLEY COUNTY (org.1920) (025)

A	B	C	D	E
1.	Hoboken, Cong.	1891	1891-1900	X

BRYAN COUNTY (org.1793) (029)

A	B	C	D	E
B1 1.	Groveland, Oak Hill Cong.(Register,Bulloch Co.PO)	1913 1914(08)	1913-1929	X

BULLOCH COUNTY (org.1796) (031)

A	B	C	D	E
pB 1.	Harville, Cong.(Hartville)	1896	1896-1900	X (1898:08)
B1 2.	Portal, Cong.(poss.same as # 3)	1895	1895-1899	X (1901:08)
B1 3.	Register, Cong.(poss.same as # 2)	1895	1905-1908	X
B1 4.	Statesboro, Cong.(Po'ell Grove)	1897	1897-1899, 1905-1908	X (1901:08)

BURKE COUNTY (org.1777) (033)

A	B	C	D	E
B1 1.	Midville, First Cong.(footnote only 1903-1904)	1901	1901-1904	X (1905:08)
2.	Waynesboro, First Pres.(f.Indep.Cong.;f.of Waynesboro & Bath, f.Burke Co.Ch.;in town;merger of #3 & Walnut Branch(Walnut Creek:63G)Pres.on Whitehead Pltn.,northwest of town(org. 1789(63G)),nl.75,m.Pby.1799;l.75:(supply 1811)btwn.1809 & 1813-btwn.1819 & 1824(prob.1819),1827-1828,1830(j1830 or 1831)-1834,1835-1839,1841 or 1842-1843(withdrew 1840),1852-(j1853)-1861(OS),1861-1975(Pres.U.S.),1973-on(PCA); specifically indep.to 1853,in 1850 Census as Cong.)	1810 M r.af.1853 (Pres.)	nl.	Tr.to Pres.; PCA
2B.	Bath(Richmond Co.), Bath Pres.(This Richmond Co.BRANCH est. 1820(52)(or 1819(65,98));98 says branch abandoned 1879;l. as a ch.75:l.1888-1983(Pres.U.S.),1983-on(Pres.);nl.24)	1889	nl.	Pres.
3.	Waynesboro, Indep.Cong.(f.Pres.of Brier Creek(Bryar Creek), northeast of town;moved 1780's to "Old Ch."site of X Epis. Ch.,south of town;l.Pres.:75;by 1773-btwn.1788 & 1797)	1760(63G,98) 1767(24) by 1790(r. Cong.) 1790(incp.)	CGA:1801- af.1803	1810 Merged to form #2(q.v.)

A	B	C	D	E
		GEORGIA - continued		
	CALHOUN COUNTY (org.1854)	(037)		
1.	Morgan, Cong.	1903	1903-1905	X
	CAMDEN COUNTY (org.1777)	(039)		
1.	Saint Mary's, Indep.Pres.(indep.cgn.,r.as Indep.Pres.1822 in Pby.;later r.as First Pres.;l.75:btwn.1819 & 1824(j1822)-1861(OS),1861-1983(Pres.U.S.),1983-on(Pres.))	1808(bldg.) 1822(75H,75Y) 1828(incp.)	nl.	Pres.
	CARROLL COUNTY (org.1826)	(045)		
1.	Whitesburg, Ratherwood Cong.(in 1859 bldg.)	1913	1913-1921	X
2.	Whitesburg, Rock Spring Cong.(at 1887 Conv.as Free Meth. Prot.)	1883	1888-1890	X
	CHARLTON COUNTY (org.1854)	(049)		
1.	Charlton, Cong.(affl.FL,l.with GA natl.;m.1895 & 1899:01S)	1893	1893-1895	X (see text)
2.	Folkston, Colerane Cong.(Coleraine)	1917	1917-1922	X
3.	Homeland, First Cong.(in 1912 bldg.)	1915	1915-1922	X
	CHATHAM COUNTY (org.1777)	(051)		
B1 1.	Louisville, Cong.(prob.here because of yokes,poss.on Louisville Rd.,rather than at Louisville,Jefferson Co.)	1874	1873-1885	X (1887:08)
B1 2.	Ogeechee, Cong.(f.Miller's of Savannah Mills,f.l.Miller's Station;f.l.Savannah;footnote only 1903-1904;prob.here because of former names & yokes,prob.nr.Ogeechee River, rather than in Ogeechee,Screven Co.)	1872 1874(s.01)	1871-1898, 1899-1904	X (1901:08)
B1 3.	Savannah, Belmont Cong.	1873 1874(08) 1878	1872-1886 or 1887 1877-1883	X (1887:08)
B1 4.	Savannah, East Cong.	1869	1868-on	X (1886:08) UCC
B1 5.	Savannah, First Cong.(some Black members of # 6)	1868(s.01)		
6.	Savannah, Indep.Pres.(Indep.Ch.(1800 incp.);org.with "doctrine of Ch.of Scotland,agreeably to Westminster Confession," claim to be a branch of Ch.of Scotland not supported as never a full member of Pby.& multi-cultural:inclu.services in Fr.(Ger.services prob.#10); served Pres.1795-1796(nl.),1811-1814 or 1815(1.75 btwn. 1798 & 1802-btwn.1809 & 1813,in northern Pbys.),1.75 btwn.:1863 & 1865-1899,1949-1983(Pres.U.S.),1983-1985 (Pres.);see also # 5)	1755(52) by 1756(land grant) c.1756(24) 1800(incp.) 1806(r.incp.)	nl.	Indep.Pres.

A	B	C	D	E Pres.U.S.;PCA
	GEORGIA - CHATHAM COUNTY - continued			
6B.	Savannah, Mary Elizabeth Blue Hull Mem.Pres.(f.Westminster Pres.;f.Second Pres.;f.Anderson St.Chap.;f.BRANCH of #6, begun 1868;l.as a ch.:75:1885(j1890)-1971(Pres.U.S., withdrew 1967);1973-on(PCA))	1886 1884(s.75Y)	nl.	Pres.U.S.;PCA
Bl 7.	Savannah, Pilgrim Cong.(f.of Woodville Canal,or Woodville))	1871	1871-1948	X (1910:08)
Bl 8.	Savannah, Second Cong.(Pilgrim in 08;footnote only 1903-1904)	1898	1898-1904	X
Bl 9.	Savannah, Wheat Hill Cong.(f.Christ Cong.;footnote only 1903-1904)	1891 1894(08)	1891-1904	X (1903:08)
10.	Savannah, White Bluff Pres.(f.Cong.of White Bluff,Cong.of Savannah;f.of Vernon or Vernonburg(h) & Acton;1810 Pastor ord.by CGA;Ger.& Eng.at start;prob.supplied from # 6 1759-1810;supply by Pres.1816-1822(l.btwn.1814 & 1818-btwn. 1819 & 1824),l.by Pres.1833-1834 or 1835,1839 or 1840-1841 or 1842,1846-1852(OS),btwn.1863 & 1865-1872,1873-1880,1944 (j1945)-1983(Pres.U.S.),1983-on(Pres.);indep.1880-1945); nl.24)	1743(65) r.1945(Pres.)	CGA 1810-?	Tr.to Pres.
	CLARKE COUNTY (org.1801) (059)			
Bl 1.	Athens, First Cong.	1882	1881-1938	X
2.	Athens, Plymouth Cong.	1890	1890-1891	X
3.	Whitehall, Mount Rest Cong.(f.Factory Cong.of Athens to c.1890;lt.1889-1890)	1888	1888-1891	X
	CLAYTON COUNTY (org.1858) (063)			
1.	Riverdale, Poplar Springs Cong.(at 1887 Conv.as Free Meth. Prot.)	1887 1882(s.01)	1888-1901, 1903-1907	X
	CLINCH COUNTY (org.1850) (065)			
1.	DuPont, Fender Cong.	1891	1891-1897	X
	COBB COUNTY (org.1832) (067)			
1.	Gilmore, Brown's Cong.	1905	1905-1908	X
Bl 2.	Marietta, First Cong.(affl.TN 1876-1877;j UCC 1962,incor.l. UCC late 1961-1962,was Sch.I)	1877 1868(s.01)	1876-1901, 1903-1964	Sch.I 1961; UCC late 1961-1964; X
3.	Smyrna, Cong.	1913	1913-1919	X
	COFFEE COUNTY (org.1854) (069)			
1.	Douglas, First Cong.	1909 r.1913	1909-1922	X

A	B	C	D	E
	GEORGIA - COFFEE COUNTY - continued			
2.	Nicholls, Cong.	1906	1906-1908	X
3.	Nicholls, Rock(y) Hill Cong.(f.of Wilsonville;f.l.Fairfax, Ware Co.)	1898 / 1897(s.01) / 1889(s.01)	1897-1922	X
	COLQUITT COUNTY (org.1856) (071)			
1.	Crosland, Huggens Cong.(lt.1902-1903)	1901	1901-1907	X
2.	Doerun, Bethany Cong.	1909	1909-1910	X
3.	Doerun, New Light Cong.	1892 / 1902(s.01) / 1904(s.01)	1902-1985	Sch.II 1961-1985; NA (affl.)1966(j 1967)- 1979,1991-on
4.	Doerun, Poplar Arbor Cong.(f.l.Tifton,Tift Co.;l.Sale City, Mitchell Co.:04)	1909 / 1910(s.01) / 1884(s.01)	1909-1985	Sch.I 1961-1985; NA(affl.)1966(j 1967)-on
5.	Hartsfield, Cong.	1901	1901-1904	X
	CRAWFORD COUNTY (org.1822) (079)			
1.	Fort Valley(Peach Co.PO), Society Hill Cong.(f.Friendship Cong.of Byron,Peach Co.;f.l.Pine Level;f.l.Taylor;at 1887 Conv.as Cong.Meth.)	1873 / 1887(s.01) r.1932	1888-1924, 1935-1959	withdrew; bec.Mission Bapt.
2.	Gaillard, Pleasant Hill Cong.(f.l.Roberta(& by 04),f.l. Clark's Mills;Gillards;l.s.Columbus,Muscogee Co.:04;lt.NA (affl.& full):1966-1983,1991-on;at 1887 Conv.as Cong. Meth.)	1883 / 1873(s.04) / 1964(s.04)	1888-1985	UCC 1961-1970; Sch.II 1970-1985; NA(full) by 1961-on
3.	Roberta, Walker's Chap.Cong.(f.l.Knoxville,f.l.Bowers(prob. Powers,Peach Co.,later Powersville);at 1887 Conv.as Cong. Meth.)	1886 / 1889(s.01)	1888-1949	X
	CRISP COUNTY (org.1905) (081)			
1.	Arabi, Athens Cong.(f.l.Wenona;lt.1902-1903)	1901	1901-1908	X
2.	Cordele, Cong.(Cordell)	1894	1894-1898	X
3.	Cordele, Wiliford Cong.(Lloyd PO;f.l.Seville,Wilcox Co.)	1891(01N) / 1892(01)	1891-1922	X
4.	Lloyd, Cong.	1892	1899-1900	X
5.	Wenona, Cong.	1894	1894-1900	X
	DADE COUNTY (org.1837) (083)			
1.	Trenton, New England Cong.	1913	1913-1923	X

A	B	C	D	E
	GEORGIA - continued			
	DAWSON COUNTY (org.1857) (085)			
	1. Dawsonville, Holly Creek Cong.(at 1887 Conv.as Cong.Meth.)	1877	1888-1934	X
	DE KALB COUNTY (org.1822) (089)			
	1. Chamblee, Poplar Springs Cong.(1.1887-1888:01S;at 1887 Conv. as Free Meth.Prot.)	by 1887 r.1890	1890-1893	X
	2. Stone Mountain, Antioch Cong.(f.l.Braden,Gwinnett Co.;at 1887 Conv.as Cong.Meth.;see also # 4)	1886	1888-1903	X
		1904	1904-1929	X
	3. Stone Mountain, Earnest Grove Cong.	1901	1901-1926	X
	4. Tucker, Union Cong.(1t.of # 2 1901-1903)	r.1903		
	DOOLY COUNTY (org.1821) (093)			
	1. Ashlern, Rayney's Chap.Cong.(or Raney's)	1890	1890-1891	X
pB Nt	Eureka, Camp Grounds Cong.(1.only in 08,prob.a mission)	1895	nl.	X 1905
	2. Richwood, Salem Cong.	1899 / 1900(s.01)	1900-1905	X
	DOUGHERTY COUNTY (org.1853) (095)			
	1. Albany, Fellowship Cong.	1910	1910-1926	X
	ELBERT COUNTY (org.1790) (105)			
	1. Dewey Rose, Liberty Cong.(f.l.Bowman,f.l.Webster Pl.,f.l. Amandaville,Hart Co.,f.l.Hartwell,Hart Co.;at 1887 Conv. as Cong.Meth.)	1878 / 1879(s.01) / 1892(s.01)	1888-on	sch.I 1961-1978; UCC 1978-on
	2. Middleton, New Hope Cong.(f.l.Rock Fence)	1900	1900-1919	X
	EMANUEL COUNTY (org.1812) (107)			
Bl	1. Garfield, Mount Zion Pilgrim Cong.	1895	1895-1899	X (1901:08)
Bl	2. Kemp, McLeod Cong.(McLerod;footnote only 1903-1904)	1895	1895-1904	X (1905:08)
pB Nt	Rountree, Cong.(1.only by 08,prob.a mission)	1900	nl.	X 1905
Bl	3. Summertown, Cong.	1903	1903-1904	X
Bl	4. Summertown, Promise Land Cong.(f.l.Swainsboro)	1899	1899-1901	X
Bl	5. Swainsboro, First Cong.	1895 / 1898(s.01)	1895-1929	X
Bl	6. Swainsboro, Green Cong.(Cribb;Summertown PO(08))	1899	1899-1901	X (1905:08)
Bl	7. Swainsboro, Mount Pleasant Cong.(f.l.Summertown)	1896(08)	1899-1900	X
Bl	8. Wade, Pilgrims Rest Cong.(f.l.Graymont)	1899 / 1895	1900-1912	X (1909:08)

GEORGIA - continued

A	B	C	D	E
	EVANS COUNTY (org.1914)	(109)		
pB	Nt			
Bl	1. Claxton, Cong.(l.only by 08,prob.a mission)	1902	nl.	X 1903
Bl	1. Daisy, Alford Cong.(f.l.Lanham PO,f.l.Hagan,f.l.Register, Bulloch Co.;lt.1901-1903)	1895	1896-1929	X
Bl	2. Hagan, Bethel Cong.(footnote only 1903-1904)	1901	1901-1922	X
Bl	3. Hagan, Eureka Cong.	1902(01S) 1894(s.01) 1895(08)	1895-1938	X
Bl	4. Hagan, Hagan Cong.	1895 1894(01S)	1895-1900	X
Bl	5. Hagan, Piney Grove Cong.(Still Ground)	1895 1895	1895-1900	X (1897:08)
Bl	6. Hagan, Shady Grove Cong.(f.l.Riggtown,Tattnall Co.;footnote only 1903-1904;l.thrice by 08,twice as Manassas,Tattnall Co.PO)	1895(lt.08) 1894(lt.08) r.1907(s.08)	1900-1914	X (1900,1907 & 1912 in 08)
pB	Nt Palaky, Cong.(l.only by 08,prob.a mission)	1897	nl.	X 1901
	FANNIN COUNTY (org.1854)	(111)		
	1. Mineral Bluff, Cong.	1903	1903-1923	X
	FLOYD COUNTY (org.1832)	(115)		
	1. Byrd, Cong.	1888	1888-1890	X
	2. Forestville, Forestville Cong.(at 1887 Conv.as Cong.Meth.)	1887	1888-1890	X
	3. Lindale, Cong.	1904	1904-1923	X
	4. Rome, East Cong.(f.Cong.)	1889	1889-1892	X
	5. Rome, North Cong.(f.of North Rome)	1891	1891-1910	X
	6. Rome, West Cong.	1891	1891-1896	X
	7. Wilkins, Cong.	1893	1893-1901	X
	FULTON COUNTY (org.1853;ab.Campbell Co.org.1828-1932 & Milton Co.org.1857-1932)	(121)		
	1. Alpharetta, Cong.(f.l.Ocee)	1900	1900-1920	X
	2. Atlanta, Berean Cong.(at 1887 Conv.as Cong.;bec.a branch of #4,m.1908)	1883(01) 1884(01N)	1884-1898	X (see text)
	3. Atlanta, Center Cong.(f.l.Woodward Station,Bolton,Center Minerva,Minerva,Clara,Howell's Mills;in 1893 bldg.)	1880 1888(s.01) 1889(s.01) 1906(s.01)	1888-1985	UCC; X
	4. Atlanta, Central Cong.(f.Piedmont,f.Ch.of the Redeemer;also l.as prps.1883-1884;at 1887 Conv.as Cong.;see also #2)	1882	1884-1931	Merged to #18 to form #5 (q.v.)
	5. Atlanta, Central Cong.(merger of #4 & #18;moved to Atlanta, De Kalb Co.1967)	1931 M	1931-on	UCC

A		B	C	D	E
		GEORGIA - FULTON COUNTY - continued			
	6.	Atlanta, East Cong.(poss.in De Kalb Co.)	1919	1919-1926	X
B1	7.	Atlanta, First Cong.(affl.TN 1870-1877)	1867	1867-on	UCC
	8.	Atlanta, Grace Cong.(at 1887 Conv.as Cong.)	1886	1885-1890	X
	9.	Atlanta, Hope Cong.	1883	1884-1885	X
	10.	Atlanta, Immanuel Cong.(Emanuel;also l.as prps.1883-1884;at 1887 Conv.as Cong.)	1884	1884-1920	X
	11.	Atlanta, Jefferson St.Cong.	1909	1909-1911	X
	12.	Atlanta, Leonard St.Cong.	1909	1909-1917	Merged to # 16 to form # 17(q.v.)
	13.	Atlanta, Marietta St.Cong.	1902	1902-1935	X
	14.	Atlanta, Pleasant Hill Cong.(f.l.Clara;at 1887 Conv.as Cong. Meth.)	by 1887 r.1888	1888-1899	X
B1	15.	Atlanta, Rush Mem.Cong.(j UCC 1962,incor.l.UCC late 1961-1962,was Sch.I)	1916 1913(s.01)	1916-on	sch.I 1961; UCC late 1961-on
	16.	Atlanta, Union Tabernacle Cong.(Tr.from United Brethren)	1902(U.B.) r.1907(20)	1907-1917	Merged to # 12 to form # 17(q.v.)
	17.	Atlanta, Union Tabernacle Cong.(merger of # 12 & # 16)	r.1917 M	1917-1934	X
	18.	Atlanta, United Cong.	1929	1929-1931	Merged to # 4 to form # 5 (q.v.)
B1	19.	Atlanta, University Cong.(1.01S:1886-1887)	1874	1873-1874	X 1895(08;see text)
B1	20.	Stonewall, Cong.(1.01S:1886-1887;1.08 1887-1888;1.01N;now part of Union City)	1887	nl.	X af.1888
	21.	Woodward, Harmony Grove Cong.(f.l.Howell's Mills;at 1887 Conv.as Cong.Meth.)	1880	1889-1892, 1895-1896	X
		GILMER COUNTY (org.1832) (123)			
	1.	Cartecay, Manoah Cong.	1889	1890-1896	X
		GORDON COUNTY (org.1850) (129)			
	1.	Calhoun, Cong.(in 1886 bldg.)	1911	1911-1923	X
	2.	Plainville, Emmanuel Cong.(at 1887 Conv.as Cong.Meth.)	1887	1888-1897	X
		GRADY COUNTY (org.1905) (131)			
B1	1.	Beachton, Evergreen Cong.(f.Duncansville Ch.;f.l.Susina;f.l. Thomasville,Thomas Co.)	1903 1911(s.01)	1903-on	UCC
		GREENE COUNTY (org.1786) (133)			
	1.	Liberty, First Cong.	1904	1904-1907	X

GEORGIA - continued

GWINNETT COUNTY (org.1818) (135)

A	B	C	D	E
1.	Buford, Duncan's Creek Cong.(f.l.Teagle,f.l.Daculah;at 1887 Conv.as Cong.Meth.)	1868 1855(s.01) 1885(s.01)	1888-on	Sch.II
2.	Daculah, Cong.	1904	1904-1908	X
3.	Duluth, Duluth Mission Cong.(f.l.Atlanta,Fulton Co.;at 1887 Conv.as Cong.Meth.)	1882(01) 1893(01N)	1888-1893, 1894-1909	X X
4.	Lawrenceville, New Trinity Cong.(f.Trinity)	1903	1903-1945	X

HABERSHAM COUNTY (org.1818) (137)

A	B	C	D	E
1.	Demorest, Meth.-Cong.Fed.(f.Union Cong.;Fed.to Meth.(?) 1947-on)	1892 1902(s.04)	1892-on	UCC; NA 1992(j 1993)-on

HALL COUNTY (org.1818) (139)

A	B	C	D	E
1.	Gainesville, Cong.	1910	1910-1920	X
2.	Oakwood, Liberty Cong.(f.l.Flowery Branch,f.l.Gainesville, f.l.Strichlow;at 1887 Conv.as Cong.Meth.)	1867 1875(s.01)	1888-1914	X

HARRIS COUNTY (org.1827) (145)

A	B	C	D	E
pB Nt	Ridgeway, Cong.(l.only by 08,prob.a mission)	1899	nl.	X 1901

HENRY COUNTY (org.1821) (151)

A	B	C	D	E
1.	Hampton, County Line Cong.(f.l.Lovejoy,Clayton Co.;on Clayton Co.line & sometimes l.in that Co.;lt.NA(affl.& full)1991-on;at 1887 Conv.as Free Meth.Prot.)	1883 1882(s.01) 1884(s.04) 1888(s.01)	1888-1985	Sch.I 1961-1962;UCC 1962-1965;Sch.II 1965-1985;NA(full) 1968 or 1969-on

HOUSTON COUNTY (org.1821) (153)

A	B	C	D	E
1.	York, York Chap.Cong.(at 1887 Conv.as Cong.Meth.)	by 1887	1888-1891	X

JACKSON COUNTY (org.1796) (157)

A	B	C	D	E
1.	Brasleton, Macedonia Cong.(f.l.Chestnut Mountain,Hall Co., f.l.Cobell,f.l.Hoschton;at 1887 Conv.as Cong.Meth.;incor. l.UCC 1988-1992)	1868 1888(s.01) 1892(s.01)	1888-1992	Sch.I 1961; UCC late 1961-1992; withdrew 1988
2.	Hoschton, First Cong.(in 1889 bldg.)	1891(01N) 1892(01) 1868(s.01)	1891-1923	X

A	B	C	D	E
	GEORGIA - continued			
	JEFFERSON COUNTY (org.1796) (163)			
Bl	1. Bartow, Danforth Cong.(Danford;footnote only 1903-1904)	1898	1899-1904	X (1906:08)
Bl	2. Bartow, Green Cong.	1896 1899(s.01) 1898(08)	1896-1901	X (1905:08)
Bl	3. Bartow, Macedonia Cong.(South Burton)	1895 1896(08)	1896-1899	X (1900:08)
Bl	4. Moxley, Cong.	1898	1899-1900	X (1901:08)
Bl	5. Wadley, Brinson Hill Cong.(footnote only 1903-1904)	1896	1900-1904	X (1905:08)
Bl	6. Wadley, First Cong.(footnote only 1903-1904)	1896 1901(01S)	1896-1898, 1900-1905, 1906-1908	X
Bl	7. Wadley, Gertrude Cong.	1899	1900-1901	X
	JENKINS COUNTY (org.1905) (165)			
pB	1. Gnat, Cong.	1899	1899-1900	X
Bl	2. Herndon, Cong.	1900 1901(08,s.01)	1900-1901, 1903-1904	X (1905:08)
Bl	3. Millen, St.John Cong.(Miller)	1917	1917-1929	X (1897:08)
Bl	4. Rogers, Bethany Cong.	1895	1895-1900	X
Bl	5. Thrift, Pilgrim Cong.(Pilgrim Rest:08;Scarboro PO;lt.08; f.l.Summit,Emanuel Co.)	1895 1900(s.08)	1895-1929	X (1901:08)
	JONES COUNTY (org.1807) (169)			
	1. Pope's Ferry(Monroe Co.PO), Sardis Cong.(Pope's Station;at 1887 Conv.as Cong.Meth.)	1885	1888-1891	X
	LAMAR COUNTY (org.1920) (171)			
	1. Barnesville, Fredonia Cong.(f.l.as in Pike Co.;f.l.in Monroe Co.:37;f.Sand Hill in 1853,f.New Prospect to 1853;j Cong. Meth.1852;at 1887 Conv.as Cong.Meth.;j UCC early 1961, incor.l.as Sch.I early 1961)	1852(18,37, s.01) 1853(s.01)	1888-on	Sch.I 1961; UCC late 1961-on
	2. Goggansville, Mount Zion Cong.(f.l.as in Monroe Co.;f.Rocky Creek to 1853;j Cong.Meth.1852;at 1887 Conv.as Cong.Meth.; first Cong.Meth.Ch.org.,a division of Rehoboth Meth.Epis. South)	1852	1888-1890	X
	LANIER COUNTY (org.1919/1920,nl.1920) (173)			
	1. Stockton, Cong.	1892	1892-1898	X

A	B GEORGIA - continued LIBERTY COUNTY (org.1777)	C (179)	D	E
B1	1. Hinesville, Shiloh Cong.(f.l.Taylor's Creek;f.l.Trinity(PO); f.l.McCann)	1898 1897(s.01)	1899-1927	X
B1	2. Hinesville, Siloam Cong.(f.Cypress Slash;f.l.Trinity;f.l. McIntosh)	1879 1881(s.01)	1878-1944	X
B1	3. McIntosh, Hammond Cong.	1905(08) 1895(01)	1904-1927	X
B1	4. McIntosh, Midway Cong.(Dorchester Center;Grove Cong.;f. Goldings Grove;f.l.Thebes;division of #5G,claimed property of # 5;lt.08 1905-1918)	1874 1872(s.01) 1879(s.01,18)	1873-on	UCC
	5. Midway, Midway Cong.(Soc.settled upon Midway & Newport; Dorchester colony;majority of Dorchester,Dorchester Co., SC(q.v.)removed here;McIntosh PO;Riceboro PO;Walthourville PO;dispersed by war 1778-1782;l.with northern Pbys.(Pres. 1791-1811(l.btwn.1788 & 1793-btwn.1809 & 1813),l.Pres. 1828-1861(OS),1861-btwn.1863 & 1865(Pres.U.S);Soc.r.1887 to care for bldg.;16 says a branch at Newport built 1806, while there was pr.there 1803,a full branch is not supported in 63)	1752(63) 1753(63G) 1754(Soc.)	nl.	Ch.X 1868 (1871:63)
	5B. Dorchester, Pres.(McIntosh PO;Riceboro PO;BRANCH of # 5 by 1854;l.as a ch.:75:1870(j1871)-1969(Pres.U.S.))	1871(63)	nl.	Pres.; X 1969
	5C. Flemington, Pres.(Gravel Hill Ch.& Mtghse.Soc.to 1850; Hinesville PO;BRANCH of # 5,begun 1833(63;1815:Sampson), l.as a ch.:75:1865(j1866)-1983(Pres.U.S.),1983-on(Pres.))	1870 1866 1865(Sampson)	nl.	Pres.
	5D. Riceboro, (Jonesville;BRANCH of # 5,begun by 1850 to c.1864, never became a ch.)		nl.	X c.1864
	5E. Sunbury, Cong.Soc.(BRANCH of # 5, begun by 1763(c.1767:24); org.Soc.in preparation to become a ch.,ch.prob.not org.;X af.1792;Pres.in 24)	1790(incp.)	nl.	X af.1792
	5F. Walthourville, Pres.(Sandy Hills(at Long Co.line);Hinesville PO;BRANCH of # 5 begun by 1820,r.as a ch.1855;l.Pres.1854 (j1856)-1861(OS),1861-1983(Pres.U.S.),1983-on(Pres.))	1855	nl.	Pres.
	5G. Midway, Midway Temple Pres.(Macedonia,Calvary;Black members of # 5;in bldg.of # 5 to 1895;divided 1874(see # 4);l. Pres.1867-1869(OS),1869-1959(Pres.);merged 1959 to Day Mem.Pres.of Dorchester(f.l.Flemington),l.1909-1959(Pres.), & Grove Pres.of Riceboro,1881-1959(Pres.),& Freedman's Grove Pres.(f.Ebenezer Second Pres.,f.Williams' Chap.) of Midway(1887)l.1888-1959(Pres.) as First Pres.(f.Liberty United)of Midway(1959 merger)1.1959-on(Pres.))	1868	nl.	Pres.; merged, Pres. (see text)
B1	5H. Riceboro, Pleasant Grove Pres.(Ch.supported by #5;l.75:1843 (j1843)-1861(OS),1861-1867(Pres.U.S.))	1843 1841(bldg.)	nl.	Pres.; X 1866

A	B	C	D	E
	GEORGIA - continued			
	LOWNDES COUNTY (org.1825) (185)			
1.	Hahira, Cong.	1908	1908-1922	X
2.	Naylor, Sweet Home Cong.(f.Pleasant Home)	1896	1897-1922	X
	LUMPKIN COUNTY (org.1832) (187)			
1.	Wier, Sprigg's Chap.Cong.(s.l.as in Dawson Co.;at 1887 Conv. as Cong.Meth.)	1879	1888-1907	X
	MC INTOSH COUNTY (org.1793) (191)			
B1 1.	Darien, Maxwell Mem.Cong.	1904 / 1905(08)	1904-1905	X (1907:08)
	MADISON COUNTY (org.1811) (195)			
1.	Comer, Ebenezer Cong.(f.l.Paoli;f.l.Gholston;f.l.Bowman, Elbert Co.;at 1887 Conv.as Cong.Meth.;lt.1889-1890)	1885	1888-1898	X
2.	Danielsville, Zoar Cong.(at 1887 Conv.as Cong.Meth.)	1880 / 1877(s.01)	1888-1929	X
3.	Five Forks, Concord Cong.(f.l.Danielsville;f.l.Colbert; prob.at Five Points;at 1887 Conv.as Cong.Meth.)	1880	1888-1920	X
	MARION COUNTY (org.1827) (197)			
1.	Brantley, Bethel Cong.	1892	1892-1895	X
2.	Juniper, Thorntonville Cong.	1892	1892-1898	X
	MERIWETHER COUNTY (org.1827) (199)			
1.	Greenville, White Chap.Cong.	1901	1901-1907	X
2.	Raleigh, Mount Pleasant Cong.(f.l.Magdalena;lt.1889-1890;j Cong.Meth.1854,prob.indep.bf.that;at 1887 Conv.as Cong. Meth.;see also # 3)	1850(18) / 1860(s.01)	1888-1900	X
3.	Woodbury, Jones' Chap.Cong.(18 sees this as successor to # 2)	1894 / 1850(s.01)	1894-on	UCC
	MILLER COUNTY (org.1856) (201)			
1.	Colquitt, Union Chap.Cong.	1918	1918-1921	X
	MUSCOGEE COUNTY (org.1826) (215)			
1.	Columbus, Bibb City Cong.	1903	1903-1926	X

A	B	C	D	E
	GEORGIA - MUSCOGEE COUNTY - continued			
2.	Columbus, First Cong.	1890 1892(01N) 1880(s.01)	1892-1931	Merged to form # 3 (q.v.)
3.	Columbus, United CC (merger of # 2 & Rose Hill Chr.(1909) & North Highland Chr.(1903);later divided & North Highland broke away 1935)	1931 M	1931-on	UCC 1961-on;NA(affl.) 1966(j 1967)-1979; (dual Cong.& Chr. 1931-1934)
	NEWTON COUNTY (org.1821) (217)			
1.	Oxford, Sardis Cong.(s.f.Liberty)	1888	1888-1963	UCC 1961-1963; NA(affl.)1966(j 1967)-on
	PAULDING COUNTY (org.1832) (223)			
1.	Braswell, Ephesus Cong.(at 1887 Conv.as Free Meth.Prot.)	1885	1888-1919	X
	PEACH COUNTY (org.1924) (225)			
B1 1.	Byron, Byron Station Cong.(First Cong.;affl.TN 1872-1877)	1873	1872-1925	X
2.	Fort Valley, First Cong.(f.specifically l.in Houston Co.;at 1887 Conv.as Cong.Meth.	1884 r.1945	1888-1931, 1945-1959	X
3.	Fort Valley, Vinesville Cong.	1888	1888-1890	X
4.	Myrtle, Union Cong.(f.Martha's Chap.)	1908	1908-1922	X
5.	Powersville, Allen's Chap.Cong.(f.l.in Houston Co.;s.incor.l. in Monroe Co.;at 1887 Conv.as Cong.Meth.)	1885 1877(s.01)	1885-1923	X
	PIERCE COUNTY (org.1857) (229)			
1.	Bristol, Antioch Cong.(f.l.Ritch,Wayne Co.PO;f.l.Hunter(prob. not Screven Co.);f.l.Baxley,Appling Co.(& by 04))	1898 1899(s.01) 1889(s.04) 1897(s.01) 1900(s.01) 1989[sic](s.04)	1899-1985	Sch.II 1961-1985; NA(affl.)1966(j 1967)-on
2.	Patterson, Louisville Cong.	1892	1892-1896	X
3.	Patterson, New Bethel Cong.(f.l.Medders,Bacon Co.PO;f.l. Coffee,Bacon Co.,PO)	1892	1892-1901, 1903-1907	X
	PIKE COUNTY (org.1822) (231)			
1.	Jolly, Cong.	1896	1896-1897	X
2.	Lifsey's Store, Culpepper Chap.Cong.(at 1887 Conv.as Cong. Meth.)	1875	1888-1892	X

A	B	C	D	E
	GEORGIA - PIKE COUNTY - continued			
3.	Meansville, First CC(f.New Hope;j Cong.Meth.1852;at 1887 Conv.as Cong.Meth.)	1852(37) r.1888 1854(s.01) 1853(s.01)	1888-1985	UCC 1961-1965; Sch.II 1965-1985; X
4.	Meansville, Liberty Chap.Cong.(f.l.Lifsey's Store)	1892(01) 1894(01N)	1894-1931, 1935-1965	Sch.I 1961-1965; X
5.	Meansville, Smyrna Cong.(in 1901 bldg.)	1908	1908-1924	X
	POLK COUNTY (org.1851) (233)			
1.	Aragon, First Cong.	1903	1903-1904	X
2.	Cedartown, First Cong.	1902	1902-1932	X
3.	Rockmart, Belleville Cong.(f.l.Aragon)	1903	1903-1905	X
	RANDOLPH COUNTY (org.1828) (243)			
pB Nt	Coleman, Cong.(l.only by 08,a mission)	1896	nl.	X 1897
	RICHMOND COUNTY (org.1777) (245)			
Bl 1.	Augusta, First Cong.	1901	1901-1938	X
	ROCKDALE COUNTY (org.1870) (247)			
1.	Conyers, Liberty Chap.Cong.(in 1882 bldg.;at 1887 Conv.as Free Meth.Prot.)	1881 1888(s.01)	1888-1923	X
	SCHLEY COUNTY (org.1857) (249)			
1.	LaCrosse, Cong.	1892 1893(01N)	1893-1895	X
	SCREVEN COUNTY (org.1793) (251)			
pB Nt	Rocky Ford, Echo Cong.(l.only by 08,prob.a mission)	1900	nl.	X 1901
Bl 1.	Rocky Ford, St.John Cong.of Gay Grove(f.l.Endicott,Bulloch Co.PO;f.l.Scarboro,Jenkins Co.PO;lt.08)	1897 1912(s.08)	1900-1924	X (1914:s.08)
	SPALDING COUNTY (org.1851) (255)			
1.	Griffin, Mount Hope Cong.(j Cong.Meth.1852;at 1887 Conv.as Cong.Meth.)	1852	1888-1890	X

A	B	C	D	E
	GEORGIA - continued			
	SUMTER COUNTY (org.1831)	(261)		
1.	Americus, Davis Chap.Cong.(at 1887 Conv.as Cong.Meth.)	1884 1892(s.01)	1888-1905	X
Bl 2.	Andersonville, Colored Cong.(affl.TN 1870-1875)	1868	1867-1876	X
Bl 3.	Andersonville, First Cong.	1887 1879(30) 1878(s.01) r.1919	1886-1925, 1930-1938	X
4.	Huntington, Cong.	1888	1890-1900	X
5.	Leslie, New Providence Cong.(f.l.Americus;at 1887 Conv.as Cong.Meth.)	1890(01N,s.01) 1883 r.1900	1888-1891, 1900-1906	X
	TALBOT COUNTY (org.1827)	(263)		
1.	Junction City, Cong.	1909	1909-1915	X
	TATTNALL COUNTY (org.1801)	(267)		
pB Nt	Collins, Cong.(l.only by 08,prob.a mission)	1896	nl.	X 1898
Bl 1.	Glenville, Griffin Cong.	1902 1903(08)	1903-1904	X (1907:08)
Bl 2.	Glenville, Oak Grove Cong.(f.l.Smiley PO;f.l.Coe)	1898 1895(s.01)	1899-1944	X
pB 3.	Glenville, Plymouth Cong.	1901 1900(s.01)	1900-1902	X (1905:08)
Bl 4.	Manassas, Mount Pleasant Cong.	1895 1896(08)	1895-1901, 1910-1911	X (1903:08)
pB 5.	Tison, St.Mark Cong.	1901	1901-1902	X
	TERRELL COUNTY (org.1856)	(273)		
1.	Dawson, New Project Cong.(f.New Prospect)	1903	1903-1920	X
	THOMAS COUNTY (org.1825)	(275)		
Bl 1.	Thomasville, Bethany Cong.(f.First)	1891	1891-1901, 1903-on	UCC
	TIFT COUNTY (org.1905)	(277)		
1.	Omega, Cong.	1910	1910-1923	X
2.	Ty Ty, Damascus Cong.(Tye Tye)	1896	1898-1901, 1903-1904	X

A	B	C	D	E
		GEORGIA - continued		
		TOOMBS COUNTY (pla.1905,org.1919) (279)		
pB Nt	Ohoopee, Cong.(l.only by 08,prob.a mission)	1896	nl.	X 1898
	TROUP COUNTY (org.1826) (285)			
1.	LaGrange, First Cong.	1909	1909-1931	Merged to form # 2 (q.v.)
2.	LaGrange, United CC (merger of # 1 & First Chr.(1903))	1931 M	1931-on	UCC (dual Cong.& Chr. 1931-1934)
	TURNER COUNTY (org.1905) (287)			
1.	Dekota, Cong.(Dakota)	1890	1891-1893	X
2.	Dekota, Cong.(Dakota)	1896	1896-1897	X
3.	Sibley, Cong.	1897	1898-1906	X
4.	Sycamore, Cong.	1900	1900-1901	X
5.	Sycamore, Womble's Chap.Cong.	1902	1902-1906	X
	UNION COUNTY (org.1832) (291)			
1.	Suches, Pleasant Union Cong.(f.Union)	1890	1890-1926	X
	UPSON COUNTY (org.1824) (293)			
1.	Crest, Hebron Cong.(f.l.Hendricks,f.l.Thunder,f.l.Thomaston, f.l.Gabbitsville(04),prob.Gabbettsville,Troup Co.,prob. home of pastor)	1889	1889-1985	Sch.I 1961-1964; Sch.II 1964-1985; NA(affl.)1966 (j 1967)-on
2.	Macksville, Cong.	1890	1890-1892	X
3.	The Rock, Bethany Cong.(at 1887 Conv.as Cong.Meth.)	1886	1888-1960	X
	WALTON COUNTY (org.1818) (297)			
1.	Windsor, Antioch Cong.	1903	1903-1905	X
2.	Woodruff, Cong.	1894	1894-1895	X
	WARE COUNTY (org.1824) (299)			
? 1.	Bickley, Cong.	1900	1900-1904	X
2.	Glenmore, Glenmore Cong.(f.l.Varn PO,f.l.Sappville)	1892	1892-1894	X
3.	Millwood, Mount Green Cong.(f.l.Fairfax;f.l.Hasty)	1899	1900-1931	X
4.	Waresboro, Cong.(Wardsboro)	1893(s.01)	1893-1896	X
5.	Waycross, Pine Bloom Cong.	1892	1892-1896	X

A	B	C	D	E
	GEORGIA - WARE COUNTY - continued			
6.	Waycross, Williams' Chap.Cong.(f.Whitehall;f.Woodard Chap.; l.Way Crop:01N)	1891 1890(s.01) r.1933	1891-1985	UCC 1961-1970; sch.II 1970-1985; NA(affl.)1966(j 1967)-on
	WASHINGTON COUNTY (org.1777/1784) (303)			
Bl 1.	Davisboro, Cong.(f.l.Francis Bridge;footnote only 1903-1904)	1898	1899-1904	X (1905:08)
Bl 2.	Davisboro, Newsum Chap.Cong.	1899	1899-1901	X
Bl 3.	Harrison, Scott's Chap.Cong.(f.l.Pringle;LeMars)	1896 r.1903	1899-1902, 1903-1954	X (1914:08)
	WAYNE COUNTY (org.1803) (305)			
Bl 1.	Jessup, Philholoway Cong.(f.Phinaway)	1898	1900-1903	X
	WILCOX COUNTY (org.1857) (315)			
Bl 1.	Rochelle, Arley Chap.Cong.(f.Asbury Chap.;f.l.Kramer)	1882 1892(s.01)	1888-1909	X
	UNLOCATED CHURCHES (999)			
Bl 1.	Cross Bays, Cong.(yoked to Appling Co.# 5)	1896	1897-1900	X
Bl 2.	Dailey, Cong.(yoked to Bulloch Co.# 1 & Evans Co.# 3,4)	1895	1895-1900	X
Bl 3.	Davisville, Cong.(1.01s 1886-1887,08 1886-1887)	1886	nl.	X af.1888
pB Nt	Emanuel Conception, Pilgrim Chap.([sic],this is poss.a confused rendering of Emanuel Co.# 8(q.v.);l.by 08 1895-1898)			
pB Nt	Greenway, Cong.(Emanuel or Fulton Co.;l.only by 08,prob.a mission)	1901	nl.	X 1905
? 4.	Hoolinville, Cong.(1.by 01N)	1890	nl.	X prob.soon (1891)
pB Nt	Lonon, Cong.(1.only by 08,prob.a mission)	1896	nl.	X 1897
pB Nt	Pierson Grove, Cong.(1.only by 08,prob.a mission)	1899	nl.	X 1901
pB Nt	Puget Grove, Cong.(1.only by 08,prob.a mission)	1896	nl.	X 1897
pB Nt	Reynoldstown, Hope Cong.(1.by 01N)	1884	nl.	X prob.soon (1885)
? 5.	Rodman, Cong.(1.only by 08,prob.a mission)	1897	nl.	X 1898
pB Nt	Ryner, Cong.(1.only by 08,prob.a mission)	1901	nl.	X 1904
pB Nt	Salem, Cong.(prob.a lt.of a ch.by this name;l.only by 08, poss.a mission)	c.1908	nl.	X 1910

70 of 159 Counties have no known Congregational Churches and are listed below. Note also that Harris, Randolph, and Toombs Counties above have no full churches.

KENTUCKY (21)

A	B	C	D	E
	BOYLE COUNTY (org.1842) (021)			
1.	Marble Hill, Cong.(Parksville PO;prob.location)	1900	1900-1905	X (1907:08)
	BRACKEN COUNTY (org.1794) (023)			
1.	Germantown, Bethesda Cong.of Hillsdale (Germantown extends into Mason Co.;l.32 as nr.Maysville,Mason Co.)	1850(01) 1849(08)	1870-1880*, 1885-1886 or 1887	X (1890:08)
	CAMPBELL COUNTY (org.1794) (037)			
Gr 1.	Newport, Cong.	1869	1870-1871	X
Gr 2.	Newport, St.Johns UCC (Tr.from Evan.Prot.1924/1925;affl.EP 1924-1947,OH 1947-on)	1847 1846(s.01)	1924-on	UCC
Gr 3.	Newport, St.Johns UCC (Licking Pike,Cold Spring;f.l.Johns Hill;Tr.from Evan.Prot.1924/1925;affl.EP 1924-1947,OH 1947-1975)	1876	1924-1975	UCC 1961-1975; prob.withdrew
Gr 4.	Newport, York St.Cong.UCC (f.Cong.;affl.OH;withdrew 1975-1980)	1877 1876(99,s.01) r.1980(s.01)	1876-1975, 1980-on	UCC 1961-1975,1980-on
	FAYETTE COUNTY (org.1780) (067)			
Bl 1.	Lexington, Emmanuel UCC(f.Chandler Mem.,f.First Cong.;affl. TN(Bl)btwn.1898 & 1903-1963,IK 1963-on;j UCC 1961,Sch.I incor.,was UCC)	1891 1890(30,s.01) 1819[sic](s. 01)	1892-on	Sch.I 1961-1962; UCC 1962-on
	GALLATIN COUNTY (org.1798) (077)			
1.	Sugar Creek, Cong.	1877	1876-1877	X
	HARLAN COUNTY (org.1819) (095)			
1.	Evarts, First Cong.	1892	1892-1978	UCC; Tr.to U.Meth. (incor.X 1907:08)
	JACKSON COUNTY (org.1858) (109)			
1.	Clover Bottom, Smith Cong.	1886	1885-1891	X (also 1.08 1895- 1897)

A	B	C	D	E
	KENTUCKY - JACKSON COUNTY - continued			
2.	Clover Bottom, Walnut Chap.of Big Hill (Big Hill in Madison Co.,but ch.specifically located here;incor.l.Pine Grove by 08)	1871	1870-1880*, 1883-1886 or 1887	X (1890:08)
3.	Gray Hawk, Cong.(Gray Hawk Creek in 01N;also l.as prps.1884-1885)	1885	1885-1894	X (1897:08)
4.	McKee, Cong.	1878	1877-1879	X
5.	McKee, Cong.(also l.as prps.1884-1885)	1885	1885-1892	X (1893:08)
6.	Middlefork, Cong.(Drip Rock PO)	1893	1893-1905	X (1907:08)
	JEFFERSON COUNTY (org.1780) (111)			
Bl 1.	Louisville, Plymouth Cong.(affl.TN(Bl) 1885-1894,1895-1962, IK 1962-1986)	1877 1881(08,s.01) 1884(s.01)	1883-1986	UCC; merged to form M.(q.v.)
Bl 1M.	Louisville, Plymouth UCC (merger of # 1 & West UCC(f.E&R,f. in Evan.Synod)(1915 or 1916);affl.IK)	1986 M	1986-on	UCC
	JESSAMINE COUNTY (org.1798) (113)			
pB 1.	Camp Nelson, Union Ch.(Ariel PO;Camp Nelson extends into Garrand Co.)	1864	1868-1880*	X (1890:08)
	KENTON COUNTY (org.1840) (117)			
Gr 1.	Covington, St.Johns Cong.(f.l.West Covington to 1947;Tr.from Evan.Prot.1925;affl.EP 1925-1947,OH 1947-1962)	1892	1925-1962	Sch.II 1961-1962; prob.withdrew
2.	Ludlow, Mabel Mem.Cong.(f.l.Fairview;in 1890 bldg.;affl.OH 1906-1910)	1906	1907-1908, 1909-1923	X
	KNOTT COUNTY (org.1884) (119)			
1.	Leburn, Com.(f.Mill Creek)	1912	1912-1925, 1932-1940	X
	LAUREL COUNTY (org.1825) (125)			
Nt	Harts, Cong.(l.only in 08 1907-1910,prob.at Hart here;prob. a mission)		nl.	X
1.	Pine Grove, Evergreen Cong.	1895	1895-1909	X (1911:08)
	LEWIS COUNTY (org.1806) (135)			
1.	Cabin Creek, Cong.	1850(01) 1847(08)	1872-1880*	X (1890:08)

KENTUCKY - continued

A	B	C	D	E
	MC CREARY COUNTY (org.1912)	(147)		
1.	Pine Knott, Com.(f.Sumner Chap.)	1927	1927-1949	X
2.	Stearns, Com.	1918	1918-1971	Sch.I 1961-1962; UCC 1962-1971; X (s.1903:08)
3.	Strunk, Cong.(Strunk's Lane;lt.08,s.incor.l.in TN 1896-1897, 1899-1903)	1899	1899-1904	X
	MC LEAN COUNTY (org.1854)	(149)		
1.	Glenville, Cong.	1845	1871-1872	X
	MADISON COUNTY (org.1785)	(151)		
1.	Berea, C of C Union (in Amer.Chr.Conv.by 1885-af.1890;ch. closed 1859-through most of Civil War)	1853 1856(s.01) r.1865	1868-1880*	Tr.to Amer.Chr.Conv.; Tr.to Counc.Com.Chs. (incor.X 08:1891)
2.	Berea, Cong.(Second in 08)	1900	1900-1911	X (1912:08)
3.	Combs, Cong.(Lone Oak PO)	1904(08) 1887	1886 or 1887-1909	X (1910:08)
	MENIFEE COUNTY (org.1869)	(165)		
1.	Tar Ridge, Cong.(Mariba PO)	1901	1901-1905	X (1907:08)
	MORGAN COUNTY (org.1822)	(175)		
Nt	Maytown, Cong.(l.only by 08 1892-1894;prob.a mission)		nl.	X
	OWSLEY COUNTY (org.1845)	(189)		
1.	South Fork, Cong.(nr.Booneville)	1870	1869-1870	X
	WHITLEY COUNTY (org.1818)	(235)		
1.	Carpenter, Poplar Creek Cong.(Teague PO)	1890	1890-1902, 1906-1908	X (1909:08)
2.	Cliffs, Cong.(Youngs Creek PO)	1897	1897-1908	X (1909:08)
3.	Corbin, Pilgrim Cong.(f.First)	1886	1885-1962	UCC; X (incor.X 1912: 08)
4.	Dowlais, Cong.(Dowliss;prob.location;Jellico,Campbell Co.,TN, PO)	1885	1885-1892	X (1897:08)
5.	Gold Bug, Fairchild Cong.	1896(01) 1897(08)	1896-1908, 1909-1911	X (1914:08)

A	B	C	D	E
	KENTUCKY - WHITLEY COUNTY - continued			
6.	Marsh Creek, Cong.(Pine Knott,McCreary Co.PO)	1890	1890-1908	X
7.	Pleasant View, Emlyn Cong.	1884(01,s.08) 1885(01N) 1850(s.08)	1884-1908, 1913-1924	X (1908:08)
8.	Red Ash, Cong.	1893	1893-1900	X (1902:08)
9.	Rockhold, Cong.(lt.08,s.incor.l.in TN 1885-1904)	1885 1884(s.01) 1889(s.08)	1884-1908	X (1904 or 1907:08)
10.	Sanders Creek, Petrey Chap.Cong.(f.Calvary;Clio PO;nr. Williamsburg)	1892 1893(08)	1892-1908	X (1910:08)
Nt	Whitley Court House, Cong.(l.only by 08 1878-1884,this is prob.an lt.of # 11(q.v.))	1878	1877-1880*,	
11.	Williamsburg, First Cong.(see also Nt above)	1881(s.01, s.08)	1883-1931	X (1917:08)
Nt	Woodbine, Cong.(l.only by 08 1900-1903,prob.a mission)		nl.	X
	WOLFE COUNTY (org.1860)	(237)		
1.	Callaboose, Cong.(Spradling PO)	1896	1897-1905	X (1907:08)
Nt	Campton, Cong.(l.only in 08 1896-1908,prob.a mission)		nl.	X
2.	Glencairn, Cong.(Gosneyville PO;affl.OH 1905-1911)	1904	1904-1908, 1909-1912	X
3.	Spradling, Bethel Cong.(Gosneyville PO;affl.OH 1898-1905)	1895 1893(08)	1895-1908, 1909-1911, 1912-1924	X (1917:08)
4.	Toliver, Cong.(Tolliver;affl.OH 1898-1910)	1895	1895-1908, 1909-1911, 1912-1919	X (1917:08)
	UNLOCATED CHURCHES (999)			
Nt	Lick Creek, Cong.(l.only by 08 1891-1898,actually in TN, see Campbell Co.,TN,# 4)			

99 of 120 Counties have no known Congregational Churches and are listed below. Note also that Morgan County above has no full churches.

LOUISIANA (22)

ALLEN PARISH (org.1912/1913) (003)

A		B	C	D	E
	1.	Bel, Barnes Creek Cong.(f.l.Pearl,Calcasieu Par.;Ward 3)	1933	1933-1945	X or poss.withdrew
	2.	Bel, Olivet Cong.(Ward 3)	1922	1922-1923	X
	3.	Cole, Clear Creek Cong.(Kinder PO;prob.Ward 2)	1894	1900-1909	X
	4.	Indian Village, Phillips Bluffs Cong.(Ward 2;nr.Jefferson Davis Par.Ward 9 Par.line)	1897	1899-1915	X
	5.	Kinder, Bethany Cong.(Ward 2)	1916	1916-1977	sch.I; withdrew
	6.	Kinder, Emad Cong.(Ward 2)	1912	1912-1927	X
	7.	Kinder, First Cong.(Ward 2)	1895	1900-1977	sch.I; withdrew
	8.	Kinder, St.Lukes Cong. (Ward 2)	1914	1913-1923	X
	9.	Oberlin, Cong.(r.1893,f.Cong.Meth.;also l.as prps.1892-1893; Ward 1)	1913(s.01) 1893	1893-1897	X
	10.	Reeves, Cong.(Ward 3)	1933	1933-1945	prob.withdrew

ASSUMPTION PARISH (org.1807) (007)

A		B	C	D	E
B1	1.	Napoleonville, Mount Zion Cong.(Ward 5)	1873	1879-1888	X (1890:08)

BEAUREGARD PARISH (org.1912/1913) (011)

A		B	C	D	E
	1.	Bundicks Creek, Cong.(prob.location,nr.Dry Creek,Ward uncertain)	1899	1900-1905	X
	2.	Dry Creek, Cong.(Ward 8)	1933	1933-1945	X or poss.withdrew
	3.	Whiskey Chitto, Cong.(prob.location;nr.Cole,Allen Par.;Ward uncertain)	1894	1900-1904	X

CALCASIEU PARISH (org.1840) (019)

A		B	C	D	E
	1.	Iowa, First Cong.(Ward 8)	1889	1889-1916	X
	2.	Lake Charles, First Cong.(Ward 3)	1888(s.01) 1890	1892-1902, 1904-1911	X
B1	3.	Lake Charles, Woodbury UCC (f.Second;Ward 3)	1899 1800([sic]08)	1900-on	UCC
	4.	Manchester, First Cong.(Ward 3)	1903	1906-1913	X
	5.	Michigan Tram Camp, Cong.(Lake Charles PO;prob.Ward 3)	1898	1900-1904	X
	6.	Vinton, First Cong.(Ward 7)	1889 1890(s.01)	1892-1916	X

LOUISIANA - continued

EAST BATON ROUGE PARISH (org.1810) (033)

A	B	C	D	E
pB 1.	Baton Rouge, Cong.(Ward 1)	1869	1868-1870	X
Bl 2.	Baton Rouge, First Cong.(Ward 1)	1908	1908-1936	X

IBERIA PARISH (org.1868) (045)

A	B	C	D	E
Bl 1.	Derouen, St.Peter's Cong.(f.l.Delcambre(Iberia/Vermilion Co. line(Delcombre;Delecambre)),f.l.Rust(or Rusk),f.l.Lake Simmonst(or Lake Simmonett);f.l.Lake Peigneur(or Little Peigneur);Parcperdue PO;Grand Marais PO;New Iberia PO;lt. 1892-1893;Ward 1)	1869 1870(s.01S) 1867(s.01) 1880(s.01,s.08) 1912(s.08)	1870-1872, 1876-1927	X
Bl 2.	Fauce Point, St.John's Cong.(Fausse Point;Ward 4)	1870	1870-1872	X
Bl 3.	Islepi Piquant, St.Luke's Cong.(Isle Piquant;Ward uncertain; poss.same as # 7)	1870	1870-1872	X
Bl 4.	New Iberia, Belle UCC (f.l.Belle Place;f.l.Fausse Point; Ward 4;nl.1891-1894:01S)	1883 1882(s.01,18) 1884(s.08,s.01)	1883-on	Sch.I 1961-1962; UCC 1962-on
Bl 5.	New Iberia, St.Paul CC (Ward 5;18 says 1869 org.followed earlier local mtgs.)	1869 1868(s.08,s.01) 1866(s.01) 1871(s.01) 1870(s.01S)	1871-on	UCC
Bl 6.	New Iberia, Teche Mission Cong.(f.l.Morbihan;Ward 5)	1931	1931-on	UCC
Bl 7.	Patoutville, St.Luke's Cong.(f.l.Little Pecan to 1891;New Iberia PO;incor.St.Mary's 1893-1894;Ward 2;lt.1890-1891; poss.same as # 3)	1879 1870(s.01)	1878-1894	X
Bl 8.	Petit Anse, St.John's Cong.(Petteance;town bec.Avery Island; Ward 1)	1878	1877-1886 or 1887	X (1894:08;drop 1885:01S)

JACKSON PARISH (org.1845) (049)

A	B	C	D	E
1.	Eros, Bethlehem Cong.(Ward 2)	1909	1909-1912	X
2.	Eros, Equality Cong.(f.l.Nash;prob.Ward 2)	1907	1907-1941	Merged to Ouachita Par. # 6 to form # 6M1.(q.v.)

JEFFERSON PARISH (org.1825) (051)

A	B	C	D	E
Bl 1.	Gretna, New Hope Cong.(Ward 1;nl.btwn.1871 & 1876-1878:01S)	1869	1868-1886 or 1887	X (1887:08;drop 1885:01S)

LOUISIANA – JEFFERSON DAVIS PARISH

LOUISIANA – continued

JEFFERSON DAVIS PARISH (org.1912/1913) (053)

A		B	C	D	E
	1.	China, Cong.(Ward uncertain)	1889; 1893(s.01)	1889-1904	X
	2.	Elton, First Cong.(Ward 4)	1916	1916-1918	X
In	3.	Elton, St.Peter's Cong.(Bayou Blue;f.l.Kinder,Allen Par.; Ward 4,nr.Allen Par.Ward 2 line;prob.serving Coushatta tribe)	1901	1901-on	Sch.I
	4.	Esterly, Cong.of Esterly (Town bec.Roanoke 1895;prob.Ward 6)	1890	1890-1897	X
Bl	5.	Jennings, First Cong.(Ward 2)	1886	1889-1931	X
	6.	Jennings, Second Providence Cong.(Ward 2)	1904	1904-1907	X
	7.	Lacassine, Cong.(Welsh PO;prob.Ward 8)	1888	1892-1894	X
	8.	Welsh, First Cong.(Ward 6;affl.Bl Assn.1888-1889)	1888	1888-1913	X
	9.	Welsh, St.Paul Cong.(Ward 6)	1897	1898-1904	X

LA FOURCHE PARISH (org.1805;s.l.as LaFourche Interior bf.1853) (057)

A		B	C	D	E
Bl	1.	Grand Bayou, Little Zion Cong.(f.l.Thibodaux;LaFourche PO; Chague Bay PO;Ward 4)	1880; 1881(s.08); r.1886	1880-1889, 1891-1991	sch.I; X
Bl	2.	Harang, St.Peter's Cong.(Harangville;Grand Bayou(08);Ward uncertain)	1879	1878-1886 or 1887	X (1890:08;drop 1885:01S)
Bl	3.	LaFourche Crossing, Equal Rights Cong.(Ward 5)	1873(01); 1880(08)	1873-1881, 1892-1894	X (1899:08)
Bl	4.	Lockport, Bethlehem Cong.(Ward 4;nl.1902-1903:01S)	1869	1868-1886 or 1887, 1890-1907	X (1904:08 & 01S; drop first time 1885:01S)
Bl	5.	Thibodaux, First Cong.(Ward 2)	1891; 1895(s.01)	1891-1940	X

LINCOLN PARISH (org.1873) (061)

A		B	C	D	E
Bl	1.	Choudrant, Longstraw Cong.(f.l.Ruston;Ward 1)	1880; 1883(s.01); 1888(s.01)	1892-1904, 1911-1917	X

NATCHITOCHES PARISH (org.1805) (069)

A		B	C	D	E
Bl	1.	Bermuda, First Cong.(Ward 4)	1917	1917-1935	X
	2.	Campti, Cong.(Clare Springs PO;Ward 2)	1892	1892-1899	X
	3.	Clare Springs, Alpha Cong.(Ward 2)	1893	1893-1904	X
	4.	Conrad, Friendship Cong.(Ward 2)	1889	1890-1904	X
	5.	Grappes Bluff, Cong.(Ward 2)	1887	1892-1904	X
	6.	Grappes Bluff, Williams Chap.(Ward 2)	c.1893	1893-1894	X
	7.	Mora, Friendship Cong.(Ward 4)	1892	1892-1893	X

LOUISIANA - continued

ORLEANS PARISH (org.1805;s.l.as New Orleans bf.1820) (071)

A		B	C	D	E
Bl	1.	Algiers, Cong.(New Orleans PO;now in city of New Orleans)	1869 1870(01S,s.01)	1868-1872	X
Bl	2.	Algiers, Mount Sinai Cong.(f.Mount Zion to 1883;now in city of New Orleans)	1872	1878-1886 or 1887	X (1887:08;drop 1885:01S)
Bl	3.	Carrollton, St.Matthew's Cong.(New Orleans PO;now in city of New Orleans)	1880(08)	1873-1879	X
Bl	4.	New Orleans, Beecher Mem.(Cong.)UCC (f.London Ave.)	1904	1904-on	UCC
Bl	5.	New Orleans, Central Cong.(division of #15)	1905(08)	1871-on	UCC
Cr	6.	New Orleans, Creole Cong.	1872	1892-1893	X (1894:08)
Bl	7.	New Orleans, First C of C,Cong.(Lafayette Square;r.1823 as First Pres.(1.Pres.:75:btwn.1819 & 1824-1833);Pby.deposed pastor 1833 & division occured,Pby.recognized seceeding group,1.Pres.(75:1833-1834);it merged 1835 to Second Pres.(1832),1.Pres.(75:1833-1834),as First Pres.(1.75:Pres.(1832),1.Pres.(75:1833-1834),as First Pres.(1.75:Pres.(OS),1861-1983(Pres.U.S.),1983-on(Pres.));Other faction bec.First Unitar.(incp.as First Cong.;1.Unitar.1845-1851),now UUA)	1818(65) 1823(r.Pres., 75H) r.1833(see text)	1892 nl.	Tr.to Pres.;1833 divided to Pres.& Unitar.(see text)
Bl	8.	New Orleans, First Cong.	1866	1865-1875, 1876-1882	X
Bl	9.	New Orleans, Howard Chap.,Cong.(f.Spain St.to 1891)	1869 1871(s.08)	1868-1927	X
Bl	10.	New Orleans, Jefferson City Cong.	1869	1868-1872	X
Bl	11.	New Orleans, Morris Brown Cong.	1870(01S,s.01) 1869 1862(s.01) 1870(s.01)	1868-1907, 1927-1937	X (1909:08)
Bl	12.	New Orleans, Mount Calvary Missionary Cong.	1891 1873(s.01)	1891-1893	X (1894:08)
Bl	13.	New Orleans, Mount Horeb Cong.of Greenville	1869	1869-1879	X
pB	14.	New Orleans, St.Andrew's Cong.(nl.01S)	1874(08)	1868-1870	X
pB	15.	New Orleans, St.James Cong.(see also #5)	1869 1848(01S)	1869-1871	Tr.to a Meth.group
Bl	16.	New Orleans, St.Luke's Cong.	1922	1923-1924	X
pB	17.	New Orleans, St.Paul's Cong.(nl.01S)	1870	1870-1871	X
Bl	18.	New Orleans, University Cong.(f.Pilgrim,Straight College Ch.)	1887	1886-1932	X (nl.1910-1915:08)
Bl	19.	New Orleans, Zion Cong.	1869	1868-1872	X
pB	Nt	New Orleans (01N lists another unnamed ch.as org.1874,could be an lt.of # 8 or # 13 or some other ch.)			

LOUISIANA - continued

OUACHITA PARISH   (org.1805/1807)   (073)

A	B	C	D	E
1.	Calhoun, Bluff Springs Cong.(Ward 6)	1911	1912-1915	X
2.	Calhoun, Cartwright Cong.(Ward 6)	1930	1930-1936	X
3.	Calhoun, Mount Ariel Cong.(Ward 6)	1883	1889-1897	X
4.	Calhoun, Pleasant Valley Cong.(f.l.Monroe;prob.Ward 5)	1914	1915-1922	X
5.	West Monroe, Drew Cong.(Drue,f.l.Monroe;prob.Ward 5)	1911	1911-1938	X
6.	West Monroe, Pleasant Hill Cong.(f.l.Eros,Jackson Par.;Ward 5)	1914	1915-1941	Merged to Jackson Par.# 2 to form M1.(q.v.)
6M1.	West Monroe, Pleasant Hill Cong.(merger of # 6 & Jackson Par. # 2;Ward 5)	1941 M	1941-1946	Merged to Appendix II.# 1 to form M2.(q.v.)
6M2.	West Monroe, Pleasant Hill Cong.(Ward 5;merger of # 6M1. & Appendix II.# 1)	1946 M	1946-on	UCC

RAPIDES PARISH   (org.1805)   (079)

A	B	C	D	E
B1 1.	Bayou Beauf, Cong.(Bayou Boeuf;1.o1S 1890-1891 or 1892 & 08; prob.location,Ward uncertain)	1890(O1S) 1869(08)	nl.	X af.1892(O1S) (1898:08)
pB 2.	Hemphill, Quadrate Cong.(f.White Bay Springs Cong.;O1(1904) confuses with # 4;either Ward 5 *Hineston,or Ward 7 *Cotile)	1889 1901(08)	1892-1903	X (1906:08)
? 3.	Oak Grove, Cong.(1.in O1N specifically here)	1894	nl.	X prob.soon (1895)
? 4.	Wilda, Liberty Cong.(f.Fellowship Cong.;f.of Quadrate,f.of Hemphill;O1(1904) confuses with # 2;l.1894,nl.1903-1904: O1S;Ward uncertain)	1890	1892-1902, 1904-1908	X

RED RIVER PARISH   (org.1871)   (081)

A	B	C	D	E
1.	Coushatta, Academy Cong.(Ward 8)	1889	1890-1892	X
2.	Coushatta, Cong.(Ward 8)	1889	1889-1904	X

SABINE PARISH   (org.1843)   (085)

A	B	C	D	E
1.	Fisher, United Cong.(Ward 4)	1908	1909-1916	X

TANGIPAHOA PARISH   (org.1869)   (105)

A	B	C	D	E
1.	Hammond, Fed.(f.First Cong.;affl. Bl Assn.1888-1904;Fed.to First Pres.(1909)(1.75:1909-1983(Pres.U.S.)1983-on(Pres.)) 1923-1948;Ward 7)	1887 1888(s.01)	1888-1948	Ab.by Pres.(incor.X 1906:08)
2.	Roseland, Fed.(f.First Union Cong.;affl. Bl Assn.1889-af. 1905;Fed.unclear;Ward 3)	1889	1889-1936	X (incor.1918:08)

A	B	C	D	E
	LOUISIANA - continued			
	TERREBONNE PARISH (org.1822) (109)			
Bl 1.	Chacahoula, Zion Chap.Cong.(s.l.Little Zion;Ward 8)	1883	1883-1991	Sch.I; X
Bl 2.	Houma, Mount Horeb Cong.(Ward 3 or 4)	1918	1918-1991	Sch.I; X
Bl 3.	Houma, St.Rock Cong.(f.Bayou du Large of Terrebonne; Ward 3 or 4;lt.08)	1880	1880-1886 or 1887	X (1887 or 1888:08; drop 1885:01S)
Bl 4.	Schriever, St.Mark Cong.(f.l.Terrebonne;Ward 1)	1870 1898(s.01) 1899(s.01)	1870-1960	X (incor.1911:08)
Bl 5.	Terrebonne, Morning Star Cong.(f.l.Terrebonne Station,f.l. Schriever,f.l.Schriever Station;prob.Ward 1)	1872 1871(s.01) 1870(08) r.1892(08)	1872-1899	X (1889:08;l.to 1902:01S)
	UNION PARISH (org.1839) (111)			
1.	Downsville, Union Cong.(f.l.Walnut Lane;f.l.Calhoun, Ouachita Par.;Ward 5)	1888 1883(s.01) 1893(s.01)	1889-1904, 1907-1945	X
2.	Oakland Springs, Cong.(Ward uncertain)	1901	1901-1904	X
3.	Walnut Lane, Willhite's Chap.Cong.(Ward uncertain)	1893 1883(s.01)	1892-1899	X
	VERMILION PARISH (org.1844) (113)			
Bl 1.	Abbeville, St.Mary's Cong.(Ward 3)	1885	1884-1889, 1890-on	Sch.II 1961; UCC late 1961-on
Bl 2.	Abbeville, Union Chap.Cong.(Ward 3)	1878(01N) 1872(s.01,08) 1877(s.01)	1877-1882	X (1884:08)
Bl 3.	Erath, Beard Cong.(Ward 1)	1912 1913(08) 1909(s.01)	1912-on	sch.I 1961-1962; UCC 1962-on
Bl 4.	Gueydan, Hubbard UCC (Ward 8)	1913 1914(08) 1912(s.01)	1914-on	Sch.II 1961; UCC late 1961-on
	VERNON PARISH (org.1871) (115)			
1.	Walnut Hill, New Prospect Cong.(Ward 8)	1889	1892-1904	X

42 of 64 Parishes have no known Congregational Churches and are listed below.

MARYLAND (24)

ALLEGANY COUNTY (org. 1789)   (001)

A	B	C	D	E
We 1.	Frostburg, First Cong.(f.Shiloh Welsh;prob.Dist.26;affl. West PA Welsh 1873-1876(and dual affl.to btwn.1887 & 1892);affl.NJ 1876-1964)	1873 1872(s.01) 1869(s.04) 1882(s.01)	1873-1964	Sch.I 1961-1964; NA 1963(j 1964)-on

ANNE ARUNDEL COUNTY (org.1650;f.Providence County 1654-1676)   (003)

A	B	C	D	E
1.	Annapolis, Providence Cong.(prob.Dist.2;majority of ch. at Nansemond Co.,VA fled 1649(16)& joined here;at Greenberry's Pt.(or Greenbury))	1644(24)	nl.	X prob.af.1660(poss.af.1700);(af.1648(24))

BALTIMORE CITY (org.1851)   (007/510)

A	B	C	D	E
1.	Baltimore, Associate Cong.(merger of # 3 & Associate Ref. Pres.(1797(s.01,53),1801(75),or 1787(s.01))(incp.1802)) (affl.Associate Ref.Ch.1801-1822,Pres.1822-1825(as Fourth Pres.)(1.75:btwn.1819 & 1824-1825),Indep.Assoc.Ref.Pby. 1825-c.1851,indep.c.1851-1900);Fed.to Messiah E&R (see below)1950-1958)	1900 M 1901 M(s.01)	1900-1958	Merged to form M. (q.v.)
1M.	Baltimore, Messiah UCC (merger of # 1 & Messiah E&R (1931 merger of Christ Ref.(1889) & Bethany Ger.Ref.(f.Friedens, Peace)(1892));retained Fed.form 1958-1961;lt.1961-1963)	1958 M	1958-on	UCC (dual CC & E&R 1958-1961)
2.	Baltimore, Canton Cong.	1891(01N) 1890(s.01)	1891-1910	Merged to # 6 to form # 7 (q.v.)
3.	Baltimore, First Cong.(affl.NJ 1869)	1865	1864-1900	Merged to form # 1 (q.v.)
4.	Baltimore, Forest Park Union Cong.	1906	1906-1908	X
5.	Baltimore, Fourth Cong.	1894	1894-1939	X
6.	Baltimore, Second Cong.(Canton PO)	1888 1867(s.05) 1850(s.05) 1895(s.01)	1888-1910	Merged to # 2 to form # 7 (q.v.)
7.	Baltimore, Second Cong.(merger of # 2 & # 6)	1910 M	1910-1955	CCCC by 1958(j 1951, (or 1955(s.05)) -1982,1983-on
We 8.	Baltimore, Welsh Cong. (affl.PA Welsh,j 1863;nl.83)	by 1858	nl.	X 1868
We 9.	Baltimore, Welsh Cong.of Canton (nl.83;not affl.)	1866	1873-1874	X

A	B	C	D	E
	MARYLAND - continued			
	CAROLINE COUNTY (org.1773) (011)			
1.	Potter's Landing, Cong.(m.1867-1868 by 01,nl.;Dist.uncertain) by 1868		nl.	X 1868
	CHARLES COUNTY (org.1658) (017)			
1.	Charles County(location uncertain), English & Scottish Pres. by 1659		nl.	X af.1679
	(this was a mixed body,not in Pby.;poss.not fully org.)			
	MONTGOMERY COUNTY (org.1776) (031)			
1.	Bethesda, Westmoreland UCC (f.Mount Pleasant Cong.of	1886	1949-on	UCC
	Washington,DC(q.v.),moved here 1949,incor.l.there 1949-	1888(s.01)		
	1981;Dist.# 7)			
	PRINCE GEORGES COUNTY (org.1695) (033)			
1.	Capitol Heights, First Cong. (Dist.# 18-Seat Pleasant)	1907	1912-1968	UCC; merged to form
		1906(s.01)		M. (q.v.)
1M.	Seat Pleasant, Maryland Park Chr.(merger of # 1 & Maryland	1967 M	1968-1988	UCC (dual Disc.); X
	Park Chr.(Disc.)of Seat Pleasant(?);Dist.# 18;l.			
	Washington,DC,PO)			
2.	Hyattsville, Pres.(f.Pres.of Bladensburg to 1875;f.Pres.at	by 1659(pr.)	nl.	Tr.to Pres.1706
	Upper Marlborough;f.Patuxent River Cong.;original bldg.	1650(21)		
	taken over by Trinity Epis.;Dist.# 3-*Marlboro,then Dist.#	1668(64)		
	2-Bladensburg,then Dist.# 16-Hyattsville;j Pres.1706,Old	r.1690(24)		
	Side 1745-1758,1.75:by 1773-1866(OS),1866-1867(Indep.	1704(53,65)		
	Patapsco Pby.),1867-1869(Pres.U.S.),1869-on(OS))			
3.	Tuxedo, Cong.(Dist.# 2-*Bladensburg)	1900	1901-1913	X
		1895(s.01)		

17 of 24 County and City units have no known Congregational Churches and are listed below.

MISSISSIPPI (28)

ADAMS COUNTY (org.1799) (001)

A		B	C	D	E
	1.	Natchez, Cong.(cited in 72 as first Prot.ch.in old southwest, 1773 prob.suppressed during War)		nl.	X c.1779

FRANKLIN COUNTY (org.1809) (037)

A		B	C	D	E
?	1.	Garden City, Cong.	1891	1891-1895	X (1892:08)

HINDS COUNTY (org.1821) (049)

A		B	C	D	E
Bl	1.	Bolton, First Cong.of Orangeville (Orange River;Clinton PO)	1903	1903-1914	X
Bl	2.	Jackson, First Cong.(01 specifies 1903 r.)	1883 r.1903	1882-1899, 1903-1910	X (1898:08,bf.r.)
Bl	3.	Jackson, First Cong.	1916	1916-1930	X

LAUDERDALE COUNTY (org.1833) (075)

A		B	C	D	E
Bl	1.	Meridian, First Cong.(affl.TN 1881-1882)	1882 1872(s.01)	1881-1960	X

LOWNDES COUNTY (org.1830) (087)

A		B	C	D	E
Bl	1.	Caledonia, Pine Grove Cong.(affl.TN 1879-1882)	1880(08) 1875(01)	1879-1883, 1884-1893, 1895-1896	Merged to # 5 to form # 2(q.v.)
Bl	2.	Caledonia, Piney Grove Cong.(Salem;f.Cherokee PO;merger of # 1 & # 5)	1896 M	1896-1952	X
Bl	3.	Caledonia, Woods Chap.(First Cong.)	1904 1906(08)	1904-1914	X
Bl	4.	Columbus, Pleasant Ridge Cong.(located in Itawamba Co.by 16 but not contiguous;affl.TN 1874-1882;08 says r.as First Cong.of Pleasant Ridge (Second)1907-af.1918)	1875 1876(s.08) 1880(s.01)	1874-1903	X (1898:08)see text
Bl	5.	Columbus, Salem Cong.(continues Indep.Pres.Ch.(see Appendix VIII.# 1);affl.TN 1870-1882;66 says this ch.was predominantly white nearly until bldg.taken over by Salem Missionary Bapt.Ch.at its org.1880,which would mean this r.late 1870's,however,50 dates that Ch.1870 which would confirm 1868 date as predominantly Black r.date)	1832 r.1868	1868-1896	Merged to # 1 to form # 2(q.v.)(drop 1898: 08)
Bl	6.	Columbus, Zion Gates Cong.(f.1.Caledonia)	1918 1917(08)	1919-1943	X

A	B	C	D	E
	MISSISSIPPI - continued			
	MADISON COUNTY (org.1828) (089)			
B1 1.	Tougaloo, Union Cong.(f.First;affl.TN 1870-1871,1873-1882; village extends into Hinds Co.)	1871 1870(s.01) 1869(s.01,18)	1870-on	UCC
	MONROE COUNTY (pla.by 1820,org.1821) (095)			
B1 1.	Hamilton, New Ruhamah Cong.(f.l.Caledonia,Lowndes Co.;f.l. Columbus,Lowndes Co.;affl.TN 1874-1882;org.is claim as r. of # 2)	1870 r.1915	1874-1903, 1915-1943	X (drop first time 1898:08)
B1 2.	Hamilton, Ruhamah Cong.(r.of Indep.Pres.,see Appendix VIII. # 1;affl.TN 1870-1874;see also # 1)	1870	1869-1875	X (see also # 1)
	TISHOMINGO COUNTY (org.1836) (141)			
B1 Nt	Yellow Creek, Cong.(l.only by 08;prob.a mission)	1916	nl.	X af.1918
	WASHINGTON COUNTY (org.1827) (151)			
B1 1.	Greenville, Cong.	1885	1885-1895	X (1892:08)
	UNLOCATED CHURCHES (999)			
pB 1.	Union Grove, Cong.(l.in 01N;poss.in Monroe Co.)	1885	nl.	X prob.soon (1886)

73 of 82 Counties have no known Congregational Churches and are listed below. Note also that Tishomingo County above has no full churches.

NORTH CAROLINA (37)

ALAMANCE COUNTY (org.1849) (001)

A	B	C	D	E
B1	1. Burlington, Clinton Mem.Cong.(f.Cong.;f.l.Glen Raven;Twn.# 4-*Morton;lt.1943-1952;incor.l.Sch.I 1962-1967,was Sch.II)	1903 1902(08) 1906(s.01) r.1969	1903-on	Sch.II 1961-1962; Sch.I 1962-1967; UCC 1967-on
B1	2. Haw River, Cedar Cliff Cong.(f.l.Mebane;f.l.Nicholson;08: nl.1894-1895;Twn.# 13-Haw River or Twn.# 10-*Melville)	1885 1882(s.01N)	1884-1916, 1917-1930	X (1916:08)
B1	3. Haw River, Melville CC (f.l.Swepsonville;Twn.# 10-Melville)	1885 1882(s.01)	1884-1970	UCC; merged to form M.(q.v.)
B1	3M. Haw River, Melfield UCC (merger of # 3 & Hawfield Chap.Chr.of Mebane(1877);Twn.# 10-Melville)	1970 M	1970-on	UCC
B1	4. Haw River, St.Andrews Chap.Cong.(l.in Graham by NA;Twn.# 13-Haw River or Twn.# 6-Graham;lt.NA(Full & Affl.)1976-1984)	1913 1914(08)	1913-on	Sch.I 1961-on; NA(Affl.)1970-1976; NA(Full)1976-1988
B1	5. Mebane, Marys Grove Chap.Cong.(f.Cedar Cliff Oaks;f.First Cong.of Oaks,Orange Co.;f.l.Graham;Moore PO;Twn.# 10-*Melville or *Cheeks Twn.,Orange Co.;lt.NA(Full & Affl.) 1980-1983;lt.1916-1918:08)	1882 1883(s.01, s.04) r.1916(08)	1881-1960	NA(Affl.)1964 or 1965-1970; NA(Full)1980-on

ANSON COUNTY (org.1749/1750) (007)

A	B	C	D	E
B1	1. Ansonville, First Cong.(08 confuses this Ch.with Snow Hill Ch.,see Montgomery Co.# 8)	1906	1906-1916	X
B1	2. Lilesville, First Cong.	1901 1900(s.01) 1902(s.01)	1901-1927	X
B1	3. Wadesboro, Cong.(l.by 08;1.01S:1894-btwn.1895 & 1899)	1895(08)	nl.	X 1898(08)

BRUNSWICK COUNTY (org.1764) (019)

A	B	C	D	E
B1	1. Cape Fear, Charlestown Puritan Settlement (location uncertain;poss.not org.as a ch.;New England settlement poss.by 1657)	c.1660 1664(58)	nl.	Abandoned 1662-1664; X 1667

BUNCOMBE COUNTY (org.1791) (021)

A	B	C	D	E
	1. Asheville, First Cong.	1914 1917(s.01)	1914-on	UCC

111

NORTH CAROLINA - continued
BURKE COUNTY (org.1777) (023)

A	B	C	D	E
Bl Nt	Valdese, Cong.(l.only by 08:1893-1894,prob.a mission; *Lovelady Twn.)			X
	CABARRUS COUNTY (org.1792) (025)			
Bl	1. Concord, Cannonville Cong.(prob.Twn.# 12-Concord)	1890	1890-1894	X
	2. Concord, First Cong.UCC (Twn.# 12-Concord)	1904 1903(s.01) 1907(08) 1913(s.01)	1904-on	UCC
Bl	3. Harrisburg, Morehead Cong.(Twn.# 1-Harrisburg)	1890 1890	1890-1900	X
	4. Mount Pleasant, Cong.(f.First;Twn.# 8-Mount Pleasant;incor. 1.UCC early 1961,never voted)	1901 1900(s.01)	1901-1965	UCC 1961; Sch.I late 1961-1965; X
	CARTERET COUNTY (org.1722) (031)			
Bl	1. Beaufort, St.Stephen's Cong.(f.First)	1870 1871(30,s.08, s.01) 1895(s.01)	1869-on	Sch.I 1961; UCC late 1961-on
	CASWELL COUNTY (org.1777) (033)			
Bl	1. Milton, Mount Olive Cong.(l.only by 01S 1915-1916)	by 1916	nl.	X prob. 1917
	CHATHAM COUNTY (org.1770) (037)			
Bl	1. Goldston, St.Luke's Cong.(f.l.Gulf(Twn.))	1922	1922-on	Sch.I 1961; UCC late 1961-on
Bl	2. Moncure, Liberty Chap.Cong.(f.l.Haywood;*Haw River Twn.)	1895 1904	1895-on 1904-1927	UCC
Bl	3. Pittsboro, Evans Cong.(f.Shiloh Cong.of Evans;*Center Twn.)	1900(01S)		X
	CLEVELAND COUNTY (org.1841) (045)			
Bl	1. Toluca, McClurd's Chap.Cong.(f.l.Knob Creek(Twn.# 10))	1880 1891(08)	1890-1900, 1903-1906	X (1905:08)
	CRAVEN COUNTY (org.1705,f.Archdale to 1712) (049)			
pB	1. New Bern, Cong.(Twn.# 8)	1866	1865-1867	X

112

NORTH CAROLINA - continued

CUMBERLAND COUNTY (org.1753/1754) (051)

A		B	C	D	E
pB	Nt	Beaver Creek, Cong.(l.only by 08:1900-1903,prob.a mission)			
Bl	1.	Cedar Creek, First Cong.	1895 1896(s.01) 1885(08)	1901-1914	X X (1915:08)
Bl	2.	Fayetteville, Douglass Chap.Cong.(*Cross Creek Twn.)	1911 1912(08)	1911-1927	X
Bl	3.	Fayetteville, First Cong.(*Cross Creek Twn.)	1899 1896(s.01) 1901(s.01)	1901-1930, 1932-1938	X
Bl	4.	Fayetteville, New Bethel Cong.(*Cross Creek Twn.)	1923	1923-1949	X
Bl	5.	Fayetteville, Shiloh CC (f.l.Vander;lt.08:1914-1915 at Sander;*Cedar Creek Twn.)	1901	1901-on	UCC
Bl	6.	Goodwin, Oak Grove Cong.(*Black River Twn.)	1900(s.01) 1916	1917-1923	X
Bl	7.	Wade, Long Branch Cong.(f.First of Long Branch;*Eastover Twn.)	1906	1906-1923	X

DURHAM COUNTY (org.1881) (063)

A		B	C	D	E
Bl	1.	Durham, First Cong.	1930	1931-1937	Merged to form M. (q.v.)
Bl	1M.	Durham, First Cong.United (merger of # 1 & Second Chr.(1902))	1937 M	1937-on	UCC

FORSYTH COUNTY (org.1849) (067)

A		B	C	D	E
Bl	1.	Winston-Salem, Wentz Mem.UCC (f.First People's Cong.;*Winston Twn.)	1919 1920(s.01)	1920-on	UCC

GASTON COUNTY (org.1846) (071)

A		B	C	D	E
pB	Nt	Gastonia, Cong.(l.only by 08 1901-1905,prob.a mission)			
Bl	1.	Kings Mountain, First UCC(f.Lincoln Academy Ch.;*Crowder Mountain Twn.;All Healing Springs;Kings Mountain extends into Twn.# 4-Kings Mountain,Cleveland Co.)	1895	1895-on	X Sch.I 1961; UCC late 1961-on
Bl	2.	Lowell, First Cong.(f.Spring Grove;*South Point Twn.)	1894	1895-1927, 1928-1933	X
Bl	3.	Lowell, Island Creek Cong.(f.l.Mountain Island;*South Point Twn.)	1889 1885(08)	1890-1894	X (1898:08)
Bl	4.	South Point, Cong.	1894 1895(s.01)	1895-1897	X (1903:08)

GUILFORD COUNTY (org.1770) (081)

A		B	C	D	E
Bl	1.	Browns Summit, Union Cong.(prob.*Madison Twn.)	1895	1895-1900	X

A	B	C	D	E
	NORTH CAROLINA - GUILFORD COUNTY - continued			
	2. Greensboro, Cooper's Chap.Cong.(f.Maryanna,Mary Ann, or Mary Annie's;f.incor.l.as First;prob.*Morehead Twn.)	1911 r.1912 1914(s.01)	1911-1912, 1913-1914, 1915-1919, 1920-1923, 1924-1938	X
B1	3. Greensboro, First Cong.(prob.*Morehead Twn.)	1895 1897(s.01)	1895-1970	UCC;Merged to Appendix III. # 2 to form M.(q.v.)
B1	3M1.Greensboro, Emmanuel UCC (merger of # 3 & Appendix III. # 2; *Gilmer Twn.)	1970 M	1970-1973	UCC; merged to form M2.(q.v.)
B1	3M2.Greensboro, Emmanuel UCC (merger of # 3M1. & Bishops Temple Chr.(1895);*Gilmer Twn.)	1973 M	1973-on	UCC
B1	4. High Point, Pilgrim UCC (f.First)	1890 1895(s.01)	1890-1972	UCC;Merged to # 5 to form M.(q.v.)
B1	4M. High Point, Cong.UCC (merger of # 4 & # 5)	1972 M	1972-on	UCC
B1	5. High Point, Washington Terrace Com.Cong.	1925	1927-1972	Sch.I 1961; UCC late 1961-1972; Merged to # 4 (q.v.)
B1	6. Jamestown, Cong.	1906	1906-1910	X (1912:08)
B1	7. McLeansville, First Cong.(f.Second;*Jefferson Twn.)	1883	1882-1924, 1925-1981	UCC; X
B1	8. McLeansville, Union Grove Cong.(lt.08 as Second of Union Grove at r.;poss.*Jefferson Twn.)	1901 1900(s.01) 1895(s.04) r.1918(08)	1901-1960	NA(Affl.)1964 or 1965-on
B1	9. Sedalia, Bethany UCC (f.First Cong.;f.First Cong.of McLeansville to 1910;f.l.Allemance(poss.Alamance,Alamance Co.);*Rock Creek Twn.)	1871 1870(s.01,18)	1871-on	UCC
B1	10. Whitsett, Wa(r)dsworth Cong.(f.l.Gibsonville;Dennysville PO; *Rock Creek Twn.);l.by 1899:01S)	1870 1899(08)	1901-1960	NA(Affl.)1964 or 1965-1983,1984-on
	HALIFAX COUNTY (org.1758) (083)			
pB Nt	Enfield, Cong.Ch.at School (l.only by 08 1905-1908,prob. a mission)			X
	HARNETT COUNTY (org.1855) (085)			
B1	1. Irwin, McBride's Temple Cong.(at Erwin;f.l.Duke(Twn.))	1922	1922-1928	X
B1	2. Rock Hill, Cong.(Norval PO;f.l.Monual PO;f.l.Morval(08); Twn.uncertain;lt.08 1897-1898)	1897	1897-1904	X
B1	3. Swan Station, Bethany Cong.(now Swanns;Twn.uncertain)	1922	1922-1928	X

A	B	C	D	E
	NORTH CAROLINA - continued			
	HOKE COUNTY (org.1911) (093)			
Bl 1.	Raeford, Stewart Mission Cong.(f.l.Stewart)	1901 1900(s.08) 1905(s.08)	1901-1911	X (1912:08)
	IREDELL COUNTY (org.1788) (097)			
Bl 1.	Mooresville, First UCC (*Codell Creek Twn.;incor.Gray's Chap.in 08(see # 3);s.incor.l.Morrisville)	1900 1901(08) r.1945	1901-1940, 1945-on	Sch.I 1961-1964, UCC 1964-on
Bl 2.	Statesville, Bethel UCC (f.Second,Plymouth Chap.;poss.same as # 4)	1904 1918(08)	1917-1928, 1932-1960, 1961-on	UCC 1961-on
Bl 3.	Statesville, Gray's Chap.Cong.(f.First)	1900	1902-on	UCC
Bl 4.	Statesville, Rankinsville Cong.(poss.same as # 2)	1896(s.01) 1902(s.01) 1899(s.01)	1902-1912, 1913-1918	X
Bl 5.	Troutman, Shinnsville Chr.,Cong.(f.Mount Zion Cong.of Shinnsville;*Fallstown Twn.)	1900 1901(s.01S) 1904(s.01S) 1900	1902-on	UCC
	LEE COUNTY (org.1907/1908) (105)			
Bl 1.	Broadway, Long St.Cong.(Twn.# 3-*Cape Fear)	1895 1898(s.01) r.1940	1895-1936, 1940-1954	X
Bl 2.	Lockville, Blacknall Cong.(Twn.# 4-*Deep River)	1895	1895-1897	Merged to # 3 to form # 4(q.v.)(X 1896:08)
Bl 3.	Lockville, Douglass Cong.(Twn.# 4-*Deep River)	1895 1884(08) 1889(s.04)	1895-1897	Merged to # 2 to form # 4(q.v.)(X 1898:08)
Bl 4.	Lockville, Ward's Mem.Cong.(l.Sanford;f.Jones Chap.;f.l. Moncure,Chatham Co.;merger of # 2 & # 3;Twn.# 4-*Deep River;j UCC 1962,incor.l.UCC late 1961-1962,was Sch.I; incor.l.Sch.I 1965-1984,was Sch.II;lt.1936-1937;lt.08: 1915-1918;lt.NA(Full & Affl.)1969 or 1970-1983)	1897 M 1915(08)	1897-on	Sch.I 1961; UCC late 1961-1965;Sch.I 1965-1984;Sch.II 1984-on; NA(Affl.)1966-1969 or 1970;NA(Full)1969 or 1970-1988
Bl 5.	Sanford, Alston Chap.UCC (f.Haw Branch Cong.;f.l.Carbonton, Chatham Co.;Twn.# 7-*Pocket)	1903 1904(s.01) 1902(s.01)	1903-on	UCC
Bl 6.	Sanford, First Cong.(Twn.# 6-*West Sanford or Twn.# 5-*East Sanford)	1895	1895-1954	X

115

A	B	C	D	E
	NORTH CAROLINA - LEE COUNTY - continued			
B1 7.	Sanford, McNeal's Chap.Cong.(of McNeill's;l.in 01S 1912 or 1913-af.1917;prob.at McNeill Rd.:Twn.# 6-*West Sanford)	1912	nl.	X af.1917
B1 8.	Sanford, Tempting Cong.(f.Egypt Cong.of Tempting;Twn.# 6-*West Sanford)	1895 1948(s.04)	1895-1960	NA(Affl.)1964 or 1965-1983,1984-on
	MC DOWELL COUNTY (org.1842) (111)			
B1 1.	Cherry Springs, Cong.(l.only by 01S 1914-1915;Twn.uncertain)	by 1915	nl.	X prob.1916
	MECKLENBURG COUNTY (org.1762) (119)			
B1 1.	Charlotte, First Cong.(Twn.# 1-Charlotte)	1889 1890(01N)	1890-1896	X
B1 2.	Charlotte, New Emanuel Cong.UCC (f.Emanuel,f.First;f.Second; f.Meth.;Twn.# 1-Charlotte)	1894 1895(08) 1900(s.01) r.1932	1895-on	UCC
B1 3.	Martindale, Prims Grove Cong.(Twn.uncertain)	1890 1883(08,01S)	1890-1895	X (1897:08)
B1 4.	Paw Creek, Cong.	1895 1894(s.01)	1895-1902	X (1903:08)
	MONTGOMERY COUNTY (org.1778/1779) (123)			
B1 1.	Biscoe, Pilgrim Cong.	1912	1912-1928	X
B1 2.	Candor, Dry Creek CC(f.First of Dry Creek(08)(poss. Moore Co.;poss.*Biscoe Twn.)	1885 1881(s.01) 1870(08) 1895(s.01)	1885-on	UCC
B1 3.	Candor, First Cong.(*Biscoe Twn.)	1895 1893(08)	1895-1921	X
B1 4.	Candor, Green Lake Cong.(f.First of Pekin(q);f.l.Mount Gilead;prob.*Cheek Creek PO)	1881 1888(s.01,s. 04) r.1936	1881-1960	NA(Affl.)1964 or 1965-on
B1 5.	Exway, First Cong.(Mount Gilead PO;prob.Mount Gilead Twn.; village at Richmond Co.line)	1901 1899(s.01)	1902-1925	X (1915:08)
B1 6.	Fly, Cong.	1900 1899(08)	1900-1903	X (1904:08)
B1 7.	Mount Gilead, Oak Ridge Cong.	1901 1900(08) 1906(s.01,s. 04)	1902-1960	NA(Affl.)1964 or 1965-1983,1984-on

A	B	C	D	E
	NORTH CAROLINA - MONTGOMERY COUNTY - continued			
B1 8.	Mount Gilead, Snow Hill Cong.(f.l.Little's Mills,Richmond Co.;f.l.Mangum,Richmond Co.;08 confuses this with Anson Co.# 1)	1895 1894(s.01) 1896(s.01) r.1906	1895-1938	X (1917:08)
B1 9.	Nalls, Moroted Cong.(First Cong.;Marotock;l.Walls:01N;Twn. uncertain)	1885	1885-1908, 1914-1921	X
10.	Star, First Cong.	1910	1910-1932	X
B1 11.	Troy, First Cong.	1881 1880(s.01) 1874(s.01) 1893(08)	1881-on	UCC
12.	Troy, Zion Cong.	1911	1911-1912	X
	MOORE COUNTY (org.1784) (125)			
B1 1.	Carthage, Shiloh Cong.(Twn.# 1-Carthage)	1924	1924-1927	X
2.	Niagara, Union First Cong.(Twn.# 7-*McNeills)	1913 1903(s.01)	1914-1916, 1920-1981	UCC; X
B1 3.	Robbins, Bear Creek Cong.(f.l.Hemp;Twn.# 3-*Sheffield;lt.NA (Full & Affl.)1970-1983)	1919 1914(s.01,s.04) 1918(s.01,s.04)	1919-1960	NA(Affl.)1964 or 1965-1969 or 1970; NA(Full)1969 or 1970-on
B1 4.	Robbins, Collins Chap.Cong.(f.First Cong.of Carters Mills; f.l.Hemp;l.04 from 1987 at Stedman,Cumberland Co.(not contiguous);Twn.# 3-*Sheffield;lt.NA(Full & Affl.)1970-1983)	1893 1894(s.01) 1882(08)	1893-1960	NA(Affl.)1964 or 1965-1969 or 1970; NA(Full)1969 or 1970-1988; X
B1 5.	Robbins, Providence Chap.Cong.(f.l.Spies;prob.Twn.# 3-*Sheffield)	1908	1910-1990	sch.I; prob.withdrew
B1 6.	Southern Pines, Ch.of Wide Fellowship(f.First;Twn.# 7-McNeills;lt.1912-1914(in both Black & White Assns.1910-1914);also l.as prps.1894-1895)	1895 1900(08)	1895-1901, 1906-on	UCC (incor.X 1902: 08)
7.	Spies, Beacon Light Cong.(Twn.# 3-*Sheffield)	1912	1912-1913	X
B1 8.	Vass, Pleasant Grove Cong.(Twn.# 7-*McNeills)	1901	1901-1914	X (1911:08)
B1 9.	West End, First Cong.(Twn.# 2-*Ben Salem)	1909 1910(08) 1901(s.01)	1910-1916	X (1915:08)
	NEW HANOVER COUNTY (org.1729) (129)			
B1 1.	Wilmington, Gregory Cong.(f.Christ,f.First)	1870	1869-on	UCC

A	B	C	D	E
	NORTH CAROLINA - continued			
	ORANGE COUNTY (org.1752/1753) (135)			
B1 1.	Chapel Hill, Cong.	1885 1894(s.08) 1865(s.08)	1884-1894, 1896-1898	X (1901:08)
2.	Chapel Hill, United CC Com.(f.Chr.;Tr.from Chr.to dual align)	1910(Chr.)	1929-on	UCC (dual Chr.1929- 1934)
[	PITT COUNTY (org.1760) (147)			]
B1 1.	Bethel, St.Augustine Cong.	1898	1900-1916	X (1915:08)
	POLK COUNTY (org.1855) (149)			
1.	Columbus, Hamilton Cross Roads Cong.	1890	1892-1897	X
2.	Green River, Cong.(poss.*Greens Creek Twn.)	1892	1892-1894	X
3.	Tryon, Cong.(UCC)(f.Erskine Mem.,f.C of C,f.Christ)	1891 1889(s.01) 1905(s.01)	1892-1901, 1903-on	UCC
	RANDOLPH COUNTY (org.1779) (151)			
1.	Asheboro, Bailey's Grove Cong.(f.l.Randleman;f.l.Spies,Moore Co.;*Richland Twn.or *Grant Twn.)	1910	1910-1974	UCC; prob.X
B1 2.	Asheboro, First Cong.UCC(in 1892 bldg.)	1896	1896-on	Sch.I 1961; UCC late 1961-on
B1 3.	Asheboro, Salem Cong.(f.New Hope;f.First Cong.of Martha;f.l. Riley's Store;f.l.Martha Mills;f.l.Farmer;f.l.Streiby; lt.08;lt.1935-1938)	1885 1884(s.08)	1884-on	UCC
B1 4.	Asheboro, Strieby Cong.(f.First Cong.of Strieby;f.l. Lassiter's Mills;f.l.Farmer;f.Randolph Co.Ch.;*New Hope Twn.)	1879 1870(s.01) 1885(s.01)	1878-on	sch.I 1961-1963; UCC 1963-on
5.	Randleman, Davis Chap.Cong.	1909	1910-1916	X
6.	Sophia, Flint Hill Com.(f.l.Randleman;*Back Creek Twn.)	1927	1928-on	UCC
7.	Sophia, UCC Com.(f.Browns Chap.f.Browns Grove Chap.;*New Market Twn.)	1910 1843(s.01)	1910-on	UCC
	RICHMOND COUNTY (org.1779) (153)			
B1 1.	Ellerbe, Malee Cong.(*Mineral Springs Twn.)	1893 1886(s.01) 1895(s.01)	1893-1931	X
B1 2.	Mangum, Cong.(*Steeles Twn.)	1901	1902-1907	X (1908:08)
B1 3.	Rockingham, Blackwell Cong.(First Cong.of Philadelphia)	1906 1902(s.01)	1906-1927	X
B1 4.	Rockingham, Long Grove Cong.	1921	1921-1927	X

A	B	C	D	E
	NORTH CAROLINA - RICHMOND COUNTY - continued			
Bl 5.	Rockingham, Louisville Cong.(Lewisville;f.l.Dockery's Store to 1911)	1900 1896(s.01)	1900-1930	X
	ROBESON COUNTY (org.1786/1787) (155)			
pB Nt	Alma, Cong.(l.only by 08 1898-1903,prob.a mission)			X
Bl 1.	Parkton, McNat Cong.(McNatt's)	1901	1902-1908	X
Bl 2.	Red Springs, Cong.	1896 1900(s.01)	1896-1900, 1901-1904	X X (1905:08)
	ROWAN COUNTY (org.1753) (159)			
1.	Salisbury, United CC (f.First Cong;dual align to Chr.1930)	1915	1915-1941	X (dual Chr.1930-1934)
	RUTHERFORD COUNTY (org.1779) (161)			
1.	Ellensboro, Cong.(*Colfax Twn.;l.in Cleveland Co.in 01S)	1879	1890-1894	X
2.	Gamble's Store, Golden Valley Cong.(Golden Valley Twn.)	1879	1890-1900	X (1898:08)
3.	Henrietta, Cong.(*High Shoals Twn.)	1879	1893-1895	X (1898:08)
	STANLY COUNTY (org.1841) (167)			
1.	Albemarle, CC (f.First Cong.;f.*North Albemarle Twn.;now *Harris Twn.)	1912	1912-on	UCC
Bl 2.	Norwood, Cong.(*Center Twn.)	1902	1902-1905	X (1906:08)
	SWAIN COUNTY (org.1871) (173)			
1.	Whittier, Cong.(*Charleston Twn.;at Jackson Co.line)	1892 1893(08)	1892-1900	X (1904:08)
	TRANSYLVANIA COUNTY (org.1861) (175)			
1.	Brevard, Dunn's Creek Cong.(nl.1894-1895:08)	1891 1893(s.08) 1895(s.08)	1892-1900	X (1898:08)
	UNION COUNTY (org.1842) (179)			
Bl 1.	Indian Trail, Cong.(*Vance Twn.)	1895	1895-1902	X (1903:08)

NORTH CAROLINA - continued

WAKE COUNTY (org.1770) (183)

A	B	C	D	E
Bl 1.	Raleigh, First Cong.	1867(s.01,18) 1874(s.01,08) 1884(s.01)	1873-on	UCC
pB Nt 2.	Raleigh, Mission (Cong.::Prison,City;l.08 1874-1908) Raleigh, United CC (f.First Chr.;Tr.from Chr.to dual align; [Fed.to Friends (1926) 1928- ?)	1881(Chr.)	1927-1969	X UCC (dual Cong.& Chr. 1927-1934); Merged to form M.(q.v.)]
[2M.	Raleigh, Com.UCC (merger of # 2 & First E&R(1954))	1969 M	1969-on	UCC

WAYNE COUNTY (org.1779) (191)

A	B	C	D	E
Bl 1.	Dudley, Cong.UCC (f.First;*Broyden Twn.)	1870 1891(s.08)	1869-on	UCC

UNLOCATED CHURCHES (999)

A	B	C	D	E
pB Nt	Banton, Cong.(l.only by 08:1901-1908,prob.a mission)			
Bl 1.	Elia, Cong.(l.only by 01S:1909 or 1910-1911,poss.a lt.of some 1891 other ch.)	1891	nl.	X X af.1911
pB 2.	Johnson's, Cong.(l.only by 01N)	1885	nl.	X prob.soon (1886)
? 3.	Sand(y) Level, Cong.(l.by 01N;01 says added to list 1895 but never appeared)	1895	nl.;see text	X prob.soon (1896)
pB Nt	Summer's Grove, Cong.(l.only by 08:1900-1903,prob.a mission)			X
Bl 4.	Woodbridge, Janesville Cong.(supplied from Carteret Co.# 1, but that was a large expansive charge at the time)	1871	1870-1874	X

60 of 100 Counties have no known Congregational Churches and are listed below. Note also that Burke and Halifax Counties above have no full churches.

OKLAHOMA (40)

	A/B	C	D	E
	ALFALFA COUNTY (org.1907) (003) [Cherokee Strip IT to 1893]			
1.	Alva(Woods Co.PO), Short Springs Cong.(Ashley PO;Marion PO)	1895	1895-1902	Merged to Woods Co. # 5 to form # 3(q.v.)
2.	Alvaretta, Cong.(nr.Major Co.line)	1895	1895-1904	X
3.	Ashley, Cong.(1.Alva,Woods Co.PO;merger of # 1 & Woods Co.# 5)	1902 M	1902-1907	X
4.	Auburn, Cong.	1896	1896-1898	X
5.	Glenella(Garfield Co.PO), Springdale Cong.(Karoma PO;bec.# 6)	1894	1894-1904	X
6.	Goltry, First Cong.UCC (r.of # 5)	r.1904	1904-on	UCC
7.	Good Hope, Cong.(Augusta PO)	1895(s.01) 1895	1895-1897	X
	ATOKA COUNTY (org.1907) (005) [Choctaw IT to 1907]			
Gr 1.	Stringtown, Prairie View Cong.(in IT,affl.OK)	1903	1903-1906	X (1907:08)
	BLAINE COUNTY (org.1895) (011)			
Gr 1.	Okeene, Ger.Cong.(affl.CO 1919-1926;drop 82:1928)	1919	1919-1929	X (see text)
	BRYAN COUNTY (org.1907) (013) [Choctaw, & Chicakasaw IT to 1907]			
In 1.	Caddo, Centennial Cong. (Choctaw Nation)	1876	1876-1893	X
In 2.	Durant, Cong.(also l.as pr.pl.1879-1881; Choctaw Nation)	1883	1882-1888	X
	CADDO COUNTY (org.1901) (015)			
Bl 1.	Anadarko, First Cong.	1901	1901-1909	X
2.	Anadarko, St.Peter's Cong.(f.Colored)	1900 1901(s.01) 1903(08)	1901-1919, 1920-1951	X
3.	Apache, Cong.	1902	1902-1905	X
4.	Binger, CC UCC	1902	1902-on	UCC
5.	Bridgeport, Cong.(on Blaine Co.line)	1898(s.01) 1901	1901-1902	X
6.	Fort Cobb, Cong.	1902	1902-1905	X
7.	Hydro, Cong.(on Blaine Co.line)	1902	1902-1909	X
8.	Hydro, Hopewell Cong.	1908	1908-1909	X

OKLAHOMA - CANADIAN COUNTY

OKLAHOMA - continued
CANADIAN COUNTY (org.1890)   (017)

A	B	C	D	E
In 1.	Darlington, Plymouth Cong.(f.Indian Mission;Cheyenne & Arapahoe Indian land;serving those tribes)	1894 1892(s.01) 1895(97) c.1899(88)	1895-1906	X (1905:97;1907:08)
2.	El Reno, Cong.(also l.as prps.1889-1890)	1890	1890-1915	X
3.	Spring Creek, Cong.(Ball PO)	1894	1894-1896	X

CHOCTAW COUNTY (org.1907)   (023)   [Choctaw IT to 1907]

A	B	C	D	E
In 1.	Doaksville, Second Cong.(Box Springs PO;Choctaw Nation)	1885	1884-1902	X
In 2.	Goodland, Cedar Bluff Cong.(Choctaw Nation;Goodland is now village of Good)	1889	1889-1892	X
In 3.	Goodland, Third Cong.of Doaksville (Trinity;Goodland is now village of Good;Choctaw Nation)	1887	1886 or 1887-1893	X

COAL COUNTY (org.1907)   (029)   [Choctaw & Chicaksaw IT to 1907]

A	B	C	D	E
In 1.	Lehigh, Knox Cong.(Choctaw Nation)	1883 1881(s.01)	1882-1893	X

COMANCHE COUNTY (org.1901)   (031)

A	B	C	D	E
Gr 1.	Indiahoma, Pilgrim Cong.(f.Ger.Com.;f.l.Chattanooga;Tr.to Eng.Assn.c.1938)	1929	1929-1971	UCC 1961-1971; NA by 1961-1967; X
2.	Lawton, First Cong.(f.Wallock Mem.)	1901	1901-1968	UCC; merged to form M.(q.v.)
2M.	Lawton, Boulevard CC (merger of # 2 & Boulevard Chr.(Disc.) (?))	1968 M	1968-on	UCC (dual Disc.)

CRAIG COUNTY (org.1907)   (035)   [Cherokee IT to 1907]

A	B	C	D	E
In 1.	Vinita, Logan Cong.(Cherokee Nation)	1889	1889-1894	X
In 2.	Vinita, Union Cong.(f.First;f.Calvary Union;Cherokee Nation; affl.MO 1878-1947;bec.predominantly White)	1879	1878-1947	X
In 3.	White Oak, Cong.(Cherokee Nation)	1883	1882-1886 or 1887	X
4.	White Oak, Cong.(l.Vinita PO)	1924	1924-1927	X

CREEK COUNTY (org.1907)   (037)   [Creek IT to 1907]

A	B	C	D	E
1.	Kellyville, Cong.(affl.IT)	1903	1903-1905	X
2.	Sapulpa, Cong.(affl.IT)	1902	1902-1905	X

122

A	No.	B	C	D	E
		OKLAHOMA - continued			
		CUSTER COUNTY (org.1891) (039)			
Gr	1.	Arapahoe, Cong.	1893	1893-1896	X
	2.	Clinton, First Ger.Cong.	1927 1908(01K)	1927-1940	X
	3.	Independence, Cong.(Independence PO)	1894	1894-1909	X
	4.	Mount Pleasant, Cong.(Independence PO)	1899	1899-1901	X
	5.	Weatherford, Fed.(f.Cong.;Fed.to First Chr.(Disc.)(1898)1918-on;& Trinity Pres.(1972)1972-on(dual Pres.U.S.1980-1983); all three chs.gradually moved from Fed.to dual form: "through inconsistency in record keeping rather than any intentional plan."(97))	1899 1900(s.01)	1899-on	UCC; (Merged:dual,see text)
Gr	6.	Weatherford, Harmony Cong.	1906	1908-1912	X
	7.	Weatherford, Zion Ger.Cong.(f.First Ger.;affl.CO 1915-1926; 01K shows as alive 1906-1915;lt.01K:1916-1917;shown in an Eng.Assn.(01S)to 1916)	1903 1906(05) r.1914 1803[sic] (s.01)	1903-1906, 1915-1971	Sch.I 1961-1971; CCCC 1977-1981; withdrew
		ELLIS COUNTY (org.1907) (045) [part in Cherokee Strip IT to 1893]			
Gr	1.	Fargo, Salem Ger.Cong.(Bereinite;f.l.Tangier,Woodward Co.; 82 incor.drop 1933;prob.affl.CO 1925-1926;incor.l.as Sch.I late 1961-1971,was Sch.II)	1925	1925-1971	Sch.I 1961-1971; withdrew
	2.	Gage, First Cong.	1901 1900(s.01)	1900-1925	X
	3.	Gage, Plymouth Cong.	1902	1902-1903	X
	4.	Gage, Sunny Slope Cong.	1907	1907-1913	X
Gr	5.	Shattuck, St.Paul Ger.Cong.(incor.drop 1936:82)	1926	1926-1971	Sch.I;withdrew
		GARFIELD COUNTY (org.1895) (047) [Cherokee Strip IT to 1893]			
Gr	1.	Bison, Cong.	1901	1901-1905	X
	2.	Breckinridge, Cong.(f.l.Paradise;North Enid PO:Cropper PO)	1895	1895-1920	X
	3.	Carrier, UCC (f.First Cong.)	1894	1894-on	UCC
	4.	Coldwater, Cong.(Hillsdale PO;Pond Creek,Grant Co.PO)	1895	1895-1909	Merged to # 10 to form # 11 (q.v.)
	5.	Drummond, CC (f.Puritan CC UCC)	1903 1904(s.01)	1905-on	UCC
Gr	6.	Enid, Evan.Luth.Ger.Cong.(l.by 82 & 01K;North Enid PO; Carrier PO(s.l.Cunier);l.01K:by 1904-btwn.1907 & 1910)	1903 1904(82)	nl.	X 1905(82;see text)
	7.	Enid, First Cong.(f.Plymouth)	1893	1893-1922	X
	8.	Enid, Turkey Creek Cong.	1894	1894-1916	X
	9.	Glenella, Cong.	1894(01N) 1900(s.01)	1894-1903	X

A	B	C	D	E
	OKLAHOMA - GARFIELD COUNTY - continued			
10.	Hillsdale, Cong.(Kremlin PO)	1894	1894-1909	Merged to # 4 to form # 11 (q.v.)
11.	Hillsdale, Cong.(merger of # 4 & # 10)	1895(s.01) 1909 M	1909-1948	withdrew; join IFCA
12.	Kremlin, Cong.	1894	1894-1895	X
13.	North Enid, Cong.(f.North of Enid)	1893	1893-1908	X
14.	Vernon, Cong.(Wilcox PO;Glenella PO)	1895(s.01) 1895	1895-1898	X
15.	Waukomis, Buffalo Springs Cong.	1895	1895-1896	X
16.	Waukomis, Cong.(Waucomis)	1894	1894-1915	X
17.	Waukomis, Mount Calvary Cong.	1895(s.01) 1894	1894-1901	X
	GRADY COUNTY (org.1907) (051) [part in Chickasaw IT to 1907]			
1.	Chickasha, Cong.(in IT to 1907,affl.OK)	1903	1903-1944	X
2.	Union Center, Cong.(Chickasha PO;in IT to 1907,but affl.OK)	1903	1903-1910	X
3.	Verden, Cong.(Chickasha PO;in IT to 1907,but affl.OK;in 1895 bldg.;on Caddo Co.line)	1905	1905-1912	X
	GRANT COUNTY (org.1895) (053) [Cherokee Strip IT to 1893]			
1.	Manchester, Cong.	1899	1899-1936	X
2.	Manchester, Victor Cong.	1897(s.01) 1901	1901-1902	X
3.	Medford, First Cong.	1894	1894-on	UCC
4.	Medford, Osage Cong.	1896	1896-1897	X
5.	Medford, Pilgrim Cong.(Renfrow PO)	1898 1897(s.01)	1897-1900, 1901-1903	X
6.	Pleasant View, Cong.(f.Nashville PO(now Nash))	1902	1902-1915	X
7.	Pondcreek, Cong.Fed.(Fed.unknown)	1893	1893-1927	X
8.	Ridgway, Cong.(Florence PO;Powell Creek PO;Lena PO;Boone, Alfalfa Co.PO;Cameron,unknown Co.,KS PO)	1895	1895-1916	X
9.	Salem, Cong.(Manchester PO;Cameron,unknown Co.,KS PO)	1897	1896-1902	X
10.	Wakita, Cong.	1895(s.01) 1895	1895-1899	X
	HARPER COUNTY (org.1905/1907) (059) [Cherokee Strip IT to 1893]			
1.	Buffalo, Fort Diamond Cong.	1911	1911-1914	X
2.	Buffalo, Greenleaf Cong.	1924	1925-1932	X
3.	Buffalo, Otter Creek Cong.(Brule PO)	1902 1903(s.01)	1903-1919	X
4.	Doby Springs, First Cong.(Dobby;l.Rosston)	1907	1908-1935	X
5.	Paruna, Willow Creek Cong.(f.l.Buffalo)	1903	1903-1919	X
6.	Rosston, Cong.	1915	1915-1925	X

A	B	C	D	E
	OKLAHOMA - HARPER COUNTY - continued			
7.	Rosston, Lone Star Cong.	1925	1925-1932	X
	HUGHES COUNTY (org.1907) (063) [Creek IT to 1907]			
1.	Holdenville, Cong.(in IT to 1907,affl.OK to 1906)	1903	1903-1907	X
	JEFFERSON COUNTY (org.1907) (067) [part in Chickasaw IT to 1907]			
1.	Addington, Cong.(in IT affl.OK)	1902	1901-1902	X
2.	Hastings, Cong.(affl.OK,in OK part of Co.)	1903	1903-1908	X
3.	Ryan, Cong.(in IT,affl.OK to 1903)	1901	1901-1902	X
4.	Waurika, Cong.(Waunika;affl.OK,in OK part of Co.)	1903	1903-1904	X
	KAY COUNTY (org.1895) (071) [part in Cherokee Strip IT to 1893]			
1.	Blackwell, Cong.(Parker PO)	1894	1894-1895	X
2.	Cross, Cong.	1893	1893-1895	X
3.	Kaw Agency, Cong.(in IT at org.;l.by O1N;now Kaw City)	1889	nl.	X prob.soon (1890)
4.	Newkirk, Cong.	1893	1893-1902	X
	KINGFISHER COUNTY (org.1890/1891) (073)			
1.	Brighton, Cong.(Downs (Twn.)PO)	1895	1895-1897	X
2.	Cashion, Cong.(f.l.Downs;Cashion on Guthrie Co.line;also l.as prps.1889-1890)	1890	1890-1919	X
3.	Cashion, Mount Zion Cong.(f.l.Downs(Twn.))	1892	1892-1899	X
4.	Dover, Cong.	1891	1891-1892	X
5.	Hennessey, First Cong.(also l.as prps.1889-1890)	1890	1890-1922	X
6.	Hennessey, Hope Cong.	1889(s.01) 1890	1890-1904	X
7.	Kingfisher, Alpha Cong.	1891(s.01) 1893	1893-1925, 1930-1948	X
8.	Kingfisher, Altona UCC (f.Beulah Cong.;f.l.Omega PO;Altona Twn.)	1892(s.01) 1895	1895-on	UCC
9.	Kingfisher, Park Cong.(Hunt(s)ville PO;Park Twn.)	1893	1893-1962	UCC; X
10.	Kingfisher, Tabor Cong.(Nagle PO)	1895	1895-1907	X
11.	Kingfisher, Union Cong.Fed.(lt.1889-1890(once on prps.l.); Fed.to First Meth.Epis.(bf.1896(incp.1908))1926-1957; incor.l.1957-1959)	1889 1898(s.01)	1889-1959	X; 1957 ab.by First (United) Meth.
12.	Okarche, First Cong.(on Canadian Co.line)	1892	1892-1981	UCC; X
13.	Okarche, Mount Pisgah Cong.	1894	1894-1902	X
14.	Okarche, Pleasant Home Cong.	1907	1907-1922	X
15.	Omega, Cong.	1892	1892-1893	X
16.	Otter, Cong.	1894	1894-1903	X

OKLAHOMA COUNTY - KINGFISHER COUNTY - continued

A	B	C	D	E
B	17. Parker, Cong.(1.Kiel(now Loyal);Oneida PO;Kingfisher PO)	1894	1894-1919	X

KIOWA COUNTY (org.1901) (075)

A	B	C	D	E
	1. Hobart, Cong.	1901	1901-1905	X

LINCOLN COUNTY (org.1891) (081)

A	B	C	D	E
	1. Agra, Cong.	1903	1903-1919	X
	2. Carney, Cong.	1892	1892-1906	X
	3. Chandler, Cong.	1891	1891-1899	X
	4. Payson, Cong.(f.l.Forest;Chandler PO;f.Mills PO)	1893 / 1892(s.01)	1893-1922	X
	5. Sparks, Cong.	1903	1903-1907	X
	6. Tohee, Cong.(Springvale,Logan Co.PO)	1895	1895-1904	X
	7. Tryon, Cong.	1899 / 1896(s.01)	1899-1905	X
	8. Union, Cong.(Parnell PO;Parnell bec.Payson)	1901	1901-1904	X
	9. Wellston, Cong.	1895	1895-1915	X
	10. Wellston, Oakdale Cong.	1911	1911-1915	X

LOGAN COUNTY (sett.1889,org.1891) (083)

A	B	C	D	E
	1. Clearwater, Cong.	1891	1891-1898	X
	2. Crescent City, Cong.	1890	1890-1891	X
	3. Evansville, Cong.	1893	1893-1895	X
	4. Guthrie, Camp Russell Cong.	1897	1897-1899	X
	5. Guthrie, Harmony Cong.(Navina PO)	1892 / 1899(s.01)	1892-1925	X
	6. Guthrie, Mount Hope Cong.(f.l.Burwick)	1891	1891-1925	X
	7. Guthrie, Oak Ridge Cong.(Seward PO)	1894 / 1895(s.01)	1894-1900, 1901-1904	X
	8. Guthrie, Pleasant Valley Cong.(f.l.Evansville PO)	1891 / r.1900	1891-1902	X
	9. Guthrie, Plymouth Cong.(lt.1889-1890(once on prps.l.);lt.01N)	1889	1889-1907	X
	10. Guthrie, Warren Ave.Cong.(f.Warner Ave.,f.Warner Oak,f.Union,f.Colored)	1891 / 1892(s.01)	1891-1922	X
B1	11. Guthrie, West Guthrie Union	1890	1890-1915	X
	12. Guthrie, Vittum Mem.Cong.(f.l.Pleasant Ridge)	1891 / 1894(s.01)	1891-1906, 1907-1927	X
	13. Langston, Cimarron Cong.(Cimarron City)	1896	1896-1900	X
	14. Langston, Langston City Cong.	1893	1893-1895	X (1896:08)
	15. Lockridge, Cong.	1912	1912-1919	X
	16. Meridian, Cong.	1903	1903-1915	X

126

A	B	C	D	E
	OKLAHOMA - LOGAN COUNTY - continued			
17.	Seward, Cong.(also l.as prps.1889-1890)	1890 1894(s.01)	1890-1927	X
	MURRAY COUNTY (org.1907) (099) [Chickasaw IT to 1907]			
1.	Sulphur, Cong.(in IT,affl.OK)	1904	1904-1906	X
	MUSKOGEE COUNTY (org.1907) (101) [Creek & Cherokee IT to 1907]			
B1				
1.	Muskogee, Colored Cong.(in IT,affl.OK to 1906)	1904 1907(s.01) 1908(08)	1904-1907, 1908-1911	X (1914:08)
2.	Muskogee, First Cong.	1911	1911-1925	X
3.	Oktaha, Cong.(in IT,affl.OK to 1906)	1905	1905-1932	X
	NOBLE COUNTY (org.1897) (103) [part in Cherokee Strip IT to 1893]			
1.	Morrison, Cong.	1895	1895-1901	X
2.	Perry, Cong.	1893	1893-1898	X
3.	Perry, Cong.	1903	1903-1905	X
4.	Perry, Cong.(f.l.Lawnview;f.l.Orlando,Logan Co.PO;Antrim PO)	1895	1895-1919	X
	NOWATA COUNTY (org.1907) (105) [Cherokee IT to 1907]			
In				
1.	Nowata, Cong.(Nuwatah,Nuhatah,Nuhatah;Chetopa,Labette Co.KS PO;affl.MO 1882-1889,1890-1891;Cherokee Nation)	1883	1882-1886 or 1887	X (see text)
	OKFUSKEE COUNTY (org.1907) (107) [Creek IT to 1907]			
B1				
1.	Boley, Eureka Colored Cong.(f.l.Rusk)	1908 1912(08)	1920-1960	X
	OKLAHOMA COUNTY (sett.1889,org.1891) (109)			
1.	Arcadia, Soldier Creek Cong.	1894	1894-1902	X
2.	Choctaw City, Cong.(also l.as prps.1889-1890)	1890	1890-1900	X
3.	Deer Creek, Cong.(Edmond PO;Waterloo,Logan Co.PO;Whisler PO)	1894	1894-1911	X
4.	Edmond, Bethel Cong.	1894 1895(s.01) 1893(s.04)	1894-1925, 1936-on	UCC 1961-1967; sch.II 1967-on; NA 1967-on
5.	Edmond, Star Chap.Cong.	1897	1897-1899	X
6.	Edmond, Victory Cong.(f.l.Waterloo,Logan Co.)	1895 1896(s.01)	1895-1904, 1905-1912, 1922-1927	X
7.	Hartzell, Cong.	1895	1895-1896	X

127

A	B	C	D	E
	OKLAHOMA - OKLAHOMA COUNTY - continued			
8.	Newalla, Cong.	1904	1904-1907	X
9.	Oklahoma City, Park Cong.(f.Harrison Ave.)	1900 1902(s.01)	1900-1924	Merged to # 10 to form # 11 (q.v.)
10.	Oklahoma City, Pilgrim Cong.(f.First;lt.1889-1890(once on prps.l.))	1889 1890(01N,s.01)	1889-1924	Merged to # 9 to form # 11 (q.v.)
11.	Oklahoma City, Pilgrim Cong.(merger of # 9 & # 10)	1924 M	1924-1965	Sch.I 1961-1962;Sch.II 1962-1965;NA by 1961-1974;Merged to Appendix IV.# 1 to form M1.(q.v.)
11M1.	Oklahoma City, Plymouth Cong.(merger of # 11 & Appendix IV.# 1;in NA to merger)	1974 M	nl.	NA 1974-1978;1979 merged to Appendix IV.# 2 to form M2.(q.v.)
11M2.	Oklahoma City, Mayflower Cong.(merger of # 11M1. & Appendix IV.# 2)	1979 M	1990-on	NA 1978-on;UCC 1990-on
12.	Oklahoma City, Plymouth Cong.	1906	1906-1912	X
B1 13.	Oklahoma City, Second Cong.(f.Colored)	1899	1899-1960	X (incor.1906:08)
	OKMULGEE COUNTY (org.1907) (111) [Creek IT to 1907]			
B1 1.	Okmulgee, Pilgrim Cong.(f.Plymouth)	1923 1928(s.01) 1921(s.01)	1926-1960, 1964-1977	UCC 1964-1977; X
	PAWNEE COUNTY (org.1897) (117) [part in Cherokee Strip IT to 1893]			
1.	Bryan, Cong.	1896	1896-1900	X
2.	Jennings, Cong.	1893	1893-1931	X
3.	Jennings, Oakwood Cong.	1911	1911-1913	X
4.	Pawnee, Cong.	1895	1895-1902	X
5.	Pawnee, Mound Center Cong.	1900	1900-1902	X
6.	Pawnee, Mount Carmel Cong.	1900	1900-1902	X
	PAYNE COUNTY (org.1890/1891) (119)			
1.	Oak Grove, Cong.(f.l.Lincoln;Chandler,Lincoln Co.PO;f.Ida PO; 1894 lt.01N)	1894	1894-1898	X
2.	Payne Center, Cong.(also l.as prps.1889-1890)	1890	1890-1891	X
3.	Perkins, Cong.	1891	1891-1942	X
4.	Perkins, Olivet Cong.	1894	1894-1910	X
5.	Stillwater, First Cong.(also l.as prps.1889-1890)	1895(s.01) 1890	1890-1902	X
6.	Stillwater, Pleasant Hill Cong.	1896	1896-1899	X
7.	Stillwater, Union Cong.	1895	1895-1900	X

128

A	B	C	D	E
	OKLAHOMA - PAYNE COUNTY - continued			
8.	Windom, Cong.	1890	1890-1892	X
	PITTSBURG COUNTY (org.1907) (121) [Choctaw IT to 1907]			
In 1.	McAlester, First Cong.(f.l.McAllister;Choctaw Nation)	1878 1880(s.01)	1879-1902	X
In 2.	McAlester, Trinity Cong.(f.l.McAllister;Choctaw Nation)	1884	1885-1902	X
In 3.	Savanna, Cong.(Choctaw Nation)	1879	1879-1888	X
	POTTAWATOMIE COUNTY (org.1893/1896) (125)			
1.	Centerview, Cong.(Brown PO)	1896	1896-1903	X
2.	Dale, Minneha(ha) Cong.(McLoud PO)	1894	1894-1911	X
Bl Nt	Keokuk Falls, Mission Cong.(1.01S:1909-1918 or later,a mission)			X
3.	McLoud, Cong.	1895	1895-1896	X
4.	Shawnee, Chap.Hill Cong.	1896	1896-1899	X
5.	Tecumseh, Cong.	1891	1891-1902	X
6.	Tecumseh, Orange Cong.	1896	1896-1898	X
7.	Tecumseh, Parker Cong.	1894	1894-1896	X
	TILLMAN COUNTY (org.1907) (141)			
Gr 1.	Manitou, Peace Ger.Cong.(Friedens,Peaceful;affl.CO 1917-1926)	1914 r.1925	1915-1971	Sch.I 1961-1963;Sch.II 1963-1971;withdrew
	TULSA COUNTY (org.1907) (143) [Cherokee & Creek IT to 1907]			
1.	Tulsa, Cong.	1924	1924-1938	X
	WASHITA COUNTY (org.1897/1899) (149)			
1.	Dill City, Cong.	1902	1902-1904	X
	WOODS COUNTY (org.1893/1895) (151) [Cherokee Strip IT to 1893]			
1.	Alva, Bethel Cong.	1896	1896-1898	X
2.	Alva, First Cong.	1893	1893-1911	X
3.	Alva, Middletown Cong.	r.1894(s.01)	1896-1898	X
4.	Capron, Cong.(f.l.Belleview(prob.in f.Belle Twn.);Alva PO)	1894	1894-1910	X
5.	Elmdale, Cong.(Alva PO)	1896	1896-1902	Merged to Alfalfa Co. # 1 to form Alfalfa Co.# 3 (q.v.)

A	B	C	D	E
	OKLAHOMA - WOODS COUNTY - continued			
6.	Waynoka, First Cong.	1893 1894(s.01)	1893-1989	UCC; X
7.	White Horse, Cong.	1896	1896-1898	X
		[Cherokee Strip IT to 1893]		
	WOODWARD COUNTY (sett.1893,org.1907) (153)			
1.	Curtis, Cong.	1901	1901-1902	X
2.	Woodward, Cong.	1893	1893-1895	X
	UNLOCATED CHURCHES (999)			
In 1.	Axtell, Cong.(Choctaw Nation IT,yoked to Bryan Co.# 1,2 & Coal Co.# 1)	1883	1882-1886 or 1887	X
In Nt	Chapel Hill, Cong.(Choctaw Nation,IT;pr.pt.only 1.1879-1881)			X
2.	Crystal, Cong.(affl.OK;prob.not in Atoka Co.,IT)	1896	1896-1897	X
3.	Fair Plains, Cong.(yoked to Harper Co.# 3)	1911	1911-1914	X
4.	Red Oak, Cong.(Sweeny PO;affl.OK;pastor s.lived in Arcadia, Oklahoma Co.;poss.Red Oak Ch.in Pontotoc Co.,then in IT nr.OK border;prob.not Red Oak of Latimer Co.,IT)	1897	1897-1900	X
In 5.	Wacoolee, Cong.(Cherokee Nation IT;Chetopa,Labette Co.,KS PO; yoked to Craig Co.# 2 & Nowata Co.# 1;affl.MO 1882-1889, 1890-1891)	1882	1882-1886 or 1887	X (see text)

37 of 77 Counties have no known Congregational Churches and are listed below.

SOUTH CAROLINA (45)

AIKEN COUNTY (org.1871) (003)

A	B	C	D	E
1.	Beech Island, Cong.(f.l.Buck Island;f.in Edgefield Dist.;f.l. Augusta,Richmond Co.,GA PO;org.as Cong.,r.Pres.;l.75:1828 (j1829)-1839(NS);report for 1837-1838 implies may be Cong.;[split 1838,OS,1.75:1838-1861(OS),1861-1953(Pres. U.S.),X;62 says OS was main ch.,& implies CUP Ch.was a Cong.split from 1838;58 & 61 imply OS was only ch.])	by 1820(Cong.) r.1828(Pres.) poss.r.c.1838 (Cong.)	CGA(supply) 1820-1822, CUPCg:1838- af.1850	X af.1850

ANDERSON COUNTY (org.1826) (007)

A	B	C	D	E
1.	Anderson, Pilgrim Cong.(affl.SC 1917-1918,NC 1918-1925)	1917	1917-1925	X

BEAUFORT COUNTY (org.Gen.Dist.1769,Dist.1799) (013)

A	B	C	D	E
1.	Beaufort, Indep.Ch.of Beaufort(at Port Royal Island,Cong.; called Pres.Ch.from 1804,although Cong.form;Pby.of SC: 1756-1772;61 says in CP approximately 1790-c.1800(1803: 75H);indep.1822-af.1831;75H continues this ch.showing in CUP 1839-1852,& connected to the 1883-1908,& 1912-on modern chs.)	btwn.1717 & 1744(55) c.1756(24,61) r.1803(61) 1804(incp.)	CGA:1803- 1821 (to 1839 [sic]61) (see text)	X af.1831 (to c.1850: 61)
2.	Stoney Creek, Indep.Pres.Ch.of Stoney Creek in Prince William Par.(Indep.Ch.of Indianland(in 1785);Cong.Ch.;Pocotaligo; Beaufort PO;Coosawhatchie,Jasper Co.PO;Pby.of SC 1756(1743 (61))-1772(c.1780:61);(Pastor in CP 1790-1803(poss.1808 (c.1819:61)),but ch.objected to Pres.powers);Pres.75:1. btwn.1819 & 1824(1822)-1826 or 1827,1831-1839(NS,Cong. forms)1846-1861(OS,Cong.forms to 1855),1861-1865(Pres. U.S.),this branch X 1865;see # 2B)	1743 1785(incp.) 1816(r.incp.) r.1855(Pres.)	CGA:1817- 1821(1801- 1822:61) CUPCg.: 1838-1846	Tr.to Pres.;this branch X 1865
2B.	McPhersonville(Hampton Co.), Stoney Creek Pres.(Yemassee, Hampton Co.,PO;this Hampton Co. BRANCH begun 1833, became main ch.1865;l.Pres.U.S.:75:1865-1967;X)	1865	nl.	Pres.; X 1967
B1 2C.	Sheldon, Beaufort Salem Pres.(f.l.Beaufort,f.l.Stoney Creek, f.l.Yemassee,Hampton Co.;f.Zion to 1870;Black members of # 2 & # 2B;l.1869-1878(Pres.U.S.),1878-on(Pres.);61 recognizes only 1878-on period)	1869	nl.	Pres.

BERKELEY COUNTY (org.1882) (015)

A	B	C	D	E
1.	Cainhoy, Pres.Ch.of Cainhoy,St.Thomas Par.(on Wando River; Indep.or Cong.in form;Pby.of SC 1720's(c.1728:61)-1740's (c.1780:61);indep.to af.1800)	c.1710(24) by 1728(58,61) 1778(incp.)	nl. (poss.:CGA: bf.1808:61)	X af.1800 (1808:61)

A	B	C	D	E
	SOUTH CAROLINA - BERKELEY COUNTY - continued			
2.	Wappetaw, Indep.Ch.in Christ Ch.Par.(Cong.;Indep.Cong.;Wando Neck;Haddrell's PO;Pby.of SC:1730's & 1760's-1772(1722-1780:75H);l.Pres.:75:btwn.1814 & 1818-btwn.1819 & 1824, 1828-1836,1849-1850,1853-1859(OS,prob.with Cong.forms); this branch X af.1877;61 designates 1696 as settlement date,& org.s.c.1700,s.1697;incp.1786,r.incp.1822;75H incor.(see text) l.in CP:1790-1801)	1696 1695(s.55) 1697(s.60) 1699(24) c.1700(75H) (see text)	CUPCg.: 1838-1849 (1852:75H) (also CGA: 1801-1822: 61)	This branch X af.1877 (c.1865:61;bldg. crumbled 1897)
2B.	Mount Pleasnt(Charleston Co.), Mount Pleasant Pres.(This Charleston Co. BRANCH begun 1827,was funded by the old Soc.as a Ch.(1867(75Y,58),or 1868(55,60));l.75:1870-1983 (Pres.U.S.),1983-on(Pres.))	1867(58,75Y) 1868(55,60)	nl.	Pres.
2C.	McClellanville(Charleston Co.), New Wappetaw Pres.(This Charleston Co.BRANCH begun 1869,r.as a Ch.1870(75Y,58,60, 61)(or 1869(55));l.1870:61;and received funds of old Soc. af.1877,l.75:1870-1983(Pres.U.S.),1983-on(Pres.))	1870 1869(55)	nl.	Pres.
	CHARLESTON COUNTY (org.Gen.Dist.1769,Dist.1798)	(019)		
B1 1.	Charleston, Battery Cong.(f.Tradd St.)	1898	1898-1909	X
2.	Charleston, Circular Ch.(f.Indep.Cong.;Brick Pres.;White Mtg.;Indep.Ch.on Meeting St.;Indep.Pres.;f.of Charles Towne to 1783;Pby.of SC:1720's-1738;Pres.:l.75:btwn.1819 & 1824(1822)-1826 or 1827,1828-1834 or 1835,1836-1839(NS, Cong.forms),1852-1858(OS,Cong.forms),1866-1877(Pres.U.S., Cong.forms),1971-on(Pres.dual(1968:18));affl.FL 1891-1917, SC 1917-1918,NC 1918-1939,GA 1939-on;lt.1912-1913:01S;see also # 3)	1897(08) 1681(01,18,65) 1684(pr.:24) bf.1690(58) & 1690(08,s.01 20) 1680(s.01) btwn.1681 & 1685(60) r.1691(01,32) 1698 or 1699 (24,27) 1784(incp.) r.1817(60)	CGA:1801-1822 CUPCg:1838-1852; 1858-1859, 1881-on	UCC (dual Pres.)
2B.	Charleston, Second Indep.Ch.(Archdale St.Ch.;this BRANCH begun 1772(02,58,60,95)(or 1773(61)),local Soc.got control of property 1815,in Pres.(nl.:75)1815-1817;Ch.org. 1817;Soc.claims 1684 as successor to # 2;bec.Unitar.by 1820;l.Unitar.1845-1851)	1772(02,58,60,95)(or 1773(61)) 1684	nl.	Pres.; Tr.to Unitar.; now UUA
2C.	Charleston, Laurel St.City Mission (This BRANCH began c.1852, X 1861;never org.as a ch.)		nl.	This branch X 1861
B1 3.	Charleston, Plymouth Cong.(First Cong.;affl.GA(Bl)1878-c.1899;Black members of # 2)	1867	1866-on	UCC

A	B	C	D	E
	SOUTH CAROLINA - CHARLESTON COUNTY - continued			
4.	Edisto(e), Pres.Ch.on Edisto Island (Indep.;f.South Edistoe River Cong.(24);lt.24(Cong.& Pres.);Pby.of SC 1730's (1722(60),c.1728(61))-1770's(1780:61);(1790 pastor in CP but ch.objected & dismissed him(incor.l.there 1790-1819: 61));l.Pres.:75:1831-1839(NS,Cong.forms),1852-1861(OS, Cong.forms),1861-1863,1864 or 1865-1983(Pres.U.S.,Cong. forms to 1870),1983-on(Pres.);see # 4B;union bldg.with Bapt.to 1722)	by 1703(24) 1710(several) 1717(s.55) c.1685(s.55) c.1690(61) 1784(incp.) r.1870(Pres.)	CUPCg.: 1838-1852	Tr.to Pres.
B1 4B.	Edisto Island, Edisto Island Pres.(f.Edisto Union Ch.;Black members of # 4;1.1866(1868:61)-1870(OS),1870-on(Pres.); nl.60)	1865	nl.	Pres.
Nt	Edistoe Island, Second Indep.Pres.(Charleston Pby.minutes imply a second ch.here in 1854,not otherwise known)	m.1854	nl.	if existed: X
5.	James Island, Indep.Pres.(Charleston PO;Pby.of SC:1720's- 1775(1722-1780:75H;CP(supply):1793(1790:60)-1796(1799:60; 1801:75H);l.Pres.btwn.1794 & 1797(prob.1796)-btwn.1798 & 1802(prob.1801),btwn.1814 & 1818-1826 or 1827,1828-1831, 1832-1836(Cong.forms),1846(1852:75H)-1861(OS,Cong.forms to 1853);1861-1983(Pres.U.S.),1983-on(Pres.))	1706(55,75Y, 61) c.1710(24,60) 1720's(58) 1734 or 1735 (Gillett) 1785(incp.) r.1853(Pres.)	CGA(supply) 1801-1816 (to 1822:61) CUPCg.: 1838-1846 (1852:75H)	Tr.to Pres.
B1 5B.	James Island, St.James Pres.(Charleston PO;Black members of # 5;1.1866-1870(OS),1870-on(Pres.);61 l.only from 1870)	1867	nl.	Pres.
	CHESTER COUNTY (org.Sub.Co.1785,Dist.1799/1800)		(023)	
B1 1.	Adamsville, Adamsville Cong.of Chester Co.	1909	1909-1917	X
B1 2.	Chester, Ebenezer Cong.	1902 1910(08)	1902-1917	X (1911:08)
	COLLETON COUNTY (org.Sub.Co.1785,Dist.1799/1800)		(029)	
1.	Jacksonboro, Bethel Pres.Ch.& Cgn.of Pon Pon,St.Bartholomew's Par.(Indep.Cong.;Bethel;First of Walterboro(from c.1835); org.at Pon Pon,moved nr.Jacksonburg(Jacksonboro) 1746; 75H says in Edinburgh Pby.,Ch.of Scotland 1728-1750;Pby.of SC:1728-1739,1740's(1750:75H)-1766;(CP:1790 pastor,but not ch.;but l.there 1790-1819:75H);l.Pres.:75:1828(1819:75H)- 1848,1849-1861(OS,Cong.forms to c.1838),1861-c.1885(Pres. U.S.);this branch X c.1885)	1728 1778(incp.) r.c.1838 (Pres.)	CGA: 1802-1822	Tr.to Pres.;This branch X c.1885
B1 1B.	Walterboro, Bethel Pres.(f.First Pres.;this BRANCH begun 1821,became dominant branch c.1835 & bec.Ch.c.1885;l. Pres.:75:c.1885-1983(Pres.U.S.),1983-on(Pres.))	c.1885	nl.	Pres.

A	B	C	D	E
	SOUTH CAROLINA - COLLETON COUNTY - continued			
B1	1C. Walterboro, Aimwell Pres.(some of Black members of #1 & #1B;1.1872(1870:75H)-1878(Pres.U.S.),1878-on(Pres.),Tr.1879:61)	c.1870	nl.	Pres.
B1	1D. Walterboro, Hopewell Pres.(some of Black members of #1 & #1B;1.1872-1878(Pres.U.S.),1878-on(Pres.),Tr.1879:61)	c.1870	nl.	Pres.
	2. Wilton, Pres.Ch.of Wilton,St.Paul's Par.(Indep.Cong.;Second Ch.of Walterboro;Adams Run PO;moved 1767;Pby.of SC 1730's (1727:61)-1771(c.1780:61);(CP Pastor 1790,but not ch.); l.Pres.1828(1823:75H)-1839(NS,Cong.forms),1850-1853,1854- 1861(OS,r.Pres.1850),1861-1928(Pres.U.S.))	1704(Pres.) 1727(61) r.early(Cong.) 1784(incp.) r.1850(Pres.)	CGA(supply) 1819-1822 (from c.1815:61) CUPCg.: 1838-1850	Tr.to Pres.; X 1928
	DORCHESTER COUNTY (org.1897) (035)			
	1. Dorchester, United Indep.Cong.of Dorchester & Beech Hill(in St.George's Par.;White Mtghse.;org.from Dorchester(at Charlestown),Suffolk Co.,MA 1695 & moved here 1696;divided 1752 & majority removed to Midway(Dorchester),Liberty Co., GA(q.v.);Pby.of SC 1720's-1734;(CP:Pastor 1793-1794,& 1798 (prob.not ch.));l.Pres.:75:btwn.1794 & 1797(j1794)-btwn. 1798 & 1802,1.btwn.1819 & 1824(1822)-1826 or 1827(1839: 75H;Cong.forms),1854(1852:75H)-1856,1858-1859(OS,Cong. forms);Ch.still alive as a Cong.Ch.1860(Edwards);Ch. inactive c.1760-1793(61),or poss.a shorter period)	1695(MA) 1696(here) 1793(incp.)	CGA(supply) 1801-1822, CUPCg.: 1838-1852	Tr.to Pres.;This branch X (no services af.1866,bldg.crumbled 1886)
	1B. Pleasant Grove(Colleton Co.), Beech Hill(St.Paul's Par., Colleton Co.)(this Colleton Co.BRANCH begun 1737,most removed to GA, c.1752, X by 1800)		nl.	This branch X by 1800
	1C. Summerville, Pres.(this BRANCH begun 1831,bec.a ch.1859;l. Pres.1859-1861(OS),1861-1983(Pres.U.S.),1983-on(Pres.);see also #1D)	1859 c.1855(61) 1882(incp.)	nl.	Pres.
B1	1D. Summerville, Pres.(Black members of #1 & #1C;l.1870-1950 (Pres.);nl.60)	c.1870	nl.	Pres.; X 1950
	FAIRFIELD COUNTY (org.Sub.Co.1785,Dist.1799/1800) (039)			
B1	1. Winnsboro, First Cong.(Plymouth)	1896	1898-1926	X
B1	2. Winnsboro, Wateree Cong.	1901 1908(08)	1901-1926	X (1914:08)
	GREENVILLE COUNTY (org.Sub.Co.1786,Dist.1799/1800) (045)			
B1	1. Greenville, Grace Cong.	1902 1903(08)	1902-1926	X
B1	2. Greenville, Mountain View Cong.	1909 1911(08)	1909-1926	X

134

SOUTH CAROLINA - continued

GREENWOOD COUNTY (org.1897) (047)

A	B	C	D	E
Bl				
1.	Greenwood, Bethany Cong.(affl.GA(Bl)1890-c.1899)	1891	1891-1898	X (1897:08)
2.	Greenwood, Rock Pres.(f.Rock Creek Pres.,f.Rock Cong.of Abbeville Dist.;s.Carmel on Rocky Creek(1809);org.as Pres.,r.Cong.,r.Pres.;l.75:btwn.1774 & 1787-btwn.1788 & 1793,btwn.1798 & 1802-1861(OS;Cong.forms 1819-1823(poss. nl.)),1861-1932(75H,minutes(1892:61)),1956-1975(Pres.U.S.) 1974-on(PCA))	1770(55,61) by 1770(58) 1772(24) r.by 1819(CG) r.1823(Pres.) r.1956	CGA(supply) 1819-1823	Tr.to Pres.(see text); PCA
3.	Ninety Six, Old Cambridge Cong.(f.in Abbeville Dist;6 miles South of Saluda River;l.Pres.75:by 1773-btwn.1788 & 1793, btwn.1819 & 1824-1828;Pres.,r.Cong.,r.Pres.)	1775(24) by 1775(58) c.1774(61) r.1819(Cong.) r.1823(Pres.) 1821(61)	CGA(supply) 1819-1823	prob. X 1794; Tr.to Pres.; X 1828 (c.1830:61;by 1833: 58)

LEXINGTON COUNTY (org.Sub.Co.1785,X:1799/1800;r.Dist.1804) (063)

A	B	C	D	E
pB				
1.	Arthur(s), Cong.	1895	1898-1899	X (1901:08)

NEWBERRY COUNTY (org.Sub.Co.1785,Dist.1799/1800) (071)

A	B	C	D	E
pB				
1.	Newberry, Plymouth Cong.	1895	1895-1902	X (1903:08)
Nt	Newberry, St.Luke's Cong.(l.17:1832-1857, not otherwise known;prob.incor.identified)	1894(08)	nl.	
pB				
2.	Pomaria, St.James Mission Cong.(l.Newberry)	1896	1897-1902	X (1903:08)

ORANGEBURG COUNTY (org.Gen.Dist.1769,Dist.1798) (075)

A	B	C	D	E
Bl				
1.	Orangeburg, Cong.(affl.GA(Bl)1877-1887,1888 or 1889-prob. 1894)	1875	1874-1894	X
2.	Orangeburg, Elliot St.Cong.(in 1910 bldg.;affl.SC 1917-1918, NC 1918-1927)	1916	1916-1927	X

RICHLAND COUNTY (org.Sub.Co.1785,Dist.1799/1800) (079)

A	B	C	D	E
Bl				
1.	Columbia, First Cong.(f.Union Com.;also l.as prps.1922-1924)	1921	1924-1935	X
2.	Columbia, People's Cong.(Blanding St.;incor.l.as Veighl Chap. (# 6)by 01N)	1895 1894(08)	1895-1898	X
Bl 3.	Columbia, Pilgrim Cong.	1894	1894-1926	X
Bl 4.	Eastover, Macedonia Cong.	1897 1898(08)	1898-1917	X (1904:08)
Bl 5.	Horrell, Cedar Creek Cong.(f.l.Columbia)	1894 1898(08)	1897-1917	X (1905:08)

A	B	C	D	E
	SOUTH CAROLINA - RICHLAND COUNTY - continued			
B1	6. Lykesland, Veighl Chap.(f.l.Columbia;l.as Sykesland by 08)	1894 1908(08)	1895-1936, 1940-1943	X (incor.:1914:08)
B1	7. Shandon, Cong.(nr.Columbia)	1894	1894-1895	X (1898:08)
	UNLOCATED CHURCHES (999)			
B1	1. Howell, Cong.(yoked to Richland Co.# 5,town is same name as Pastor)	1898	1898-1899	X

31 of 46 Counties have no known Congregational Churches and are listed below.

TENNESSEE (47)

A	B	C	D	E
	ANDERSON COUNTY (org.1801) (001)			
	1. Coal Creek, Heatherly Chap.(f.l.Willison's Grove)	1895	1895-1912	X (1909:08)
We	2. Coal Creek, Welsh Cong.(also l.as prps.1883-1884)	1870	1871-1875, 1884-1886 or 1887	X
	CAMPBELL COUNTY (org.1806) (013)			
	1. Jellico, First Cong.(f.Indep.Cong.;Jellicho)	1885	1884-1909	X (1907:08)
	2. Lafollette, Big Creek Gap Cong.(f.Rutherford Chap.of Big Creek Gap;f.Pilgrim;f.of College Hill(s.Cottage Hill))	1888 / 1886(08) / 1890(s.01)	1890-1913	X (1917:08)
	3. Lafollette, College Hill Cong.(f.First)	1900 / 1901(08) / 1892(s.01)	1900-1912, 1913-1925	X (1917:08)
	4. Lick Creek, Cong.(Pine Mountain PO;incor.in KY in 08)	1891	1891-1892, 1893-1907	X
	5. Pine Mountain, Calvary Cong.	1887 / 1888(s.08)	1886 or 1887-1909	X (1908:08)
	6. Pioneer, Cong.	1892 / 1890(s.01) / 1882(08)	1892-1893, 1895-1901	X (1897:08)
	CLAIBORNE COUNTY (org.1801) (025)			
	1. Cumberland Gap, Pilgrim Cong.	1891	1891-1909	X (1901:08)
	CUMBERLAND COUNTY (org.1856) (035)			
	1. Crossville, Cross Roads Union Cong.(f.l.Genesis)	1908 / 1909(08)	1908-1915	Merged to # 3 to form # 4 (q.v.)
	2. Crossville, First Cong.	1887 / 1888(s.01)	1886 or 1887-1942	Merged to # 4,# 8,& Morgan Co.# 10 to form M.(q.v.); (incor.X 1917:08)
	2M. Crossville, First Cong.(merger of # 2,# 4,# 8,& Morgan Co.# 10)	1942 M	1942-1982	UCC 1961-1982; NA 1986(j 1987)-on
	3. Genesis, Cong.	1908 / 1909(08)	1911-1915	Merged to # 1 to form # 4(q.v.)(X 1917:08)
	4. Genesis, Cross Roads Cong.(Union of Cross Roads;merger of # 1 & # 3)	1915 M	1915-1942	Merged to # 2,# 8,& Morgan Co.# 10 to form # 2M.(q.v.)

A	B	C	D	E
	TENNESSEE - CUMBERLAND COUNTY - continued			
		1896	1896-1912	X
5.	Lantana, Cong.		nl.	X
Nt	Mayland, Cong.(l.in 08:1914-1916,prob.a mission)			
6.	Pleasant Hill, Pleasant Hill Com.(First Cong.)	1885	1884-on	UCC (incor.X 1917:08)
7.	Pomona, Benedict Mem.Cong.	1871	1870-1876,	X (1917:08)
		r.1884	1883-1890,	
		1885(s.01)	1891-1920	
8.	Rinnie, Cold Springs Cong.(f.l.Isoline)	1911	1913-1942	Merged to # 2,# 4,&
		1912(08)		Morgan Co.# 10 to
				form # 2M,(q.v.);
				(incor.X 1917:08)
9.	Westel, Isham Cong.(prob.not Isham of Scott Co.)	1903	1903-1907	X (1908:08)
		1902(08)		
	DAVIDSON COUNTY (org.1783) (037)			
Bl 1.	Gootlettsville, Cong.	1886	1885-1912	X (1916:08)
		1885(s.01)		
Bl 2.	Nashville, Collegeside Cong.(*Belmont Twn.)	1929	1928-1952	X
		1928(s.01)		
Bl 3.	Nashville, Fisk Union (f.Union,University;*Fisk Twn.)	1868	1868-1982	UCC; X
		1867(42,s.08)		
		1876(s.01)		
Bl 4.	Nashville, Howard Cong.UCC (f.Howard Chap.,Knowles St.;*North	1876	1875-on	Sch.I 1961-1962;
	Twn.;in 1869 bldg.;Sch.I l.incor.,was UCC)	1869(s.01,18)		UCC 1962-on
Bl 5.	Nashville, Jackson St.Cong.(Third)	1884	1883-1901	X
	FRANKLIN COUNTY (org.1807) (051)			
1.	Sherwood, Com.	1928	1928-1949	X (1893:08)
2.	Sherwood, Union Cong.	1884	1883-1891	X (1893:08)
		1885(s.01)		
		1883(s.08)		
	GREENE COUNTY (org.1783) (059)			
1.	Cedar Creek, Cong.	1894	1895-1909	X (1898:08)
	GRUNDY COUNTY (org.1844) (061)			
1.	Monteagle, Smith's Chap.Cong.(on Marion Co.line)	1894	1895-1909	X (1908:08)
		1895(01)		
2.	Tracy City, Cong.	1894	1895-1899	X (1905:08)
		1893(01)		

TENNESSEE - HAMILTON COUNTY

TENNESSEE - continued (org.1819)
HAMILTON COUNTY (org.1819) (065)

A	B	C	D	E
Bl	1. Chattanooga, Central Cong.	1891	1893-1905	X Sch.I 1961;
	2. Chattanooga, First Cong.	1867	1866-on	UCC late 1961-on
	3. Chattanooga, Pilgrim Cong.(l.in 01N)	1889	nl.	X (prob.soon:1890)
	4. Chattanooga, Pilgrim Cong.	1914	1914-1969	UCC; merged to #11 to form M.(q.v.)
	4M. Chattanooga, Pilgrim Cong.(merger of #4 & #11)	1969 M	1969-on	UCC
	5. Chattanooga, Union Cong.	1871	1870-1874	X
	6. Chattanooga, Union Cong.(f.of East Lake;East Lake Twn.)	1893; 1892(43,48); 1883(s.01)	1893-1944	X
	7. Daisy, First Cong.(f.Com.;Sch.I l.incor.,was Sch.II)	1924; 1925(s.01); 1929(s.01)	1924-1989	UCC 1961-1975; sch.I 1975-1989; prob.withdrew
We	8. Rock Creek, Welsh Cong.(f.l.Sale Creek to 1883)	1883	1882-1886 or 1887	X
	9. Signal Mountain, Cong.	1927	1927-1930	X
	10. Soddy, Clifftown Cong.	1933	1933-1940	X
We	11. Soddy, First Cong.(Welsh)	1863(s.01)	1881-1969	UCC; merged to #4 to form 4M.(q.v.); (incor.X 1917:08)
	12. Soddy, Mount Tabor Cong.	1931	1931-1940	X (1915:08)
	13. Welshtown, First Cong.(f.Cong.of Welshtown & Hodgetown; incor.l.as Sale Creek of Harriman 1907-1912:while Sale Creek is here,Harriman is in Roane Co.and not contiguous)	1899	1899-1912	X (1915:08)

KNOX COUNTY (org.1792) (093)

A	B	C	D	E
We	1. Knoxville, First Welsh Cong.	1869; 1870(s.01); 1868(s.01); 1860(s.01)	1871-1896	X (1895:83;1897:44)
	2. Knoxville, Pilgrim Cong.(lt.01N)	1886; 1887(s.01S)	1886 or 1887-1912	X (1913:44)
Bl	3. Knoxville, Second Cong.	1883	1882-1931	X (1928:44)

MC MINN COUNTY (org.1819) (107)

A	B	C	D	E
pB	1. Athens, Cong.	1889	1889-1891	X (1894:08)
	2. McCulley, Cong.	1896	1897-1899	X (1902:08)

139

A	B	C	D	E
	TENNESSEE - continued			
	MARION COUNTY (org.1817) (115)			
B1	1. Whiteside, First Cong.	1885 1886(s.08,s.01)	1885-1888	X (1890:08)
	MORGAN COUNTY (org.1817) (129)			
	1. Deer Lodge, CC (f.First)	1887	1886 or 1887-on	UCC (incor.X 1917:08)
	2. Deer Lodge, Pleasant Green Com.	1924	1924-1931	X
	3. Frankfort, Pilgrim Cong.	1917	1917-1925	X
	4. Islandford, Bethel Cong.(Lancing PO)	1914	1914-1925	X (1917:08)
	5. Lancing, Cong.	1916(08)	1895-1899	X (1917:08)
	6. Lancing, Pleasant View Union Cong.(f.l.Robbins,Scott Co.,PO)	1894 1893(s.01)	1896-1929	X (1917:08)
	7. Mill Creek, First Cong.(Glenmary,Scott Co.PO)	1893	1893-1918	X (1917:08)
	8. Mossy Grove, Cong.(f.of Whetstone)	1894	1895-1912	X (1909:08)
	9. Oakdale, First Cong.	1897	1897-1909	X
	10. Oakdale, Rankin's Chap.(First Cong.;f.l.Harriman,Roane Co. to 1912;lt.1909-1912;lt.08)	1899 1897(s.01S) 1903(s.01) 1900(s.01)	1899-1942	Merged to Cumberland Co.:# 2,# 4,& # 8 to form Cumberland Co. # 2M.(q.v.);(X:1915: s.08)
	11. Pine Flat, New Sage Cong.(Deer Lodge PO)	1914 1915(08)	1914-1924	X (1917:08)
	12. Piney, People's Ch.,Cong.(Oakdale PO)	1917	1917-1920	X (1915:08)
	13. Piney, United Cong.(First;Oakdale PO)	1901	1901-1912	X (1898:08)
	14. Rugby, Cong.	1890	1890-1893, 1895-1906	
	OBION COUNTY (org.1823) (131)			
?	1. Moffatt, Cong.	1876	1875-1878	X
	RHEA COUNTY (org.1807) (143)			
	1. Grand View, First Cong.	1885	1884-1950	X (1917:08)
	2. Salem, Cong.(Ogden PO)	1901	1901-1906	X
	3. Salem, Cong.(Ogden PO;St.Elmo,Hamilton Co.PO)	1902	1902-1906	X
	ROANE COUNTY (org.1801) (145)			
?	1. Harriman, Pilgrim Chap.,Cong.	1890	1890-1909	X (1908:08)

TENNESSEE - continued

A	B	C	D	E
	SCOTT COUNTY (org.1849) (151)			
1.	Elgin, Union Cong.	1901	1901-1909	X
2.	Glenmary, CC (f.Com.)	1929	1929-on	UCC
		1885(s.01)		
3.	Glenmary, Glenmary Cong.(f.Second Cong.)	1891	1891-1909	X (1901:08)
4.	Glenmary, Glenmary Mines Cong.(f.First)	1888	1888-1892	X (1894:08)
5.	Helenwood, Piedmont Cong.	1885	1884-1907	X (1904:08)
6.	Robbins, Barton Chap.Com.(f.Plymouth,f.First)	1885	1884-on	UCC (incor.X 1916:08)
7.	Slick Rock, Union Cong.	1886	1885-1888	X (1890:08)
8.	Wolf Creek, Union Cong.(Elgin PO;Black Wolf Creek in 08;	1894	1895-1899,	X (1916:08)
	drop 08:1900(first time))	r.1901	1903-1908,	
			1909-1917	
	SHELBY COUNTY (org.1819) (157)			
1.	Memphis, First Cong.(f.Ch.of Strangers;*Madison Heights Twn.;	1863(45,s.01)	1864-1878,	UCC
	affl.TN 1870-1873,1874-1876,1886-1904,1914-1956,MO (dual	1864(s.01,01N)	1883-on	
	1889-1904)1904-1914,1956-on)	1866(s.01)		
		1867(s.01)		
		r.1884		
B1 2.	Memphis, Second Cong.(*Elmwood Twn.;affl.TN(B1)1870-1876,	1868	1867-on	UCC
	1878-1966,MO 1966-on)	1867(45,s.01)		
	WARREN COUNTY (org.1807) (177)			
B1 1.	McMinnsville, Highland Cong.	1872	1871-1873	X
	WASHINGTON COUNTY (Dist.1776,Co.org.1777) (179)			
B1 1.	Jonesborough, Union Ch.,Cong.	1885	1884-1909	X
B1 2.	Mount Earley, Washington College Cong.	1896	1896-1909	X
		1884(s.01S)		
	WHITE COUNTY (org.1806) (185)			
1.	Bon Air, Cong.	1891	1891-1909	X
2.	Rock House, Cong.(Bon Air PO)	1893	1893-1909	X
	UNLOCATED CHURCHES (999)			
Nt	Proctor, Cong.(l.only in 08:1896-1898,prob.a mission;prob.		nl.	X
	not the town in Crockett Co.)			
Nt	Rockhold(1.08 incor.,this is actually Whitley Co.,KY # 9)			

A

B
TENNESSEE - UNLOCATED CHURCHES - continued

C

D

E

Nt Strunk's Lane(lt.08 incor.;actually this is McCreary Co.KY #
3)

74 of 95 Counties have no known Congregational Churches and are listed below.

TEXAS (48)

ANDERSON COUNTY (org.1846) (001)

A	B	C	D	E
Bl	Nt Bois D'Arc, Cong.(PO Palestine;l.by 08:1887-1897,prob. a mission)		nl.	X
	1. Palestine, First Cong.	1881	1880-1944	X

BASTROP COUNTY (pla.1836,org.1837) (021)

A	B	C	D	E
pB	1. Colorado, Cong.(l.by 01N)	1884	nl.	X prob.soon (1885)

BEE COUNTY (pla.1857,org.1858) (025)

A	B	C	D	E
pB	Nt Beeville, Cong.(l.by 08:1915-1918,prob.a mission)		nl.	X
pB	1. Skidmore, Cong.	1877	1876-1877	X

BEXAR COUNTY (pla.1836,org.1837) (029)

A	B	C	D	E
	1. San Antonio, Pilgrim Cong.(f.First,Central)	1913	1913-1978	UCC; merged to form M. (q.v.)
	1M. San Antonio, Bethany Cong.(UCC)(merger of # 1 & Bethany E&R (f.in Evan.Synod)(1904))	1978 M	1978-on	UCC
Bl	2. San Antonio, Second Cong.	1922	1922-1928	X

BOWIE COUNTY (pla.1840,org.1841) (037)

A	B	C	D	E
	1. Texarkana, First Cong.(moved from Texarkana,Miller Co.,AR, 1956(q.v.))	1908	1956-1965	UCC 1961-1965; NA 1964 or 1965 (j1965)-1974; X

CALDWELL COUNTY (org.1848) (055)

A	B	C	D	E
Bl	1. Luling, Cong.	1879	1879-1886 or 1887, 1891-1892	X (1893:08)

CAMERON COUNTY (org.1848) (061)

A	B	C	D	E
Bl	1. Brownsville, First Cong.	c.1867 r.1869	1867-1872	X
Bl	2. Brownsville, Second Cong.	1870	1869-1872	X

TEXAS - continued

CAMP COUNTY (org.1874) (063)

A	B	C	D	E
	1. Spring Hill, Cong.(Newsome PO;f.Scroggins,Franklin Co.PO; f.Winnsboro,Franklin & Wood Co.line)	1900	1900-1908	X

CASS COUNTY (org.1846,f.Cass Co.to 1861,f.Davis Co.to 1871) (067)

A	B	C	D	E
?	1. Rocky Point, Cong.(Naples,Morris Co.PO)	1903	1903-1908	X

CHEROKEE COUNTY (org.1846) (073)

A	B	C	D	E
?	1. Morrill, First Cong.	1905	1907-1911	X

DALLAM COUNTY (pla.1876,org.1891) (111) [PANHANDLE]

A	B	C	D	E
?	1. Texline, Cong.(on Union Co.,NM line;assume predominantly White)	1906	1906-1908	X

DALLAS COUNTY (org.1846) (113)

A	B	C	D	E
	1. Dallas, Central Cong.	1902	1902-1941	Merged to # 4 to form M.(q.v.)
	1M. Dallas, Central Cong.UCC (merger of # 1 & # 4)	1941 M	1941-on	UCC
	2. Dallas, First Cong.(see also # 3)	1877	1876-1923	withdrew
	3. Dallas, Grand Ave.Cong.(a branch of # 2:1893-1897;also l.as prps.1896-1897)	1897	1897-1905	X
	4. Dallas, Junius Heights Cong.(in 1911 bldg.;merged to # 1 (q.v.))	1913	1913-1941	Merged to # 1 (q.v.)
Bl	5. Dallas, People's Cong.	1923	1923-1945	Merged to # 7 (q.v.)
Bl	6. Dallas, Pilgrim Cong.	1884	1883-1886 or 1887	X
Bl	7. Dallas, Plymouth Cong.	1884	1883-1885, 1886 or 1887-1945	Merged to # 5 to form M.(q.v.)
Bl	7M. Dallas, Plymouth Cong.(merger of # 5 & # 7)	1945 M	1945-1953	X
Bl	8. Dallas, Winnetka Cong.	1914	1914-1934	X
Bl	9. Dallas, Witness Cong.(in 1905 bldg.)	1909	1908-1934	X

EL PASO COUNTY (org.1850) (141) [WEST]

A	B	C	D	E
Sp	1. El Paso, El Buen Pastor Cong.(Good Shepherd;f.Mexican;affl.NM btwn.1913 & 1915-1928)	1892 1891(s.01)	1892-1928	X
	2. El Paso, First Cong.(assume predominantly white)	1893	1893-1897	X

TEXAS - EL PASO COUNTY - continued

A	B	C	D	E
3.	El Paso, Pilgrim Cong.UCC(f.Modern Liberal,First;r.as Pilgrim 1908 & Saturday House Chs.1972-1974;affl.NM btwn.1913 & 1915- r.1972 1974;poss.Fed.to unknown)		1908-1974	UCC 1961-1974; X
Sp 4.	El Paso, Trinity Cong.,East El Paso(Iglesia Cong.La Trinidad; f.La Santesema Trinity;j UCC 1964,incor.l.Sch.I 1964-1966, was UCC; affl.NM)	1924 1920(18)	1924-on	Sch.I 1961-1966; UCC 1966-on
5.	El Paso, Valley Cong.UCC (affl.NM)	1922 1937(s.01)	1923-on	UCC

FANNIN COUNTY (pla.1837,org.1838) (147)

A	B	C	D	E
Bl 1.	Dodds (City), First Cong.(f.Pilgrim;Dodd's Station)	1883 1884(01N)	1883-1896, 1897-1914	X (1916:08)
? 2.	Honey Grove, Cong.	1877	1876-1877	X

FAYETTE COUNTY (pla.1837,org.1838) (149)

A	B	C	D	E
Bl 1.	Schulenberg, Flatonia Cong.	1878(s.01) 1880(08) 1875(s.01)	1877-1886 or 1887	X (1887:08)

GALVESTON COUNTY (pla.1838,org.1839) (167)

A	B	C	D	E
Bl 1.	Galveston, First Cong.	1916 1918(08)	1917-1922	X

GOLIAD COUNTY (pla.1836,org.1837) (175)

A	B	C	D	E
Bl 1.	Goliad, First Cong.	1872 1873(s.01)	1871-1915, 1917-1919	X (1907:08)

GRAYSON COUNTY (org.1846) (181)

A	B	C	D	E
? 1.	Denison, First Cong.	1889	1889-1908	X
? 2.	Sherman, Cong.	1874	1873-1876	X
3.	Sherman, First Cong.(f.St.Paul's;pastor expelled from Assn. 1897,relisted 1900;see also # 4;prob.White)	1883	1882-1897, 1900-1901	X
4.	Sherman, First Cong.(f.St.Paul's;in 1878 bldg.;claim is as continuation of # 3;prob.White)	1900 1883(claim)	1900-1911	X

HARRIS COUNTY (pla.1836,org.1837,f.Harrisburg to 1839) (201)

A	B	C	D	E
1.	Houston, Bellaire Union Cong.	1916	1916-1921	X
2.	Houston, First Cong.(in 1900 bldg.)	1909	1909-1934	X

A	B	C	D 1907-on	E UCC
	TEXAS - HARRIS COUNTY - continued			
B1	3. Houston, Pilgrim Cong.UCC	1904(01,18) 1907(08)	1907-on	X
	JEFFERSON COUNTY (pla.1836,org.1837) (245)			
B1	1. Beaumont, First Cong.	1923	1923-1931	X
B1	2. Beaumont, Graham Cong.(f.Douglass Chap.)	1915 1918(s.01,18)	1917-1944	Merged to form M.(q.v.) sch.I 1961; UCC late 1961-on
B1	2M. Beaumont, Plymouth UCC (f.Graham;merger of # 2 & Appendix II. # 1)	1944 M	1944-on	
B1	3. Port Arthur, Beacon Cong.	1927	1927-1933	X
B1	4. Port Arthur, Cong.(see also # 5;assume predominantly white because of claim of # 5)	1899	1899-1906	X
B1	5. Port Arthur, Groves Com.(f.First Cong.;in 1898(s.01)or 1899 (s.01)bldg.;claim is as # 4)	1910(s.01) 1915(08) 1899(claim) r.1929	1910-1934	X (1918:08)
	JOHNSON COUNTY (org.1854) (251)			
	1. Cleburne, Trinity Cong.(prob.White)	1883	1882-1904	X
	KARNES COUNTY (org.1854) (255)			
B1	1. Karnes City, First Cong.(Flaccus;lt.08)	1915(01) 1895(08)	1917-1919	X (1918:08)
B1	2. Runge, Helena Cong.(f.l.Flaccus;f.l.Goliad,Goliad Co.;X 1907 & r.1914:08)	1874 1872(08) 1884(s.01) r.1914(08)	1873-1946	X
	LAMAR COUNTY (pla.1840,org.1841) (277)			
	1. Paris, First Cong.(f.Second,Main St.)	1874 1875(s.01)	1873-1927	X
B1	2. Paris, Grace Cong.(f.African,Rusk St.,First)	1868 1872(01N,s.01)	1872-1946	X
B1	3. Paris, New Hope Cong.(f.l.Stilltwon(Stelltown);f.l.Davis; (Second of Stelltown in 08))	1869 1872(s.01) 1879(08) r.1918(08)	1878-1879, 1897-1905, 1907-1914, 1917-1927	X (1908:08)
pB	4. Pattonville, Cong.	1869 1868(08) 1877(s.01) 1883(01N)	1876-1877, 1878-1879, 1890-1897, 1898-1899	X (1908:08)

A	B	C	D	E
	TEXAS - LAMAR COUNTY - continued			
Bl 5.	Petty, Cong.	1887	1886 or 1887-1892	X (1888:08)
Bl 6.	Red Hill, Cong.(Paris PO)	1919	1920-1922	X
Bl 7.	Roxton, Bethel Cong.(First Cong.;High PO;in 1883 bldg.)	1887 1885(s.01) 1866(s.01)	1888-1914, 1917-1922	X
Bl 8.	Stilltown, Cong.(Davis PO;Stelltown in 08)	1898 1884(08)	1898-1907	X (1898:08)
	LAMB COUNTY (pla.1876,org.1908) (279) [PANHANDLE]			
1.	Hurley, Union Cong.(Pleasant Valley PO)	1912	1912-1926	X
2.	Spring Lake, Fed.(f.Cong.;affl.OK 1910-1911 or 1912,& 1932-1945;Fed.to Meth.Epis.South(?)unknown-1945;in 1907 bldg.)	1908	1909-1945	X
	LIPSCOMB COUNTY (pla.1876,org.1887) (295) [PANHANDLE]			
Gr 1.	Darrouzett, Emmanuel Ger.Cong.(Immanuel;f.First Ger.Cong.of Booker;drop 01K btwn.1959 & 1961;never in South Central records other than natl.01;may be X by 1963 & incor.l.)	1927	1927-on	Sch.I (see text)
Gr 2.	Follett, St.John Cong.(St.Johannes;affl.CO 1925-1926;incor. l.as Sch.I,was Sch.II;although in South Central Conf.on natl.list 1963-on,never in their minutes,but in the KS-OK minutes 1963-1971,prob.transferred there 1963 & not reported correctly by natl.01)	1925 1924(s.05)	1925-on	Sch.I; CCCC 1973-on
3.	Lipscomb, Cong.(assume predominantly White)	1905	1906-1909	X
	MARION COUNTY (org.1860) (315)			
? 1.	Jefferson, Cong.(Tr.from Cumberland Pres.)	? (Pres.) r.1869(Cong.)	1868-1869	X (poss.Tr.back to Cumberland Pres.)
	NACOGDOCHES COUNTY (org.1836) (347)			
Bl 1.	Nacogdoches, Wesley Chap.Cong.	1912 1910(s.01)	1922-1945	X (1915:08)
	NUECES COUNTY (org.1846) (355)			
Bl 1.	Corpus Christi, First UCC (affl.MI 1866-1867,1870-1871;j UCC 1961,incor.l.Sch.I,was UCC;see also # 2)	1866 1867(01N) 1886(s.01)	1866-1867, 1870-on	Sch.I 1961-1962; UCC 1962-on
Bl 2.	Corpus Christi, Freedman's Cong.(poss.this ch.became First, & # 1 was X)	1867(01N) 1866(01)	1866-1867	X

TEXAS - continued

PARKER COUNTY (pla.1855,org.1856) (367)

A	B	C	D	E
1.	Weatherford, Cong.(prob.White)	1883	1882-1885	X

PARMER COUNTY (pla.1876,org.1907) (369) [PANHANDLE]

A	B	C	D	E
1.	Bovina, Pilgrim Cong.(assume predominantly White)	1905	1906-1908	X
2.	Farwell, Cong.(Texico,Curry Co.,NM,PO)	1906	1906-1917	X
3.	Friona, Union Cong.(affl.OK 1932-1963)	1908 1906(s.01)	1909-on	UCC

POTTER COUNTY (pla.1876,org.1887) (375) [PANHANDLE]

A	B	C	D	E
1.	Amarillo, First Cong.(affl.OK 1910-1911 or 1912)	1906	1906-1920	X
2.	Amarillo, First Cong.(affl.OK 1932-1933)	1927	1927-1933	X

SMITH COUNTY (org.1846) (423)

A	B	C	D	E
1.	Coplen, Cong.(Flint PO)	1901	1902-1908	X
2.	Galena, Garden Valley Cong.(Van,Van Zandt Co.PO)	1898	1898-1916	X
3.	Swan, Mount Lebanon Cong.	1902	1902-1907	X
4.	Tyler, Cong.	1900	1900-1909	X

TARRANT COUNTY (pla.1849,org.1850) (439)

A	B	C	D	E
? 1.	Fort Worth, Cong.	1891	1891-1893	X
2.	Fort Worth, First Cong.UCC	1903	1903-on	UCC
? 3.	Fort Worth, Union Cong.	1884	1883-1886 or 1887	X

TRAVIS COUNTY (pla.1840,org.1843) (453)

A	B	C	D	E
pB 1.	Austin, Central Cong.	1896	1896-1901	X (1899:08)
2.	Austin, Cong.UCC (f.First,University Com.)	1901 1902(s.01) 1904(s.01)	1903-on	UCC
B1 3.	Austin, Tillotson Cong.(Tillostin;f.First Cong.of Tillotson)	1885	1884-1915, 1919-1921	X

TRINITY COUNTY (org.1850) (455)

A	B	C	D	E
? 1.	Groveton, Cong.	1885	1886 or 1887-1892	X

A	B	C	D	E
	TEXAS - continued			
	UPSHUR COUNTY (org.1846) (459)			
1.	Grice, Pilgrim Cong.(f.l.Rhonesboro;Pittsburg,Camp Co.PO)	1899 1900(s.01)	1899-1912	X
	VAN ZANDT COUNTY (org.1848) (467)			
?	1. Edgewood, Rainey's Chap.Cong.(Wills Point PO;in 1898 bldg.)	1908	1908-1927	X
	2. Fruitvale, Cong.	1912	1912-1943	X
	3. Grand Saline, Cong.(l.as prps.1899-1900)	1900	1900-1901	X
	4. Martins Mills, Cong.	1899 1898(s.01)	1898-1905	X
	5. Pruett, First Cong.(Grand Saline PO)	1904	1907-1916	X
	6. Round Flat, Cong.(Fruitvale PO)	1904	1909-1911	X
	7. Sexton, Cong.(Ben Wheeler PO)	1899	1899-1905	X
	8. Silver Lake, Cong.	1908	1908-1917	X
	UNLOCATED CHURCHES (999)			
Gr	1. Kiowa, Ger.Cong.(l.only in 82;poss.01K:lacuna in records; poss.in Lipscomb Co.)	1926	nl.	X 1934
pB	2. Paradise, Cong.(yoked to # 3 & Lamar Co. # 1 & # 5)	1879	1878-1879	X
pB	3. Shiloh, Cong.(yoked to # 2 & Lamar Co. # 1 & # 5)	1879	1878-1879	X
?	4. Tuscambia, Cong.(l.in 01N)	1872	nl.	X prob.soon (1873)

217 of 254 Counties have no known Congregational Churches and are listed below.

149

VIRGINIA (51)

A	B	C	D	E
	ACCOMACK COUNTY (org. 1661/1662) (001)			
	1. Guilford, Cong.(Gilford;*Metompkin Dist.;affl.NJ 1869-1870)	1868	1867-1870	X
	ALBEMARLE COUNTY (org.1744) - CHARLOTTESVILLE CITY (003)			
pB	1. Greenwood, Indep.Hill Cong.(*White Hall Dist.;not affl.)	1867(01N) 1866(s.01)	1867-1871	X
	ARLINGTON COUNTY (in DC 1791-1846;org.1801;f.Alexandria Co.(DC):1801-1846;f.Alexandria Co.(VA) 1846(org.1847)-1920) - ALEXANDRIA CITY (013)			
	1. Alexandria, Cong.(affl.NJ)	1891	1891-1892	Tr.to "Zion's Connection" (Chr. Catholic Ch.)
	2. Arlington, Rock Spring Cong.(f.Cong.of Vanderwerken;affl.NJ)	1912	1914-on	UCC
	BUCKINGHAM COUNTY (org.1761) (029)			
We	1. Arvonia, Welsh Cong.(1.01N;nl.83;*Marshall Dist.)	1891	nl.	X prob.soon (1892)
	[ELIZABETH CITY COUNTY (org.1634,X 1952)] - HAMPTON CITY (055/650)			
B1	1. Hampton, Cong.at Normal School (m.NJ 1884-1885;otherwise not affl.)	1869	1869-1884	X (1894:08)
	FAIRFAX COUNTY (org.1742) - FALLS CHURCH CITY - FAIRFAX CITY (059)			
	1. Falls Church, Cong.(affl.NJ)	1876	1875-1914	X
	2. Herndon, Cong.(*Dranesville Dist.;affl.NJ 1869-1949)	1868	1867-1949	X
	ISLE OF WIGHT COUNTY (org.1634,f.Warrosqueyoacke to 1642) (093)			
	1. Warwisqueake, Indep.Puritan (sett.by 1618:16;Dist.unclear)	c.1621	nl.	X af.1624(poss.ab.by Epis.Par.org.1642)
	[NANSEMOND COUNTY (org.1637,f.Upper Norfolk to 1642,X 1972)] - SUFFOLK CITY (inclu.f.NANSEMOND CITY) (123/800)			
	1. Suffolk, Nansemond Puritan of Providence(Upper Norfolk Farms (in West,or Chuckatuck Par.);majority removed to Providence,Anne Arundel Co.MD 1649)	c.1641	nl.	X (c.1660(remnant prob.removed to Cape Fear,Brunswick Co.,NC))

150

VIRGINIA - continued

A	B	C	D	E
	[NORFOLK COUNTY (org.1693,X 1963)] - NORFOLK CITY - PORTSMOUTH CITY - CHESAPEAKE CITY (inclu.f.SOUTH NORFOLK CITY) (129/710)			
1.	Portsmouth, First UCC (f.Shelton Mem.Cong.;affl.NJ 1906-1938, Southern 1938-1975)	1905	1906-1975	UCC; X
	PRINCE GEORGE COUNTY (org.1702/1703) - HOPEWELL CITY (149)			
Sk 1.	Disputanta, Bethlehem CC (f.Begonia;f.l.Prince George PO; *Templeton Dist.;affl.NJ 1904-1936,Southern 1938-1979)	1896 1898(s.01)	1904-1936, 1938-1979	Sch.I 1961-1979; CCCC 1967 or 1968 (j 1969)-on
	PRINCE WILLIAM COUNTY (org.1730/1731) - MANASSAS CITY - MANASSAS PARK CITY (153)			
? 1.	Occoquan, First Cong.(not affl.;m.1867-1868)	1868	1868-1869	X

89 of 100 county equivalent units have no known Congregational Churches and are listed below.

151

A	B	C	D	E
	WEST VIRGINIA (54)			
	BERKELEY COUNTY (org.1772) (003)			
1.	Martinsburg, Cong.(also l.as prps.1880-1881;affl.NJ)	1881	1882-1885	X
	CABELL COUNTY (org.1809) (011)			
1.	Huntington, First Cong.(UCC)(*Gideon Dist.;affl.OH)	1872	1871-on	UCC
	OHIO COUNTY (org.1777) (069)			
1.	Wheeling, Cong.(Dist.uncertain)	bf.1851	nl.	X by 1851
	RITCHIE COUNTY (org.1843) (085)			
1.	Lone Valley, Cong.(Goose Creek PO;*Grant Dist.;affl.OH;also l.as prps.1879-1880)	1880	1880-1883	X
	WAYNE COUNTY (org.1842) (099)			
1.	Ceredo, Cong.(affl.OH)	1874 1883(s.04)	1873-1968	UCC 1961-1968; NA 1967(j 1968)-on

50 of 55 Counties have no know Congregational Churches and are listed below.

A	B	C	D	E
	SOUTHERN CHURCHES UNLOCATED BY STATE (99)			
1.	Angoria, Cong.(affl.to West FL-South AL Conference,in one of those states)	1892	1907-1908	X

ALABAMA - 17 of 67

Choctaw Co.(org.1847) (023)
Clarke Co.(org.1812) (025)
Fayette Co.(org.1824) (057)
Franklin Co.(org.1818) (059)
Greene Co.(org.1819) (063)
Hale Co.(org.1867) (065)
Lowndes Co.(org.1830) (085)
Macon Co.(org.1832) (087)
Madison Co.(org.1809) (089)
Marengo Co.(org.1818) (091)
Marshall Co.(org.1836) (095)
Monroe Co.(org.1815) (099)
Pickens Co.(org.1820) (107)
Sumter Co.(org.1832) (119)
Tuscaloosa Co.(org.1818) (125)
Walker Co.(org.1823) (127)
Wilcox Co.(org.1819) (131)

ARKANSAS - 63 of 75

Ashley Co.(org.1848) (003)
Baxter Co.(org.1873) (005)
Bradley Co.(org.1840) (011)
Calhoun Co.(org.1850) (013)
Chicot Co.(org.1823) (017)
Clay Co.(org.1873,f.Clayton to
  1875) (021)
Cleburne Co.(org.1883) (023)
Cleveland Co.(org.1873,f.Dorsey to
  1885) (025)
Columbia Co.(org.1852) (027)
Conway Co.(org.1825) (029)
Craighead Co.(org.1859) (031)
Crawford Co.(org.1820) (033)
Cross Co.(org.1862) (037)
Dallas Co.(org.1845) (039)
Drew Co.(org.1846) (043)
Faulkner Co.(org.1873) (045)
Franklin Co.(org.1837) (047)
Fulton Co.(org.1842) (049)
Garland Co.(org.1873) (051)
Grant Co.(org.1869) (053)
Greene Co.(org.1833) (055)
Hempstead Co.(org.1818) (057)
Hot Spring Co.(org.1829) (059)
Howard Co.(org.1873) (061)
Independence Co.(org.1820) (063)
Izard Co.(org.1825) (065)
Jackson Co.(org.1829) (067)
Jefferson Co.(org.1829) (069)
Johnson Co.(org.1833) (071)
Lafayette Co.(org.1827) (073)
Lawrence Co.(org.1815) (075)
Lee Co.(org.1873) (077)
Lincoln Co.(org.1871) (079)
Little River Co.(org.1867) (081)
Logan Co.(org.1871,f.Sarber to
  1875) (083)

Madison Co.(org.1836) (087)
Marion Co.(org.1835,f.Searcy(old)
  to 1836) (089)
Mississippi Co.(org.1833) (093)
Monroe Co.(org.1829) (095)
Montgomery Co.(org.1842) (097)
Nevada Co.(org.1871) (099)
Newton Co.(org.1842) (101)
Ouachita Co.(org.1842) (103)
Perry Co.(org.1840) (105)
Phillips Co.(org.1820) (107)
Pike Co.(org.1833) (109)
Poinsett Co.(org.1838) (111)
Polk Co.(org.1844) (113)
Pope Co.(org.1829) (115)
Prairie Co.(org.1846) (117)
Randolph Co.(org.1835) (121)
St. Francis Co.(org.1827) (123)
Saline Co.(org.1835) (125)
Scott Co.(org.1833) (127)
Searcy Co.(new)(org.1838) (129)
Sevier Co.(org.1828) (133)
Sharp Co.(org.1868) (135)
Stone Co.(org.1873/1875) (137)
Union Co.(org.1829) (139)
Van Buren Co.(org.1833) (141)
White Co.(org.1835) (145)
Woodruff Co.(org.1862) (147)
Yell Co.(org.1840) (149)

DELAWARE - 0 of 3

DISTRICT OF COLUMBIA - 0 of 1

FLORIDA - 25 of 67

Bradford Co.(org.1858,f.New River
  to 1861) (007)
Charlotte Co.(org.1921) (015)
Collier Co.(org.1923) (021)
De Soto Co.(org.1887) (027)
Dixie Co.(org.1921) (029)
Flagler Co.(org.1917) (035)
Franklin Co.(org.1832) (037)
Gadsden Co.(org.1823) (039)
Gilchrist Co.(org.1925) (041)
Gulf Co.(org.1925) (045) [WEST]
Hamilton Co.(org.1827) (047)
Hardee Co.(org.1921) (049)
Hendry Co.(org.1923) (051)
Jefferson Co.(org.1827) (065)
Lafayette Co.(org.1856) (067)
Levy Co.(org.1845) (075)
Liberty Co.(org.1855) (077)
Madison Co.(org.1827) (079)
Manatee Co.(org.1855) (081)
Nassau Co.(org.1824) (089)
Okeechobee Co.(org.1917) (093)
Osceola Co.(org.1887) (097)
St. Johns Co.(org.1821) (109)

Taylor Co.(org.1856) (123)
Wakulla Co.(org.1843) (129)

GEORGIA - 70 of 159

Baldwin Co.(org.1803) (009)
Banks Co.(org.1858) (011)
Barrow Co.(org.1914/1915) (013)
Berrien Co.(org.1856) (019)
Brooks Co.(org.1858) (027)
Butts Co.(org.1825) (035)
Candler Co.(org.1914) (043)
Catoosa Co.(org.1853) (047)
Chattahoochee Co.(org.1854) (053)
Chattooga Co.(org.1838) (055)
Cherokee Co.(org.1831) (057)
Clay Co.(org.1854) (061)
Columbia Co.(org.1790) (073)
Cook Co.(org.1918/1919) (075)
Coweta Co.(org.1826) (077)
Decatur Co.(org.1823) (087)
Dodge Co.(org.1870) (091)
Douglas Co.(org.1870) (097)
Early Co.(org.1818) (099)
Echols Co.(org.1858) (101)
Effingham Co.(org.1777) (103)
Fayette Co.(org.1821) (113)
Forsyth Co.(org.1832) (117)
Franklin Co.(org.1784) (119)
Glascock Co.(org.1857) (125)
Glynn Co.(org.1777) (127)
Hancock Co.(org.1793) (141)
Haralson Co.(org.1856) (143)
Hart Co.(org.1853) (147)
Heard Co.(org.1830) (149)
Irwin Co.(org.1818) (155)
Jasper Co.(org.1807,f.Randolph to
  1812) (159)
Jeff Davis Co.(org.1905) (161)
Johnson Co.(org.1858) (167)
Laurens Co.(org.1807) (175)
Lee Co.(org.1827) (177)
Lincoln Co.(org.1796) (181)
Long Co.(org.1920) (183)
McDuffie Co.(org.1870) (189)
Macon Co.(org.1837) (193)
Mitchell Co.(org.1857) (205)
Monroe Co.(org.1821) (207)
Montgomery Co.(org.1793) (209)
Morgan Co.(org.1807) (211)
Murray Co.(org.1832) (213)
Oconee Co.(org.1875) (219)
Ogelthorpe Co.(org.1793) (221)
Pickens Co.(org.1853) (227)
Pulaski Co.(org.1808) (235)
Putnam Co.(org.1807) (237)
Quitman Co.(org.1858) (239)
Rabun Co.(org.1819) (241)
Seminole Co.(org.1920) (253)
Stephens Co.(org.1905) (257)

Stewart Co.(org.1830) (259)
Taliaferro Co.(org.1825) (265)
Taylor Co.(org.1853) (269)
Telfair Co.(org.1807) (271)
Towns Co.(org.1856) (281)
Treutlen Co.(org.1917/1919) (283)
Twiggs Co.(org.1809) (289)
Walker Co.(org.1833) (295)
Warren Co.(org.1793) (301)
Webster Co.(org.1853,f.
  Kinchafoonee to 1856) (307)
Wheeler Co.(org.1912/1913) (309)
White Co.(org.1857) (311)
Whitfield Co.(org.1851) (313)
Wilkes Co.(org.1777) (317)
Wilkinson Co.(org.1803) (319)
Worth Co. (org.1852) (321)

KENTUCKY - 99 of 120

Adair Co.(org.1901) (001)
Allen Co.(org.1815) (003)
Anderson Co.(org.1827) (005)
Ballard Co.(org.1842) (007)
Barren Co.(org.1798) (009)
Bath Co.(org.1811) (011)
Bell Co.(org.1867,f.Josh Bell to
  1873) (013)
Boone Co.(org.1798) (015)
Bourbon Co.(org.1785) (017)
Boyd Co.(org.1860) (019)
Breathitt Co.(org.1839) (025)
Breckinridge Co.(org.1799) (027)
Bullitt Co.(org.1796) (029)
Butler Co.(org.1810) (031)
Caldwell Co.(org.1809) (033)
Calloway Co.(org.1822) (035)
Carlisle Co.(org.1886) (039)
Carroll Co.(org.1838) (041)
Carter Co.(org.1838) (043)
Casey Co.(org.1806) (045)
Christian Co.(org.1792) (047)
Clark Co.(org.1792) (049)
Clay Co.(org.1806) (051)
Clinton Co.(org.1835) (053)
Crittenden Co.(org.1842) (055)
Cumberland Co.(org.1796) (057)
Daviess Co.(org.1815) (059)
Edmonson Co.(org.1825) (061)
Elliott Co.(org.1869) (063)
Estill Co.(org.1808) (065)
Fleming Co.(org.1798) (069)
Floyd Co.(org.1799) (071)
Franklin Co.(org.1794) (073)
Fulton Co.(org.1845) (075)
Garrard Co.(org.1796) (079)
Grant Co.(org.1820) (081)
Graves Co.(org.1823) (083)
Grayson Co.(org.1810) (085)
Green Co.(org.1792) (087)

Greenup Co.(org.1803) (089)
Hancock Co.(org.1829) (091)
Hardin Co.(org.1792) (093)
Harrison Co.(org.1793) (097)
Hart Co.(org.1819) (099)
Henderson Co.(org.1793) (101)
Henry Co.(org.1798) (103)
Hickman Co.(org.1821) (105)
Hopkins Co.(org.1808) (107)
Johnson Co.(org.1843) (115)
Knox Co.(org.1799) (121)
Larue Co.(org.1843) (123)
Lawrence Co.(org.1821) (127)
Lee Co.(org.1870) (129)
Leslie Co.(org.1878) (131)
Letcher Co.(org.1842) (133)
Lincoln Co.(org.1780) (137)
Livingston Co.(org.1798) (139)
Logan Co.(org.1792) (141)
Lyon Co.(org.1854) (143)
McCracken Co.(org.1824) (145)
Magoffin Co.(org.1860) (153)
Marion Co.(org.1834) (155)
Marshall Co.(org.1842) (157)
Martin Co.(org.1870) (159)
Mason Co.(org.1789) (161)
Meade Co.(org.1823) (163)
Mercer Co.(org.1785) (167)
Metcalfe Co.(org.1860) (169)
Monroe Co.(org.1820) (171)
Montgomery Co.(org.1796) (173)
Muhlenburg Co.(org.1798) (177)
Nelson Co.(org.1784) (179)
Nicholas Co.(org.1799) (181)
Ohio Co.(org.1798) (183)
Oldham Co.(org.1823) (185)
Owen Co.(org.1819) (187)
Pendleton Co.(org.1798) (191)
Perry Co.(org.1820) (193)
Pike Co.(org.1821) (195)
Powell Co.(org.1852) (197)
Pulaski Co.(org.1798) (199)
Robertson Co.(org.1867) (201)
Rockcastle Co.(org.1810) (203)
Rowan Co.(org.1856) (205)
Russell Co.(org.1825) (207)
Scott Co.(org.1792) (209)
Shelby Co.(org.1792) (211)
Simpson Co.(org.1819) (213)
Spencer Co.(org.1824) (215)
Taylor Co.(org.1848) (217)
Todd Co.(org.1819) (219)
Trigg Co.(org.1820) (221)
Trimble Co.(org.1836) (223)
Union Co.(org.1811) (225)
Warren Co.(org.1796) (227)
Washington Co.(org.1792) (229)
Wayne Co.(org.1800) (231)
Webster Co.(org.1860) (233)
Woodford Co.(org.1788) (239)

LOUISIANA - 42 of 64

Acadia Par.(org.1886) (001)
Ascension Par.(org.1807) (005)
Avoyelles Par.(org.1807,r.1873)
  (009)
Bienville Par.(org.1848) (013)
Bossier Par.(org.1843) (015)
Caddo Par.(org.1838) (017)
Caldwell Par.(org.1838) (021)
Cameron Par.(org.1870) (023)
Catahoula Par.(org.1808) (025)
Claiborne Par.(org.1828) (027)
Concordia Par.(org.1805) (029)
De Soto Par.(org.1843) (031)
East Carroll Par.(org.1877) (035)
East Feliciana Par.(org.1824) (037)
Evangeline Par.(org.1910/1911)
  (039)
Franklin Par.(org.1843) (041)
Grant Par.(org.1869) (043)
Iberville Par.(org.1805) (047)
Lafayette Par.(org.1823) (055)
La Salle Par.(org.1908/1910) (059)
Livingston Par.(org.1832) (063)
Madison Par.(org.1838) (065)
Morehouse Par.(org.1844) (067)
Plaquemines Par.(org.1807) (075)
Pointe Coupee Par.(org.1805) (077)
Richland Par.(pla.1852(nl.1860,
  org.1868) (083)
St.Bernard Par.(org.1807) (087)
St.Charles Par.(org.1807) (089)
St.Helena Par.(org.1810) (091)
St.James Par.(org.1807) (093)
St.John the Baptist Par.(org.1807)
  (095)
St.Landry Par.(org.1807) (097)
St.Martin Par.(org.1807) (099)
St.Mary Par.(pla.1811(nl.1820,l.
  1830),org.1833) (101)
St.Tammany Par.(org.1810) (103)
Tensas Par.(org.1843) (107)
Washington Par.(org.1819) (117)
Webster Par.(org.1871) (119)
West Baton Rouge Par.(org.1807,f.
  Baton Rogue to 1810) (121)
West Carroll Par.(org.1877) (123)
West Feliciana Par.(org.1824) (125)
Winn Par.(org.1852) (127)

MARYLAND - 17 of 24

Baltimore Co.(org.1659) (005)
Calvert Co.(org.1650) (009)
Carroll Co.(org.1836) (013)
Cecil Co.(org.1674) (015)
Dorchester Co.(org.1668/1669) (019)
Frederick Co.(org.1748) (021)
Garrett Co.(org.1872) (023)

Harford Co.(org.1773) (025)
Howard Co.(org.1851) (027)
Kent Co.(org.1642) (029)
Queen Annes Co.(org.1706) (035)
St. Marys Co.(org.1637) (037)
Somerset Co.(org.1666) (039)
Talbot Co.(org.1662) (041)
Washington Co.(org.1776) (043)
Wicomico Co.(org.1867) (045)
Worcester Co.(org.1742) (047)

MISSISSIPPI - 73 of 82

Alcorn Co.(org.1870) (003)
Amite Co.(org.1809) (005)
Attala Co.(org.1833) (007)
Benton Co.(org.1870) (009)
Bolivar Co.(org.1836) (011)
Calhoun Co.(org.1852) (013)
Carroll Co.(org.1833) (015)
Chickasaw Co.(org.1836) (017)
Choctaw Co.(org.1833) (019)
Claiborne Co.(org.1802) (021)
Clarke Co.(org.1833) (023)
Clay Co.(org.1871/1872,f.Colfax to
  1876) (025)
Coahoma Co.(org.1836) (027)
Copiah Co.(org.1823) (029)
Covington Co.(org.1819) (031)
DeSoto Co.(org.1836) (033)
Forrest Co.(org.1908) (035)
George Co.(org.1910) (039)
Greene Co.(org.1811) (041)
Grenada Co.(org.1870) (043)
Hancock Co.(org.1812) (045)
Harrison Co.(org.1841) (047)
Holmes Co.(org.1833) (051)
Humphreys Co.(org.1918) (053)
Issaquena Co.(org.1844) (055)
Itawamba Co.(org.1836) (057)
Jackson Co.(org.1812) (059)
Jasper Co.(org.1833) (061)
Jefferson Co.(org.1799,f.Pickering
  to 1802) (063)
Jefferson Davis Co.(org.1906) (065)
Jones Co.(org.1826) (067)
Kemper Co.(org.1833) (069)
Lafayette Co.(org.1836) (071)
Lamar Co.(org.1904) (073)
Lawrence Co.(org.1814) (077)
Leake Co.(org.1833) (079)
Lee Co.(org.1866) (081)
Leflore Co.(org.1871) (083)
Lincoln Co.(org.1870) (085)
Marion Co.(org.1811) (091)
Marshall Co.(org.1836) (093)
Montgomery Co.(org.1871) (097)
Neshoba Co.(org.1833) (099)
Newton Co.(org.1836) (101)
Noxubee Co.(org.1833) (103)

Oktibbeha Co.(org.1833) (105)
Panola Co.(org.1836) (107)
Pearl River Co.(org.1890) (109)
Perry Co.(org.1820) (111)
Pike Co.(org.1815) (113)
Pontotoc Co.(org.1836) (115)
Prentiss Co.(org.1870) (117)
Quitman Co.(org.1877) (119)
Rankin Co.(org.1828) (121)
Scott Co.(org.1833) (123)
Sharkey Co.(org.1876) (125)
Simpson Co.(org.1824) (127)
Smith Co.(org.1833) (129)
Stone Co.(org.1916) (131)
Sunflower Co.(org.1844) (133)
Tallahatchie Co.(org.1833) (135)
Tate Co.(org.1873) (137)
Tippah Co.(org.1836) (139)
Tunica Co.(org.1836) (143)
Union Co.(org.1870) (145)
Walthall Co.(org.1914) (147)
Warren Co.(org.1809) (149)
Wayne Co.(org.1809) (153)
Webster Co.(org.1874,f.Sumner to
  1882) (155)
Wilkinson Co.(org.1802) (157)
Winston Co.(org.1833) (159)
Yalobusha Co.(org.1833) (161)
Yazoo Co.(org.1823) (163)

NORTH CAROLINA - 60 of 100

Alexander Co.(org.1847) (003)
Alleghany Co.(org.1859) (005)
Ashe Co.(org.1799) (009)
Avery Co.(org.1911) (011)
Beaufort Co.(org.1705,f.Pamptecough
  to 1712) (013)
Bertie Co.(org.1722) (015)
Bladen Co.(org.1732/1734) (017)
Caldwell Co.(org.1841) (027)
Camden Co.(org.1777) (029)
Catawba Co.(org.1842) (035)
Cherokee Co.(org.1839) (039)
Chowan Co.(org.1670/1672) (041)
Clay Co.(org.1861) (043)
Columbus Co.(org.1847) (047)
Currituck Co.(org.1670/1672) (053)
Dare Co.(org.1870) (055)
Davidson Co.(org.1822) (057)
Davie Co.(org.1836) (059)
Duplin Co.(org.1749/1750) (061)
Edgecombe Co.(org.1732/1741) (065)
Franklin Co.(org.1779) (069)
Gates Co.(org.1778/1779) (073)
Graham Co.(org.1872) (075)
Granville Co.(org.1746) (077)
Greene Co.(org.1791,f.Glasgow to
  1799) (079)
Haywood Co.(org.1808) (087)

Henderson Co.(org.1838) (089)
Hertford Co.(org.1759) (091)
Hyde Co.(org.1705,f.Wickham to
  1712) (095)
Jackson Co.(org.1851) (099)
Johnston Co.(org.1746) (101)
Jones Co.(org.1778/1779) (103)
Lenoir Co.(org.1791) (107)
Lincoln Co.(org.1779) (109)
Macon Co.(org.1828) (113)
Madison Co.(org.1851) (115)
Martin Co.(org.1774) (117)
Mitchell Co.(org.1861) (121)
Nash Co.(org.1777) (127)
Northampton Co.(org.1741) (131)
Onslow Co.(org.1731/1734) (133)
Pamlico Co.(org.1872) (137)
Pasquotank Co.(org.1670/1672) (139)
Pender Co.(org.1875) (141)
Perquimans Co.(org.1670/1672) (143)
Person Co.(org.1791) (145)
Rockingham Co.(org.1785) (157)
Sampson Co.(org.1784) (163)
Scotland Co.(org.1899/1900) (165)
Stokes Co.(org.1789) (169)
Surry Co.(org.1770) (171)
Tyrrell Co.(org.1729) (177)
Vance Co.(org.1881) (181)
Warren Co.(org.1779) (185)
Washington Co.(org.1799) (187)
Watauga Co.(org.1849) (189)
Wilkes Co.(org.1777) (193)
Wilson Co.(org.1855) (195)
Yadkin Co.(org.1850) (197)
Yancey Co.(org.1833) (199)

OKLAHOMA - 37 of 77

Adair Co.(org.1907) (001) [Cherokee
  IT to 1907]
Beaver Co.(org.1890) (007)
Beckham Co.(org.1907) (009)
Carter Co.(org.1907) (019)
  [Chickasaw IT to 1907]
Cherokee Co.(org.1907) (021)
  [Cherokee IT to 1907]
Cimarron Co.(org.1907) (025)
Cleveland Co.(org.1890) (027)
Cotton Co.(org.1912) (033)
Delaware Co.(org.1907) (041)
  [Cherokee & Seneca IT to 1907]
Dewey Co.(org.1895) (043)
Garvin Co.(org.1907) (049)
  [Chicakasw IT to 1907]
Greer Co.(pla.TX 1860,org.TX 1886,
  org.OK 1890(TX claim to 1896))
  (055)
Harmon Co.(org.1909) (057)
Haskell Co.(org.1907) (061)
  [Choctaw IT to 1907]

Jackson Co.(org.1907) (065)
Johnston Co.(org.1907) (069)
  [Chickasaw & Choctaw IT to 1907]
Latimer Co.(org.1907) (077)
  [Choctaw IT to 1907]
Le Flore Co.(org.1907) (079)
  [Choctaw IT to 1907]
Love Co.(org.1907) (085) [Chickasaw
  IT to 1907]
McClain Co.(org.1907) (087)
  [Chickasaw IT to 1907]
McCurtain Co.(org.1907) (089)
  [Choctaw IT to 1907]
McIntosh Co.(org.1907) (091)
  [Cherokee & Creek IT to 1907]
Major Co.(org.1907) (093) [Cherokee
  Strip IT to 1893]
Marshall Co.(org.1907) (095)
  [Chickasaw IT to 1907]
Mayes Co.(org.1907) (097) [Cherokee
  & Creek IT to 1907]
Osage Co.(org.1907) (113)
Ottawa Co.(org.1907) (115)
  [Cherokee,Seneca & 6 small tribes
  IT to 1907]
Pontotoc Co.(org.1907) (123)
  [Chickasaw & Choctaw IT to 1907]
Pushmataha Co.(org.1907) (127)
  [Choctaw IT to 1907]
Roger Mills Co.(org.1895) (129)
Rogers Co.(org.1907) (131)
  [Cherokee & Creek IT to 1907]
Seminole Co.(org.1907) (133)
  [Seminole & Creek IT to 1907]
Sequoyah Co.(org.1907) (135)
  [Cherokee IT to 1907]
Stephens Co.(org.1907) (137) [part
  Chickasaw IT to 1907]
Texas Co.(org.1907) (139)
Wagoner Co.(org.1907) (145)
  [Cherokee & Creek IT to 1907]
Washington Co.(org.1907) (147)
  [Cherokee IT to 1907]

SOUTH CAROLINA - 31 of 46

Abbeville Co.(org.Sub Co.1785,Dist.
  1799/1800) (001)
Allendale Co.(org.1919) (005)
Bamberg Co.(org.1897) (009)
Barnwell Co.(org.1798) (011)
Calhoun Co.(org.1908) (017)
Cherokee Co.(org.1897) (021)
Chesterfield Co.(org.Sub Co.1785,
  Dist.1799/1800) (025)
Clarendon Co.(org.1855) (027)
Darlington Co.(org.Sub Co.1785,
  Dist.1799/1800) (031)
Dillon Co.(org.1910) (033)

Edgefield Co.(org.Sub.Co.1785,Dist.
  1799/1800) (037)
Florence Co.(org.1888) (041)
Georgetown Co.(org.Gen.Dist.1769,
  Dist.1798) (043)
Hampton Co.(org.1878) (049)
Horry Co.(org.1801) (051)
Jasper Co.(org.1912) (053)
Kershaw Co.(org.Sub Co.1791,Dist.
  1799/1800) (055)
Lancaster Co.(org.Sub Co.1785,Dist.
  1799/1800) (057)
Laurens Co.(org.Sub Co.1785,Dist.
  1799/1800) (059)
Lee Co.(org.1902) (061)
McCormick Co.(org.1914/1917) (065)
Marion Co.(org.1799/1800) (067)
Marlboro Co.(org.Sub Co.1785,Dist.
  1799/1800) (069)
Oconee Co.(org.1868) (073)
Pickens Co.(org.1826) (077)
Saluda Co.(org.1895/1896) (081)
Spartanburg Co.(org.Sub Co.1785,
  Dist.1799/1800) (083)
Sumter Co.(org.1799/1800) (085)
Union Co.(org.Sub Co.1785,Dist.
  1799/1800) (087)
Williamsburg Co.(org.Sub Co.)1785,
  X:1799/1800;r.Dist.1804) (089)
York Co.(org.Sub Co.1785,Dist.1799/
  1800) (091)

TENNESSEE - 74 of 95

Bedford Co.(org.1807/1808) (003)
Benton Co.(org.1835) (005)
Bledsoe Co.(org.1807) (007)
Blount Co.(org.1795) (009)
Bradley Co.(org.1835) (011)
Cannon Co.(org.1836) (015)
Carroll Co.(org.1821) (017)
Carter Co.(org.1796) (019)
Cheatham Co.(org.1856) (021)
Chester Co.(org.1882) (023)
Clay Co.(org.1870) (027)
Cocke Co.(org.1797(nl.1800)) (029)
Coffee Co.(org.1836) (031)
Crockett Co.(org.1872) (033)
Decatur Co.(org.1845) (039)
DeKalb Co.(org.1837/1838) (041)
Dickson Co.(org.1803) (043)
Dyer Co.(org.1823) (045)
Fayette Co.(org.1824) (047)
Fentress Co.(org.1823) (049)
Gibson Co.(org.1823) (053)
Giles Co.(org.1809) (055)
Grainger Co.(org.1796) (057)
Hamblen Co.(org.1870) (063)
Hancock Co.(org.1844) (067)
Hardeman Co.(org.1823) (069)

Hardin Co.(org.1819) (071)
Hawkins Co.(org.1786/1787) (073)
Haywood Co.(org.1823) (075)
Henderson Co.(org.1821) (077)
Henry Co.(org.1821) (079)
Hickman Co.(org.1807) (081)
Houston Co.(org.1871) (083)
Humphreys Co.(org.1809) (085)
Jackson Co.(org.1801) (087)
Jefferson Co.(org.1792) (089)
Johnson Co.(org.1836) (091)
Lake Co.(org.1870) (095)
Lauderdale Co.(org.1835) (097)
Lawrence Co.(org.1817) (099)
Lewis Co.(org.1843) (101)
Lincoln Co.(org.1809) (103)
Loudon Co.(org.1870,f.Christiana to
  1870) (105)
McNairy Co.(org.1823) (109)
Macon Co.(org.1842) (111)
Madison Co.(org.1821) (113)
Marshall Co.(org.1836) (117)
Maury Co.(org.1807) (119)
Meigs Co.(org.1836) (121)
Monroe Co.(org.1819) (123)
Montgomery Co.(org.1796) (125)
Moore Co.(org.1871/1872) (127)
Overton Co.(org.1806) (133)
Perry Co.(org.1818) (135)
Pickett Co.(org.1881) (137)
Polk Co.(org.1839) (139)
Putnam Co.(org.1854) (141)
Robertson Co.(org.1796) (147)
Rutherford Co.(org.1803) (149)
Sequatchie Co.(org.1857) (153)
Sevier Co.(org.1794) (155)
Smith Co.(org.1799) (159)
Stewart Co.(org.1803) (161)
Sullivan Co.(org.1779) (163)
Sumner Co.(org.1786/1787) (165)
Tipton Co.(org.1823) (167)
Trousdale Co.(org.1870) (169)
Unicoi Co.(org.1875) (171)
Union Co.(org.1850/1854) (173)
Van Buren Co.(org.1840) (175)
Wayne Co.(org.1819) (181)
Weakley Co.(org.1823) (183)
Williamson Co.(org.1799) (187)
Wilson Co.(org.1799) (189)

TEXAS - 217 of 254

Andrews Co.(pla.1876,org.1910)
  (003)
Angelina Co.(org.1846) (005)
Aransas Co.(org.1871) (007)
Archer Co.(pla.1858,org.1880) (009)
Armstrong Co.(pla.1876,org.1890)
  (011)
Atascosa Co.(org.1856) (013)

Austin Co.(pla.1836,org.1837) (015)
Bailey Co.(pla.1876,org.1917) (017)
Bandera Co.(org.1856) (019)
Baylor Co.(pla.1858,org.1879) (023)
Bell Co.(org.1850,l.1860) (027)
Blanco Co.(org.1858) (031)
Borden Co.(pla.1876,org.1892) (033)
Bosque Co.(org.1854) (035)
Brazoria Co.(org.1836) (039)
Brazos Co.(pla.1841,org.1843,f.
  Navasota to 1842) (041)
Brewster Co.(org.1887) (043)
Briscoe Co.(pla.1876,org.1892)
  (045)
Brooks Co.(pla.1911,org.1912) (047)
Brown Co.(pla.1856,org.1858) (049)
Burleson Co.(org.1846) (051)
Burnet Co.(pla.1852,org.1854) (053)
Calhoun Co.(org.1846) (057)
Callahan Co.(pla.1858,org.1877)
  (059)
Carson Co.(pla.1876,org.1888) (065)
Castro Co.(pla.1876,org.1891) (069)
Chambers Co.(org.1858) (071)
Childress Co.(pla.1876,org.1887)
  (075)
Clay Co.(pla.1857,org.1873) (077)
Cochran Co.(pla.1876,org.1924)
  (079)
Coke Co.(org.1889) (081)
Coleman Co.(pla.1858,org.1924)
  (083)
Collin Co.(org.1846) (085)
Collingsworth Co.(pla.1876,org.
  1890) (087)
Colorado Co.(pla.1836,org.1837)
  (089)
Comal Co.(org.1846) (091)
Comanche Co.(org.1856) (093)
Concho Co.(pla.1858,org.1879) (095)
Cooke Co.(org.1848) (097)
Coryell Co.(org.1854) (099)
Cottle Co.(pla.1876,org.1892) (101)
Crane Co.(pla.1887,org.1927) (103)
Crockett Co.(pla.1875,org.1891)
  (105)
Crosby Co.(pla.1876,org.1886) (107)
Culberson Co.(pla.1911,org.1912)
  (109)
Dawson Co.(pla.1876,org.1905) (115)
Deaf Smith Co.(pla.1876,org.1890)
  (117)
Delta Co.(org.1870) (119)
Denton Co.(org.1846) (121)
De Witt Co.(org.1846) (123)
Dickens Co.(pla.1876,org.1891)
  (125)
Dimmit Co.(pla.1858,org.1880) (127)
Donley Co.(pla.1876,org.1882,f.
  Wegefarth to 1882) (129)

Duval Co.(pla.1858,org.1876) (131)
Eastland Co.(pla.1858,org.1873)
  (133)
Ector Co.(pla.1887,org.1891) (135)
Edwards Co.(pla.1858,org.1883)
  (137)
Ellis Co.(pla.1849,org.1850) (139)
Erath Co.(org.1856) (143)
Falls Co.(org.1850) (145)
Fisher Co.(pla.1876,org.1886) (151)
Floyd Co.(pla.1876,org.1890) (153)
Foard Co.(org.1891) (155)
Fort Bend Co.(org.1837) (157)
Franklin Co.(org.1875) (159)
Freestone Co.(pla.1850,org.1851)
  (161)
Frio Co.(pla.1858,org.1871) (163)
Gaines Co.(pla.1876,org.1905) (165)
Garza Co.(pla.1876,org.1907) (169)
Gillespie Co.(org.1848) (171)
Glasscock Co.(pla.1887,org.1893)
  (173)
Gonzales Co.(pla.1836,org.1837)
  (177)
Gray Co.(pla.1876,org.1902) (179)
Gregg Co.(org.1873) (183)
Grimes Co.(org.1846) (185)
Guadalupe Co.(org.1846) (187)
Hale Co.(pla.1876,org.1888) (189)
Hall Co.(pla.1876,org.1890) (191)
Hamilton Co.(pla.1842,org.1858)
  (193)
Hansford Co.(pla.1876,org.1889)
  (195)
Hardeman Co.(pla.1858,org.1884)
  (197)
Hardin Co.(org.1858) (199)
Harrison Co.(pla.1839,org.1842)
  (203)
Hartley Co.(pla.1876,org.1891)
  (205)
Haskell Co.(pla.1858,org.1885)
  (207)
Hays Co.(org.1848) (209)
Hemphill Co.(pla.1876,org.1887)
  (211)
Henderson Co.(org.1846) (213)
Hidalgo Co.(org.1852) (215)
Hill Co.(org.1853) (217)
Hockley Co.(pla.1876,org.1921)
  (219)
Hood Co.(pla.1865,org.1866) (221)
Hopkins Co.(org.1846) (223)
Houston Co.(org.1837) (225)
Howard Co.(pla.1876,org.1882) (227)
Hudspeth Co.(org.1917) (229)
Hunt Co.(org.1846) (231)
Hutchinson Co.(pla.1876,org.1901)
  (233)
Irion Co.(org.1889) (235)

Jack Co.(pla.1856,org.1857) (237)
Jackson Co.(pla.1836,org.1837)
  (239)
Jasper Co.(org.1836) (241)
Jeff Davis Co.(org.1887) (243)
Jim Hogg Co.(org.1913) (247)
Jim Wells Co.(pla.1911,org.1912)
  (249)
Jones Co.(pla.1858,org.1881) (253)
Kaufman Co.(pla.1848,org.1878)
  (257)
Kendall Co.(org.1862) (259)
Kenedy Co.(org.1911,f.Willacy to
  1921) (261)
Kent Co.(pla.1876,org.1892) (263)
Kerr Co.(org.1856) (265)
Kimble Co.(pla.1858,org.1876) (267)
King Co.(pla.1876,org.1891) (269)
Kinney Co.(pla.1850,org.1869) (271)
Kleberg Co.(org.1913) (273)
Knox Co.(pla.1858,org.1886) (275)
Lampasas Co.(org.1856) (281)
La Salle Co.(pla.1858,org.1880)
  (283)
Lavaca Co.(org.1846) (285)
Lee Co.(org.1874) (287)
Leon Co.(org.1846) (289)
Liberty Co.(org.1836) (291)
Limestone Co.(org.1846) (293)
Live Oak Co.(org.1856) (297)
Llano Co.(org.1856) (299)
Loving Co.(pla.1887,org.1931) (301)
Lubbock Co.(pla.1876,org.1891)
  (303)
Lynn Co.(pla.1876,org.1903) (305)
McCulloch Co.(pla.1856,org.1876)
  (307)
McLennan Co.(org.1850) (309)
McMullen Co.(pla.1858,org.1877)
  (311)
Madison Co.(pla.1842,org.1854)
  (313)
Martin Co.(pla.1876,org.1884) (317)
Mason Co.(org.1858) (319)
Matagorda Co.(org.1836) (321)
Maverick Co.(pla.1856,org.1871)
  (323)
Medina Co.(org.1848) (325)
Menard Co.(pla.1858,org.1871) (327)
Midland Co.(org.1885) (329)
Milam Co.(pla.1836,org.1837) (331)
Mills Co.(org.1887) (333)
Mitchell Co.(pla.1876,org.1881)
  (335)
Montague Co.(pla.1857,org.1858)
  (337)
Montgomercy Co.(org.1837) (339)
Moore Co.(pla.1876,org.1892) (341)
Morris Co.(org.1875) (343)
Motley Co.(pla.1876,org.1891) (345)

Navarro Co.(org.1846) (349)
Newton Co.(org.1846) (351)
Nolan Co.(pla.1876,org.1881) (353)
Ochiltree Co.(pla.1876,org.1889) (357)
Oldham Co.(pla.1876,org.1880) 359)
Orange Co.(org.1852) (361)
Palo Pinto (pla.1856,org.1857) (363)
Panola Co.(org.1846) (365)
Pecos Co.(pla.1871,org.1875) (371)
Polk Co.(org.1846) (373)
Presidio Co.(pla.1850,org.1875) (377)
Rains Co.(org.1870) (379)
Randall Co.(pla.1876,org.1889) (381)
Reagan Co.(org.1903) (383)
Real Co.(org.1913) (385)
Red River Co.(pla.1836,org.1837) (387)
Reeves Co.(pla.1883,org.1884) (389)
Refugio Co.(pla.1836,org.1837) (391)
Roberts Co.(pla.1876,org.1889) (393)
Robertson Co.(pla.1837,org.1838) (395)
Rockwall Co.(org.1873) (397)
Runnels Co.(pla.1858,org.1880) (399)
Rusk Co.(org.1843) (401)
Sabine Co.(pla.1836,org.1837) (403)
San Augustine Co.(pla.1836,org. 1837) (405)
San Jacinto Co.(org.1870) (407)
San Patricio Co.(pla.1836,org.1837) (409)
San Saba Co.(org.1856) (411)
Schleicher Co.(pla.1887,org.1901) (413)
Scurry Co.(pla.1876,org.1884) (415)
Shackelford Co.(pla.1858,org.1874) (417)
Shelby Co.(pla.1836,org.1837) (419)
Sherman Co.(pla.1876,org.1889) (421)
Somervell Co.(org.1875,f.Somerville to 1876) (425)
Starr Co.(org.1848(l.with Cameron 1850)) (427)
Stephens Co.(pla.1858,f.Buchanan to 1861,org.1876) (429)
Sterling Co.(org.1891) (431)
Stonewall Co.(pla.1876,org.1888) (433)
Sutton Co.(pla.1887,org.1890) (435)
Swisher Co.(pla.1876,org.1890) (437)
Taylor Co.(pla.1858,org.1878) (441)

Terrell Co.(org.1905) (443)
Terry Co.(pla.1876,org.1904) (445)
Throckmorton Co.(pla.1858,org.1879) (447)
Titus Co.(org.1846) (449)
Tom Green Co.(org.1874) (451)
Tyler Co.(org.1846) (457)
Upton Co.(pla.1887,org.1910) (461)
Uvalde Co.(pla.1850,org.1856) (463)
Val Verde Co.(org.1885) (465)
Victoria Co.(pla.1836,org.1837) (469)
Walker Co.(org.1846) (471)
Waller Co.(org.1873) (473)
Ward Co.(pla.1887,org.1892) (475)
Washington Co.(pla.1836,org.1837) (477)
Webb Co.(org.1848(l.with Cameron 1850)) (479)
Wharton Co.(org.1846) (481)
Wheeler Co.(pla.1876,org.1879) (483)
Wichita Co.(pla.1858,org.1882) (485)
Wilbarger Co.(pla.1858,org.1881) (487)
Willacy Co.(org.1921) (489)
Williamson Co.(org.1848) (491)
Wilson Co.(org.1860) (493)
Winkler Co.(pla.1887,org.1910) (495)
Wise Co.(org.1856) (497)
Wood Co.(org.1850) (499)
Yoakum Co.(pla.1876,org.1907) (501)
Young Co.(org.1856) (503)
Zapata Co.(org.1858) (505)
Zavala Co.(pla.1858,org.1884) (507)

VIRGINIA - 89 of 100

Alleghany Co.(org.1822) - Clifton Forge City - Covington City (005)
Amelia Co.(org.1734) (007)
Amherst Co.(org.1761) (009)
Appomattox Co.(org.1845) (011)
Augusta Co.(org.1745) - Staunton City - Waynesboro City (015)
Bath Co.(org.1790/1791,l.1800) (017)
Bedford Co.(org.1753/1754) - Bedford City (019)
Bland Co.(org.1861) (021)
Botetourt Co.(org.1769/1770) (023)
Brunswick Co.(org.1732) (025)
Buchanan Co.(org.1858) (027)
Campbell Co.(org.1781/1782) - Lynchburg City (031)
Caroline Co.(org.1727/1728) (033)
Carroll Co.(org.1842) - Galax City (035)

Charles City Co.(org.1634) (036)
Charlotte Co.(org.1764/1765) (037)
Chesterfield Co.(org.1749) - Colonial Heights City (041)
Clarke Co.(org.1836) (043)
Craig Co.(org.1851) (045)
Culpeper Co.(org.1748/1749) (047)
Cumberland Co.(org.1748/1749) (049)
Dickenson Co.(org.1880) (051)
Dinwiddie Co.(org.1752) - Petersburg City (053)
Essex Co.(org.1692) (057)
Fauquier Co.(org.1759) (061)
Floyd Co.(org.1831) (063)
Fluvanna Co.(org.1777) (065)
Franklin Co.(org.1785/1786) (067)
Frederick Co.(org.1743) - Winchester City (069)
Giles Co.(org.1806) (071)
Gloucester Co.(org.1651) (073)
Goochland Co.(org.1727/1728) (075)
Grayson Co.(org.1792/1793) (077)
Greene Co.(org.1838) (079)
Greensville Co.(org.1780/1781) - Emporia City (081)
Halifax Co.(org.1752) - South Boston City (083)
Hanover Co.(org.1720/1721) (085)
Henrico Co.(org.1634) - Richmond City (inclu.f.Manchester City) (087)
Henry Co.(org.1776/1777) - Martinsville City (089)
Highland Co.(org.1847) (091)
James City Co.(org.1634) - Williamsburg City (095)
King and Queen Co.(org.1691) (097)
King George Co.(org.1720/1721) (099)
King William Co.(org.1701/1702) (101)
Lancaster Co.(org.1651) (103)
Lee Co.(org.1792/1793) (105)
Loudoun Co.(org.1757) (107)
Louisa Co.(org.1742) (109)
Lunenburg Co.(org.1746) (111)
Madison Co.(org.1792/1793) (113)
Mathews Co.(org.1790/1791) (115)
Mecklenburg Co.(org.1764/1765) (117)
Middlesex Co.(org.1673/1674) (119)
Montgomery Co.(org.1776/1777) - Radford City (121)
Nelson Co.(org.1807/1808) (125)
New Kent Co.(org.1654) (127)
Northampton Co.(org.1634,f. Accawmack to 1642) (131)
Northumberland Co.(org.1648) (133)
Nottoway Co.(org.1788/1789,nl.1790) (135)

Orange Co.(org.1734) (137)
Page Co.(org.1831) (139)
Patrick Co.(org.1790/1791,l.1800)
 (141)
Pittsylvania Co.(org.1766/1767) -
 Danville City (143)
Powhatan Co.(org.1777) (145)
Prince Edward Co.(org.1753/1754)
 (147)
[Princess Anne Co.(org.1691,X
 1963)] - Virginia Beach City (151/
 810)
Pulaski Co.(org.1839) (155)
Rappahannock Co.(org.1833) (157)
Richmond Co.(org.1692) (159)
Roanoke Co.(org.1838) - Roanoke
 City - Salem City (161)
Rockbridge Co.(org.1778) - Buena
 Vista City - Lexington City (163)
Rockingham Co.(org.1778) -
 Harrisonburg City (165)
Russell Co.(org.1787) (167)
Scott Co.(org.1814) (169)
Shenandoah Co.(org.1772,f.Dunmore
 to 1778) (171)
Smyth Co.(org.1832) (173)
Southampton Co.(org.1749) -
 Franklin City (175)
Spotsylvania Co.(org.1720/1721) -
 Fredericksburg City (177)
Stafford Co.(org.1664) (179)
Surry Co.(org.1652) (181)
Sussex Co.(org.1753/1754) (183)
Tazewell Co.(org.1799/1800) (185)
Warren Co.(org.1836) (187)
[Warwick Co.(org.1634,X 1957)] -
 Newport News City (inclu.f.Warwick
 City) (189/700)
Washington Co.(org.1776/1777) -
 Bristol City (191)
Westmoreland Co.(org.1653) (193)
Wise Co.(org.1856) - Norton City
 (195)
Wythe Co.(org.1789/1790,l.1800)
 (197)
York Co.(org.1634,f.Charles River
 to 1642) - Poquoson City (199)

WEST VIRGINIA - 50 of 55

Barbour Co.(org.1843) (001)
Boone Co.(org.1847) (005)
Braxton Co.(org.1836) (007)
Brooke Co.(org.1796) (009)
Calhoun Co.(org.1856) (013)
Clay Co.(org.1858) (015)
Doddridge Co.(org.1845) (017)
Fayette Co.(org.1831) (019)
Gilmer Co.(org.1845) (021)
Grant Co.(org.1866) (023)

Greenbrier Co.(org.1778) (025)
Hampshire Co.(org.1753) (027)
Hancock Co.(org.1848) (029)
Hardy Co.(org.1785) (031)
Harrison Co.(org.1784) (033)
Jackson Co.(org.1831) (035)
Jefferson Co.(org.1801) (037)
Kanawha Co.(org.1789) (039)
Lewis Co.(org.1816) (041)
Lincoln Co.(org.1867) (043)
Logan Co.(org.1824) (045)
McDowell Co.(org.1858) (047)
Marion Co.(org.1842) (049)
Marshall Co.(org.1835) (051)
Mason Co.(org.1804) (053)
Mercer Co.(org.1837) (055)
Mineral Co.(org.1866) (057)
Mingo Co.(org.1895) (059)
Monongalia Co.(org.1776) (061)
Monroe Co.(org.1799) (063)
Morgan Co.(org.1820) (065)
Nicholas Co.(org.1818) (067)
Pendleton Co.(org.1787) (071)
Pleasants Co.(org.1851) (073)
Pocahontas Co.(org.1821) (075)
Preston Co.(org.1818) (077)
Putnam Co.(org.1848) (079)
Raleigh Co.(org.1850) (081)
Randolph Co.(org.1787) (083)
Roane Co.(org.1856) (087)
Summers Co.(org.1871) (089)
Taylor Co.(org.1844) (091)
Tucker Co.(org.1856) (093)
Tyler Co.(org.1814) (095)
Upshur Co.(org.1851) (097)
Webster Co.(org.1860) (101)
Wetzel Co.(org.1846) (103)
Wirt Co.(org.1848) (105)
Wood Co.(org.1798) (107)
Wyoming Co.(org.1850) (109)

APPENDIX I. - UNITARIAN CHURCHES (org.by 1851 outside primary Cong.fellowship)

A	B	C	D	E
	ALABAMA (01)			
	MOBILE COUNTY (097)			
1.	Mobile, Unitar.	1838	1845-1851	X af.1851
	DISTRICT OF COLUMBIA (11)			
	WASHINGTON (001)			
1.	Washington, All Souls Ch.,Unitar.(NW;f.First;lt.1846-1847)	1821	1845-1851	UUA
	GEORGIA (13)			
	CHATHAM COUNTY (051)			
1.	Savannah, Unitar.	1832	1845-1851	X af.1860
	RICHMOND COUNTY (245)			
1.	Augusta, First Unitar.	1831	1845-1851	X 1856
	KENTUCKY (21)			
	JEFFERSON COUNTY (111)			
1.	Louisville, First Unitar.Ch.of Messiah (also inclu. Ministry- at-large org.1845,l.1845-1849,X af.1846)	1830	1845-1851	UUA
	MARYLAND (24)			
	BALTIMORE CITY (007/510)			
1.	Baltimore, First Unitar.,Unitar.& Univ.(f.First Indep.Chr.; ab.Second Univ.Ch.of Our Father(1839)in c.1935;also inclu.Ministry-at-large org.1843,l.1845-1849,X af.1846)	1817	1845-1851	UUA
	VIRGINIA (51)			
	HENRICO COUNTY - RICHMOND CITY (087)			
1.	Richmond, First Indep.Chr.(l.27)	1830	nl.	X 1863

APPENDIX II. - CONGREGATIONAL CHRISTIAN CHURCHES

ALABAMA (01)

A	B	C	D	E
	CHAMBERS COUNTY (017)			
1.	Valley, Pine Forest Cong.UCC (f.Huguley CC;f.Highway CC; f.l. Lanett;incor.l.as Sch.I was Sch.II)	1941 1944(s.01)	1944-on	sch.II 1961-1962; sch.I 1962-1981; UCC 1981-on
2.	Valley, Todd CC (f.l.Shawmut to 1985)	1950	1950-on	UCC
	CHILTON COUNTY (021)			
1.	Jemison, Archie's Chap.CC(f.l.Clanton;f.Archer's Chap.)	1940	1940-1950	X
	COVINGTON COUNTY (039)			
1.	Andalusia, First CC	1943	1943-on	UCC
	LAWRENCE COUNTY (079)			
1.	Moulton, Bethlehem CC	1940	1940-1960	X
	RANDOLPH COUNTY (111)			
1.	Roanoke, Sweet Home CC	1957	1957-1965	Sch.II 1961; UCC late 1961-1965; x
	RUSSELL COUNTY (113)			
1.	Phenix City, Russell Woods CC	1957	1957-on	UCC
	TALLAPOOSA COUNTY (123)			
1.	Alexander City, First Cong.(UCC)(f.Hunt CC;j UCC 1962, incor. 1945 UCC late 1961-1962)	1945 1942(s.01)	1945-on	Sch.I 1961; UCC late 1961-on

FLORIDA (12)

A	B	C	D	E
	BREVARD COUNTY (009)			
1.	Cocoa Beach, Com.United	1942 1944(s.01) 1945(s.01)	1945-on	UCC

161

APPENDIX II. – CONGREGATIONAL CHRISTIAN CHURCHES – FLORIDA – continued

BROWARD COUNTY (011)

A	B	C	D	E
1.	Fort Lauderdale, First Cong.	1954	1954-on	UCC
2.	Hallandale, Union Cong.(poss.grew from 1901 Union Com.(49))	1942	1942-on	Sch.I 1961-1962; UCC 1962-on
3.	Hollywood, First Cong.UCC	1958	1958-1968	UCC; merged to form M.(q.v.)
3M.	Hollywood, First UCC (f.First United to 1970;l.Pres.:75:1968-1970;Merger of #3 & United Pres.(1966,l.75:1966-1968); Pres.withdrew (continues,l.Pres.:75:1970-on))	1959(s.01) 1968 M	1968-on	UCC (dual Pres.1968-1970,Pres.withdrew)
4.	Plantation, Com.(j NA(full)1979,incor.l.full 1978-1979)	1950 1948(s.04) 1974(s.04)	1950-1989	UCC 1961-1989; NA(Asso.)1976-1978; NA(Full)1978-on

DADE COUNTY (025)

A	B	C	D	E
1.	Bal Harbour, Ch.by the Sea(f.Surfside of Miami Beach)	1945	1945-on	UCC
2.	Miami, Christ Cong.(South of city)	1956	1956-on	UCC
3.	Miami, Key Biscayne Com.(not in city)	1952	1952-on	UCC
4.	Miami, Ch.of the Open Door	1959	1959-on	UCC
B1 5.	Miami Shores, Com.(f.Cooperative;Affl.only 1943-1959;s.in Counc.Com.Chs.)	1933 r.1968	1943-1959, 1968-on	UCC 1968-on (f.dual Disc.)

HILLSBOROUGH COUNTY (057)

A	B	C	D	E
1.	Tampa, Park Manor CC	1947	1947-1950	X

LEE COUNTY (071)

A	B	C	D	E
1.	Lehigh Acres, First Com.	1956	1957-on	UCC

MANATEE COUNTY (081)

A	B	C	D	E
1.	Bradenton, Cong.UCC (f.First UCC)	1958	1957-on	UCC

MONROE COUNTY (087)

A	B	C	D	E
1.	Key West, Poinciana Com.(also l.as SS: 1949-1951)	1945	1945-1949	X

ORANGE COUNTY (095)

A	B	C	D	E
1.	Windermere, Union	1916 1917(s.01)	1959-on	UCC

APPENDIX II. - CONGREGATIONAL CHRISTIAN CHURCHES - FLORIDA - continued

A	B	C	D	E
	PALM BEACH COUNTY (099)			
1.	Lake Park, Com.UCC	1926(49) 1929(s.01) r.1943(s.01)	1943-on	UCC
	PINELLAS COUNTY (103)			
1.	Indian Rocks Beach, Ch.of the Isles	1953	1953-on	UCC
2.	Madeira Beach, Ch.by the Sea (f.l.Saint Petersburg)	1944	1944-on	UCC
3.	Pass-a-Grille Beach, Com.	1915(s.01) 1917(s.01) r.1950	1949-on	UCC
4.	Saint Petersburg, Pilgrim Cong.	1955	1955-on	UCC
	SANTA ROSA COUNTY (113) [WEST]			
1.	Milton, Union Valley CC	1937	1937-1939	X
	SARASOTA COUNTY (115)			
1.	Sarasota, First Cong.	1954	1954-on	UCC
2.	Sarasota, Wide Fellowship Cong.(l.in 41,49)	1935	nl.	prob.X (af.1942)
	VOLUSIA COUNTY (127)			
1.	Samsula, CC (Christ Cong.Com.)	1930(01) 1939(49)	1938-1945	X
	WALTON COUNTY (131) [WEST]			
1.	Lakewood, First United CC (EARLY LIST:CC)	1932	1932-1937	X (dual Cong. & Chr. 1932-1934)
	GEORGIA (13)			
	COFFEE COUNTY (069)			
1.	Douglas, First Cong.	1950	1950-1985	UCC 1961-1963;Sch.II 1963-1985; NA(Affl.) 1966(j 1967)-on
	FULTON COUNTY (121)			
B1 1.	Atlanta, Carroll Heights CC	1960	1960-on	UCC

APPENDIX II. - CONGREGATIONAL CHRISTIAN CHURCHES - GEORGIA - continued

A	B	C	D	E
	TIFT COUNTY (277)			
1.	Tifton, First CC	1952	1952-1985	Sch.II 1961-1985; NA (Affl.)1968 or 1969-1979; X
	TROUP COUNTY (285)			
1.	West Point, Bethel CC	1948	1948-1990	UCC 1961-1990; withdrew
	KENTUCKY (21)			
	CARTER COUNTY (043)			
1.	Smiths Creek, Grassy Chr. (Affl.KY North)	1937	1938-1948	prob. withdrew
	FAYETTE COUNTY (067)			
1.	Lexington, Southside Cong.	1950	1950-1952	X
	LOUISIANA (22)			
	ALLEN PARISH (003)			
1.	LeBlanc, Cong. (Ward 3)	1937	1937-1945	X
	BEAUREGARD PARISH (011)			
1.	Ragley, Gaytine CC (Ward 6)	1942	1943-on	Sch.I
	CALCASIEU PARISH (019)			
1.	Lake Charles, East Broad Com. (prob.Ward 3)	1944	1944-1945	X
2.	Lake Charles, Moss Bluff Chap. (Ward 1)	1943	1944-1955	withdrew
	JEFFERSON DAVIS PARISH (053)			
1.	Kinder, Edna Cong. (Ward 5)	1935	1935-1977	Sch.I; X
	OUACHITA PARISH (073)			
1.	West Monroe, CC (Ward 5)	1945	1945-1946	merged to # 6M1. (main list) (q.v.)

APPENDIX II. - CONGREGATIONAL CHRISTIAN CHURCHES - LOUISIANA - continued

UNION PARISH (111)

A	B	C	D	E
	1. Downsville, Mount Nebo Cong.(Ward 5)	1935	1935-1938	X
	2. Linville, UCC (or Lineville;f.l.Marion;Ward 2 or 8)	1935	1935-1938,	UCC; X
		r.1950	1950-1965	

MARYLAND (24)

MONTGOMERY COUNTY (031)

A	B	C	D	E
	1. Bethesda, UCC (f.Cong.;Dist.7)	1957	1957-on	UCC
	2. Silver Spring, Christ Cong.(Dist.13)	1944	1944-on	UCC
	3. Spencerville, Mount Calvary Cong.(Dist.5)	1942	1944-1956	X

PRINCE GEORGES COUNTY (033)

A	B	C	D	E
	1. Greenbelt, Com. (Dist.21:*Berwyn)	1937	1948-on	UCC

NORTH CAROLINA (37)

ALAMANCE COUNTY (001)

A	B	C	D	E
B1	1. Burlington, Beverly Hills CC (Twn.# 4-*Morton)	1951	1951-on	UCC
B1	2. Burlington, Chr.Tabernacle UCC (Twn.# 4-*Morton;incor.l.as Sch.I,was Sch.II)	1947	1951-on	Sch.II 1961-1962; sch.I 1962-1967; UCC 1967-on
	3. Burlington, Lakeview CC (Twn.# 5-*Faucette)	1952	1952-on	UCC
	4. Burlington, Zion CC (Twn.# 2-*Coble,nr.Glen Raven)	1948	1948-on	UCC
B1	5. Graham, Ruffins Chap.(f.l.Burlington;Twn.# 6-Graham,or Twn.# 12-Burlington)	1948(04)	1951-1955	NA(Affl.)1964 or
		1950(01)		1965-on

BRUNSWICK COUNTY (019)

A	B	C	D	E
B1	1. Leland, Chr.Hope (*Northwest Twn.)	1943	1943-1965	Sch.I; X

CHATHAM COUNTY (037)

A	B	C	D	E
B1	1. Siler City, Goldston Mission CC (*Matthews Twn.)	1935	1935-1951	X
		1925(s.01)		

CUMBERLAND COUNTY (051)

A	B	C	D	E
B1	1. Fayetteville, Eutaw Com.UCC (*Cross Creek Twn.)	1951	1951-on	UCC
	2. Hope Mills, CC (*Rockfish Twn.)	1939	1939-on	UCC

APPENDIX II. - CONGREGATIONAL CHRISTIAN CHURCHES - NORTH CAROLINA - continued

A	B	C	D	E
	DURHAM COUNTY (063)			
B1	1. Durham, Mount Calvary CC	1898	1935-on	UCC
	EDGECOMBE COUNTY (065)			
B1	1. Bricks, Franklinton Com.(Twn.# 6-*Upper Fishing Creek)	1955	1955-1990, 1992-on	UCC
	FORSYTH COUNTY (067)			
	1. Pfafftown, Com.(*Old Town Twn.)	1941 1940(s.01)	1941-on	UCC
	2. Winston-Salem, Parkway UCC (f.United CC;f.First CC;EARLY LIST:CC;*Winston Twn.)	1933 1932(s.01)	1932-on	UCC (dual Cong.& Chr. 1932-1934)
	GUILFORD COUNTY (081)			
	1. Gibsonville, CC (*Rock Creek Twn.)	1939	1939-1970	Sch.II; withdrew
	2. Greensboro, Calvary CC (*Jamestown Twn.)	1940	1951-1992	Sch.I; withdrew
	3. High Point, East Green CC	1934	1934-1939	X
	HENDERSON COUNTY (089)			
	1. Hendersonville, First Cong.(f.CC)	1950	1953-on	UCC
	HERTFORD COUNTY (091)			
B1	1. Tunis, First Chr.(*Winton Twn.)	1954	1954-1960	X
	LEE COUNTY (105)			
	1. Sanford, Northview UCC(f.Com.;Twn.# 6-*West Sanford)	1958	1958-on	UCC
	MONTGOMERY COUNTY (123)			
	1. Biscoe, Flint Hill Chr.(Star PO)	1932	1934-1982	UCC;prob. withdrew
	NORTHAMPTON COUNTY (131)			
B1	1. Jackson, Spring CC	1936	1936-1939	X

APPENDIX II. - CONGREGATIONAL CHRISTIAN CHURCHES - NORTH CAROLINA - continued

ONSLOW COUNTY (133)

A		B	C	D	E
B1	1.	Jacksonville, First CC	1957	1957-on	Sch.I 1961; UCC late 1961-on

ORANGE COUNTY (135)

A		B	C	D	E
B1	1.	Chapel Hill, Alston Grove CC (f.l.Auston Grove(s.04))	1926	1952-1990	Sch.I 1961-1990; NA(Affl.)1970-on
B1	2.	Chapel Hill, Neville's Chap.(f.Children's Chap.)	1944	1945-on	Sch.I 1961-1969; UCC 1969-on

RANDOLPH COUNTY (151)

A		B	C	D	E
B1	1.	Asheboro, UCC (f.CC)	1939	1939-on	UCC

RICHMOND COUNTY (153)

A		B	C	D	E
B1	1.	Hamlet, First CC (*Marks Creek Twn.)	1935	1935-1939	X

VANCE COUNTY (181)

A		B	C	D	E
B1	1.	Henderson, Ebenezer CC (f.l.Clarksville,Mecklenburg Co.,VA; j UCC late 1961;incor.l.Sch.I late 1961-1969,was UCC)	1926	1935-1982	Sch.I 1961-1969; UCC 1969-1982; X

WAKE COUNTY (183)

A		B	C	D	E
B1	1.	Garner, Trinity Com.(*Saint Marys Twn.)	1960	1960-1971	UCC; X
B1	2.	Zebulon, New Bethel UCC (*Marks Creek Twn.)	1940 1896(s.01)	1940-on	Sch.I 1961-1965; UCC 1965-on

WARREN COUNTY (185)

A		B	C	D	E
B1	1.	Elam, Elam Chap.(f.l.Keats,Mecklenburg Co.,VA PO;*Roanoke Twn.)	1930	1935-on	Sch.I 1961-1973; UCC 1973-on

WAYNE COUNTY (191)

A		B	C	D	E
B1	1.	Mount Olive, Stanley Chap.(*Broyden Twn.)	1940	1940-1954	X

OKLAHOMA (40)

PAWNEE COUNTY (117)

A		B	C	D	E
B1	1.	Jennings, Com.	1938	1938-1946	X

APPENDIX II. - CONGREGATIONAL CHRISTIAN CHURCHES - OKLAHOMA - PAWNEE COUNTY - continued

A	B	C 1925	D 1936-1940	E
2.	Ralston, Fed. (Fed.unknown)			X
	TEXAS COUNTY (139)			
Gr 1.	Hooker, St.Johnannes Ger.Cong.(St.John;also l.(82)1932-1934)	1906 1905(82)	1936-1958	X
	TULSA COUNTY (143)			
1.	Tulsa, Fellowship Cong.	1950	1950-on	UCC
	TENNESSEE (47)			
	DAVIDSON COUNTY (037)			
1.	Nashville, Brookmeade United Cong.(f.Pilgrim Chap.)	1953	1953-on	UCC
	KNOX COUNTY (093)			
1.	Knoxville, Ch.of the Saviour, UCC (f.First Cong.)	1956	1957-on	UCC
	WHITE COUNTY (185)			
1.	DeRossett, Com.	1934	1934-1936	X
	TEXAS (48)			
	DALLAS COUNTY (113)			
1.	Dallas, First Com.UCC	1949	1953-on	UCC
	HARRIS COUNTY (201)			
1.	Houston, First Cong.(*Hunters Creek Village)	1955	1956-on	UCC
2.	Houston, First Unitar.(affl.only;f.Unitar.)	1914	1946-1950	(Dual Unitar.); Tr. to Unitar.;UUA
3.	Pasadena, Cong.	1956	1956-1960	X
	JEFFERSON COUNTY (245)			
B1 1.	Beaumont, Mayflower Cong.	1938	1938-1944	Merged to # 2 (main list) (q.v.)

APPENDIX II. - CONGREGATIONAL CHRISTIAN CHURCHES - continued

VIRGINIA (51)

A	B	C	D	E
	CAMPBELL COUNTY - LYNCHBURG CITY (031)			
1.	Lynchburg, Ch.of the Covenant	1954	1954-on	UCC
	CARROLL COUNTY - GALAX CITY (035)			
1.	Fancy Gap, Ivy Hill CC	1936	1936-1949	X
	FAIRFAX COUNTY - FALLS CHURCH CITY - FAIRFAX CITY (059)			
1.	Annadale, Little River UCC (f. CC of Fairfax Co.)	1955	1955-on	UCC
	HALIFAX COUNTY - SOUTH BOSTON CITY (083)			
1.	South Boston, Center CC	1954	1954-on	UCC
	HENRICO COUNTY - RICHMOND CITY (087)			
B1 1.	Richmond, Beautiful Star CC	bf.1947 r.1952	1952-1983	Sch. I; withdrew
B1 2.	Richmond, Rising Union CC	1938	1939-1954	X
	[NORFOLK COUNTY] CHESAPEAKE CITY - NORFOLK CITY - PORTSMOUTH CITY (129/710)			
1.	Chesapeake, Com.of South Norfolk	1957 1956(s.01)	1957-1959	X
B1 2.	Norfolk, Coronado UCC	1958	1957-1968	UCC; X
3.	Norfolk, Little Creek Chr.	1938 1939(s.01)	1938-1991	UCC; withdrew
4.	Portsmouth, United CC	1958	1958-on	UCC
	PRINCE GEORGE COUNTY - HOPEWELL CITY (149)			
1.	Prince George, CC (*Bland Dist.)	1958	1958-on	Sch.II 1961; UCC late 1961-on
	[PRINCESS ANNE COUNTY] VIRGINIA BEACH CITY (151/810)			
1.	Virginia Beach, Bayside UCC (f.l.Norfolk,Norfolk Co.)	1954	1954-on	UCC
2.	Virginia Beach, Lynnhaven Colony Cong.(f.Com.)	1958	1959-on	UCC

169

A	B	C	D	E

APPENDIX. II. - CONGREGATIONAL CHRISTIAN CHURCHES - VIRGINIA - continued
ROCKBRIDGE COUNTY - LEXINGTON CITY - BUENA VISTA CITY (163)

A	B	C	D	E
	1. Oak Dale, Associate CC (Dist.uncertain)	1952	1952-1956	X

SUSSEX COUNTY (183)

A	B	C	D	E
B1	1. Wakefield, Pocohontas Temple CC	1938 1838([sic] s.01)	1939-1983	sch.I 1961-1963; UCC 1963-1983; withdrew

[WARWICK COUNTY] NEWPORT NEWS CITY (189/700)

A	B	C	D	E
B1	1. Newport News, Angelic CC	1956	1957-1959	X
B1	2. Newport News, CC of Warwick	1954	1954-on	UCC

170

APPENDIX III. - UNITED CHURCH OF CHRIST CONGREGATIONS

A	B	C	D	E
	ALABAMA (01)			
	MADISON COUNTY (089)			
1.	Huntsville, UCC (lt.1961-1963)	1960	1961-on	UCC
	MONTGOMERY COUNTY (101)			
1.	Montgomery, United Ch.of South Montgomery	1961	1961-1972	UCC; X
	ARKANSAS (05)			
	MILLER COUNTY (091)			
Bl 1.	Texarkana, Bethel United (f.New Bethel United Pres.,Tr.from Pres.(1.75:1939-1969;*Garland Twn.)	c.1939	1969-1975	UCC; X
	DELAWARE (10)			
	NEW CASTLE COUNTY (003)			
1.	Newark, New Ark UCC	1981	1981-on	UCC
	DISTRICT OF COLUMBIA (11)			
	WASHINGTON (001)			
Bl 1.	Washington, Faith UCC (NE)	1980	1980-on	UCC
Hu 2.	Washington, Hungarian Ref.(moved to Bethesda, Montgomery Co., MD (q.v.);affl.Calvin Synod;Fed.unknown)	1971	1982-1983	UCC; moved (see text)
	FLORIDA (12)			
	ALACHUA COUNTY (001)			
1.	Gainesville, United	1965	1966-on	UCC
	BREVARD COUNTY (009)			
1.	Melbourne, Crossroads Com.UCC (f.UCC of Eau Gaille to 1988)	1964	1965-on	UCC
Nt	Palm Bay, West UCC (1.as prps.1989-on)	1965(s.01)		UCC
2.	Rockledge, Hope UCC	1964	1964-on	UCC

171

APPENDIX III. - UNITED CHURCH OF CHRIST CHURCHES - FLORIDA - continued

A	B	C	D	E
	BROWARD COUNTY (011)			
1.	Tamarac, Faith UCC (f.l.PO:Fort Lauderdale(Oakland Park))	1968	1968-on	UCC
Nt	Weston, West Broward Co.UCC (l.as prps.1988-1989)			UCC; X
	CHARLOTTE COUNTY (015)			
1.	Port Charlotte, Pilgrim United	1967	1966-on	UCC
2.	Punta Gorda, Cong.United	1984	1983-on	UCC
	CITRUS COUNTY (017)			
1.	Citrus Springs, Com.CC(f.l.Dunnellon PO,Marion Co.)	1973 1977(s.04)	1973-1974	UCC 1973-1974; NA 1982-on
	CLAY COUNTY (019)			
1.	Middleburg, Family of God Ch.	1987	1988-on	UCC
2.	Orange Park, Morningside Cong.(f. of Jacksonville, Duval Co.to 1978;f.Morningside Bapt.(f.in American Bapt.Chs.,poss.f. dual))	1988(s.01) 1959 r.1978	1965-1992	UCC (see text); X
	COLLIER COUNTY (021)			
1.	Marco Island, United	1968	1968-on	UCC
2.	Naples, Mayflower UCC (f.Southeast;also l.as prps.1988-1989)	1989	1989-on	UCC
3.	Naples, Naples UCC	1973	1973-on	UCC
	DADE COUNTY (025)			
1.	Miami, Carol City UCC (also l.as prps.1989-1990)	1990	1990-on	UCC
Sp 2.	Miami, Casa de Oracion UCC (*Hialeah)	1984 r.1988	1988-on	UCC
Sp 3.	Miami, El Shaddai UCC(f.Kendall Hispanic UCC (also l.as prps. 1989-1990))	1992 1990(s.01)	1990-on	UCC
Hu 4.	Miami, Magyar Chr.Ref.(f.Chr.Ref.;affl.Calvin Synod;west of city)	1963	1963-1972	UCC; X
Sp 5.	Miami, Spanish UCC (west of city;*Coral Gables)	1978	1978-1986	UCC; X
6.	Miami, Sunset Cong.UCC (f.Cross of Glory UCC;f.Southwest United;west of city)	1963	1963-on	UCC
7.	Miami Lakes, Cong.UCC	1964	1964-on	UCC
Fl 8.	Miami Shores, Spanish-Filipino UCC (f.First Filipino UCC; f.l.Miami;m.1980 in 80)	1978(01)	1986-1989	UCC; X

APPENDIX III. - UNITED CHURCH OF CHRIST CHURCHES - FLORIDA - continued

DUVAL COUNTY (031)

A	B	C	D	E
B1				
1.	Jacksonville, Amistad UCC (f.Northwest)	1978	1978-1985	UCC; X
2.	Jacksonville, First Coast UCC of Jacksonville Beach (l.as prps.1991-1992)	1992	1992-on	UCC
	ESCAMBIA COUNTY (033) [WEST]			
1.	Pensacola Beach, Com.United (affl.FL Conf.)	1978	1978-on	UCC
	FLAGLER COUNTY (035)			
1.	Palm Coast, UCC (nr.Flagler Beach)	1986	1982-1988	UCC; X 1987
	HERNANDO COUNTY (053)			
1.	Ridge Manor, All Faiths Com.UCC	1960	1982-on	UCC
2.	Spring Hill, Spring Hill Cong.UCC	1961(s.01) 1978	1978-on	UCC
	HIGHLANDS COUNTY (055)			
1.	Sebring, Emmanuel UCC (also l.as prps.1988-1989)	1989	1989-on	UCC
	HILLSBOROUGH COUNTY (057)			
1.	Brandon, St.Mark United Ch.of Brandon/Valrico (f.UCC, Riverview PO)	1983 1981(s.01)	1981-on	UCC
2.	Sun City Center, United Com.	1963	1963-on	UCC
3.	Tampa, Faith UCC (f.Northwest)	1986	1982-1991	UCC; X
4.	Tampa, United Com.Ch.of North Tampa	1990	1992-on	UCC
	INDIAN RIVER COUNTY (061)			
1.	Sebastian, United Ch.,UCC	1986	1985-on	UCC
2.	Vero Beach, Com.(s.in Counc.Com.Chs.;lt.41;f.l.Vero(s.41))	1924 r.1974	1974-on	UCC
	LAKE COUNTY (069)			
1.	Leesburg, Pilgrim's UCC	1990 1988(s.01)	1989-on	UCC

APPENDIX III. – UNITED CHURCH OF CHRIST CHURCHES – FLORIDA – continued

A	B	C	D	E
	LEE COUNTY (071)			
1.	Bonita Springs, Com.Cong.UCC	1982	1981-on	UCC
2.	Cape Coral, Colonial UCC	1983	1982-on	UCC
3.	Fort Myers, First UCC	1963	1963-1967	UCC; X
4.	Fort Myers, Fort Myers Cong.UCC	1976	1976-on	UCC
5.	Fort Myers, Reconciler UCC (Fed.to Colonial Rd.United Pres. (f.Mount Hope Pres,1.75:1956-1972)1970-1972)	1970	1970-1972	UCC; merged to form M. (q.v.)
5M.	Fort Myers, St. Marks Com.(merger of # 5 & Colonial Rd.United Pres.(see under # 5);1.75:1972-1975)	1972 M	1972-1974	UCC(dual Pres.); X (1975 in Pres.)
6.	Fort Myers, The Pilgrims Ch.	1987	1990-on	UCC
7.	Sanibel Island, Sanibel UCC	1977	1977-on	UCC
	LEON COUNTY (073)			
1.	Tallahassee, United Ch.	1975	1975-on	UCC
	MANATEE COUNTY (081)			
1.	Bradenton, Faith UCC	1988	1988-on	UCC
	MARION COUNTY (083)			
1.	Ocala, First Cong. (f.UCC)	1984, 1985(s.01)	1983-on	UCC
2.	Ocala, UCC (f.The Lord's Chap.)	1974	1987-on	UCC
	MARTIN COUNTY (085)			
1.	Jensen Beach, Com.(f.Union;f.of Jensen;f.in Counc.Com.Chs.bf. 1980)	1908(49) r.1980	1980-on	UCC
2.	Stuart, Christ Ch.	1984	1984-on	UCC
	MONROE COUNTY (087)			
1.	Tavernier, Coral Isle UCC (f.l.Islamorada)	1963	1963-on	UCC
	ORANGE COUNTY (095)			
1.	Orlando, First UCC (EARLY LIST;lt.1961-1962)	1959, 1960(s.01)	1959-on	UCC(dual CC & E&R 1959-1961)
2.	Orlando, Friends UCC (f.Southwest)	1986	1985-1989	UCC; X
3.	Orlando, University UCC (f.l.Winter Park to 1983)	1969	1969-on	UCC
B1 4.	Orlando, Victory UCC (f.Victory Chr.Assembly)	1988	1989-on	UCC

APPENDIX III. - UNITED CHURCH OF CHRIST CHURCHES - FLORIDA - continued

A	B	C	D	E
	OSCEOLA COUNTY (097)			
1.	Kissimmee, Emmanuel UCC (f.Southeast of Orlando, Orange Co. to 1989)	1987 1986(s.01)	1985-on	UCC
	PALM BEACH COUNTY (099)			
1.	Boca Raton, Cong.(UCC)	1964	1964-on	UCC
2.	Boynton Beach, Cong.UCC	1975	1975-on	UCC
3.	Delray Beach, Ch.of the Palms	1961	1961-on	UCC
4.	Jupiter, First UCC	1983	1982-on	UCC
5.	West Palm Beach, Pine Lake UCC	1971	1971-1974	UCC; X
	PASCO COUNTY (101)			
Nt	East Pasco Co., (l.as prps.1989-1990)			
1.	Holiday, UCC (Forest Hills Com.)	1967 1968(s.01)	1968-on	UCC; X UCC
Nt	Mid Pasco Co., (l.as prps.1989-1990)			
2.	New Port Richey, St.Marks United Ch.of Bayonet Point (supposedly dual to Pres.U.S.,but nl.there)	c.1973	1973-1974	UCC; X UCC(dual see text); X
3.	Zephyrhills, Bradford UCC	1977	1977-on	UCC
	PINELLAS COUNTY (103)			
1.	Clearwater, Faith UCC (EARLY LIST;lt.1961-1962;on CC list as a note 1959-1960)	1960	1959-on	UCC (dual CC & E&R 1959-1961)
2.	Pinellas Park, Good Samaritan Ch.(1.Pres.(75):1970-on)	1970	1970-on	UCC (dual Pres.,see text)
3.	Saint Petersburg, Lakewood UCC (f.All Saints Luth.)	1960 r.1967	1968-on	UCC
4.	Seminole, Chap.on the Hill UCC (f.Ridgewood Com.)	1963	1963-on	UCC
	POLK COUNTY (105)			
1.	Babson Park, Com. (poss.f.Pres.)	1921(01,97) 1932(49) r.1981	1981-1989	UCC; withdrew
2.	Lakeland, UCC	1968	1968-1970	UCC; X
Nt	Lakeland, UCC (l.as prps.1989-1990)			
3.	Winter Haven, Trinity Cong.UCC	1982 1981(s.01)	1981-on	UCC; X UCC

175

APPENDIX III. - UNITED CHURCH OF CHRIST CHURCHES - FLORIDA - continued

A	B	C	D	E
	SAINT JOHNS COUNTY (109)			
1.	Saint Augustine, Pilgrim Ch.,UCC	1987	1984-on	UCC
	SAINT LUCIE COUNTY (111)			
1.	Fort Pierce, First Cong.(f.Pilgrim Way Ch.)	1985	1982-on	UCC
2.	Port Saint Lucie, Faith UCC (f.St.Lucie West;also l.as prps. 1989-1990)	1990	1990-on	UCC
3.	Port Saint Lucie, First Cong.UCC	1979	1979-on	UCC
	SARASOTA COUNTY (115)			
Nt	Englewood, Englewood UCC of Englewood-Murdock(Murdock, Collier Co.);l.as prps.1989-1990)			UCC; X
1.	Northport, Northport Com.United (f.l.Warm Mineral Springs, Englewood PO)	1969 1970(s.01)	1970-on	UCC
2.	Sarasota, St. Andrew UCC	1965	1965-on	UCC
3.	Venice, Venice UCC	1962 1963(s.01)	1963-on	UCC
	SEMINOLE COUNTY (117)			
1.	Altamonte Springs, Altamonte Chap.Com.(UCC)(f.Altamonte Chap.,f.Lake Brantley Union Chap.to 1906(49);41:lt.as Union of Alamonte(here) & Lake Brantley Union Chap.in Orange Co.;18 says moved Lake Brantley to Altamonte Springs af.1897;see # 3 main list;in 1884 bldg.)	1885(01) 1884(49)	1965-on	UCC
2.	Sanford, Chr.Fellowship UCC (f.Northwest of Orlando, Orange Co.to 1988)	1987	1985-on	UCC
3.	Winter Springs, St.Gabriels UCC (f.Tuscawilla UCC,f. Northeast,f.North;l.Orlando,Orange Co.)	1986	1985-on	UCC
	VOLUSIA COUNTY (127)			
1.	Deltona, UCC (f.United,f.l.Orange City)	1965	1965-on	UCC
2.	Edgewater, Edgewater Union (f.Com.;New Smyrna PO(41);nl.49; s.in Counc.Com.Chs.)	1914	1988-on	UCC
3.	Port Orange, United UCC	1979	1979-on	UCC
	UNLOCATED CHURCHES (999)			
Nt	Viera, East UCC (l.as prps.1989-1990)			UCC; X

APPENDIX III. - UNITED CHURCH OF CHRIST CHURCHES - continued

A	B	C	D	E
	GEORGIA (13)			
	CLAYTON COUNTY (063)			
1.	Jonesboro, Trinity United (f.Bonanza Com.UCC)	1968	1968-on	UCC
	COBB COUNTY (067)			
1.	Marietta, Pilgrimage UCC (f.Fellowship of the United Ch.in Cobb Co.)	1977	1977-on	UCC
	FULTON COUNTY (121)			
Bl 1.	Atlanta, Atlanta UCC	1986	1986-on	UCC
Bl 2.	Atlanta, Southwest Cong.(f.AME)	1978(AME) 1979(01)	1979-1981	UCC; X
	GWINNETT COUNTY (135)			
1.	Lilburn, Button Gwinnett UCC	1979	1979-on	UCC
	KENTUCKY (21)			
	BOONE COUNTY (015)			
Nt	Florence, Boone County UCC(l.as prps. 1990-on;affl.OH)			UCC
	JEFFERSON COUNTY (111)			
1.	Louisville, Calvary UCC (f.Fern Creek,SE of city)	by 1965	1965-1969	UCC; X
2.	Louisville, Chapel Hill UCC (*Shivley)	1963	1962-on	UCC
3.	Louisville, Faith UCC (*Middletown)	1984	1984-on	UCC
	LOUISIANA (22)			
	EAST BATON ROUGE PARISH (033)			
1.	Baton Rouge, First United (Ward 1)	1984	1984-on	UCC

A	B	C	D	E
	APPENDIX III. - UNITED CHURCH OF CHRIST CHURCHES - continued			
	MARYLAND (24)			
	ANNE ARUNDEL COUNTY (003)			
1.	Annapolis, UCC Edgewater (Dist.2;lt.1962-1965; claim is as successor to St.Martin's Evan.(f.Markus,org.1874,1875, or 1876;majority Tr.to United Luth.1962(l.there 1961) divided))	1962 / 1876(claim)	1962-on	UCC
2.	Glen Burnie, Ch.of the Good Shepherd (Dist.5;lt.1962-1965)	1963	1962-1967	UCC; X
	BALTIMORE CITY (007/510)			
Bl 1.	Baltimore, Heritage UCC (f.Northwest;lt.1963-1965)	1963	1963-on	UCC
	CARROLL COUNTY (013)			
1.	Eldersburg, Our Saviour UCC (Dist.# 5-*Freedom;lt.1963-1965)	by 1963	1963-1970	UCC; X
	HOWARD COUNTY (027)			
1.	Columbia, United Chr.(f.Oakland Mills Uniting Cgn.to r.; Dist.# 6-*Savage;pr.1970)	1972 / r.1988	1970-on	UCC (dual Ch.of the Brethren)
	MONTGOMERY COUNTY (031)			
Hu 1.	Bethesda, Hungarian Ref.(moved from Washington,DC (q.v.) 1983;affl.Calvin Synod;Fed.unknown;Dist.7)	1971	1983-on	UCC
2.	Germantown, UCC of Seneca Valley (f.l.Gaithersburg;Dist.9)	1980 / 1984(s.01)	1984-on	UCC
3.	Wheaton, Pilgrim UCC (f.North Wheaton of Silver Spring;lt. 1962-1965;Dist.13)	1963	1961-on	UCC
	PRINCE GEORGES COUNTY (033)			
1.	Bowie, United Par.Ch.,Belair Village (l.Pres.(75) 1977-on, (also to Pres.U.S.1977-1983);Dist.7-*Queen Anne)	1977(full) / 1970(s.01)	1970-on	UCC (dual Pres., see text)
2.	Oxon Hill, United Cgn.(dual unknown;Dist.12-Oxon Hill)	1970	1970-1974	UCC(dual);Tr.to other denomination
Bl Nt	Upper Marlboro, Amistad UCC (Dist.# 3-*Marlboro;l.as prps. 1989-on)			UCC

APPENDIX III. - UNITED CHURCH OF CHRIST CHURCHES - continued

MISSISSIPPI (28)

HINDS COUNTY (049)

A	B	C	D	E
1.	Jackson, Ecumenical Fellowship of Reconciliation	1969	1971-1972	UCC; X

NORTH CAROLINA (37)

ALAMANCE COUNTY (001)

A	B	C	D	E
1.	Burlington, Edgewood UCC (EARLY LIST,lt.1961-1966;Twn.# 12)	1959	1959-1978	UCC(dual CC & E&R 1959-1961);merged to form M. (q.v.)
1M.	Burlington, First Chr.(merger of # 1 & First Chr.(1884);Twn.# 4-*Morton)	1978 M	1978-on	UCC
2.	Burlington, New Mission UCC (prob.Twn.# 12)	1989	1989-on	UCC
B1 3.	Burlington, Vistors Chap.UCC (Twn.# 4-*Morton)	1974	1974-on	UCC

CATAWBA COUNTY (035)

A	B	C	D	E
1.	Hickory, Ch.of the Master, UCC	1964	1964-on	UCC

CHATHAM COUNTY (037)

A	B	C	D	E
1.	Siler City, Mission UCC (*Matthews Twn.)	1964	1965-1967	UCC; X

DURHAM COUNTY (063)

A	B	C	D	E
B1 1.	Durham, Monroe Chap.	1980	1980-1987	UCC; withdrew

GUILFORD COUNTY (081)

A	B	C	D	E
1.	Browns Summit, Shalom Com.(f.l.Greensboro;*Monroe Twn.)	1974	1974-1991	UCC; X
2.	Greensboro, St.Peter UCC (EARLY LIST,lt.1961-1966;*Gilmer Twn.)	1958	1958-1970	UCC(dual CC & E&R 1958-1961); merged to main list # 3 (q.v.)

IREDELL COUNTY (097)

A	B	C	D	E
1.	Statesville, Cgn.of the Chap.at White Mill	1974	1974-on	UCC

APPENDIX III. - UNITED CHURCH OF CHRIST CHURCHES - NORTH CAROLINA - continued

A	B	C	D	E
	LEE COUNTY (105)			
	1. Sanford, Emmanuel UCC (Twn.# 6-*West Sanford)	1975	1975-on	UCC
	LENOIR COUNTY (107)			
Bl	1. Kinston, New Hope UCC	1981	1981-on	UCC
	MECKLENBURG COUNTY (119)			
	1. Charlotte, Clanton Park UCC (EARLY LIST,l.bf.fully org. & org.as UCC;Sch.I because not fully org.;lt.1961-1963; Twn.# 1)	1961	1960-1963	Sch.I 1961;UCC late 1961-1963; X
	2. Charlotte, Mint Hill Mission UCC (Twn.# 6-*Clear Creek)	1978	1978-1981	UCC; X
	3. Charlotte, Pilgrim UCC (f.Southeast Mission;Twn.# 1)	1968	1966-on	UCC
	MOORE COUNTY (125)			
	1. Pinehurst, Cong.(f.Chr.Fellowship of Friends;Twn.uncertain)	1988	1989-on	UCC
	NEW HANOVER COUNTY (129)			
Bl	1. Wilmington, Zion Metropolitan UCC	1977	1982-on	UCC
	ONSLOW COUNTY (133)			
Bl	1. Holly Ridge, Chap.of Peace (Tr.from another denomination; *Stump Sound Twn.)	by 1987	1987-1988	UCC; withdrew
	ORANGE COUNTY (135)			
Bl	1. Chapel Hill, New Covenant Chr.	1989	1989-on	UCC
	2. Hillsborough, Hillsborough UCC	1989	1989-on	UCC
	RANDOLPH COUNTY (151)			
Bl	1. Ramseur, First UCC (f.Mission;*Columbia Twn.)	1965 1945(s.01)	1965-on	UCC
	UNION COUNTY (179)			
	1. Monroe, Christ Com.UCC (f.Com.)	1982 r.1989	1989-on	UCC

APPENDIX III. - UNITED CHURCH OF CHRIST CHURCHES - NORTH CAROLINA - continued

A	B	C	D	E
	VANCE COUNTY (181)			
B1 1.	Henderson, Union Grove UCC	1979 / 1978(s.01)	1979-on	UCC
2.	Henderson, West Hills Chap.(f.UCC,f.Mission)	1971	1971-1988	UCC; withdrew
	WAKE COUNTY (183)			
1.	Cary, Good Shepherd UCC	1987	1987-on	UCC
	YADKIN COUNTY (197)			
B1 1.	Yadkinville, Tabernacle UCC (*Liberty Twn.)	1967	1967-on	UCC
	OKLAHOMA (40)			
	OKLAHOMA COUNTY (109)			
1.	Oklahoma City, Com.UCC House Ch.(Del City)	1970	1970-1983	UCC; X
	SOUTH CAROLINA (45)			
	RICHLAND COUNTY (079)			
1.	Columbia, Pilgrim Cgn.UCC	1983	1986-1990	UCC; X
	TENNESSEE (47)			
	CUMBERLAND COUNTY (035)			
1.	Crossville, Ch.of the Good Shepherd (joint services with Fellowship Chr.(Disc.)(1981)1988-1990)	1983	1982-1989	UCC; 1990 merged to form M.(q.v.)
1M.	Crossville, United Chr.(merger of # 1 & Fellowship Chr.(Disc.)(1981))	1990	1989-on	UCC;(dual,see text)
2.	Fairfield Glade, Faifield Glade Com.(dual Pres.(1.75:1977-on))	1977 / 1975(s.01)	1977-on	UCC; (dual, see text)
	HUMPHREYS COUNTY (085)			
1.	Waverly, United Com.(f.Indep.)	r.1989	1989-on	UCC
	MONROE COUNTY (123)			
B1 1.	Sweetwater, First UCC (Tr.from Colored Cumberland Pres.)	r.1964	1964-on	UCC

APPENDIX III. - UNITED CHURCH OF CHRIST CHURCHES - continued

TEXAS (48)

A	B	C	D	E
	BEXAR COUNTY (029)			
Sp 1.	San Antonio, Iglesia Unida de Cristo (Bethania)	1980	1980-on	UCC
	BRAZOS COUNTY (041)			
1.	College Station, Friends UCC	1978	1978-on	UCC
	COLLIN COUNTY (085)			
1.	Plano, First Cong.UCC (f.United Fellowship UCC)	1980	1980-on	UCC
	COMAL COUNTY (091)			
1.	New Braunfels, Faith UCC	1967	1967-on	UCC
	CORYELL COUNTY (099)			
Sa 1.	Fort Hood, American Samoa First CC (Copperas Cove PO;Fort Hood extends into Bell Co.;f.Indep.)	r.1989	1988-on	UCC
	EL PASO COUNTY (141) [WEST]			
1.	El Paso, Desert View UCC	1980	1980-on	UCC
	GREGG COUNTY (183)			
1.	Longview, Ch.of the Holy Trinity	1986	1986-on	UCC
	HARRIS COUNTY (201)			
1.	Houston, Clear Lake UCC	1965	1966-1973	UCC; merged to form M.(q.v.)
1M.	Houston, United Ch.of Clear Lake (Seabrook,a Uniting Ch.; merger of # 1 & Seabrook Pres.(Pres.U.S.,(1.75:1970-1973); United Ch.dual Pres.U.S.(1.75:1973-1983)1973-1983;dual Pres.(1.75:1980-on)1980-on))	1973 M	1973-on	UCC (dual,see text)
2.	Houston, Ecumenical Fellowship UCC	1964	1965-1971	UCC; X
3.	Houston, Garden Villas Com.UCC (s.in Counc.Com.Chs.)	1937	1963-1988	UCC; X
4.	Houston, Gethsemane UCC	1964	1963-on	UCC
Bl 5.	Houston, Transitional UCC	1963(s.01) 1974	1974-1980	UCC; X

APPENDIX III. - UNITED CHURCH OF CHRIST CHURCHES - TEXAS - HARRIS COUNTY - continued

A	B	C	D	E
6.	LaPorte, Com.(1964 merger of chs.f.Fed.(1925-1964)as Com.Ch.: Pres.(c.1896)(1.75:1895-1964)& Chr.(Disc.)(by 1925);f.in Fed.were Meth.(1925-1948)& Bapt.(1925-bf.1964);dual Chr. (Disc.)1964-on)	1925(01,97) 1929(75);f.in r.1964 M	1966-on	UCC (dual Disc., see text)
7.	Spring, Plymouth United Ch.,UCC	1978	1978-on	UCC
8.	Spring, Plymouth United Ch.,UCC - Filipino Cgn.	1985	1985-1989	UCC; X 1988
	JEFFERSON COUNTY (245)			
B1 1.	Port Arthur, First UCC	1976	1976-1982	UCC; X
	LUBBOCK COUNTY (303) [PANHANDLE]			
1.	Lubbock, First United Ch.,UCC (f.Com.Fellowship)	1969	1969-on	UCC
	MONTGOMERY COUNTY (339)			
1.	Woodlands, Shepherd of the Woods UCC	1978	1978-on	UCC
	TARRANT COUNTY (439)			
Sa 1.	Arlington, First Samoan CC	1988	1991-on	UCC
	TRAVIS COUNTY (453)			
1.	Lago Vista, Rolling Hills Com.(f.l.Round Rock,Williamson Co.; dual Pres.(1.75:1984-on),Disc.(1984-on)& U.Meth.(1984-on))	1984	1984-on	UCC (dual see text)
	VIRGINIA (51)			
	FAIRFAX COUNTY - FALLS CHURCH CITY - FAIRFAX CITY (059)			
B1 1.	Alexandria (Arlington Co.,PO), Hope UCC (f.United Ch.of the Covenant of South Alexandria;EARLY LIST,1.bf.fully org.& org.as UCC;Sch.I because not fully org.;lt.1962-1965;*Lee Dist.)	1963	1960-on	Sch.I 1961; UCC late 1961-on
2.	Herndon, Heritage Fellowship (*Dranesville Dist.;f.l.Reston to 1990,f.*Centreville Dist.)	1983	1985-on	UCC
3.	Reston, United Chr.Par.(f.Redeemer United Meth.to r.;dual to U.Meth.(1972-on),Disc.(1973-on),Pres.(1.75:1973-on),Pres. U.S.(1973-1983);three branches:Lake Anne(Redeemer)1964-on; Hunters Woods 1972-on;South Lakes 1979-on;*Centreville Dist.)	1964(U.Meth.) r.1972	1973-on	UCC (dual see text)
4.	Vienna, Emmaus UCC (f.l.McLean;*Centreville Dist.)	1966	1963-on	UCC

APPENDIX III. - UNITED CHURCH OF CHRIST CHURCHES - VIRGINIA - continued
HENRICO COUNTY - RICHMOND CITY (087)

A	B	C	D	E
B1 1.	Richmond, New Hope UCC (s.l.Midlothian,Chesterfield Co.;also l.as a note:1982-1983)	1982	1983-1988	UCC; X
B1 2.	Richmond, St.Andrews UCC (EARLY LIST;lt.1961-1962)	1959	1958-1962	UCC(dual CC & E&R 1958-1961); X

[NORFOLK COUNTY] CHESAPEAKE CITY - NORFOLK CITY - PORTSMOUTH CITY (129/710)

A	B	C	D	E
B1 1.	Chesapeake, Fellowship Chr.(f.l.Portsmouth to 1972)	1961 1962(s.01)	1966-on	UCC
B1 2.	Portsmouth, Mount Sinai UCC	1964	1964-1990, 1992-on	UCC
B1 3.	Portsmouth, Trinity UCC (f.Chesapeake Trinity)	1972	1972-on	UCC

[PRINCESS ANNE COUNTY] VIRGINIA BEACH CITY (151/810)

A	B	C	D	E
B1 1.	Virginia Beach, Pembroke Manor UCC	1964 1963(s.01)	1963-on	UCC
B1 2.	Virginia Beach, Trinity Ch.in Green Run (Thalia;dual Pres. U.S.(1.75:1959-1983),Epis.)	c.1959(Pres.) r.1974(01)	1974-1984	UCC (dual see text);X

ROCKINGHAM COUNTY - HARRISONBURG CITY (165)

A	B	C	D	E
Nt	Harrisonburg, Sanctuary UCC (1.as prps.1992-on;affl.CAC)			UCC

WEST VIRGINIA (54)

KANAWHA COUNTY (039)

A	B	C	D	E
Nt	Dunbar, St.Gregory UCC (1.as prps.1991-1992;affl.OH;Dist.#4)			UCC; X

A	B	C	D	E

APPENDIX IV. - CONTINUING CONGREGATIONAL CHRISTIAN CHURCHES

ALABAMA (01)

JEFFERSON COUNTY (073)

[

1. Birmingham, St.John's Evan.(f.in Evan.Synod & E&R;left UCC & 1898 1961-1982 UCC 1961-1969;
became CC;poss.f.Friedens Evan.(Peace)) sch.II 1969-1982;
withdrew

DISTRICT OF COLUMBIA (11)

WASHINGTON (001)

1. Washington, Universalist National Mem.Ch.(NW;f.Univ.) 1869 nl. NA(Hon.)1983-on;
Dual UUA

FLORIDA (12)

LAKE COUNTY (069)

1. Grand Island, Frontier Com. 1971 nl. NA 1976-1990; X

LEE COUNTY (071)

1. Cape Coral, First Cong.(Com.) 1979 nl. NA 1979-on

LEON COUNTY (073)

1. Tallahassee, Good Shepherd Chr.Fellowship 1982 nl. NA 1981(j 1982)-1988;
prob.X

ORANGE COUNTY (095)

1. Orlando, Edgewood Com.(f.Cong.) 1967 nl. CCCC 1969 or 1970 (j
1970)-1992; X

PALM BEACH COUNTY (099)

1. Riviera Beach, Sunrise Com. 1987 nl. NA 1992(j 1993)-on

SARASOTA COUNTY (115)

1. Laurel, Cong.(f.Full Circle) 1977 nl. NA 1985-on
1976(s.04)

A	B	C	D	E
	APPENDIX IV. - CONTINUING CONGREGATIONAL CHRISTIAN CHURCHES - FLORIDA - SARASOTA COUNTY - continued	1977	nl.	NA 1977-1979; X
2.	Sarasota, First Com.			
	VOLUSIA COUNTY (127)			
1.	Holly Hill, Colony Com.(Daytona Beach;j CCCC but left in year)	by 1978	nl.	CCCC (j 1978)nl.; X prob.soon (1979)
2.	Orange City, Pilgrim Com.Cong.(s.in Counc.Com.Chs.)	1954 1967(s.04)	nl.	NA 1983-on
	MARYLAND (24)			
	GARRETT COUNTY (023)			
1.	Friendsville, Mem.Cong.(f.Chr.;r.of Disc.;Dist.2)	1964	nl.	NA 1966-on
	NORTH CAROLINA (37)			
	ALAMANCE COUNTY (001)			
B1 1.	Graham, New Mount Zion Chr.(f.l.Haw River;Twn.# 6-Graham,or Twn.# 13-Haw River)	1948 1950(s.04)	nl.	NA(Affl.)1964 or 1965-on
	OKLAHOMA (40)			
	OKLAHOMA COUNTY (109)			
1.	Oklahoma City, First Cong.	1972	nl.	NA 1972(j 1973)-1974; merged to main list # 11(q.v.)
2.	Oklahoma City, Mayflower Com.Cong.(in NA to merger)	1958 1957(s.04)	nl.	NA by 1961-1978; 1979 merged to main list # 11M1.(q.v.)
	TULSA COUNTY (143)			
1.	Tulsa, Trinity Chr.	1984	nl.	CCCC 1984-on
	TENNESSEE (47)			
	SHELBY COUNTY (157)			
1.	Memphis, Brethren C of C	1950	nl.	NA(Affl.)1968 or 1969-1976;poss. withdrew

APPENDIX IV. - CONTINUING CONGREGATIONAL CHRISTIAN CHURCHES - continued

TEXAS (48)

DENTON COUNTY (121)

A	B	C	D	E
1.	Flower Mound, Mayflower Cong.(f.l.Lewisville to 1986;l.as pr.pl.1974-1975)	1976 1977(s.04) 1975(s.04)	nl.	NA 1974-on
2.	Lake Dallas, Union Mem.	1972	nl.	CCCC 1974(j 1973)-1975; prob.X

EL PASO COUNTY (141) [WEST]

A	B	C	D	E
1.	El Paso, Cong.Ch.of Hope	1976	nl.	NA 1976-on

HARRIS COUNTY (201)

A	B	C	D	E
1.	Bellaire, Plymouth Cong.of Houston (f.All Souls Cong.of Houston to 1964 or 1965)	1962	nl.	NA 1963-1967; X
2.	Houston, Central Cong.(f.First Evan.,f.First Ger.Evan.Luth.; f.in Evan.Synod & E&R(1883-1961);left UCC & became CC)	1851	1961-1968	UCC 1961-1968; NA 1968 or 1969-on

SWISHER COUNTY (437) [PANHANDLE]

A	B	C	D	E
1.	Tulia, First Cong.	1961 1962(s.05)	nl.	CCCC 1961(j 1962)-1974; X

187

APPENDIX V. - AMERICAN BOARD OF COMMISSIONERS FOR FOREIGN MISSIONS - INDIAN CONGREGATIONS

A	B	C	D	E

ALABAMA (01)

COLBERT COUNTY (033)

A	B	C	D	E
In Nt	Caney Creek, Mission (on Tennessee River; serving Chickasaw tribe;mission of Pres.Synod of SC & GA to 1827/1828 when Tr.to ABCFM)	1826(19) 1827(88)	nl.	X 1833(88);1835(92)

DE KALB COUNTY (049)

A	B	C	D	E
In 1.	Willstown, Ch.(nr.Fort Payne;serving Cherokee tribe;1.Pres. 1826(j 1824)-1839(OS);poss.Cong.)	1824(ch.) 1823(mission)	nl.	X 1839

MARSHALL COUNTY (095)

A	B	C	D	E
In 1.	Creek Path, Ch.(at Guntersville nr.Tennessee River; serving Cherokee tribe;1.Pres.btwn.1819 & 1824-1838;poss.Cong.)	1820	nl.	X 1837 (88)

ARKANSAS (05)

CRAWFORD COUNTY (033)

A	B	C	D	E
In Nt	Mulberry, Mission (serving Cherokee tribe; moved to Fairfield,Adair Co.,OK)	1828	nl.	X 1829

POPE COUNTY (115)

A	B	C	D	E
In 1.	Dwight, Ch.(west side of Arkansas Creek,5 miles north of Arkansas River;serving Cherokee tribe;nl.Pres.;prob.Cong.; moved to OK)	1822(Ch.) 1821(92) 1820(mission)	nl.	X 1829

GEORGIA (13)

FLOYD COUNTY (115)

A	B	C	D	E
In 1.	Haweis, Turnip Mtn.Ch.(nr.Rome,nr.west border of GA;serving Cherokee tribe;nl.Pres.;prob.Cong.)	1826(ch.) 1823(mission)	nl.	X 1834

FORSYTH COUNTY (117)

A	B	C	D	E
In 1.	Hightower, Ch.(on Etowah River;serving Cherokee tribe;1.Pres. 1823 btwn.1819 & 1824(j 1824)-1833,poss.Cong.)	1823	nl.	X 1831

APPENDIX V. - AMERICAN BOARD INDIAN CHURCHES - GEORGIA - continued

A		B	C	D	E
		GILMER COUNTY (123)			
In	1.	Talona (Taloney), Carmel Ch.(serving Cherokee tribe;l.Pres. btwn.1819 & 1824(j 1824)-1837;poss.Cong.)	1823(Ch.) 1819(mission)	nl.	X 1836
		GORDON COUNTY (129)			
In	1.	New Echota, Ch.(Capital of Cherokee Nation;1827-1834 in 92; serving Cherokee tribe;l.Pres.1831-1837;poss.Cong.)	1825(Ch.) 1824(mission)	nl.	X 1839
		UNLOCATED CHURCHES (999)			
In	Nt	Running Waters, Mission (residence of two Cherokee leaders; prob.in GA; serving Cherokee tribe)	1835	nl.	X 1836
		MISSISSIPPI (28)			
		ADAMS COUNTY (001)			
[In	1.	Natchez, Pine Ridge Pres.(f.Salem Ch.of Washington to 1820;f. Bethel Ch.to 1807;not technically an ABCFM mission,this was begun by a New England Yale educated missionary commissioned by the NY Missionary Soc.;serving Chickasaw tribe;Indians left c.1807,considered parent of Choctaw Co.#1;continuing ch.here bec.predominantly white c.1807; l.Pres.btwn.1814 & 1818-1861(OS),1861-1983(Pres.U.S.), 1983-1987(Pres.),1987 or 1988-on(PCA))	1804(ch.) 1807(ch.r.) 1799(mission)	nl.	X Indians gone c.1807;(white ch. continues Pres., PCA)
		CHOCTAW COUNTY (019)			
In	1.	French Camps, Bethel Ch.(western District Choctaw;considered r.of ch.in Adams Co.(q.v.) which served Chickasaw tribe; this serving Choctaw tribe;nl.Pres.)	1822(Ch.) 1821(mission r.)	nl.	X 1827
		GRENADA COUNTY (043)			
In	1.	Eliot, Ch.(Upper Towns,nr.Holcomb;serving Choctaw tribe;l. Pres.1830-1834)	1819(ch.) 1818(mission)	nl.	X 1833
		JASPER COUNTY (061)			
In	1.	Goshen, Ch.(nr.Hoo-la-ta-hoomah;Southeast District Choctaw, serving Choctaw tribe;l.Pres.1829(j 1830)-1834)	by 1825(ch.) 1823(mission)	nl.	X 1833

APPENDIX V. - AMERICAN BOARD INDIAN CHURCHES - MISSISSIPPI - continued

LOWNDES COUNTY (087)

A	B	C	D	E
In Nt	Hebron Mission (Northeast Choctaw area;serving Choctaw tribe)	1827	nl.	X c.1832(88);1833(92)
In 1.	Mayhew, Ch.(Lower Towns;nr.Starkville, Oktibbeha Co.; Northeast Choctaw Nation,nr.Choctaw/Chickasaw boundary; serving Choctaw tribe;1.Pres.1826-1827,1829(j 1830)-1842, most removed to OK by 1840)	1821(ch.) 1820(mission)	nl.	X 1833

MARSHALL COUNTY (093)

A	B	C	D	E
In Nt	Martyn Station, Mission (Pigeon Roost;nr.Holly Springs; serving Chickasaw tribe;88 says local work replaced by an unamed mixed blood Pres.Ch.;mission of Pres.Synod of SC & GA to 1827/1828, when Tr.to ABCFM)	1827	nl.	X 1832 or 1833(88) (to 1835:92)

PONTOTOC COUNTY (115)

A	B	C	D	E
In 1.	Monroe, Pres.Ch.(Monroe Station;nr.McIntoshville;Chickasaw Agency;Pontotoc PO;moved to Algoma 1915;serving Chickasaw tribe;mission of Pres.Synod of SC & GA to 1827/1828 when Tr.to ABCFM;Indians forced out 1834,pastor went to OK to serve them 1837,continuing ch.here predominantly white; 1.Pres.1831-1861(OS),1861-1983(Pres.U.S.),1983-on(Pres.))	1823(ch.) 1821(mission)	nl.	X 1834,(1830:92); Indians left (see text)
In 2.	To(c)kshish Station, Ch.(2 miles north of # 1;serving Chickasaw tribe;Mission of Pres.Synod of SC & GA to 1827/1828,when Tr.to ABCFM;nl.Pres.;99 says only a mission,not a ch.)	by 1830(ch.) 1827(mission) 1823(70)	nl.	X 1835

WAYNE COUNTY (153)

A	B	C	D	E
In Nt	Hachah Mission at Bok-e-tun-nuh (Bok-i-tun-nah,Bokitunnuh; now Buckatunna;lt.88;serving Choctaw tribe)	1824 1825(s.88)	nl.	X 1826(or 1827(s.88))
In 1.	Long Prairie, Emmaus Ch.(prob.location;nr.#Nt;poss.Six Towns (19);Southeast Choctaw Nation;140 miles south of Lowndes Co.# 1;nr.AL border;serving Choctaw tribe;1.Pres.1830-1834)	by 1831(ch.) 1822(mission: 88) 1825(19)	nl.	X 1833

UNLOCATED CHURCHES (999)

A	B	C	D	E
In Nt	Bethany Mission (serving Choctaw tribe)	1825	nl.	X 1826
In Nt	Captain Harrison's Mission (serving Choctaw tribe)	1825	nl.	X 1826
In Nt	Hik-a-shub-a-ha Mission(Northeast Choctaw area;serving Choctaw tribe)	1830	nl.	X 1831

APPENDIX V. - AMERICAN BOARD INDIAN CHURCHES - MISSISSIPPI - UNLOCATED CHURCHES - continued

A	B	C	D	E
In	Nt	I-ik-hun-nuk Mission(or Ai-ik-hun-nuh,Ai-ik-hun-nah;Northeast Choctaw area;30 miles west of Lowndes Co.# 1;serving Choctaw tribe)	1824 nl.	X 1831
In	Nt	Mr. Juzon's Mission (Southeast District Choctaw;serving Choctaw tribe)	1823 nl.	X 1832
In	Nt	Mushulatubees Mission (Mooshoolatubbees;Northeast Choctaw Distrcit;serving Choctaw tribe)	1823 nl.	X 1824
In	Nt	Yok-nok-cha-ya Mission (Gibeon;Northeast Choctaw area;serving Choctaw tribe)	1826 nl.	X 1833

OKLAHOMA (40)

ADAIR COUNTY (001)

A	B	C	D	E
In	1.	Fairfield, Ch.(nr.Lyons;group from Mulberry,Crawford Co.,AR removed here;serving Cherokee tribe;nl.Pres.,prob. Cong.)	c.1834(ch.) 1829(mission) nl.	alive 1860; X thereafter
In	2.	Lee's Creek, Ch.(serving Cherokee tribe;earlier ch.became ABCFM mission 1849;nl.Pres.,prob.Cong.)	by 1835 nl.	alive 1860; X thereafter

ATOKA COUNTY (005)

A	B	C	D	E
In	1.	Boggy Depot, Boggy Chickasaw Ch.in Boggy River(serving Chickasaw tribe although on Choctaw land;Tr.ABCFM to Pres. Bd.(OS)1853;l.Pres.btwn.1843 & 1846-1861(OS),1861-1905 (Pres.U.S.))	c.1841 nl.	Pres.; X 1905
In	2.	Boggy Depot, Mount Pleasant Ch.(serving Choctaw tribe;Tr. ABCFM to Pres.Bd.,1859;l.Pres.btwn.1843 & 1846-1861(OS), 1861-1898(Pres.U.S.))	1845(ch.) c.1844 (mission) nl.	Pres.; X 1898

BRYAN COUNTY (013)

A	B	C	D	E
In	1.	Bennington, Old Bennington Ch.(west of Boggy River,nr.Atoka Co.# 2;serving Choctaw tribe;Tr.ABCFM to Pres.Bd.1859; l.Pres.1849-1861(OS),1861-1983(Pres.U.S.),1983-on(Pres.); lt.1887-1889(Pres.))	1849 nl.	Pres.
In	2.	Bennington, Chish Oktak Ch.(Chishoktok;serving Choctaw tribe; Tr.ABCFM to Pres.Bd.,1859;l.Pres.1853-1861(OS),1861-1870, 1874-1983(Pres.U.S.),1983-on(Pres.))	1854 nl.	Pres.
In	Nt	Bokchito Mission (Box Chito;nr.Red River;serving Choctaw tribe)	1854 nl.	X 1859
In	3.	Caddo, Six Towns Ch.(on Blue River;serving Choctaw tribe;88 suggests ch.separated from Chickasaw mission at Atoka Co.# 1;Tr.ABCFM to Pres.Bd.1859;l.Pres.btwn.1843 & 1846-1861(OS),1861-1910(Pres.U.S.))	1845 nl.	Pres.; X 1910

APPENDIX V. - AMERICAN BOARD INDIAN CHURCHES - OKLAHOMA - continued

CHEROKEE COUNTY (021)

A	B	C	D	E
In Nt	Forks of Illinois Mission (prob.location;20 miles North of Sequoyah Co.# 1;serving Cherokee tribe;moved to # 1)	1830	nl.	X 1836
In 1.	Tallequah, Park Hill Ch.(moved from Forks of Illinois mission; serving Cherokee tribe;Tr.ABCFM to Pres.Bd.1859, but missionaries withdrew from OS service;l.Pres.1870-1882,1884-1983(Pres.U.S.),1983-on(Pres.);prob.Cong.to 1870)	1837(ch.) 1836(mission)	nl.	Tr.to Pres.c.1870

CHOCTAW COUNTY (023)

A	B	C	D	E
In 1.	Doaksville, Pine Ridge Ch.(Cedron;2 miles from Fort Towson; divided from McCurtain Co.# 6;serving Choctaw tribe;Tr.-ABCFM to Pres.Bd.1859;l.Pres.1834 or 1835-1861(OS),1861-1877(Pres.U.S.),1838-1839(NS));r.Pres.U.S.A.,l.1890-1946)	1835	nl.	Pres.; X 1877 (r.,see text)
In 2.	Hugo, Good Land Ch.(serving Choctaw tribe;divided from McCurtain Co.# 6;Tr.ABCFM to Pres.Bd.1859;l.Pres.1853-1861(OS),1861-1962(Pres.U.S.))	1853 c.1848 (mission)	nl.	Pres.; X 1962
In 3.	Mayhew Ch.(nr.Boggy River;serving Choctaw tribe;Tr.ABCFM to Pres.Bd.1859;l.Pres.1839-1861(OS))	1840	nl.	X 1861

JOHNSTON COUNTY (069)

A	B	C	D	E
In Nt	Washita Mission (nr.Fort Washita;in Chickasaw country,serving Choctaw tribe)	1847	nl.	X 1848

LE FLORE COUNTY (079)

A	B	C	D	E
In 1.	Buck's Creek Ch.(serving Choctaw tribe;Tr.ABCFM to Pres.U.S. Bd.1876;l.Pres.1874-1879(Pres.U.S.);prob.location)	by 1874	nl.	Pres.; X 1879
In 2.	Green Hill Ch.(prob.location,20 miles from Fort Smith,AR; serving Choctaw tribe;ABCFM aided from 1873,Tr.ABCFM to Pres.U.S.Bd.1876;l.Pres.1870-1886(Pres.U.S.))	by 1871(ch.)	nl.	Pres.; X 1886
In 3.	Lenox, Ch.(ABCFM aided from 1873,Tr.to Pres.U.S.Bd.1876; serving Choctaw tribe;l.Pres.1854-1861(OS),1861-1886,1887-1907(Pres.U.S.)) r.1873	by 1855	nl.	Pres.; X 1907

MC CURTAIN COUNTY (089)

A	B	C	D	E
In 1.	Battiest, Mount Zion Ch.(serving Choctaw tribe;Tr.ABCFM to Pres.Bd.1859;nl.75H but in Pres.records,l.Pres.1849-1861(OS),1861-1983(Pres.U.S.),1983-on(Pres.))	by 1849	nl.	Pres.
In 2.	Bok Toklo Ch.(Bok Tuklo;nr.Red River;serving Choctaw tribe; nl.Pres.;mission ended 1836)	1834	nl.	1842 merged to # 9 to form # 10(q.v.)

APPENDIX V. - AMERICAN BOARD INDIAN CHURCHES - OKLAHOMA - MC CURTAIN COUNTY - continued

A	B	C	D	E
In Nt	Clear Creek Mission (10 miles from Fort Towson,nr.Red River; serving Choctaw tribe)	1833	nl.	X 1837
In 3.	Eagletown, Bethabara Ch.(nr.chief ford of Little River; serving Choctaw tribe;nl.Pres.)	1832	nl.	X 1837(92); (c.1840:88)
In 4.	Eagletown, Greenfield Ch.(Luk-fo-a-ta;serving Choctaw tribe; l.Pres.1836-btwn.1840 & 1846(OS),1838-1839(NS))	by 1837(ch.) 1836(mission)	nl.	X c.1840
In 5.	Eagletown, Mountain Fork Ch.(serving Choctaw tribe;88 incor. shows this ch.X c.1841 & # 8 continuing;Tr.ABCFM to Pres. Bd.1859;l.Pres.1834 or 1835-1861(OS),1861-1886(Pres.U.S.), 1887-on(Pres.),1838-1839(NS))	by 1836	nl.	Pres.
In 6.	Hugo(Choctaw Co.PO), Good Water Ch.(serving Choctaw tribe; Tr.ABCFM to Pres.Bd.af.1853,by 1859;l.Pres.1846-1861(OS), 1861-1909(Pres.U.S.);see also Choctaw Co. # 1 & # 2)	1836(88) 1837(92)	nl.	Pres.; X 1909
In Nt	McCurtain City(not Haskell Co.), Bethel Mission (m.as temporary 1832;serving Choctaw tribe;lt.88)	1834	nl.	X 1837
In Nt	Norwalk Mission (serving Choctaw tribe;5 miles from # 9, 12 miles east of Fort Towson)	1842	nl.	X 1854
In 7.	Living Land Ch.(Yokini Okchaga,Yakni Okehaya,Yakni Okchaya; serving Choctaw tribe;Tr.ABCFM to Pres.Bd.1859;l.Pres. 1856-1861(OS),1861-1886(Pres.U.S.))	1856	nl.	Pres.; X 1886
In 8.	Stockbridge Ch.(serving Choctaw tribe;s.l.Mountain Fork;88 confuses this with # 5;l.Pres.1834 or 1835-1836 or 1837)	by 1836	nl.	X c.1841
In 9.	Wheelock Ch.(serving Choctaw tribe;6 miles south of Little River branch of Red River;l.Pres.1834 or 1835-1842(OS), 1838-1839(NS))	1832	nl.	1842 merged to # 2 to form # 10 (q.v.)
In 10.	Wheelock Ch.(nr.Garvin;McCurtain City(not Haskell Co.);merger of # 2 & # 9;Tr.ABCFM to Pres.Bd.1859;serving Choctaw tribe;l.Pres.1842-1861(OS),1861-1905(Pres.U.S.))	1842 M	nl.	Pres.; X 1905

MAYES COUNTY (097)

A	B	C	D	E
In Nt	Hopefield Mission (UFMS mission Tr.to ABCFM 1826;begun on Neosho River 5 miles from Union,Wagoner Co.,in Mayes Co., nr.Rogers Co.line;af.1825 moved 25 or 30 miles farther up river:prob.in Labette Co.KS;served Osage and Neosho tribes;nl.Pres.)	1823(88) 1820(70)	nl.	prob.moved out of state af.1825; X 1835 or 1836

MUSKOGEE COUNTY (101)

Nt Fort Gibson, First Pres.Ch.(this Pres.Ch.,claims to continue mission begun to Osage tribe 1824,then Cherokee tribe,then Creek tribe,formally org.1873/1874,l.1874-on(Pres.);we can not connect this with any particular mission)

APPENDIX V. - AMERICAN BOARD INDIAN CHURCHES - OKLAHOMA - continued

PUSHMATAHA COUNTY (127)

A	B	C	D	E
In 1.	Wade's Settlement Ch.on Kiamichi River (serving Choctaw tribe;nl.Pres.;ABCFM mission to 1859 & 1873-1876)	by 1855(ch.) 1853(mission)	nl.	X af.1876

SEQUOYAH COUNTY (135)

A	B	C	D	E
In 1.	Dwight Ch.(west bank of Sallican Creek flowing into Arkansas River from North;later Vian, Marble City, Sallisaw PO; moved from Dwight,Pope Co.,AR;serving Cherokee tribe;l. Pres.1887-1948(Pres.),prob.Cong.to btwn.1860 & 1888;Tr. ABCFM to Pres.Bd.1859,but missionaries withdrew from OS service;bec.Pres.mission by 1888)	1829	nl.	r.as Pres.by 1888; X 1948
In 2.	Hanson, Mount Zion Ch.(serving Cherokee tribe;nl.Pres.,prob. Cong.;later r.as a Pres.Ch.)	1840	nl.	X c.1848 (see text)

WAGONER COUNTY (145)

A	B	C	D	E
In 1.	Creek Station Ch.(at Arkansas & Verdigris River junction; serving Creek tribe;nl.Pres.,prob.Cong.)	1832(19,92) 1830(ch.:88) 1829(mission: 88)	nl.	X 1837
In 2.	Union Ch.(on Neosho River,20 miles from Fort Gibson;serving Osage,Neosho & other tribes;explored 1819;Tr.UFMS to ABCFM 1826;nl.Pres.,poss.Cong.)	1821(ch.) 1820(mission)	nl.	X 1837

UNLOCATED CHURCHES (999)

A	B	C	D	E
In Nt	Bushpotupa's Mission (serving Choctaw tribe)	1848	nl.	X 1849
In 1.	Honey Creek Ch.(serving Cherokee tribe;nl.Pres.,prob.Cong.; prob.in Delaware or Rogers Co.)	c.1840	nl.	X af.1859
In Nt	Yazoo Creek Mission (serving Choctaw tribe)	1854	nl.	X 1855

TENNESSEE (47)

BRADLEY COUNTY (011)

A	B	C	D	E
In Nt	Ahmohee Mission (nr.Candy's Creek;serving Cherokee tribe)	1831	nl.	X 1833
In 1.	Candy's Creek, Ch.(10 miles west of Cherokee Agency;serving Cherokee tribe;l.Pres.1825-1837,poss.Cong.)	1825(ch.) 1824(mission)	nl.	X 1839
In 2.	Red Clay, Ch.(20 miles east of Hamilton Co.# 1; & 14 miles south of # 1;prob.nr.present Red Hill;serving Cherokee tribe;nl.Pres.,prob.Cong.)	1835	nl.	X 1839

A	B	C	D	E
	APPENDIX V. - AMERICAN BOARD INDIAN CHURCHES - TENNESSEE - continued			
	HAMILTON COUNTY (065)			
In 1.	Brainerd Station, C of C in Chickamaugah (Chicamauga Creek; now in city of Chattanooga;serving Cherokee tribe; specifically Cong.forms;l.Pres.btwn.1819 & 1824(j1824)-1837;continues mission of Pres.General Assembly plan 1803, 1804-1810,supported by Western Missionary Soc.of NJ & New England Chs.,no ch.that period)	1817	nl.	X 1839
	TIPTON COUNTY (167)			
In Nt	Tipton Co.Mission (serving Chickasaw tribe)	1833	nl.	X 1835

APPENDIX VI. - ATTEMPTED MERGER

(All these churches were organized before or during the Civil War. They are probably all Black. They were reported by the Pastor of Chattanooga (First) on December 6,1867;in 01)

A	B	C	D	E
	GEORGIA (13)			
	MURRAY COUNTY (213)			
pB	1. Spring Place, unnamed	?	1866-1867	drop
	WHITFIELD COUNTY (313)			
pB	1. Dalton, unnamed	?	1866-1867	drop
	UNLOCATED CHURCHES (999)			
pB	1. Whitefield, Center Hill	?	1866-1867	drop
	TENNESSEE (47)			
	BRADLEY COUNTY (011)			
pB	1. Cleveland, Pleasant Valley	?	1866-1867	drop
pB	2. Cleveland, Zion Hill	?	1866-1867	drop
	HAMILTON COUNTY (067)			
pB	1. Hamilton, unnamed	?	1866-1867	drop
	POLK COUNTY (139)			
pB	1. Ducktown, unnamed	?	1866-1867	drop
	UNLOCATED CHURCHES (999)			
pB	1. C___ Creek, unnamed	?	1866-1867	drop
pB	2. Smith Chap. (unlocated;yoked to Murray Co.,GA # 1)	?	1866-1867	drop

APPENDIX VII. - PRESBYTERIAN CHURCHES SERVED BY CHARLESTON UNION PRESBYTERY WHILE IT WAS INDEPENDENT NEW SCHOOL (1838-1852)

SOUTH CAROLINA (45)

AIKEN COUNTY (003)

A	B	C	D	E
1.	Aiken, First Pres.(62 suggests this ch.was not Pres.in 1838; poss.Cong.,r.as Pres.;l.Pres.:75:1837-1839(NS),1858-1861 (OS),1861-1983(Pres.U.S.),1983-on(Pres.);poss.X & new org.1858)	by 1838 r.1858(75Y, 55,61)	CUPPr.: 1838-1852	Pres.

BARNWELL COUNTY (011)

A	B	C	D	E
1.	Barnwell Court House, Pres.(l.Pres.:75:1852-1860 or 1861(OS), btwn.1863 & 1865-1983(Pres.U.S.),1983-on(Pres.);c.1851 ab. Boiling Springs Pres.(pr.1820,org.1842)1.75:1841 or 1842- 1851(OS);Boiling Springs Pres.later r.1896-on)	1840 1832(pr.:61) early 1830's (55)	CUPPr.: 1840-1852	Pres.

CHARLESTON COUNTY (019)

A	B	C	D	E
1.	Charleston, First Pres.(Old Scots;f.of Charles Towne to 1783; 62 suggests this was not Pres.in 1838;Pby.of SC 1734(1731: 60,61)-1776(c.1780:61);CP 1790-1810(c.1819:61);l.Pres.:75: (Tr.1810)btwn.1819 & 1824-1826 or 1827,1828-1830(Pres.), 1854-1861(OS),1861-1869(Pres.U.S.),1869-1881(Indep. Charleston Union Pby.),l.1881(j 1882)-1983(Pres.U.S.),1983- on(Pres.);closed 1776-1784,1863-1866(Wars);during CUP pastor indep.,but ch.included in that circle)	1731 1734(24) r.1882	poss. CUPPr.: 1838-1852	Pres.
Fr 2.	Charleston, French Prot.(Calvinistic Ch.of French Prots.; French Huguenot Ch.;Ref.Ch.;French Ref.;Huguenot Ch.;f.of Charles Towne to 1783;pastor in CP:1816-1818,Ref.Ch.in America 1859-1864,l.1866-1900(Pres.U.S.);ch.dispersed late 1820's-1830;pastor emeritus in Pres.U.S.to 1916;prob.not in CUP,but included in same circle)	1687 c.1681(60) 1686(pr.,24; 75H) 1783(incp.)	poss. CUPPr.: to 1852 (see text)	Indep.
Nt	Charleston, Mariner's (not clear if a ch.or a mission;l.Pres. btwn.1819 & 1824-1826 or 1827,1828-1831,1834 or 1835-1839 (NS))	by 1825 c.1822(75H)	CUPPr.: 1838- X (by 1852)	X by 1852 (indep. Chap.here to 1898)

APPENDIX VII. - CHARLESTON UNION PRESBYTERY PRESBYTERIAN CHURCHES (1838-1852) - continued
SOUTH CAROLINA - CHARLESTON COUNTY - continued

A	B	C	D	E
3.	Charleston, Third Pres.(bec.Central Pres.1850(1857:58);bec. United Zion & Central Pres.1882;bec.Westminster Pres.1883; l.Pres.:75:1823 or 1824-1839(NS),1852-1855,1856-1861(OS), 1861-1983(Pres.U.S.),1983-on(Pres.);ab.1882 Zion & Glebe St.Pres.(1866(l.1867(1875:75H)-1882(Pres.U.S.)),merger of Glebe St.Pres.(1847;l.75:1847-1861(OS),1861-btwn.1863 & 1865(Pres.U.S.))& Zion Pres.(white members only;f.Anson St.to 1858(Chap.1847(58,60)or 1850(61)),org.as white led Black Ch.1854(60,61)or 1859(55),l.1853-1855,1856-1857, 1858-1861(OS),1861-1867(Pres.U.S.),(divided 1867(71)or 1869(60)or 1875(75H)));ab.1925(61;1927(55,59)Knox Pres. (1914)(1.1914-1925(Pres.U.S.));ab.1926(61(1924:59))Com. Pres.(1921)(1.1921-1927(Pres.U.S.));ab.1970 Covenant Pres. (1964)(1.1964-1970(Pres.U.S.)))	1823 1882 M 1925 M 1926 M 1970 M	CUPPr: 1838-1852	Pres., merged Pres. (see text)
B1 Nt	Charleston, Wallingford United Pres.(f.Siloam Pres.,f.First Colored Pres.;Black members from various chs.;prob. particularly # 1 & # 3;l.1866-1870(OS),1870-on(Pres.);61 incor.suggests f.in Pres.U.S.)	1867	nl.	Pres.
B1 Nt	Charleston, Zion Pres.(f.Anson St.to 1858;Black Chap. sponsored by Second Pres.(1809,OS);set up as a mission 1847(58,60)1850(61));r.as a white led predominantly Black ch.1854(1858(s.75H),1859(55));divided:whites left 1867(60, minutes(1869:71;1875:75H))to form ch.later merged to Third Pres.(q.v.);l.1853-1855,1856-1857,1858-1861(OS),1861-1867 (Pres.U.S.);l.1867-1868,1869-1878(Pres.U.S.),1878-1959 (Pres.);merged to Olivet Pres.(1879)(1.1879-1959(Pres.)), as Zion-Olivet Pres.(1959),l.1959-on(Pres.)	1854 1859(55) 1847(mission) 1850(mission: 61) r.1867(see text) 1959 M	nl.	Pres.;merged Pres. (see text)
4.	Johns Island, Johns Island Pres.(Indep.Pres.Ch.,St.John's Par.(in 1785);bec.Pres.Ch.of Johns Island & Wadmalaw 1835 (58),1792(55);Pby.of SC:1730's(1722:60,75H)-1737,1755- 1770's(1780:75H);CP 1790's-by 1798,by 1808-1814;Pres.l.75: (m.1792)1.btwn.1794 & 1797-btwn.1798 & 1802(poss.served to 1808;1790-1801:75H),(pastor j1814,nl.),l.btwn.1819 & 1824- 1839(NS),1838 voted indep.Pres.,l.1852(j1853)-1861(OS), 1861-1983(Pres.U.S.),1983-on(Pres.);[divided 1838,OS org.: 1.1838-1849,court gave property to OS 1846,X 1849];Johns Island Soc.org.1799,ab.by ch.1822;61 contends in OS when we show in CUP,not supported by OS minutes;61 & 75H say in CGA 1801-1822,which would imply this ch.is Cong.;see also #4D,#4E)	1710 by 1720(58) 1734 or 1735 (Gillett) 1785(incp.) 1792(r.incp.) 1835(r.incp.)	CUPPr.: (j 1846) 1846-1852 (poss.CGA, see text)	Pres.
4B.	Wadmalaw Island, Rockville Pres.(this BRANCH begun 1792(58; 1809(55)),(c.1710:61);separated from main ch.1909(1. 1909-1983(Pres.U.S.),1983-on(Pres.));claims 1710 as successor to main ch.;see also #4F)	1909	nl.	Pres.

APPENDIX VII. - CHARLESTON UNION PRESBYTERY PRESBYTERIAN CHURCHES (1838-1852) - continued
SOUTH CAROLINA - CHARLESTON COUNTY - continued

A	B	C	D	E
	4C. Legareville, Pres.(this BRANCH alive 1846,other dates uncertain;did not bec.a ch.)			prob.X
B1	4D. Johns Island, St.Andrews Pres.(f.Buleau;some of Black members by 1867 of # 4;1.1866-1870(OS),1.1870-on(Pres.);nl.60)		nl.	Pres.
B1	4E. Johns Island, Zion Pres.(f.Pres.of Johns Island;some of Black by 1867 members of # 4;1.1866-1870(OS),1870-1990(Pres.);merged to c.1870 Hebron Pres.of Johns Island(1.1875-1990(Pres.)),as Hebron- 1990 M Zion Pres.(1.1990-on(Pres.));nl.60)		nl.	Pres.;merged Pres. (see text)
B1	4F. Wadmalaw Island, Salem Pres.(Black members of # 4C;1.1867- 1870(OS),1870-on(Pres.);61 incor.l.in Pres.U.S.bf.1879; incor.l.OS & NS:75H;nl.60)	1868	nl.	Pres.

COLLETON COUNTY (029)

A	B	C	D	E
	1. Saltcatcher, Indep.Pres.Ch.(Salkehatchie;Salt Ketcher;Pby.of SC 1766-1772(1780:75H);CP 1790-1811;1.Pres.:75:btwn.1809 & 1813(prob.1811)-btwn.1814 & 1818,1827(j1826)-1834 or 1835, 1836-1839(NS,1836-1838 reports imply Cong.form);[divided 1838,62 says main ch.bec.OS,1.1838-1844,1845-1853,OS r.as predominantly Bl 1844,X 1855];61 does nl.NS Ch.)	1766(24,61) by 1770(58) 1808(incp.)	CUPPr.: 1838-X by 1852	X by 1852

ORANGEBURG COUNTY (075)

A	B	C	D	E
	1. Orangeburg, First Pres.(1.Pres.:75:1834 or 1835-1839(NS), 1852-1855,1856-1861(OS),1861-1983(Pres.U.S.),1983-on (Pres.))	1835	CUPPr.: 1838-1852	Pres.

APPENDIX VIII. - INDEPENDENT PRESBYTERIAN CHURCH

ALABAMA (01)

FAYETTE COUNTY (057)

A	B	C	D	E
1.	Olney, Indep.Pres.(prob.western group btwn.1840 & 1843- Civil War;nl.75H)	c.1840	j c.1840- btwn.1840 & 1843	withdrew; in western group to Civil War; X (c.1861)

MISSISSIPPI (28)

LOWNDES COUNTY (087)

A	B	C	D	E
1.	Columbus, Salem Indep.Pres.(see main list # 5;prob.western group btwn.1840 & 1843 to bec.Cong.& eventually predominantly Black by c.1868;drop 1844 75H)	1832	1832(j)- btwn.1840 & 1843	withdrew; in western group; bec.Cong.(see text)

MONROE COUNTY (095)

A	B	C	D	E
1.	Hamilton, Ruhamah Indep.Ch.(Pres.;see main list # 2;prob. western group btwn.1840 & 1843 to r.as Cong.& predeominantly Black 1870;nl.75H)	1837	1838(j)- btwn.1840 & 1843	withdrew; in western group; r.Cong. 1870; (see text)

NORTH CAROLINA (37)

GASTON COUNTY (071)

A	B	C	D	E
1.	Bessemer City, Hephzibah Indep.Pres.(f.of Lincoln Co.;l. Pres.U.S.:75:1866-1983,1983-on(Pres.))	1830(69) 1838(75Y,75H)	btwn.1824 & 1832(j1828) -1863	opposed 1863 merger; j Pres.U.S.1865
2.	Gastonia, Olney Indep.Pres.(f.of Lincoln Co.;[division from 1793 Olney Pres.(1.75:btwn.1788 & 1797-1861(OS),1861-1866 (Pres.U.S.)];1864 merged to that Ch.as Olney(1.75:1866- 1983(Pres.U.S.),1983-on(Pres.))	1810	1813(j)- 1863	opposed 1863 merger; merged to Pres.U.S. 1864(66;1866:75H)
3.	Gastonia, Union Indep.Pres.(j IPC by 1855 & Tr.to Pres.U.S. 1863(1.btwn.1863 & 1865-1983,1983-on(Pres.))	1850(66,75H, 75Y) by 1855(69) by 1843(pr.)	btwn.1844 & 1854-1863	btwn.1844 & Tr.to Pres.U.S.

APPENDIX VIII. - INDEPENDENT PRESBYTERIAN CHURCH - continued

SOUTH CAROLINA (45)

CHEROKEE COUNTY (021)

A	B	C	D	E
1.	Gaffney, Salem Indep.Pres.(f.of Union Dist.;incor.in NC (16);[division from Salem Pres.(c.1805:61),l.75:unclear early years,by 1818-1838(X,r.1840)1840-1864;]61 says these merged 1854 as an IPC Ch.,however,66 cites clear minutes on 1864 merger;Merged Ch.l.Pres.U.S.1863-1974,PCA 1973-on)	by 1809(58,66)1813(j)-1813(61) 1804(pr.)	1813(j)-1863	Tr.to Pres.U.S.; merged 1864,Pres.; PCA
2.	Jonesville(Union Co.PO), Tabor Indep.Pres.(Tr.to Pres.U.S.,l. 75:btwn.1862 & 1865(j1863)-1983,Pres.1983-on;61 incor. transfers from IPC to Pres.(OS) 1841,but that is not supported in OS minutes or 66)	by 1829(16) 1832(61,75Y)	btwn.1824 & 1832(j1829) -1863	Tr.to Pres.U.S., bec. Mount Tabor Pres.
3.	Kings Creek, Hopewell Indep.Pres.(f.of York Dist.;j IPC 1829 (16);75H view that ch.split & reg.Pres.l.by 1824-1863 is unsubstantiated,he & 61 confuse with ch.in York Co.nr. Lesslie & Rock Hill(1808(61),1810(75H)))	c.1829	btwn.1824 & 1832(j1829) -1863	opposed 1863 merger but agreed to go along with majority; Tr.to Pres.U.S.; X 1864
4.	York District(f.location,but in Cherokee Co.,nr.NC line), Shiloh Indep.Pres.(nl.61;[a division of Shiloh Pres.of York Dist.(s.in NC,s.in York Dist:58)(1780(75Y),1785(61; r.1828))(f.Calvary Pres.to 1795),l.:75:btwn.1798 & 1802 (supply from NC,j SC Pby.1786)-1861(OS),1861-1884(Pres. U.S.);moved to Grover,Cleveland Co.,NC,l.75:1884-1983 (Pres.U.S.),1983-on(Pres.)])	c.1811(75H) by 1813	1813(j)- btwn.1813 & 1824	X by 1821(66) (1823:75H)

CHESTER COUNTY (023)

A	B	C	D	E
1.	Chester, Bethany Indep.Pres.(s.l.Clover,York Co.;1841 bldg.)	1844(69) 1837(pr.) 1834(16) 1835(61,69)	btwn.1836 & 1843-1863 1834 or 1835(j1835) -btwn.1836 & 1843	Reported as Tr.to Pres.U.S.,but nl.;X btwn.1836 & 1843 (1844:75H;pr.to 1844)
2.	Chester (f.Chesterville), Center Indep.Pres.(Chesterville)			
3.	Chester, Edmonds Indep.Pres.(f.Pres.;incor.in NC:16;Edmonds Pres.(l.75:btwn.1798 & 1802-btwn.1819 & 1824),withdrew 1812(61))	1802 r.1811(75H)	1813(j)- 1834 or 1835	X 1834 or 1835 (c.1825:61)
4.	Rodman, Carmel Hill Indep.Pres.(Carmel Pres.from 1907;61 incor.shows in IPC from c.1813,but nl.by IPC to btwn.1844 & 1854;l.Pres.U.S.:75:btwn.1863 & 1865-1898,1907-1917)	by 1854 c.1810(61)	btwn.1844 & 1854- 1863	Tr.to Pres.U.S.; X 1917

APPENDIX VIII. - INDEPENDENT PRESBYTERIAN CHURCH - SOUTH CAROLINA - continued
YORK COUNTY (091)

A	B	C	D	E
1.	McConnells(ville), Olivet Pres.(McConnells PO;York PO;f. Olivet Indep.Pres.;1836 bldg.;l.75:1867-1975(Pres.U.S.), 1973-on(PCA))	1844(69) 1842(61) r.1868(75Y,55)	btwn.1836 & 1844(j1843) -1863	Tr.to Pres.U.S.; PCA
2.	Sharon, Bullock('s) Creek Indep.Pres.([division of Pres.or Cong.Ch.of Bullock's Creek(1769(or 1765(59));incp.:1784) l.75:by 1773-btwn.1798 & 1802,btwn.1803 & 1808-btwn.1809 & 1813,btwn.1814 & 1818-1861(OS),1861-1864(Pres.U.S.);] merged 1864,l.75:1864-1983(Pres.U.S.),1983-1985(Pres.), 1984 or 1985-on(PCA))	1810 1811(75H)	1813(j)- 1863	Tr.to Pres.U.S.; Merged (see text); Pres.;PCA
3.	York, Beth-Shiloh Indep.Pres.(l.Pres.U.S.::75:btwn.1863 & 1865-1983,Pres.1983-on)	1828(59,67, 75Y;pr.:61) 1830(61)	btwn.1824 & 1832(j1831) -1863	Tr.to Pres.U.S.
4.	York, Harmony Indep.Pres.(l.Pres.U.S.::btwn.1863 & 1865-1909)	1827	btwn.1824 & 1832(j1827) -1863	Tr.to Pres.U.S.; X 1910
5.	York, Indep.Pres.of Yorkville([Yorkville Pres.l.75:btwn.1809 & 1813-1830,1835-1836,may be Ch.from which this split,but 61 says that is a l.of a division of this ch.;66 does not recognize a reg.Pres.Ch.here at this time];Merged to First Pres.Ch.here at this time];Merged to First Pres.of York(1842)(l.75:1841-1861(OS),1861-1863(Pres. U.S.)), as First Pres.of York(l.75:1863-1983(Pres.U.S.), 1983-on(Pres.)))	1825(69) c.1822(66) c.1813(61)	btwn.1813 & 1824- 1863	Tr.to Pres.U.S.; Merged 1864(see text); Pres.
6.	York, Mill Creek Indep.Pres.(poss.Rooker's Mtghse.(61))	1835(69)	1834 or 1835(j 1835)-btwn. 1836 & 1843	X c.1841 or c.1842 (66)(by 1844:75H)

TENNESSEE (47)

RUTHERFORD COUNTY (149)

A	B	C	D	E
1.	Rutherford Co.(location uncertain), Ebenezer Indep.Pres.(nl. c.1815 75H)	c.1815	nl.,prob. c.1815-af. 1821	X prob.1822 or 1823

ABBREVIATIONS USED IN THE TEXT
(Many common bibliographic abbreviations are not shown.)

ab.	absorbed	e.g.	for example
ABCFM	American Bd.of Commissioners for Foreign Missions	Eng.	English
		EP	Evan.Prot.Conf.
af.	after	Epis.	Episcopal
affl.	affiliated	E&R	Evangelical & Reformed
AHMS	American Home Missionary Soc.	et al.	and others
AL	Alabama	etc.	et cetera (and so forth)
AMA	American Missionary Assn.	Evan.	Evangelical
Amer.	America(n)	f.	formerly
AR	Arkansas	Fed.	Federated
Assn.	Association	ff.	following
Assns.	Associations	Fl	Filipino
Asso.	Associate	FL	Florida
Ave.	Avenue	Fr	French
Bapt.	Baptist	GA	Georgia
bB	bec.Black	Gen.	General
Bd.	Board	Ger.	German
bec.	became	Gr	German
bf.	before	Hon.	Honorary
Bl	Black	Hu	Hungarian
bldg.	building	Hung.	Hungarian
btwn.	between	IFCA	Indep.Fundamental Chs.of Amer.
c.	circa (about)	IK	Indiana/KY Conf.
CAC	Central Atlantic Conf.	In	American Indian (all tribes)
CC	Congregational Christian	inclu.	included/including
CCCC	Conservative Congregational Christian Conference	incor.	incorrect/incorrectly
		incp.	incorporated
CGA	Cong.Assn.of SC	indep.	independent
cgn.	congregation	IPC	Indep.Pres.Ch.
ch.	church	IT	Indian Territory
Chap.	Chapel	j	joined
Chr.	Christian	KS	Kansas
chs.	churches	KY	Kentucky
CO	Colorado	l.	listed/listing
Co.	County	LA	Louisiana
C of C	Church of Christ	lt.	listed twice
Com.	Community	Luth.	Lutheran
Conf.	Conference	m.	mentioned
Cong.	Congregational	M	Merger
Conv.	Convention	MA	Massachusetts
Cos.	Counties	MD	Maryland
Counc.	Council of Community	Mem.	Memorial
Com.Chs.	Churches	Meth.	Methodist
CP	Charleston Pby.	MI	Michigan
Cr	Creole	MO	Missouri
CUP	Charleston Union Pby.	mos.	months
CUPCg.	CUP:Cong.Ch.	MS	Mississippi
CUPPr.	CUP:Pres.Ch.	Mt.	Mount
DC	District of Columbia	mtghse.	meetinghouse
DE	Delaware	Mtn.	Mountain
Disc.	Christian Church (Disciples of Christ)	NA	Cong.Chr.Chs.,Natl.Assn.
		natl.	national
Dist.	District	NC	North Carolina
Ed.	Editor(s)	n.d.	no date

ABBREVIATIONS USED IN THE TEXT
(Many common bibliographic abbreviations are not shown.)

NE	Northeast		Tr.	Transferred
NJ	New Jersey		Twn.	Township
nl.	not listed		TX	Texas
NM	New Mexico		UCC	United Church of Christ
no.	number		UDMS	United Domestic Missionary Soc.
n.p.	no place			
nr.	near		UFMS	United Foreign Missionary Soc.
NS	New School		U.Meth.	United Methodist
Nt	Note		Unitar.	Unitarian
NW	Northwest		Univ.	Universalist
NY	New York		U.S.	United States
OH	Ohio		U.S.A.	United States of America
OK	Oklahoma		UT	Utah
org.	organized/organization		UUA	Unitar.Univ.Assn.
OS	Old School		VA	Virginia
p.	page		Vol.	Volume
PA	Pennsylvania		X	Extinct
Par.	Parish		We	Welsh
pB	prob.Black		WV	West Virginia
Pby.	Presbytery			
Pbys.	Presbyteries			
PCA	Pres.Ch.in Amer.		SYMBOLS	
pl.	place			
pla.	plotted		&	and
pltn.	plantation		?	unknown or possibly
PO	Post Office		#	number (used for one, two, or three digit number of a church; and for numbered minor civil divisions)
poss.	possibly			
pp.	pages			
pr.	preaching			
Pres.	Presbyterian		*	In KY Column D for churches dropped as inter-church not being Congregational (1880)
prob.	probably			
Prot.	Protestant			
pr.pl.	preaching place			
prps.	proposed			
Pt.	Point			
q.v.	which see			
r.	reorganized/reorganization			
Rd.	Road			
Ref.	Reformed			
reg.	regular			
s.	sometime/sometimes			
Sa	Samoan			
SC	South Carolina			
Sch.	Schedule			
sett.	settled			
sic	thus so (literal quote)			
Sk	Slovak			
Soc.	Society			
Sp	Hispanic			
SS	Sunday School			
St.	Saint or Street			
Sub.Co.	Subordinate County			
Sub.Dist.	Subordinate District			
TN	Tennessee			

ANNOTATED BIBLIOGRAPHY

Bibliographic
Reference
Number

(01) ANNUAL STATISTICAL LISTS

This single reference number refers to the continuous annual statistics and lists of the churches. Generally we have used the national listings for this information, which usually conform to the state lists (see below).

National Publications:

The Congregational Almanac for 1846-1848
     (3 volumes) (C.C.Dean(1846 volume), James French(1847 & 1848 volumes), Boston, 1845-1847)
These three volumes have reproduced a variety of state reports without consistency.

American Congregational Yearbook 1854-1859
     (6 volumes) (American Congregational Union, New York, 1854-1859)
[first issue called Yearbook of the American Congregational Union]
We have used these lists for statistics for the years c.1852-c.1857. During these years there are often large discrepancies with state lists when the latter are available.

Congregational Quarterly 1859-1878
     (20 volumes) (American Congregational Association and American Congregational Union, Boston and New York, 1859-1878)
This magazine, beginning in 1860, devoted one issue per year to the publication of statistics which we have used to cover the years c.1858-c.1876, nineteen years of statistics. The Quarterly from the start also printed information on new churches organized or received beginning with 1858.(See code 01N)

Congregational Yearbook 1879-1928
     (51 volumes)(National Council of Congregational Churches, New York and Boston, 1879-1929)
We have generally followed these listings. The user of this set should be aware of two problems in dating these volumes. The 1888 Yearbook was the first to make statistics uniform for the calendar year before the date of publication. (That volume printed the January 1 to December 31, 1887 statistics.) The earlier volumes printed variously dated reports covering c.1877-c.1885. Thus there may be a c.1886 report available from the state minutes which could fill in the continuity (See below). The other problem involves the dating of these volumes themselves. Volumes 1 to 24 bore the date of the year of their publication (1879 to 1902). Volumes 25 to 36 bore two dates, the year of publication and the year the enclosed statistics covered (1903 to 1914, statistics for 1902-1913). Volumes 37 to 51 carry the date of the covered statistics (statistics for 1914-1928). Thus, depending on the method followed, many libraries have two 1902 volumes, two 1914 volumes, or have erroneously discarded one issue. These volumes generally have statistics for c.1877-c.1885, 1887-1928. The Quarterly practice of separate lists for new churches organized or received was followed through the 1896 Yearbook. (See code 01N). These volumes also included a chart of building dates in the issues from 1911(statistics for 1910) through 1926, inclusive, which we have used to find congregations which may have had an earlier ecumenical or other denominational origin revealed through such a date.(Whenever we use a building date, either the original building, or the building is use during this period is implied.) These books also include a directory of independent or mission Sunday Schools related to the denomination from 1893 to 1914 (statistics for 1913) inclusive. Also summary totals of these from 1914 to 1926. We have not picked up any of this Sunday School information for this volume.

205

<u>Yearbook of the Congregational (and) Christian Churches 1929-1960</u>
(32 volumes)(General Council of the Congregational (and) Christian Churches, New York and Dayton (Ohio) 1930-1961)
We have followed these lists with statistics for 1929-1960.

<u>Yearbook of the United Church of Christ 1962-1993</u>
(32 volumes)(United Church of Christ, New York or Cleveland, 1962-1993)
We have followed these lists with statistics for 1961-1992.

Related national references:
<u>CC Churches which by their action reported as of June 15, 1961 will be counted as part of the UCC</u> (Report of the Co-Secretaries of the United Church of Christ) (mimeo,1961). This was the first list of United Church congregations.
<u>File of Votes of Congregational Christian Churches on the formation of the United Church of Christ</u> 1960 ff. This file from the office of the Secretary of the United Church of Christ, formerly in New York, (now at the United Church of Christ Archives in Lancaster, PA), was used to find exact dates of congregations votes on the United Church of Christ, Schedule II., etc..

Proposed Churches:
Beginning in the 1875 Quarterly (for c.1873) churches not yet fully organized were added in brackets. This continued through the 1922 Yearbook (for 1922). Occasionally these churches were designated other ways, such as with an asterisk or at the end of the list without a number. On rare occasion this also happened in years other than those specified. A new listing entitled "Proposed Churches," was added to the 1989 Yearbook (for 1988) and has appeared each year since then. We have indicated all such churches as proposed churches and note them in the column B text rather than in Column D.

Preaching Places:
It is generally not our policy to report on preaching places where there are no organized congregations. Nor was it the policy of any of the above publications to print such material.

Calendar Dating:
Statistics and reports are on a calendar year basis for all states from 1888 on. In addition calendar year listings were given for churches with the following affiliations: Alabama: from 1882; Florida: from 1885; New Jersey: from 1879.
Listings before these dates were collected either by the national Yearbook at various (usually designated) dates in the year, or at meetings of the various Associations. For example an 1879 Association meeting would collect data for a year which included part of 1878 and part of 1879. We have designated such a report as 1878 (since that is the year that ended in the period covered). All years before calendar dating was introduced (except for the exceptions noted below) should therefore be taken to mean "in this year or in the immediately following year."
The 1887 national Yearbook covers c.1885 reports, while the 1888 Yearbook includes the entire year 1887. This change left one year of data not collected by the national Yearbook. We have inserted calendar year data for 1886 from the Alabama, Florida, and New Jersey minutes. We have inserted c.1886 data from Georgia (Black), Louisiana, and North Carolina minutes. (In these three latter cases "1887" therefore only refers to the latter part of that year.) No insert data has been found for churches affiliated with Arkansas, Georgia (White), Mississippi, Tennessee, Texas, Missouri, and Ohio bodies, nor for unaffiliated churches. In such cases, changes occurring between the 1887 and 1888 national Yearbook lists are shown as 1886 or 1887, and cover part of 1886 and all of 1887.
Even though calendar year reports were given in the New Jersey minutes, the national Yearbook printed mid-year reports for the District of Columbia in 1880 for Virginia in 1880,1882,1883,1884,1885, and 1886, and for West Virginia in 1880,1882, 1883, and 1884. We have checked all such reports to make sure all churches are given.

Even though the national Yearbook printed calendar year reports, mid-year reports appear in the minutes of the following bodies: Georgia (Black): 1888,1890; Louisiana (Black): 1888,1890,1892,1893,1894,1895; North Carolina (Black): 1888,1889,1890,1891, 1892,1893. We have checked all such cases to make sure all churches are given.

In addition to the above, the following variants to calendar dating exist in the reports of churches affiliated with the following bodies: Alabama: reported 1881 is part of that year, reported 1879 is actually only part of 1880; Florida: 1884 is part of that year; Louisiana: 1876 is part of that year, 1870 is part of that year; Indian Territory: reported 1877 is actually only part of 1878, 1876 is part of 1876 and all of 1877; New Jersey: 1878 is part of that year; Ohio: reported 1875 is all of 1875 and part of 1876, 1874 and 1873 are calendar years, 1872 is part of that year.

Summary Remarks:
These entries taken as a whole, are the primary source material on which these studies are based. Unless otherwise specified, all references on listing, not listed, listed twice etc. refer to these publications.

The first date in the listing column indicates that the church first appeared in the report issued for the end of that year. The year shown as the year dropped means this is the first year end report in which the church does not appear. (The last appearance was actually in the report for one year earlier.) The number of reports a church appeared in could be easily computed by subtracting the first year from the second. Thus a church listed 1918 to 1920 appeared in two statistical reports, those for the ends of 1918 and 1919.

(01N)   As stated above, in addition to the regular church lists, lists of newly organized churches were printed in the Congregational Quarterly in all issues, and continuing in the Yearbook from the first issue through the 1896 issue. These are indicated with the code 01N. (In my earlier volumes these entries were designated with the code ncl.01).

(01S)   State Publications:

The weakness of Congregationalism in the South led to many marginal inter-church organizations which were often not able to publish their minutes, often even unable to meet. This was further complicated by segregation which divided the churches in an area into two even weaker organizations. Some minutes were never published, others are probably permanently lost. In addition, when minutes were published, they were often only the actual meeting minutes and lack a church directory. Sometimes the minutes of several years would be published in one booklet without comparable church lists. Thus it is impossible to use the state records to make ongoing lists. Therefore the various state records are used only as secondary materials to the national church lists. In modern years a few Conferences have published Directories separate from the minutes. These are, however, hard to date exactly.

One place where inter-church bodies have been helpful has been in identifying ethnic churches. Since many forces in the national church sought to integrate work in the South, records submitted by racially defined bodies were often combined in the national Yearbook. The state records found help us to see where the churches were affiliated.

We have used the national lists in all cases, except as noted. Where discrepancies appear we have used the 01S code. Many churches were reported in the national publications long before there was a state body in their area. The best collections of state minutes that we have found are at the Congregational Library in Boston, the Andover Harvard Library at Harvard Divinity School in Cambridge, MA, and the Chicago Theological Seminary Library. Charleston Union Presbytery minutes (1822-1839) are at the Presbyterian Historical Center in Montreat, NC.

ANNOTATED BIBLIOGRAPHY

State or state equivalent bodies in the south, including the years they existed, ethnic identity, states served(for the entire life of the inter-church body unless otherwise specified), and years for which we have found minutes are as follows:

Information on all states served by southern oriented groups is given. However, only southern states served by non-southern oriented groups are shown. Also minutes found are not identified for primarily non-Southern groups.

State Oriented Southern Bodies: (Arranged alphabetically by state;chronologically within states, except that successor organizations follow directly their originating bodies.)

General Conference of Congregational Churches of the State of Alabama
   (Congregational Association of Alabama) Org.1876 (Multi-racial, then Black from
   1890) Minutes found: 1877-1895,1897-1899,1901-1905,1909-1911,1913-1921. A
   library I have not visited says they also have 1896,1900,1906-1908,1912. Served
   AL. Merged 1929 to form following:
Alabama Mississippi Congregational Association (Alabama Mississippi Congregational
   Christian Conference) Org.1929 (Black) Minutes found: None. Served AL,MS. Joined
   Convention of the South 1950 (q.v.)
United Congregational Conference of South Alabama.Org.1890 (White) Minutes found:
   1890-1891. (The 1890 minutes include two District minutes, while the 1891
   minutes include five District minutes.) Also found District minutes for Mount
   Jefferson:1890;Tallassee:1890;Clanton:1891. Served AL. Succeeded by General
   Convention 1892.
United Congregational Conference of North Alabama.Org.1891 (White) Minutes found:
   1891. Also found District minutes for Bear Creek:1891;Warrior:1891.Served AL.
   Succeeded by General Convention 1892.
General Congregational Convention of Alabama (General Congregational Conference of
   Alabama; Congregational Conference of Alabama) Org.1892 (White) Minutes found:
   1892,1894-1896,1898-1915,1923-1929. (Did not meet 1893;1923 minutes report that
   1918,1920 and 1921 minutes already missing.1919 was apparently printed.) Also
   found District minutes for Echo:1898-1899. Served AL,FL(1919-1931). Merged to
   Christian group 1931 to form:
Alabama Conference of Congregational and Christian Churches. Org.1931 (White)
   Affiliated to Southern Convention 1931-1934. Minutes found: None. Served AL,FL.
   Joined Southeast Convention 1949(q.v.).
West Florida and South Alabama Congregational Association. Org.1907 (White) Minutes
   found: None. Served AL,FL. X 1908
Arkansas Congregational Association. Org.1887 (White) Minutes found:None. Served AR.
   Inactive 1890. Probably X 1894 or 1895, reported as such 1898; listed until
   1902.
Congregational Association of the District of Columbia. Org.1867. (probably Multi-
   racial) Minutes found: None. Served DC (possibly elsewhere). Probably a
   ministerial Association. Succeeded by NJ Association 1869/1870.
General Congregational Association of Florida (General Congregational Association of
   Florida and the Southeast; General Congregational Conference of Florida and the
   Southeast; Florida Congregational Conference; Florida Congregational Christian
   Conference; Florida Conference of the United Church of Christ) Plan 1883, Org.
   1884. (Multi-racial;White 1903-af.1924;Multi-racial by 1959) Minutes found:
   1883-1907,1909-1920,1922,1924-1926,1928-1930,1932-1935,1939. Served FL,GA(1893-
   1899,1903-1918),SC(1891-1918),Cuba(1901-1919). Received E&R Churches 1962.
   Alive.
West Florida and South Alabama... (see above under Alabama)
Southeastern Congregational Conference (mentioned in GA 1874, probably not fully
   org.)
Georgia Congregational Conference (Georgia Congregational Association) Org.c.1878.
   (Multi-racial;Black from 1885) Minutes found:1878-1888,1890-1891.(Last year as
   part of General Convention) Served GA,SC. Absorbed under General Convention
   1890.

Atlanta Congregational Union. Org.1885 (White) Minutes found: None. Served GA. Merged into United Conference 1888.

United Congregational Conference of Georgia.Plan 1887,Org.1888. (White) Minutes found:1887-1892 (two meetings 1888).(Last two years served bodies also in General Convention) Also found District minutes for Vann's Valley & Chattahoochie:1888;Broad River:1888;Gainesville:1888;Atlanta:1888;Flint River:1888. Served AL,GA. Absorbed under General Convention 1890.

General Congregational Convention of Georgia (General Congregational Convention of Georgia and South Carolina; General Congregational Christian Convention of Georgia and South Carolina) Org.1890 (Multi-racial to 1903,then Black) Minutes found:1890,1892-1893,1904-1907,1915. Also found District minutes for Blue Ridge: 1890;Gainesville:1892,1897;Atlanta:1891,1897;Flint River:1891. Served FL(1921-1924),GA,SC(1927-1950). Joined Convention of the South 1950(q.v.).

United Congregational Conference of Georgia Org.1918. (White) Minutes found: None. Served GA. Merged to Christian group 1931/1932 to form:

Georgia Congregational Christian Conference (Georgia-South Carolina Congregational Christian Conference) Org.1932. (White) Affiliated to Southern Convention 1931-1934. Minutes found: None. Served GA,SC(1939-1949). Joined Southeast Convention 1949 (q.v.).

State Association of Christian Churches and Ministers of Kentucky. Org.by 1870. (Multi-racial) Minutes found: None. Served KY. Reported as not a Congregational body 1879, dropped 1880. (Although most churches later rejoined denomination.)

Cumberland Valley Congregational Association. mentioned 1892. shown as Org.1896. (probably White) Minutes found: None. Served KY. Extinct 1897.

General Congregational Association of Kentucky (Kentucky Congregational State Conference) Org.1898. (White) Minutes found: None. Served KY. Merged to Tennessee 1941 (q.v.)

New Orleans Congregational Ministers Association. Org.by 1869. (probably Multi-racial; probably derived from an interdenominational fellowship which is existed in 1864 and was supportive of the AMA.) Minutes found: None. Served LA. Ministerial body, succeeded by:

South Western Conference of Congregational Churches and Ministers (Louisiana Congregational Association;Louisiana Congregational Conference; Louisiana Congregational Christian Conference) Plan 1869,Org.1870(incp.1910). (Multi-racial (had some White churches as late as 1905);then Black) Minutes found:1870-1871,1877-1895,1900-1905,1907-1911,1925. Served LA,MS(1870-1872). Merged to Plymouth Conference of the Southwest 1948(q.v.).

West Central Congregational Association (or Calcasieu Congregational Association) Org.by 1889. (White) Minutes found: None. Served LA. Extinct after 1895.

Louisiana State Congregational Association (Louisiana State Congregational Christian Association) Org.1914. (White) Minutes found: None. Served LA. Joined Central South Convention 1947 (q.v.).

Mississippi Congregational Association (Mississippi Conference of Congregational Churches) Org.1883 (Multi-racial,later considered Black) Minutes found: 1884-1886. Served MS. Merged to Alabama 1929 (q.v.)

Alabama Mississippi...   (see above under Alabama)

Conference of Congregational Churches and Ministers of North Carolina (Association of Congregational Churches of North Carolina; General Association of Congregational Churches (and Ministers) of North Carolina; (Annual) Conference of Congregational Churches of North Carolina; North Carolina State Conference of Congregational Churches) Org.1879 (Multi-racial(had White churches as late as 1914);later considered Black) Minutes found: 1879-1895,1900-1905,1907,1909,1911-1912,1914-1917. Served NC. Merged to Christian groups 1932 to form:

State Conference of Congregational and Christian Churches of North Carolina. Org. 1932. (Black) Minutes found: None. Served NC,VA. Joined Convention of the South 1950 (q.v.).

Golden Valley Congregational District Conference of North Carolina. Org.1890 (White) Minutes found:1890. Served NC. Merged 1897 into Western North Carolina.

Piedmont Congregational Conference. Org.by 1892 (White) Minutes found: None. Served NC. Merged 1897 into Western North Carolina.

ANNOTATED BIBLIOGRAPHY

Western North Carolina Congregational Association. Org.1897 by merger of above. (White) Minutes found: None. Served NC. Extinct after 1900.

Middle North Carolina Congregational Association. Org.1910 (White) Minutes found: 1915-1917. Served NC. Merged 1917 to form:

Congregational Conference of the Carolinas (Congregational Christian Conference of the Carolinas) Org.1917 by merger. (White) Minutes found: 1918. Served NC,SC. Joined Southern Convention 1932 (q.v.).

Indian Mission Association. Mentioned 1845. (Multi-racial) Minutes found: None. Served Indian Territory (OK) Other information unknown.

Red River Congregational Association. Org.by 1880. (Multi-racial) Minutes found: None. Served OK,and TX. Extinct 1882.

Oklahoma Congregational Association (Oklahoma General Association of Congregational Churches;Oklahoma General Conference of Congregational Churches;Oklahoma General Conference of Congregational Christian Churches) Org.1890. (Multi-racial;White 1925-1947) Minutes found: 1890-1911,1913-1918,1922. Served AR(1925-1939), Indian Territory (OK) (1901-1907),KS(1902-1906,btwn.1910 & 1912-1932),OK,TX (1910-1911 or 1912,1932-1947). Joined Central South Convention 1947 (q.v.).

Congregational Association of South Carolina. Org.1801. (White) Minutes found: None. Served GA(1801-af.1811),SC. Possibly only Ministerial in form. 1822 merged to Presbyterian Churches to form Charleston Union Presbytery.

Charleston Union Presbytery. (A Presbyterian body affiliated to Presbyterian Church, U.S.A.;Perhaps a majority of the clergy served Congregational Churches.) Org. 1822. (White) Minutes found: 1822-1839. Divided 1838 and became an independent body outside regular Presbyterian Church. Extinct 1852, merged to Charleston Presbytery of Presbyterian Church,U.S.A.(Old School).

South Carolina State Congregational Association. Org.1899 (or 1918 in some sources). (Black) Minutes found: None. Served SC. 1927 merged to Georgia Convention (q.v.).

South Carolina Congregational Association. Org.1917. (White) Minutes found: None. Served SC. 1918 Merged to Middle North Carolina Association to form Conference of the Carolinas (q.v.,with North Carolina)

Central South Conference of Congregational Ministers and Churches (Central South Congregational Association; Tennessee Association of Congregational Churches; Tennessee Association of Congregational Christian Churches) plan 1869, Org.1871. (Multi-racial;then Black c.1915) Minutes found:1869,1871-1887,1889-1896,1898, 1903-1904,1926. Served AL,AR(1881-1898,1901-1950),GA(1871-1878),KY(1885-1950),MS (1871-1883),TN. Joined Convention of the South 1950 (q.v.).

Tennessee Conference of Congregational Churches (Tennessee Conference of Congregational Christian Churches) Org.1915 (incp.1925)(White) Minutes found: None. Served TN. 1941 Merged to Kentucky Conference to form:

Kentucky-Tennessee Congregational Christian Association. Org.1941 (White) Minutes found: None. Served KY,TN. Joined Southeast Convention 1949 (q.v.).

Congregational Conference of Texas (Congregational Association of Texas; Southwest Texas Congregational Association) Org.1871. (Multi-racial;(Inactive c.1884-1894) became Black by 1894) Minutes found: 1894.Served TX.Extinct af.1904.

North Texas Congregational Association (Texas Congregational Association;Lone Star Congregational Association;Lone Star Conference of Congregational Churches and Ministers;Conference(or Association) of Congregational Ministers and Churches of Texas) Org.1882(incp.1928) (possibly Multi-racial at start,became White early) Minutes found:1912-1920,1922-1927. Served Indian Territory (OK) (1882-af.1884), TX. Joined Central South Convention 1947 (q.v.)

Texas Congregational Conference (Plymouth Congregational Conference of Texas; Plymouth Congregational Christian Conference of Texas) Org.1900 or 1911(incp. 1927) (Black) Minutes found: None. Served OK(1925-1948);TX. Joined Plymouth Conference of the Southwest 1948(q.v.).

Virginia Congregational Christian Conference. Org.1939 (Black) Minutes found: None. Served VA. Joined Convention of the South 1950 (q.v.).

Northern Bodies Serving Southern States: (Arranged alphabetically except that successor organizations follow their predecessor body. All of these groups were considered Multi-racial. However, if they only served one ethnic group in the South that is identified.)

Colorado State Association Conference (Congregational Association of
     Colorado; Colorado Congregational Conference) Org.1868 Served OK(1916-1926),
     TX(1925-1926). Extinct 1962.
Congregational Association of Pennsylvania (Congregational Conference of
     Pennsylvania;Pennsylvania State Conference of Congregational Churches;
     Congregational Christian Conference of Pennsylvania) Org.1886,r.1931. Served
     MD(1931-1935). Extinct 1963.
Congregational Conference of Ohio (Congregational Association of Ohio;
     Congregational Conference of Ohio) Plan 1852, Org.1853(incp.1907) Served KY
     (1877-1931),WV(1872-1931). Received Christian Churches 1930 and r.1931 as:
Ohio Conference of Congregational Christian Churches Org.1931. Served KY,WV. Merged
     1963 into:
Ohio Conference of the United Church of Christ. Org.1963. Served KY,WV. Alive.
Evangelical Protestant Conference of Congregational Churches. Received by merger
     1924/1925. Served KY. Disbanded 1947, Churches transferred to Ohio.
General Association of Arizona and New Mexico (New Mexico Congregational
     Association;New Mexico Congregational Conference) Org.1884. (Related to
     Tri-State Congregational Conference of Arizona,New Mexico and Texas 1924-1925);
     Served TX(between 1913 & 1915-1930) Merged 1930 into:
Southwest Congregational Conference. Org.1930. Served TX. Merged 1943 into:
General Congregational Association of Southern California (General Conference of
     Congregational Churches and Ministers of Southern California; Southern
     California Congregational Conference; Congregational Conference of Southern
     California and the Southwest; Southern California and Southwest Conference of
     the United Church of Christ; Southern California Conference of the United Church
     of Christ) Org. 1887. Served TX(1943-1965). Alive. (Churches transferred to:)
Southwest Conference of the United Church of Christ. Org.1965. Served TX. Alive.
General Association of Congregational Churches and Ministers of New Jersey
     (Congregational Association of New Jersey; Congregational Conference of New
     Jersey; Middle Atlantic Conference of Congregational Churches) Org.1869 (incp.
     1927/1928) Served DE(1898-1902,1927-1931),DC,MD,VA,WV(1880-1881,1882-1885).
     1931 merged into:
Middle Atlantic Congregational Christian Conference. Org.1931. Served DE,DC,MD,VA.
     1964 merged into:
Central Atlantic Conference of the United Church of Christ. Org.1964. Served DE,DC,
     MD,VA,WV. Alive.
General Association of Congregational Ministers and Churches of Michigan (General
     Association of Congregational Churches and Ministers in Michigan; Michigan
     Congregational Association; Michigan Congregational Conference; Michigan
     Congregational and Christian Conference) Organized 1842. Served TX (Black: 1866-
     1867,1870-1871) Extinct 1963.
General Association of New York Congregational Churches and Ministers
     (Congregational Association of New York; Congregational Conference of New York;
     New York Congregational Christian Conference) Plan 1834,Org.1835. Served DE
     (1836-1843). Extinct 1963.
General Conference of Missouri Congregational Churches and Ministers (General
     Association of Congregational Churches of Missouri; Congregational Association
     of Missouri; Missouri Congregational Conference; Congregational Christian
     Conference of Missouri) Org.1865. Served AR(1881-1887,1894-1963(White 1881-1887,
     1894-1956;Black 1955-1963)),Indian Territory(OK)(1879-1907),OK(1907-1947),TN
     (1889-1914,1956-1963(White)). Merged 1963 into:
Missouri Conference of the United Church of Christ. Org.1963. Served AR,TN(White
     1963-1966,Multi-racial 1966-on) Alive.
Indiana-Kentucky Conference of the United Church of Christ. Org.1963. Served KY,TN
     (1963-1965). Alive.
Kansas-Oklahoma Conference of the United Church of Christ. Org.1963. Served OK,
     TX(claimed churches 1963-1971,although they were reported in South Central

Conference in the national Yearbook.). Alive.
Penn West Conference of the United Church of Christ. Org.1962. Served MD. Alive.
Welsh Gymanfa of Pennsylvania. Org.1838,r.1839. Served MD 1858-1868. Divided 1871.
West Pennsylvania Welsh Congregational Association. Org.1871. Served MD(1873-1876).
    Joined Congregational Association of Pennsylvania 1886(q.v.).

Former Christian Bodies Serving in the South 1931-on:

Southern Based Groups:
Afro-Christian Convention. Org.1892,r.1908. (Black) Minutes found: None. Served MD
    (1931-1934),NJ,NY,NC(1931-1932),VA. Divided 1939. (Continued as a fellowship
    group to 1950).
Southern Christian Convention (Southern Congregational Christian Convention)
    Org.1856. (White) (Received Congregational Churches 1932;in Association with
    Alabama and Georgia bodies (q.v.) 1931-1934 [two meetings held 1932 and 1934 as
    South Eastern Convention of Congregational Christian Churches]) Minutes found:
    1931-1932,1934,1944,1946-1947,1956,1960,1962,1964,1965(met every other year
    except that 1931,1947 & 1965 were special meetings.Also found 1933 & 1947 local
    Conference reports. Served AL(-1931),DE(-1931),GA(-1931),MD(1931-1932),NC,SC
    (1932-1939),VA,WV(1931-1964). Also claimed AL(1931-1934),FL(1931-1934),GA(1931-
    1934) through temporary affiliations. Merged into Southern Conference of the
    United Church of Christ 1965(q.v.).

Formerly part of Primarily Northern Based Groups:
The following Conferences were part of the Metropolitan Christian Convention,org.
    1919,disbanded 1931:
New Jersey Christian Conference: Served DE(-1931). Merged into Middle Atlantic
    Conference 1931(q.v.).
Rays Hill and Southern Pennsylvania Christian Conference: Served MD(-1931). Merged
    into Congregational Christian Conference of Pennsylvania (q.v.).
Southwestern West Virginia Christian Conference: Served WV. withdrew 1935.
West Virginia Christian Conference: Served WV. withdrew 1934.
The following Conferences were part of the Central Christian Convention,org.1920,
    disbanded 1931:
Kentucky Christian Conference (Kentucky North Congregational Christian Conference)
    Served KY,OH. withdrew 1934. Reinstated 1938. withdrew 1948.
Kentucky State Christian Conference. Served KY,WV. withdrew 1934.

Regional Southern Bodies: (listed alphabetically)

Central South Congregational Christian Convention. Org.1947 (White) Minutes found:
    1952-1953,1960. Served LA,OK,TX. Divided 1963 to Kansas-Oklahoma and South
    Central Conferences.
Convention of the South of Congregational Christian Churches. Org.1950 (Black)
    Minutes found: None. Served AL,AR(1950-1955),GA,KY(1950-1963),LA(1950-1963),MS,
    NJ(1950-1960),NY(1950-1960),NC,OK(1950-1960),SC,TN,TX(1950-1963),VA. Churches
    variously transferred to the Missouri, New York, Indiana-Kentucky, Kansas-
    Oklahoma, South Central, Southeast and Southern Conferences, extinct 1965.
Plymouth Congregational Christian Conference of the Southwest. Org. 1948 (Black)
    Minutes found:None. Served LA,OK,TX. Joined Convention of the South 1950 (q.v.).
South Central Conference of the United Church of Christ. Org.1963 (Multi-racial)
    Minutes found:1981(Bluebook),1980/1981 Directory. Served AR(1969-1975),LA,MS
    (1963-1975),TX. Alive.
Southeast Convention of Congregational Christian Churches (Southeast Conference of
    the United Church of Christ) Org. 1949,r.1965 (White to 1965; then Multi-racial)
    Minutes found: 1975,1981. Served AL,FL,GA,KY(1949-1978),MS,SC,TN. Alive.
Southern Conference of the United Church of Christ. Org.1965 (Multi-racial) Minutes
    found: 1965-1968,1970-1986, also reports from Associations 1966-1981 (only some
    Associations 1966-1969). Served NC,VA. Alive.

ANNOTATED BIBLIOGRAPHY

Evangelical and Reformed Synods Serving in the South 1961-on: (Listed alphabetically)

Kansas City Synod of the E&R Church. Served OK(1961-1963).
Magyar Synod of the E&R Church (Calvin Synod Acting Conference of the United Church of Christ) Served DC(1982-1983),FL(1963-1972),MD(1983-on),VA(1961-1968),WV(1961-1982). Alive.
Missouri Valley Synod of the E&R Church. Served AR(1961-1963).
Pittsburgh Synod of the E&R Church. Served MD(1961-1963).
Potomac Synod of the E&R Church. Served DC(1961-1964),MD(1961-1964),VA(1961-1964),WV (1961-1964).
South Indiana Synod of the E&R Church. Served AL(1961-1963),KY(1961-1963),TN(1961-1963).
Southeast Ohio Synod of the E&R Church. Served WV(1961-1963).
Southwest Ohio Synod of the E&R Church. Served KY(1961-1963).
Texas Synod of the E&R Church. Served LA(1961-1963),MS(1961-1963),TX(1961-1963).

(01K)   German Listings:
The General Conference of German Congregational Churches, organized 1883, could have its various churches traced through its constituent sub-bodies in their respective state bodies. These can also be traced through its annual publication Kirchenbote Kalender (later Illustrierter Kirchenbote Kalender). This booklet, in almanac form also published regular church statistical lists. We have found the issues of 1905, 1907,1911,1913-1921,1924,1926,1939-1942,1945,1949,1959,1962-1963. These would cover statistical reports for the years 1903,1905,1909,1911-1919,1922,1924,1937-1940, 1943,1947,1957,1960-1961. The statistical report for 1936 is reported in 82.
The sub-group of the German Conference in Colorado also belonged to the Colorado state group and served German churches in OK and TX, as reported under Colorado in the 01S section. The Southern German Congregational Conference was related to the national German Conference but not to any English state body. It was organized in 1926, and served its entire life in KS,OK,and TX. While many of its churches appear with the UCC Kansas-Oklahoma Conference from 1964, and its TX churches were probably erroneously claimed by the UCC South Central Conference, the group probably withdrew.

Other Listings:

Early Unitarian listings come from:
(02)   Unitarian Congregational Register for 1846-1851 (6 volumes)(Crosly and Nichols, Boston, 1846-1851)[The first two issues were published as the Unitarian Annual Register] Statistics are for c.1845-c.1850. We have dropped all regular Unitarian listings in 1851, although they continue thereafter.
Modern Unitarian listings come from:
(03)   Unitarian Universalist Association Directory (Unitarian Universalist Association, Boston) [We have used the issues of 1965,1966,1968, and 1981/1982, 4 volumes published 1965,1966,1968 and 1982 with statistics for c.1964,c.1965, c.1967 and c.1981.]

(04) Congregational Christian Churches, National Association, organized 1955 began to act as a denomination 1961. Its records are compiled jointly from these publications:
Member Churches of the National Association 9/15/61 (mimeo) This earliest list of National Association Churches is the first printed after they began to function as a denomination, and is used to indicate churches listed "by 1961."
Handbook (National Association of Congregational Christian Churches, Milwaukee) (9 volumes published as January 1962; 1963; 1964; 1965/66; 1966/67; 1967/68; 1968/69; 1970; 1971/72; published on an irregular basis (1962-1971)) These lists cover approximately one year each. Changes in listings between the 1964 and 1965/66 Handbooks are shown as 1964 or 1965. Changes from the 1965/1966 Handbook to the

1966/1967 Handbook are shown simply as 1965. Changes between the 1968/69 and 1970 Handbooks are shown as 1968 or 1969. Dates are always approximate because of publication irregularity. The last issue (1971/72) included statistics for the calendar year 1970, although changes in the church lists run through part of 1971. Therefore the list information may be in the year shown or in the year thereafter.

Yearbook (Congregational Christian Churches, National Association, Milwaukee or Oak Creek (WI))(22 volumes published as 1972/73 to 1984/85, and 1986 to 1994;published 1972-1993) Statistics for 1971 to 1992, although list changes may be in the year following the statistical data.

Most National Association congregations are full member churches, and listings undesignated may be assumed to be such. However two state bodies (North Carolina State Conference; South Georgia Association) are affiliated to the NA. Their churches are all listed, but they may or may not also be full members churches. In addition the NA also has Associate members churches, which while usually foreign, may be in the U.S.. There is also one Honorary member church in this study. All such special categories are designated.

(05) The Conservative Congregational Christian Conference was organized in 1948. We have found no publications before the 1959 minutes. However, later issues of listings give dates when churches joined the Conference, and we have been able to reconstruct some of the earlier membership from this information. Listings are compiled from the following publications:

Minutes of the Eleventh Annual Meeting of the Conservative Congregational Christian Conference (n.p.,1959). Statistics for c.1958.

Annual Report 1966-67, The Conservative Congregational Christian Conference (mimeo) Church lists here are inserted to the listing continuity for c.1965.

Year Book (of the) Conservative Congregational Christian Conference (1960-1961; 1963-1966; 1968; 1970-1994) (32 volumes, various places, published 1961-1966, 1968, 1970-1994). Statistics for c.1959-c.1964,c.1966,c.1968,1970-1993. In the continuity of these volumes, the 1970 issue notes changes for 1967 or 1968. The 1971 issue was the first issue with calendar year reports, and notes changes 1969 or 1970.

General Studies: (Arranged randomly)

(08)   "The Amistad Event," Special Issue of New Conversations (Vol.II, #2 & 3, Winter/Spring 1989). Includes these articles of particular note: "Southern and Western Churches Affiliated with the American Missionary Association, 1865-1918," pp.77-82; "Churches in the South and Among Native Americans Founded by the American Missionary Association and Under Its Support in 1888," pp.83-84.

(14)   Zikmund, Barbara Brown,Ed.,Hidden Histories of the United Church of Christ, (United Church Press, New York, 1984) This is a general history but includes chapters here of importance, particularly "American Indians, Missions, and the United Church of Christ," (by Serge F.Hummon), and "Blacks and the American Missionary Association" (by Clara Merritt DeBoer).

(15)   Zikmund, Barbara Brown,Ed.,Hidden Histories in the United Church of Christ 2 (United Church Press, New York, 1987) This is a general history, continuing the above, but with little that relates directly to Southern Congregationalism.

(16)   Punchard, George, History of Congregationalism Volume V. (Congregational Publishing Society, Boston, 1881) [Congregationalism in America Volume II.] This interesting general history takes various parts of the country and traces the early development of Congregationalism in that area. Some of its southern materials, particularly on the relation to the Independent Presbyterian Church, are unique and valuable.

(17)   Kirkham, E.Kay, A Survey of American Church Records IV Edition (Everton Publishers, Logan (UT), 1978) This is a listings of local church records which could provide historical parameters, but has few southern entries related to our

group of churches.

(18)   Goddard, Carolyn E., <u>On the Trail of the UCC</u> (United Church Press, New York, 1981) This non-exhaustive book includes several brief comments of the histories of many of the more historic churches in this area.

(19)   Gaustad, Edwin Scott, <u>Historical Atlas of Religion in America: Revised Edition</u> (Harper & Row, NY,Hagerstown,San Francisco, 1978) See particularly "Indians," pp.141-149.

<u>General Southern and Congregational Studies:</u> (Arranged alphabetically)

    "The Color Line" (a collection of articles on southern strategy) <u>The American Missionary</u> (Vol.37 # 9, Sept.1883) pp.267-278.

    Goodwin, Edward Lewis, <u>The Colonial Church in Virginia</u> (Morehouse Publishing Co., Milwaukee, 1927) Deals primarily with the Anglican Church in VA, but helpful in an overview of early Puritanism.

(20)   Jenkins, Frank E., <u>et al.</u>, <u>Anglo Saxon Congregationalism in the South</u> (Franklin Turner Co., Atlanta, 1908) This is a terrible book. While purporting to be a book on southern church history it gives few dates and limited information. Instead the book is an appeal for support for a southern mission strategy aimed at "Anglo Saxon" populations. To do that, it contends that only a strong "Anglo Saxon" strategy will help Black congregations to grow. It includes a long chapter to defend the southern point of view on "the race question," which regards Blacks as inferiors and confines them to agricultural and industrial learning opportunities.

(21)   Kirbye, J. Edward, <u>Puritanism in the South</u> (Pilgrim Press, Boston, 1908) This interesting book is probably the most complete treatment of seventeenth and early eighteenth century Puritanism in the south.

    Strieby, M.E., "History of Congregationalism in the Southern States," A paper read before the National Council of Congregational Churches, 1883 <u>Minutes</u> (Congregational Publishing House, Boston, 1883) pp.117-129. A well informed summary history for its time, Strieby (an officer of the AMA) enters the southern mission strategy debate by using the history to defend the idea of a mission "coming down to the lowliest" is society, Black or White, rather than seeking out the "Congregational element."

(22)   Sweet, William Warren, <u>Religion on the American Frontier 1783-1850, Vol.III.: The Congregationalists</u> (Cooper Square Publishers Inc., New York, 1964 [reprint of 1939 edition]) The best overview of Congregational mission strategy on the frontier in the period studied.

(23)   Walker, Williston, <u>The Creeds and Platforms of Congregationalism</u>, (Pilgrim Press, Boston, 1960 [reprint of 1893 edition]) An essential book for understanding Congregational history.

(24)   Weis, Frederick Lewis, <u>The Colonial Churches and the Colonial Clergy of the Middle and Southern Colonies 1607-1776</u> (Society of the Descendants of the Colonial Clergy, Lancaster,MA, 1938) This interesting directory of all denominations is helpful, but is not as complete as the New England volume.

(25)   Weis, Frederick Lewis, <u>The Colonial Clergy of Maryland, Delaware, and Georgia</u> (Genealogical Publishing Co., Baltimore, 1978 [reprint of 1950 edition]) These ministerial biographical collections, published later, are more complete than the church lists (24).

(26)   Weis, Frederick Lewis, <u>The Colonial Clergy of Virginia, North Carolina, and</u>

<u>South Carolina</u> (Genealogical Publishing Co., Baltimore, 1976 [reprint of 1955 edition]) These ministerial biographical collections, published later, are more complete than the church lists (24).

(27)   Weis, Frederick Lewis, <u>List of the Unitarian Churches and Their Ministers in th</u> <u>United States and Canada</u> (Meadville Theological Seminary, typescript, n.d.(c.1960) This helpful directory pinpoints Unitarian churches.

<u>General Black Congregational Studies</u>: (see also 81)   (arranged alphabetically)

(30)   DeMond, A.L., "The Negro in the Congregational Churches of America," <u>Louisiana Congregational Association Minutes, 1902</u> pp.12-20. This short early summary gives some helpful information on specific churches.

(32)   Drake, Richard B., "The Growth of Segregation in American Congregationalism in the South," <u>Negro History Bulletin</u> (Vol.XXI #6, Mar.1958, pp.135-138) This important article clarifies the issues in the mission board debate over racial issues.

(33)   Stanley, A.Knighton, <u>The Children Is Crying: Congregationalism Among Black</u> <u>People</u> (Pilgrim Press, New York/Philadelphia, 1979) An important overview of the work of the American Missionary Association among Black people in the South 1861-1926.

(34)   Stanley, J.Taylor, <u>A History of Black Congregational Christian Churches of the</u> <u>South</u> (United Church Press/American Missionary Association, New York, 1978) A significant overview of the history of the Black Churches, with particular emphasi on the Twentieth Century.

<u>Specific Area and Congregational Methodist Related Items</u>: (arranged alphabetically)

<u>The Alabama Churches and the National Council</u> (n.p.,n.p.,c.1895, 4 p. pamphlet) A spirited defense from the Black Alabama Association to the imposition of segregated inter-church bodies in the fellowship.

Butler, E.W., <u>The Future of Alabama Congregationalism</u>, 1927 address to the Congregational Conference of Alabama. Points out that the Congregational Methodist merger was not as advantageous as promoted.

Clark, Almon Taylor, <u>Alabama: The Facts Stated and the Proof Given</u> (Roberts & Sons, Birmingham, 1898) Meant to be a defense of the Congregational Methodist merger.

<u>Coming of Age: A History of the Southwest Conference of the United Church of</u> <u>Christ</u> (Conference, n.p., c.1978) Includes churches in the El Paso, TX area.

(37)   McDaniel, S.C., <u>The Origin and Early History of the Congregational Methodist</u> <u>Church</u> (James P. Harrison & Co., Atlanta, 1881) This is the most important document for understanding the origins and ideas behind the Congregational Methodist movement.

(38)   "Oklahoma Congregationalism - Decennial Year MDCCCC," <u>Oklahoma Congregational</u> <u>Association Minutes 1900</u> (11p. insert including 3 articles and Biographical Sketches) An overview of the development of the denomination in this Territory from 1889 to 1900.

Ross, A.Hastings, "Ecclesiastical Questions to the National Council," <u>Bibliotheca Sacra</u> Vol.L(1893),No.CC,pp.561-587. A defense of the position of the White churches in the reorganization of the southern church bodies.

ANNOTATED BIBLIOGRAPHY

Silsby, E.C., <u>Congregationalism in Alabama</u> (no publisher,n.p.,1900) Continues merger/segregation controversy.

Wright, W.E.C., "Christian Fellowship As Affected By Race," <u>Bibliotheca Sacra</u> Vol.LI(1894),No.CCIII,pp.421-428. A review of the racial issue in the Churches.

<u>Work Projects Administration Studies</u> (arranged alphabetically except for 41):

(39)   <u>A Directory of Churches and Religious Organizations in the District of Columbia,</u>
<u>Preliminary Edition</u> (Historical Records Survey, Washington, 1939) Only a list of
living churches.

(40)   <u>Directory of Churches and Religious Organizations in New Orleans</u> (Historical
Records Survey, Department of Archives, Louisiana State University, University,LA,
1941) Only a list of living churches.

(41)   <u>A Preliminary List of Religious Bodies in Florida</u> (Historical Records Survey,
Jacksonville, 1939) An incomplete list of living churches.

(42)   <u>Directory of Churches, Missions, and Religious Institutions of Tennessee #19 -</u>
<u>Davidson County - Nashville</u> (Tennessee Historical Records Survey, Nashville, 1940)
Gives dates for churches covered.

(43)   <u>Directory of Churches, Missions, and Religious Institutions of Tennessee #33 -</u>
<u>Hamilton County - Chattanooga</u> (Tennessee Historical Records Survey, Nashville,
1940) Gives dates for churches covered.

(44)   <u>Directory of Churches, Missions, and Religious Institutions of Tennessee #47 -</u>
<u>Knox County - Knoxville</u> (Tennessee Historical Records Survey, Nashville, 1941)
Gives dates for churches covered.

(45)   <u>Directory of Churches, Missions, and Religious Institutions of Tennessee #79 -</u>
<u>Shelby County - Memphis</u> (Tennessee Historical Records Survey, Nashville, 1941)
Gives dates for covered churches.

(46)   <u>Directory of Churches, Missions, and Religious Institutions of Tennessee #90 -</u>
<u>Washington County - Jonesboro</u> (Tennessee Historical Records Survey, Nashville,
1942) Gives dates for covered churches.

(48)   <u>Guide to Church Vital Statistics in Tennessee</u> (War Services Section, Nashville,
1942) Gives dates for covered churches, but unfortunately a large part of this
repeats the data in the five county studies above.

(49)   <u>Guide to Supplementary Vital Statistics from Church Records in Florida</u> (Florida
Historical Records Survey, Jacksonville, 3 Volumes, 1942) Gives dates for covered
churches, but list is incomplete.

(50)   <u>Guide to Vital Statistics Records in Mississippi - Volume II. - Church Archives</u>
(Mississippi Historical Records Survey, Jackson, 1942) Gives dates for covered
churches, but list is incomplete.

(51)   <u>The Historical Records Survey - Florida</u> (An Extract Copy of parts of 49 at
Presbyterian Historical Society, Philadelphia)

(52)   <u>Inventory of the Church Archives of Georgia - Presbyterian Churches</u> (Georgia
Historical Records Survey, arranged and indexed by Candace W. Belfield,
Presbyterian Historical Society, Philadelphia, 1969) Includes dates and historic
sketches, but list is incomplete.

(53)   <u>Inventory of the Church Archives of Maryland - Presbyterian Churches</u> (Maryland

Historical Records Survey (1936), arranged and indexed by Candace W. Belfield and Ellis Archer Wasson, Presbyterian Historical Society, Philadelphia, 3 Volumes, 1969) Includes dates and historic sketches, but list is incomplete.

(54)   Inventory of the Church Archives of Mississippi - Presbyterian Churches (Mississippi Historical Records Survey, arranged and indexed by Candace W. Belfield, Presbyterian Historical Society, Philadelphia, 2 volumes, 1969) Includes dates and historic sketches, but list is incomplete.

(55)   Inventory of the Church Archives of South Carolina - Presbyterian Churches (Historical Records Survey, arranged and indexed by Candace W. Belfield and Elizabeth M. Irving, Presbyterian Historical Society, Philadelphia, 5 Volumes, 1969) Includes dates and historic sketches, but list is incomplete.

(56)   Inventory of the Church Archives of West Virginia - The Presbyterian Churches (West Virginia Historical Records Survey, Charleston, 1941) Includes dates and historic sketches, but list is incomplete.

(57)   Preliminary Bibliography of Material Related to Churches in West Virginia, Kentucky, and Southern Ohio (West Virginia Historical Records Survey, Charleston, 1940) A resource for tracking down other sources.

Low Country South Carolina and Georgia Materials: (arranged alphabetically)

    Edwards, George N., A History of the Independent or Congregational Church of Charleston, S.C. (Commonly Known as Circular Church) (Pilgrim Press, Boston, 1947) A well written history of what could be called the most important southern Congregational Church. This is very valuable for understanding much about pre-Civil War southern Congregationalism in general.

    History of the Independent Presbyterian Church and Sunday School, Savannah, GA (George N. Nichols, Savannah, 1882) An individual history of this one important church.

(58)   Howe, George, History of the Presbyterian Church in South Carolina
        Volume I. (Duffie & Chapman, Columbia, 1870)
        Volume II. (W.J.Duffie, Columbia, 1883)
    Howe's monumental two volumes contain a wealth of information on all the Calvinist Churches in this state. He seemed to have access to the records of the Congregational Association of South Carolina, and presents more information on that group than any other source. However, his chronological writing style is very hard to follow if you are trying to find information on a specific church.

(59)   Jones, F.D. and W.H.Mills, Editors, History of the Presbyterian Church in South Carolina since 1850 (Synod of South Carolina, Columbia, 1926) This book is meant to continue Howe's work, but covers the period after the high point of Congregational Presbyterian interaction.

(60)   Legerton, Clifford L. & Edward G. Lilly,Ed., Historic Churches of Charleston, South Carolina (Legerton & Co., Charleston, 1966) Excellent histories of all of the early city churches we have cited, and many of the suburban churches.

(61)   Martin, Joseph B.,III, "Guide to Presbyterian Ecclesiastical Names and Places In South Carolina 1685-1985," South Carolina Historical Magazine (Vol.90, #1 & 2, Jan.-Apr.1989,pp.3-212) A fascinating and extensive study of local Presbyterian churches in the state. We wish that other states had similar sources. However, while generally excellent, Martin's work shows its greatest problems in the areas where our interaction is most pronounced: the Independent Presbyterian Church, and the early churches with both Congregational and Presbyterian sentiments. For some reason he does not always follow Howe in the latter group.

ANNOTATED BIBLIOGRAPHY

   Minutes of Charleston Presbytery 1839-1864 At Presbyterian Historical Center,
Montreat, NC. This is the Old School body.

   Minutes of the Charleston Union Presbytery 1822-1839 At Presbyterian Historical
Center, Montreat, NC.

   Report and Resolution Adopted by the Charleston Union Presbytery, February 20th,
1845 (Charleston Union Presbytery, n.p.,c.1845) A paper published by the CUP
indicating that they wished to be in the Presbyterian General Assembly and accepted
its acts "though not approving." They consider themselves a part of the Synod and
Assembly, a step which led to the later reunion.

   Sampson, Gloria, Historic Churches and Temples of Georgia (Mercer University
Press, Macon, 1987) A collection of some local church histories, including more of
ours than you might expect from our size in the state.

(62)   Smyth, Thomas, The Late Charleston Union Presbytery (Observer Office Press,
Charleston, 1840) An Old School tract contending that many pastors in the CUP were
not serving real Presbyterian churches, and that the opposition to the Old School
was from these people who were not Presbyterian at all.

(63)   Stacy, James, History and Published Records of the Midway Congregational Church,
Liberty County, Georgia (Reprint Co.Publishers, Spartanburg,SC, 1987 [reprint of
two volumes 1903 and 1894 respectively]) This is a mammoth collection relating to
this one important congregation.

(63G) Stacy, James, A History of the Presbyterian Church in Georgia (Presbyterian
Synod of Georgia, n.p., c.1912) After writing about Midway Church, Stacy turned his
attention to all Presbyterian development in the state. This gives specific
information on some churches, and a list of congregations.

   Tankersley, Allen P., "Midway District: A Study of Puritanism in Colonial
Georgia," Georgia Historical Quarterly (Vol. XXXII #3, Sept.1948, 11p. reprint) A
brief summary of the Midway community.

General Presbyterian and Independent Presbyterian Materials: (arranged alphabetically)

(64)   American Presbyterian Churches - 17th Century - Chronologically Listed (A
document at the Presbyterian Historical Society, Philadelphia)

(65)   Blade,Robert E., "Pioneer Presbyterian Congregations," American Presbyterians
(Journal of Presbyterian History) (Vol.67, # 1 & 2, Spring/Summer, 1989) pp.1-188.
A collection of histories of the oldest living congregation in each Presbytery of
the Presbyterian Church U.S.A.

(66)   Bynum, William B. (of the Presbyterian Historical Center, Montreat, NC)
Correspondence with this author about the Independent Presbyterian Church,
Charleston Presbytery, and related matters. Mar.14,1990;Apr.24,1990;June 3,1992.

(67)   Feemster, Samuel Calvin, History of the Independent Presbyterian Church in the
Carolinas (typed manuscript, before 1875, at Presbyterian Historical Society,
Philadelphia) An overview of the Independent Presbyterian Church from the
perspective of a leader of the western group that separated from the main body.

   Gillett, E.H., History of the Presbyterian Church in the U.S.A. (Presbyterian
Board of Publication, Philadelphia, 1873) A general history.

   Green, Ashbel, Presbyterian Missions (Anson D.F.Randolph & Co., New York, 1893)
Helpful in reviewing Indian work.

(68)   Minutes and Pastoral Letter of the Tenth Session of General Convention of the Independent Presbyterian Church, 1833; Also Eleventh Session, 1834 (at Presbyterian Historical Society, Philadelphia) Annual reports.

(69)   Parker, Harold M. Jr., "The Independent Presbyterian Church and Reunion in the South 1813-1863," Journal of Presbyterian History (Vol. 50 #2, Summer 1972) An important overview of this group, but without access to the materials in Feemster (67) or Punchard (16).

        Parker, Harold M. Jr., The United Synod of the South: The Southern New School Presbyterian Church (Greenwood Press, New York/Westport,CT, 1988) This is perhaps the best source on the latter years of the Plan of Union in the South (after 1837). While particularly interested in the independent southern New School church which existed 1858 to 1864, he attempts to show its origins in the entire New School group in the south. However, the overall knowledge of out and out Congregationalism in the south is either confused or non-existent. While admitting that the Southern Aid Society when organized in 1853 sought to serve both New School and Congregational Churches "at the South," (p.86), he later reports that "Congregationalists...had no churches in the South." (p.297)

(70)   Posey, Walter Brownlee, The Presbyterian Church in the Old Southwest 1778-1838 (John Knox Press, Richmond, 1952) A helpful overview of the earliest Presbyterian work, which often interacted with Congregationalists.

        Sweet, William Warren, Religion on the American Frontier 1783-1840: Vol.II The Presbyterians (Cooper Square Publishers, New York, 1964 [reprint of 1936 edition]) A massive documentary overview of frontier missions in the period named.

        Thompson, Ernest Trice, Presbyterian Missions in the Southern United States (Presbyterian Committee on Publication, Richmond/Texarkana, 1934) Helpful information on Indian work.

(71)   Thompson, Ernest Trice, Presbyterianism in the South
            Vol.I. 1607-1861 (John Knox Press, Richmond, 1963)
            Vol.II. 1861-1890 (John Knox Press, Richmond, 1973)
            Vol.III. 1890-1972 (John Knox Press, Richmond, 1973) The major modern history of southern Presbyterianism.

        Trinterud, Leonard J., The Forming of An American Tradition: A Re-examination of American Presbyterianism (Westminster Press, Philadelphia, 1949) This is a ground breaking seminal work that documents the early connections of American Congregationalism and Presbyterianism.

(72)   Voss, Louis, Presbyterianism in New Orleans and Adjacent Points (Presbyterian Board of Publication of the Synod of Louisiana, n.p., 1931) While focused on one local area, this includes helpful early information for adjacent areas as well.

        Weeks, Louis B., Kentucky Presbyterians (John Knox Press, Atlanta, 1983) A modern overview of Presbyterianism in this state.

Presbyterian Listing Interface:

(75)   This number is used to indicate listings in Presbyterian judicatories. General Listings: In 1774 a list of congregations was published as "A List of the Ministers and Congregations, Whether Settled or Vacant, Belonging to the Rev.Synod of New York and Philadelphia," in Aitken's General American Register, and the Gentleman's and Tradesman's Complete Annual Account Book and Calendar, etc. (Joseph Cruickshank for R.Aitken, Philadelphia, 1774) We have used the list republished in Sweet (Presbyterians,pp.12-20) Thereafter church lists were published in the Synod

Minutes of 1788 and in the <u>Minutes of the General Assembly of the Presbyterian Church, U.S.A.</u> for 1794,1798,1803,1809,1814,1819,and 1825-1834 and 1836-1958. This continuity follows the Old School minutes 1838-1869. The 1948 General Assembly minutes covered the part of the year for 1947. Thereafter all reports were for full calendar years. The 1952 Minutes include two complete calendar reports from 1951 and 1952. To conform to our usage for Congregational Churches, all years of listings contained here before the General Assembly minutes of 1947, mean in that year or the year later. For example, 1946 or 1947 is shown on the listings as 1946. New School lists were published by their General Assembly in 1839,1840,1843,1846, 1849-1869. There were no lists in their 1838 Minutes. These are also reports for the year before the minutes or the year of the minutes, and are shown as the previous year. These two bodies reunited in 1870. This body then united with the United Presbyterian Church of North America in 1958 to form the United Presbyterian Church,U.S.A.. Its Minutes of 1959 to 1979 include reports for 1959 to 1979.

Southern Listings: The Presbyterian Church in the U.S. (formerly the Presbyterian Church in the Confederate States of America) broke away in 1861. There are no new lists in its 1861,1862,1864,and 1865 Minutes. Lists appear in the 1863 and 1866-1980 minutes. The 1955 Minutes include a calendar year report for 1954. The 1954 Minutes covered part of 1953. In the 1953 and earlier Minutes reports are for part of the year of the Minutes and for part of the previous year. Here we have also conformed to our policy that the year shown in a non-calendar period as the year listed or dropped means in that year or the following year.

Merged reports: These two groups published their statistics together for the three years 1980-1982 (designated as part of the 1980-1982 Minutes of the United Presbyterian Church and the 1981-1983 Minutes of the Presbyterian Church U.S.). These two groups reunited in 1983 as the Presbyterian Church,U.S.A.. The Minutes of 1983-on have the calendar year statistics for 1983-on. The last year used was the 1992 statistics.

Labeling: In showing listings for these churches: "Pres." always refers to churches in the continuity of the New York and Philadelphia Synod, General Assembly, United Presbyterian Church,U.S.A., and Presbyterian Church U.S.A.. During the period 1837 to 1870 Old School (OS) or New School (NS) are always specified. "Pres.U.S." always refers to the southern church (1861-1983). Other Presbyterian bodies are specifically identified.

Sources: Most of the data included in this book for Presbyterian listings is based on the Russell Hall cards at the Presbyterian Historical Society in Philadelphia. (See first Hall entry below.) However, Hall began with the 1825 lists, and limits himself to the national Minutes. We have inserted from the Minutes data from before 1825 and from the date that the cards were written to the present. Where possible we have also used lists in Synod or Presbytery minutes to fill in the pre-1825, 1835, and New School lacunas when lists were not published. We have also researched and corrected some errors which appear in his lists.

Hall, Russell E., <u>Index of Congregations of the Presbyterian Churches in the United States</u> (Written card file of churches in the Presbyterian Historical Society,Philadelphia) Unfortunately Mr. Hall has kept some key churches in South Carolina out of the main card file. They are included in the following booklet.

Hall, Russell E., <u>Congregations in the Carolina Low Country (Charleston, S.C.) Identified as Presbyterian, Independent Presbyterian, Independent and Congregational (1690-1882)</u> (manuscript, 1988)

(75H) In the Hall cards in Philadelphia and the booklet (see above two entries) he has sometimes in the South also added organization dates or other information in addition to listing dates. Where that is the case we indicate by using this code. Oftentimes he merely repeats the 75Y data, and where that is the case we have usually only entered the 75Y code.

(75Y) In the Minutes of the Presbyterian Church U.S., local church organization dates are often given. Where that is the case we use this code.

Ethnic Studies: (Arranged randomly, so as to conform use to numbering in the New
    England volume)

(80)   Directory of the United Church of Christ Congregations of Minority
    Background (United Church Board for Homeland Ministries, New York, 1980) A
    listing of living Hispanic, Black, American Indian, and Pacific Asian
    congregations. The latter group are not broken down into sub-groups.

(81)   Directory of UCC Black Churches and Ministers (Black Church Development
    Program, New York, 1976) A list of living Black churches.

(82)   Eisenach, George J., History of the German Congregational Churches in the
    United States, (Pioneer Press, Yankton (SD), 1938) An exhaustive study of
    living and extinct German churches.

(83)   Hartmann, Edward George, Americans from Wales, (Christopher Publishing
    House, Boston, 1967) Includes a supposedly exhaustive list of living and
    extinct Welsh churches.

(85)   Directory of United Church of Christ Congregations with Black, Hispanic,
    Native American, Asian or Pacific Island Members, as of January 1988, (United
    Church Board for Homeland Ministries, New York, 1989) The most exhaustive study
    ever done of living churches, it not only breaks down each Pacific Asian group,
    but also shows ethnic percentages within congregations.

(88)   Norton, Margery J., American Indian Missions of the Constituent
    Denominations of the UCC: A Preliminary Bibliography, (United Church Board for
    Homeland Ministries, typescript, 1980) An excellent overview of pre-1870 Indian
    work, with some outlines of later work.

(91)   Strong, William E., The Story of the American Board (Pilgrim Press, Boston,
    1910) Some help on Indian work.

(92)   Tracy, Joseph, "History of the American Board of Commissioners for Foreign
    Missions," and "History of the Board of Foreign Missions of the General Assembly of
    the Presbyterian Church in the United States of America," in History of American
    Missions to the Heathen from their Commencement to the Present Time (Spooner &
    Howland, Worcester, 1840) A helpful delineation of the early mission groups.

Building Study:

(95)   Rose, Harold Wickliffe, The Colonial Houses of Worship in America (Hastings
    House, New York, 1963) Includes all pre-1776 buildings surviving, with information
    on their congregations.

Special References:

(97)   Correspondence carried on by this author with federated and dual churches
    and sometimes with other churches, libraries or scholars.

(98)   The present author has looked over a large number of county histories and
    other local history sources too numerous to list.

(99)   All other references.

Local, County, and State Histories and Location sources: (arranged alphabetically)

Locating towns and cities was done by the use of a wide range of atlases and gazetteers both modern and from the historic periods involved. Correspondence with state and local historical societies and libraries was also used for difficult locations. These are too many in number to add to this bibliography. Other sources for state and county histories and related matters came from:

Clements, John, Florida Facts, (Clements Research, Dallas, 1987)

Clements, John, Texas Facts: Flying the Colors, (Clements Research, Dallas, 1984)

Corbitt, David Leroy, The Formation of the North Carolina Counties 1663-1943, (State Department of Archives and History, Raleigh, 1950)

Gannett, Henry, A Gazateer of Maryland and Delaware, (Genealogical Publishing Co., Baltimore, 1979)

Gannett, Henry, A Gazateer of Virginia and West Virginia, (Genealogical Publishing Co., Baltimore, 1980)

Halverson, F.Douglas, County Histories of the United States Giving Present Name, Date Formed, Parent County, and County Seat, (mimeo,n.d.)

Kane, Joseph Nathan, The American Counties, (The Scarecrow Press, New York, 1960)

Kavenagh, W. Keith, Foundations of Colonial America: A Documentary History, (Vol.II:Middle Atlantic Colonies; Vol.III:Southern Colonies) (Chelsea House, New York, 1983)

Kirkham, E.Kay, A Genealogical And Historical Atlas Of The United States Of America,(Keith W. Watkins & Sons, Providence,Utah, 1980)

Ten Years of Change in ... Will Be Measured by the 1970 Census, (A series of pamphlets, one for each state, named at the ... location)(U.S.Department of Commerce, Bureau of the Census, Census '70, c.1969)

Thornapple, William and William Dollarhide, Map Guide to the U.S. Federal Censuses 1790-1920, (Genealogical Publishing Co.Inc.,Baltimore, 1987)

INDEX TO COMMUNITIES

Indexes to finding the County location of each community follow in alphabetical order by state.

In the left hand column for each state are all community, town, city, village, post office, or similar names. In the right hand column is the appropriate county where the community name may be found.

When a community extends over a county line two counties are shown in the right hand column with the word "and." When a community is clearly in one county, but is referred to in the entry of another county, the county of location is given first and the other county where the community is mentioned follows the words "see also." The latter situation could happen if a church is located by a post office in a different county, moved, and sometimes for other reasons.

Where there is a wide variation is the spelling of a location it is shown under both spellings in the index. Some minor variations are shown with alternative spellings in parentheses.

All entries are for the main Congregational church lists unless the community name is followed by a number in parentheses. If a plus sign (+) and a number appear, then that community name can be found in both the main regular Congregational lists and in the appendix of that number. (+2 would mean in the main list and in Appendix II.) If a number appears in parentheses by itself, that means that the community may be found only in the appendix with that number. (3 would mean in Appendix III. only.) These references are not repeated for the County designation except in cases where there are more than one county reference for a given community with a designation "and" or "see also." In such cases to clarify in what cases the second county is to be checked, parentheses numbers have been added under the same system as above.

An asterisk (*) indicates that this is the name of a minor civil division, but this name was never used as a location name by any church. (Some communities not shown with asterisks here, will sometimes have one in the main text. If that is the case, it is because this name was used for some church, but not for every church referred to this minor civil division.)

A hatch symbol (#) indicates that the name shown is actually the church name, but it was at some point also used as a location reference.

INDEX TO COMMUNITIES

INDEX TO COMMUNITIES

INDEX TO COMMUNITIES

TOWN/CITY	COUNTY	TOWN/CITY	COUNTY

DELAWARE

TOWN/CITY	COUNTY
Canterbury	Kent
Glasgow	New Castle
Milton	Sussex
New Amstel	New Castle
New Castle	New Castle
Newark (+3)	New Castle
Pencader	New Castle
Welsh Tract	New Castle
Wilmington	New Castle

DISTRICT OF COLUMBIA

TOWN/CITY	COUNTY
Cleveland Park	District
Temple Park	District
Washington (+1,3,4)	District, see also Montgomery,MD(+3) & Prince Georges, MD

FLORIDA

TOWN/CITY	COUNTY
Alamonte	Seminole
Alamonte Springs (3)	Seminole
Apopka	Orange
Arch Creek	Dade
Avon Park	Highlands
Babson Park (3)	Polk
Bagdad	Santa Rosa
Baker	Okaloosa
Bal Harbour (2)	Dade
Bascom	Jackson
Bayonet Point (3)	Pasco
Bearhead	Walton
Belleair	Pinellas
Belleview	Marion
Black Oak	Walton
Blountsville	Calhoun
Boca Raton (3)	Palm Beach
Boggy	Walton
Bonifay	Holmes
Bonita Springs (3)	Lee
Boynton Beach (3)	Palm Beach
Bradenton (2,3)	Manatee
Brandon (3)	Hillsborough
Cameron City	Seminole
Campton	Okaloosa
Cantonment	Escambia
Cape Coral (3,4)	Lee
Careyville	Washington, see also Holmes
Carol City (3)	Dade
Caryville	Washington
Center Ridge	Santa Rosa
Cerro Gordo	Holmes
Chipley	Washington
Citrus Springs (3)	Citrus
Clarcona	Orange
Clearwater (3)	Pinellas
Cluster Springs	Walton
Coatesville	Holmes
Cobb	Okaloosa
Cocoa Beach (2)	Brevard
Coconut Grove	Dade
Coral Gables (+3)	Dade
Coral Isle (3)	Monroe
Cottondale	Jackson
Cottonville	Okaloosa
County Line	Jackson
Crestview	Okaloosa
Crystal Springs	Pasco
Cypress Grove	Baker
Daytona	Volusia
Daytona Beach (+4)	Volusia
Deerland	Okaloosa
DeFuniak Springs	Walton
Delray Beach (3)	Palm Beach
Deltona (3)	Volusia
Destin	Okaloosa

INDEX TO COMMUNITIES

TOWN/CITY	COUNTY	TOWN/CITY	COUNTY
	GEORGIA		GEORGIA
Acton	Chatham	Clark's Mills	Crawford
Albany	Dougherty	Claxton	Evans
Alpharetta	Fulton	Cobell	prob.Jackson
Amandaville	Hart, see also Elbert	Cochran	Bleckley
		Coe	Tattnall
Americus	Sumter	Coffee	Bacon, see also Pierce
Andersonville	Sumter		
Antioch #	Pierce	Cohran	Bleckley
Arabi	Crisp	Cohren	Bleckley
Aragon	Polk	Colbert	Madison
Ashlern	Dooly	Coleman	Randolph
Athens	Clarke	Coleraine	Charlton
Atlanta (+2,3)	Fulton and De Kalb, see also Gwinnett	Colerane	Charlton
		Collins	Tattnall
Augusta (+1)	Richmond, see also Aiken,SC	Colquitt	Miller
		Columbus	Muscogee, see also Crawford
Axson	Atkinson		
Barnesville	Lamar	Comer	Madison
Bartow	Jefferson	Conyers	Rockdale
Bath	Richmond, see also Burke	Cordele	Crisp
		Cordell	Crisp
Baxley	Appling, see also Pierce	Crest	Upson
		Cribb	Emanuel
Beachton	Grady	Crosland	Colquitt
Belleville	Polk	Cross Bays	Unlocated
Belmont	Chatham	Cypress Slash	Liberty
Bethel #	Marion	Daculah	Gwinnett
Bibb City	Muscogee	Dailey	Unlocated
Bickley	Ware	Daisy	Evans
Bolton	Fulton	Dakota	Turner
Bowers	Crawford	Dalton (6)	Whitfield
Bowman	Elbert, see also Madison	Danielsville	Madison
		Darien	Mc Intosh
Braden	Gwinnett, see also DeKalb	Davisboro	Washington
		Davisville	Unlocated
Brantley	Marion	Dawson	Terrell
Brasleton	Jackson	Dawsonville	Dawson
Braswell	Paulding	Dekota	Turner
Brier Creek	Burke	Demorest	Habersham
Bristol	Pierce	Dewey Rose	Elbert
Bryar Creek	Burke	Doerun	Colquitt
Buford	Gwinnett	Dorchester	Liberty
Burkett's Store	Bibb	Dorchester Center	Liberty
Byrd	Floyd	Douglas (+2)	Coffee
Byron	Peach, see also Crawford	Duluth	Gwinnett
		Duncansville	Grady
Byron Station	Peach	DuPont	Clinch
Calhoun	Gordon	Emanuel Conception	Unlocated
Carmel # (5)	Gilmer	Endicot(t)	Bulloch, see also Screven
Cartecay	Gilmer		
Cedartown	Polk	Eureka	Dooly
Center Minerva	prob.Fulton	Fairfax	Ware, see also Coffee
Chamblee	De Kalb		
Charlton	Charlton	Fender	Clinch
Chestnut Mountain	Hall, see also Jackson	Fitzgerald	Ben Hill
		Five Forks	Madison
Clara	Fulton	Five Points	Madison

231

INDEX TO COMMUNITIES

TOWN/CITY	COUNTY	TOWN/CITY	COUNTY
GEORGIA		GEORGIA	
Flemington	Liberty	Junction City	Talbot
Flowery Branch	Hall	Juniper	Marion
Folkston	Charlton	Kemp	Emanuel
Folsom	Bartow	Knoxville	Crawford
Forestville	Floyd	Kramer	Wilcox
Fort Valley	Peach, see also Crawford	LaCrosse	Schley
		LaGrange	Troup
France(i)s Bridge	prob.Washington	Lanhan	prob.Evans
Gabbettsville	Troup, see also Upson	Lawrenceville	Gwinnett
		LeMars	prob.Washington
Gabbitsville	Unlocated, see also Upson	Leroy	Bacon
		Leslie	Sumter
Gaillard	Crawford	Liberty	Greene
Gainesville	Hall	Lifsey's Store	Pike
Garfield	Emanuel	Lilburn (3)	Gwinnett
Gay Grove	Screven	Lindale	Floyd
Gholston	Madison	Lizella	Bibb
Gillards	Crawford	Lloyd	Crisp
Gilmore	Cobb	Lonon	Unlocated
Glenmore	Ware	Louisville	Jefferson, see also Chatham
Glenville	Tattnall		
Gnat	Jenkins	Louisville #	Pierce
Goggansville	Lamar	Lovejoy	Clayton, see also Henry
Goldings Grove	Liberty		
Gravel Hill	Liberty	Mack(s)ville	Upson
Graymont	Emanuel	Macon	Bibb
Greenville	Meriwether	Magdalena	Meriwether
Greenway	Unlocated	Manassas	Tattnall, see also Evans
Griffin	Spalding		
Griffin #	Tattnall	Marietta (+3)	Cobb
Groveland	Bryan	McCann	Liberty
Hagan	Evans	McDonald's Mills	Atkinson
Hahira	Lowdnes	McIntosh	Liberty
Hampton	Henry	McLeod	Emanuel
Harrison	Washington	Meansville	Pike
Hartsfield	Colquitt	Medders	Bacon, see also Pierce
Hartville	Bulloch		
Hartwell	Hart, see also Elbert	Meridian	Appling
Harville	Bulloch	Middleton	Elbert
Hasty	Ware	Midville	Burke
Haweis (5)	Floyd	Midway	Liberty, see also Dorchester,SC
Hendricks	Upson		
Herndon	Jenkins	Milford	Baker
Hinesville	Liberty	Millen	Jenkins
Hoboken	Brantley	Miller	Jenkins
Homeland	Charlton	Miller's Station	Chatham
Hoolinville	Unlocated	Millwood	Ware
Hoschton	Jackson	Mindian	Appling
Howell's Mills	Fulton	Mineral Bluff	Fannin
Huggens	Colquitt	Minerva	prob.Fulton
Hunter	Screven, see also Pierce	Morgan	Calhoun
		Moxley	Jefferson
Huntington	Sumter	Myrtle	Peach
Jessup	Wayne	Naylor	Lowdnes
Jolly	Pike	New Echota (5)	Gordon
Jonesboro (3)	Clayton	New England #	Dade
Jonesville	Liberty	New Lacy	Bacon

INDEX TO COMMUNITIES

INDEX TO COMMUNITIES

TOWN/CITY	COUNTY	TOWN/CITY	COUNTY
KENTUCKY		**LOUISIANA**	
Pine Grove	Laurel, see also Jackson	Abbeville	Vermilion
Pine Knott	McCreary, see also Whitley	Algiers	Orleans
		Avery Island	Iberia
Pleasant View	Whitley	Barnes Creek	Allen
Poplar Creek	Whitley	Baton Rouge (+3)	East Baton Rouge
Red Ash	Whitley	Bayou Beauf	prob.Rapides
Rockhold	Whitley	Bayou Blue	Jefferson Davis
Sanders Creek	Whitley	Bayou Boeuf	prob.Rapides
Shivley (3)	Jefferson	Bayou du Large	Terrebonne
Smiths Creek (2)	Carter	Beard	Vermilion
South Fork	Owsley	Bel	Allen
Spradling	Wolfe	Belle	Iberia
Stearns	McCreary	Belle Place	Iberia
Strunk	McCreary	Bermuda	Natchitoches
Strunk's Lane	McCreary	Bluff Springs	Ouachita
Sugar Creek	Gallatin	Bundicks Creek	prob.Beauregard
Tar Ridge	Menifee	Calhoun	Ouachita, see also Union
Teague	Whitley		
Toliver	Wolfe	Campti	Natchitoches
Tolliver	Wolfe	Carrollton	Orleans
West Covington	Kenton	Chacahoula	Terrebonne
Whitley Court House	Whitley	Chague Bay	La Fourche
Williamsburg	Whitley	China	Jefferson Davis
Woodbine	Whitley	Choudrant	Lincoln
Youngs Creek	Whitley	Clare Springs	Natchitoches
		Clear Creek	Allen
		Cole	Allen, see also Beauregard
		Conrad	Natchitoches
		Cotile*	Rapides
		Coushatta	Red River
		Delcambre	Iberia & Vermilion
		Delcombre	Iberia
		Delecambre	Iberia
		Derouen	Iberia
		Downsville (+2)	Union
		Dry Creek	Beauregard
		Edna (2)	Jefferson Davis
		Elton	Jefferson Davis
		Emad	Allen
		Erath	Vermilion
		Eros	Jackson
		Esterly	Jefferson Davis
		Fauce Point	Iberia
		Fausse Point	Iberia
		Fisher	Sabine
		Gaytine (2)	Beauregard
		Grand Bayou	La Fourche
		Grand Marais	Iberia
		Grappe's Bluff	Natchitoches
		Greenville	Orleans
		Gretna	Jefferson
		Gueydan	Vermilion
		Hammond	Tangipahoa
		Harang	LaFourche
		Harangville	LaFourche
		Hemphill	Rapides

INDEX TO COMMUNITIES

TOWN/CITY	COUNTY	TOWN/CITY	COUNTY
MARYLAND		**MISSISSIPPI**	
Annapolis (+3)	Anne Arundel	Ai-ik-hun-nah (5)	Unlocated
Baltimore (+1,3)	Baltimore City	Ai-ik-hun-nuh (5)	Unlocated
Belair Village (3)	Prince Georges	Algoma (5)	Pontotoc
Berwyn Dist.* (2)	Prince Georges	Bethany (5)	Unlocated
Bethesda (+2,3)	Montgomery,see also	Bethel (5)	Choctaw
	Washington,DC(+3)	Bok-i-tun-nah (5)	Wayne
Bladensburg	Prince Georges	Bokitunnuh (5)	Wayne
Bowie (3)	Prince Georges	Bolton	Hinds
Canton	Baltimore City	Buckatunna (5)	Wayne
Capitol Heights	Prince Georges	Caledonia	Lowndes, see also
Columbia (3)	Howard		Monroe
Eldersburg (3)	Carroll	Captain Harrison's	Unlocated
Forest Park	Baltimore City	(5)	
Freedom Dist.* (3)	Carroll	Cherokee	prob.Lowndes
Friendsville (4)	Garrett	Chickasaw Agency (5)	Pontotoc
Frostburg	Allegany	Clinton	Hinds
Gaithersburg (3)	Montgomery	Columbus (+8)	Lowndes, see also
Germantown (3)	Montgomery		Monroe
Glen Burnie (3)	Anne Arundel	Eliot (5)	Grenada
Greenbelt (2)	Prince Georges	Emmaus (5)	prob.Wayne
Greenberry Point	Anne Arundel	French Camps (5)	Choctaw
(Greenbury)		Garden City	Franklin
Hyattsville	Prince Georges	Gibeon (5)	Unlocated
Marlboro Dist.* (+3)	Prince Georges	Goshen (5)	Jasper
North Wheaton (3)	Montgomery	Greenville	Washington
Oakland Mills (3)	Howard	Hachah (5)	Wayne
Oxon Hill (3)	Prince Georges	Hamilton (+8)	Monroe
Patuxent River	Prince Georges	Hebron (5)	Lowndes
Potter's Landing	Caroline	Hik-a-shub-a-ha (5)	Unlocated
Providence	Anne Arundel, see	Holcomb (5)	Grenada
	also Nansemond, VA	Holly Springs (5)	Marshall
Queen Anne Dist.* (3)	Prince Georges	Hoo-la-ta-hoomah (5)	Jasper
Savage Dist.* (3)	Howard	I-ik-hun-nuk (5)	Unlocated
Seat Pleasant	Prince Georges	Jackson (+3)	Hinds
Seneca Valley (3)	Montgomery	Long Prairie (5)	prob.Wayne
Silver Spring (2,3)	Montgomery	Lower Towns (5)	Lowndes
Spencerville (2)	Montgomery	Martyn Station (5)	Marshall
Tuxedo	Prince Georges	Mayhew (5)	Lowndes
Upper Marlboro(ugh)	Prince Georges	McIntoshville (5)	Pontotoc
(+3)		Meridian	Lauderdale
Wheaton (3)	Montgomery	Monroe (5)	Pontotoc
		Monroe Station (5)	Pontotoc
		Mooshoolatubbees (5)	Unlocated
		Mr. Juzon's (5)	Unlocated
		Mushulatubees (5)	Unlocated
		Natchez (+5)	Adams
		New Ruhamah	Monroe
		Orange River	Hinds
		Orangeville	Hinds
		Pigeon Roost (5)	Marshall
		Pine(y) Grove	Lowndes
		Pleasant Ridge	Lowndes
		Pontotoc (5)	Pontotoc
		Ruhamah (+8)	Monroe
		Six Towns (5)	Unlocated, see also
			Wayne

INDEX TO COMMUNITIES

239

INDEX TO COMMUNITIES

TOWN/CITY	COUNTY	TOWN/CITY	COUNTY
NORTH CAROLINA		**NORTH CAROLINA**	
		Sander	Cumberland
Moncure	Chatham, see also Lee	Sanford (+2,3)	Lee
		Sedalia	Guilford
Monroe (3)	Union	Sheffield Twn.*	Moore
Monroe Twn.* (3)	Guilford	Shinnsville	Iredell
Monual	Harnett	Siler City (2,3)	Chatham
Moore	Alamance	Snowhill	Montgomery, see also Anson
Mooresville	Iredell		
Morehead	Cabarrus	Sophia	Randolph
Morehead Twn.*	Guilford	South Point	Gaston
Moroted	Montgomery	Southern Pines	Moore
Morrisville	Iredell	Spies	Moore, see also Randolph
Morton Twn.* (+2,3)	Alamance		
Morval	Harnett	Spring Grove	Gaston
Mount Gilead	Montgomery	Star (+2)	Montgomery
Mount Olive (2)	Wayne	Statesville (+3)	Iredell
Mount Pleasant	Cabarrus	Stedman	Cumberland, see also Moore
Mountain Island	Gaston		
Nalls	Montgomery	Steeles Twn.*	Richmond
New Bern	Craven	Stewart	Hoke
New Hope Twn.*	Randolph	Strieby	Randolph
New Market Twn.*	Randolph	Stump Sound Twn.* (3)	Onslow
Niagara	Moore	Summer's Grove	Unlocated
Nicholson	Alamance	Swan Station	Harnett
North Albemarle Twn.*	Stanly	Swanns *	Harnett
Northwest Twn.* (2)	Brunswick	Swepsonville	Alamance
Norval	Harnett	Tempting	Lee
Norwood	Stanly	Toluca	Cleveland
Oaks	Orange, see also Alamance	Troutman	Iredell
		Troy	Montgomery
Old Town Twn.* (2)	Forsyth	Tryon	Polk
Olney (8)	Gaston	Tunis (2)	Hertford
Parkton	Robeson	Union #	Guilford
Paw Creek	Mecklenburg	Union Grove	Guilford
Pekin(g)	Montgomery	Upper Fishing Creek Twn.* (2)	Edgecombe
Pfafftown (2)	Forsyth		
Philadelphia	Richmond	Valdese	Burke
Pinehurst (3)	Moore	Vance Twn.*	Union
Pittsboro	Chatham	Vander	Cumberland
Pleasant Grove	Moore	Vass	Moore
Pocket Twn.*	Lee	Wade	Cumberland
Raeford	Hoke	Wadesboro	Anson
Raleigh	Wake	Wadsworth	Guilford
Ramseur (3)	Randolph	Walls	Montgomery
Randleman	Randolph	Wardsworth	Guilford
Rankinsville	Iredell	West End	Moore
Red Springs	Robeson	West Sanford Twn.* (+2,3)	Lee
Richland Twn.*	Randolph		
Riley's Store	Randolph	White Mill (3)	Iredell
Roanoke Twn.* (2)	Warren	Whitsett	Guilford
Robbins	Moore	Whittier	Swain
Rock Creek Twn.* (+2)	Guilford	Wilmington (+3)	New Hanover
Rock Hill	Harnett	Winston Salem (+2)	Forsyth
Rockfish Twn.* (2)	Cumberland	Winston Twn.* (+2)	Forsyth
Rockingham	Richmond	Winton Twn.* (2)	Hertford
Saint Marys Twn.* (2)	Wake	Woodbridge	Unlocated
Salisbury	Rowan	Yadkinville (3)	Yadkin
Sand(y) Level	Unlocated	Zebulon (2)	Wake

INDEX TO COMMUNITIES

TOWN/CITY	COUNTY	TOWN/CITY	COUNTY
OKLAHOMA		**OKLAHOMA**	
Fort Washita (5)	Johnston	Luk-fo-a-ta (5)	McCurtain
Gage	Ellis	Lyons (5)	Adair
Garvin (5)	McCurtain	Manchester	Grant
Glenella	Garfield, see also Alfalfa	Manitou	Tillman
		Marble City (5)	Sequoyah
Goltry	Alfalfa	Marion	prob.Alfalfa
Good	Choctaw	Mayhew (5)	Choctaw
Good Hope	prob.Alfalfa	McAlester	Pittsburg
Goodland (+5)	Choctaw	McAllister	Pittsburg
Green Hill # (5)	LeFlore	McCurtain City (5)	McCurtain
Greenfield (5)	McCurtain	McLoud	Pottawatomie
Greenleaf #	Harper	Medford	Grant
Guthrie	Logan	Meridian	Logan
Hanson (5)	Sequoyah	Middletown #	Woods
Harmony #	Logan	Mills	Lincoln
Hartzell	Oklahoma	Minnehaha	Pottawatomie
Hastings	Jefferson	Morrison	Noble
Hennessey	Kingfisher	Mound Center	Pawnee
Hillsdale	Garfield	Mount Calvary #	Garfield
Hobart	Kiowa	Mount Carmel #	Pawnee
Holdenville	Hughes	Mount Hope #	Logan
Honey Creek (5)	Unlocated	Mount Pisgah #	Kingfisher
Hooker (2)	Texas	Mount Pleasant	prob.Custer
Hope #	Kingfisher	Mount Pleasant # (5)	Atoka
Hopefield (5)	Mayes	Mount Zion #	Kingfisher
Hugo (5)	Choctaw, see also McCurtain	Mount Zion # (5)	Sequoyah
		Mount Zion (5)	McCurtain
Hunt(s)ville	Kingfisher	Mountain Fork # (5)	McCurtain
Hydro	Caddo & Blaine	Muskogee	Muskogee
Ida	Lincoln, see also Payne	Nagle	Kingfisher
		Nash	Grant
Independence	Custer	Nashville	Grant
Indiahoma	Comanche	Navina	Logan
Jennings (+2)	Pawnee	Newalla	Oklahoma
Karoma	Alfalfa	Newkirk	Kay
Kaw Agency	Kay	North Enid	Garfield
Kaw City	Kay	Norwalk (5)	McCurtain
Kellyville	Creek	Nowata	Nowata
Keokuk Falls	Pottawatomie	Nuhatah	Nowata
Kiel	Kingfisher	Numatah	Nowata
Kingfisher	Kingfisher	Nuwatah	Nowata
Kremlin	Garfield	Oak Grove	Payne
Langston	Logan	Oak Ridge #	Logan
Lawnview	prob.Noble	Oakdale #	Lincoln
Lawton	Comanche	Oakwood #	Pawnee
Lee's Creek (5)	Adair	Okarche	Kingfisher & Canadian
Lehigh	Coal	Okeene	Blaine
Lena	prob.Grant	Oklahoma City (+3,4)	Oklahoma
Lenox (5)	LeFlore	Okmulgee	Okmulgee
Lincoln	Unlocated(poss. Lincoln), see also Payne	Oktaha	Muskogee
		Old Bennington (5)	Bryan
		Olivet #	Payne
Living Land (5)	McCurtain	Omega	Kingfisher
Lockridge	Logan	Oneida	Kingfisher
Logan #	Craig	Orange #	Pottawatomie
Lone Star #	Harper	Orlando	Logan, see also Noble
Loyal	Kingfisher		

INDEX TO COMMUNITIES

TOWN/CITY	COUNTY	TOWN/CITY	COUNTY
OKLAHOMA		**OKLAHOMA**	
Osage	Grant	Tangier	Woodward, see also
Otter	Kingfisher		Ellis
Otter Creek	Harper	Tecumseh	Pottawatomie
Paradise	Garfield	Tohee	Lincoln
Park	Kingfisher	Tryon	Lincoln
Park Hill (5)	Cherokee	Tulsa (+2,4)	Tulsa
Parker	Kay	Turkey Creek	Garfield
Parker	prob.Kingfisher	Union	Lincoln
Parker #	Pottawatomie	Union # (5)	Wagoner
Parnell	Lincoln	Union Center	Grady
Paruna	Harper	Verden	Grady
Pawnee	Pawnee	Vernon	prob.Garfield
Payne Center	Payne	Vian (5)	Sequoyah
Payson	Lincoln	Victor	Grant
Perkins	Payne	Victory #	Oklahoma
Perry	Noble	Vinita	Craig
Pine Ridge # (5)	Choctaw	Wacoolee	Unlocated
Pleasant Hill #	Payne	Wade's Settlement (5)	Pushmataha
Pleasant Home #	Kingfisher	Wakita	Grant
Pleasant Ridge	Logan	Washita (5)	Johnston
Pleasant Valley #	Logan	Waterloo	Logan, see also
Pleasant View	prob.Grant		Oklahoma
Pondcreek	Grant, see also	Waucomis	Garfield
	Garfield	Waukomis	Garfield
Powell Creek	prob.Grant	Waunika	Jefferson
Ralston (2)	Pawnee	Waurika	Jefferson
Red Oak	Unlocated	Waynoka	Woods
Renfrow	Grant	Weatherford	Custer
Ridgway	prob.Grant	Wellston	Lincoln
Rosston	Harper	West Guthrie	Logan
Rusk	prob.Okfuskee	Wheelock (5)	McCurtain
Ryan	Jefferson	Whisler	Oklahoma
Salem	prob.Grant	White Horse	Wood
Sallisaw (5)	Sequoyah	White Oak	Craig
Sapulpa	Creek	Wilcox	Garfield
Savanna	Pittsburg	Willow Creek	prob.Harper
Seward	Logan	Windom	Payne
Shattuck	Ellis	Woodward	Woodward
Shawnee	Pottawatomie	Yakni Okchaya (5)	McCurtain
Short Springs	Alfalfa	Yakni Okehaya (5)	McCurtain
Six Towns (5)	Bryan	Yazoo Creek (5)	Unlocated
Soldier Creek #	Oklahoma	Yokini Okchaga (5)	McCurtain
Sparks	Lincoln		
Spring Creek	prob.Canadian		
Springdale	prob.Alfalfa		
Springvale	Logan, see also		
	Lincoln		
Star Chapel #	Oklahoma		
Stillwater	Payne		
Stockbridge (5)	McCurtain		
Stringtown	Atoka		
Sulphur	Murray		
Sunny Slope	Ellis		
Sween(e)y	Unlocated		
Tabor #	Kingfisher		
Tahequah (5)	Cherokee		
Tallequah (5)	Cherokee		

INDEX TO COMMUNITIES

TOWN/CITY	COUNTY	TOWN/CITY	COUNTY
SOUTH CAROLINA		SOUTH CAROLINA	
Adams Run	Colleton	Mount Pleasant	Charleston, see also Berkeley
Adamsville	Chester		
Aiken (7)	Aiken	Mountain VIew	Greenville
Anderson	Anderson	New Wappetaw	Charleston, see also Berkeley
Arthur(s)	Lexington		
Barnwell Court House (7)	Barnwell	Newberry	Newberry
		Ninety Six	Greenwood
Beaufort	Beaufort	Old Cambridge	Greenwood
Beech Hill	Colleton, see also Dorchester	Orangeburg (+7)	Orangeburg
		Pleasant Grove	Colleton, see also Dorchester
Beech Island	Aiken		
Boiling Springs (7)	Barnwell	Pocotaligo	Beaufort
Buck Island	Aiken	Pomaria	Newberry
Bullock's Creek (8)	York	Pon Pon	Colleton
Cainhoy	Berkeley	Port Royal	Beaufort
Cambridge	Greenwood	Port Royal Island	Beaufort
Carmel Hill (8)	Chester	Prince William Par.	Beaufort
Cedar Creek	Richland	Rock	Abbeville
Charles Towne (+7)	Charleston	Rockville (7)	Charleston
Charleston (+7)	Charleston	Rocky Creek	Abbeville
Chester (+8)	Chester	Rodman (8)	Chester
Chesterville (8)	Chester	Saint Bartholomew's Par.	Colleton
Christ Ch. Par.	Berkeley		
Clover (8)	York, see also Chester	Saint George's Par.	Dorchester
		Saint John's Par. (7)	Charleston
Columbia (+3)	Richland	Saint Paul's Par.	Colleton, see also Dorchester
Coosawhatchie	Jasper, see also Beaufort		
		Saint Thomas' Par.	Berkeley
Dorchester	Dorchester	Salkehatchie (7)	Colleton
Eastover	Richland	Salt Ketcher (7)	Colleton
Edisto(e)	Charleston	Saltcatcher (7)	Colleton
Edisto(e) Island	Charleston	Shandon	Richland
Edmonds (8)	Chester	Sharon (8)	York
Gaffney (8)	Cherokee	Sheldon	Beaufort
Greenville	Greenville	South Edistoe River	Charleston
Greenwood	Greenwood	Stoney Creek	Beaufort
Haddrell's	Berkeley	Summerville	Dorchester
Horrell	Richland	Sykesland	Richland
Howell	Unlocated	Wadmalaw (Island) (7)	Charleston
Indianland	Beaufort	Walterboro	Colleton
Jacksonboro	Colleton	Wando Neck	Berkeley
Jacksonburg	Colleton	Wando River	Berkeley
James Island	Charleston	Wappetaw	Berkeley
Johns Island (7)	Charleston	Wateree	Fairfield
Jonesville (8)	Union, see also Cherokee	Wilton	Colleton
		Winnsboro	Fairfield
Kings Creek (8)	Cherokee	Yemassee	Hampton, see also Beaufort
Legareville (7)	Charleston		
Lykesland	Richland	York (8)	York
McClellanville	Charleston, see also Berkeley	Yorkville (8)	York
McConnells (8)	York		
McConnellsville (8)	York		
McPhersonville	Hampton, see also Beaufort		
Mill Creek (8)	York		

INDEX TO COMMUNITIES

INDEX TO COMMUNITIES

246

INDEX TO COMMUNITIES

INDEX TO COMMUNITIES

INDEX TO TOPICS DISCUSSED IN THE INTRODUCTORY TEXT

(Counties are not shown except when they are a church location. Full names of
inter-church bodies may be found in the annotated bibliography.)

INDEX TO TOPICS DISCUSSED IN THE INTRODUCTORY TEXT

(Counties are not shown except when they are a church location. Full names of
inter-church bodies may be found in the annotated bibliography.)

(Counties are not shown except when they are a church location. Full names of
inter-church bodies may be found in the annotated bibliography.)

INDEX TO TOPICS DISCUSSED IN THE INTRODUCTORY TEXT

(Counties are not shown except when they are a church location. Full names of
inter-church bodies may be found in the annotated bibliography.)

(Counties are not shown except when they are a church location. Full names of
inter-church bodies may be found in the annotated bibliography.)

(Counties are not shown except when they are a church location. Full names of
inter-church bodies may be found in the annotated bibliography.)